jasper tudor

jasper tudor

Dynasty Maker

TERRY BREVERTON

AMBERLEY

First published 2014

Amberley Publishing
The Hill, Stroud
Gloucestershire, GL5 4EP

www.amberley-books.com

British Library Cataloguing in Publication Data.
A catalogue record for this book is available from the British Library.

ISBN 978 1 4456 3391 6 (hardback)
ISBN 978 1 4456 3402 9 (ebook)

Typesetting and Origination by Amberley Publishing.
Map illustration by Thomas Bohm, User design
Printed in the UK.

Contents

Insomuch that men commonly report that, seven hundred and ninety seven years past, it was by a heavenly voice revealed to Cadwaladr, last king of Britons, that his stock and progeny should reign in this land, and bear dominion again; whereupon most men were persuaded in their own opinion, that by the heavenly voice he [Henry VII] was provided and ordained long before, to enjoy and obtain this kingdom.

The Union of the Two Noble and Illustre Families of Lancastre and Yorke, commonly known as *Hall's Chronicle* (1548 and 1550, collated 1809)

Genealogical Tables

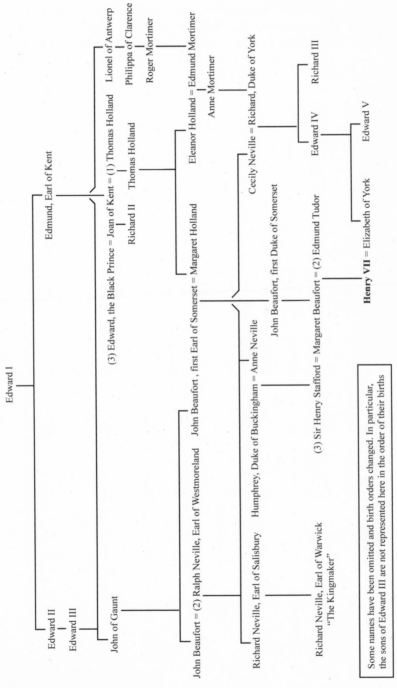

The royal descent from Edward I

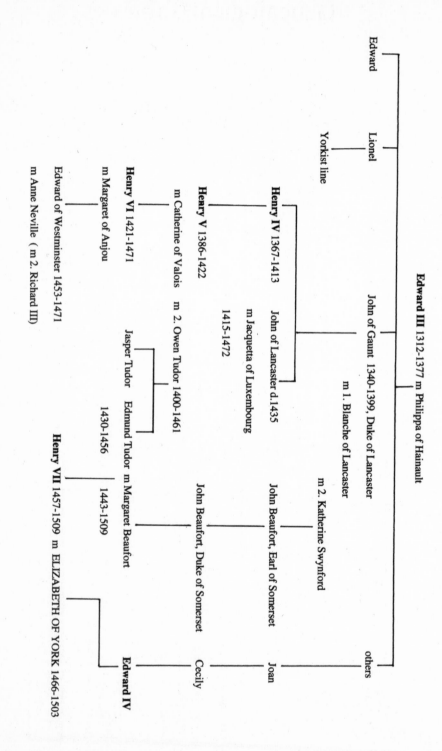

The Lancastrian line of descent from Edward III

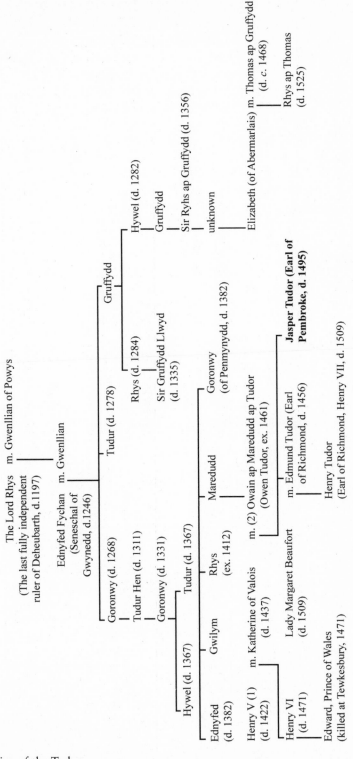

The origins of the Tudors

Introduction

There has never been a book on one of Britain's most selfless and brave nobles, Jasper Tudor, the uncle of Henry VII. Yet without Jasper's almost lone efforts at times, the Wars of the Roses would have surely petered out in 1471, after a mere sixteen years, with the battles of Barnet and Tewkesbury and the murders of the Lancastrian Henry VI and his heir Prince Edward of Westminster. As Ross in *Edward IV* states:

> Tewkesbury destroyed the Lancastrian cause as Barnet had destroyed the Nevills. The arch-enemies of the house of York, the Beauforts, had now been totally eliminated in the male line. The House of Lancaster was on the verge of extinction, with Prince Edward dead and Henry VI soon to perish in the Tower. Only Jasper Tudor, Earl of Pembroke, and his young nephew, Henry of Richmond, remained even of the half-blood branch of the family. Soon after the battle, Queen Margaret, who had taken refuge in a house of sanctuary, fell into Edward's hands...

These blood-drenched familial wars for the crown seemed over in 1471, but instead lasted for over another quarter of a century. And Jasper was the single peer who was present at the first and last battles between the Houses of York and Lancaster, being at St Albans on 22 May 1455, and at Stoke Field on 16 June 1497. It would be tempting to say that the eventual Lancastrian victory, and the end of the wars, owed to Jasper's loyalty alone. However, it was greatly assisted by the Yorkist usurper Edward IV's killing of his brother the Duke of Clarence, leaving his remaining brother, Richard of Gloucester, placed nearer the crown. When Edward IV died unexpectedly in 1483, he left two young princes. Richard of Gloucester immediately usurped the crown from the young Edward V. When Richard III killed the Duke of Buckingham, and incarcerated his nephews Edward V and Prince Richard in the Tower, all adult Plantagenet claimants to the crown had been wiped out, except for Jasper's nephew Henry, Earl of Richmond, the sole survivor of John of Gaunt's line. Richard now wanted Henry Tudor dead, and Jasper's role now was to protect Henry. The Tudors would only be safe if they killed the new king.

During Jasper's strange childhood, he and his elder brother Edmund had been made earls of Richmond and Pembroke respectively by their half-brother Henry VI. Edmund died mysteriously in 1456, and after the comparative safety of the Lancastrian court, Jasper's next four decades and more were spent in periods of fighting, being hunted and exiled. Apart from leading the Lancastrian forces at Mortimer's Cross, waging guerrilla warfare across Wales, being besieged in Northumberland and closely accompanying his brother Edmund's son Henry Tudor at the decisive Battle of Bosworth, Jasper was close to Henry in the long years of exile in Brittany and France. Jasper's personal charisma, reputation and hold upon the Welsh nobility and people enabled Henry Tudor to march unopposed through Wales, gathering Welsh forces to defeat Richard III at Bosworth in 1485. Jasper helped Henry cement a new Tudor dynasty into place. He was not merely a 'kingmaker' like the Earl of Warwick, killed fourteen years previously, but a true 'dynasty maker'.

1

Why Did the Wars of the Roses Happen?

The reader must forgive the skimming over of certain familial rifts and events during the sixty-five years of Jasper Tudor's life. His remarkable time included the thirty-two years of the convoluted series of battles and alliances that we now call the Wars of the Roses. Many recent historians and novelists have tried to simplify matters by omitting shades of grey in favour of a heroes-and-villains approach, as, for example, in the recent hagiographical accounts of Richard III, which this writer has attempted to leaven in a recent account of that king by comparing him to his successor, Henry VII. Also, recent writers seem to look upon Richard III, a Yorkist king, as a hero of the north of England, against the rich Southerners. Nothing could be further from the truth. His father, Richard of York, held hegemony in the Marches rather than the North, and very generally the Yorkist nobles were southern-based and the Lancastrians northern-based. Also, such was the animosity raised by the disappearance of the rightful king Edward V and his brother Richard of Cornwall in the Tower of London that Yorkist sympathisers in the south of England rebelled against Richard of Gloucester, in the very first months of his reign as Richard III. Many Yorkists fled to join Henry Tudor, the Lancastrian pretender in exile, and few Yorkist lords assisted the new king at Bosworth Field.

The wars were a series of battles between rival Plantagenet claims to the English throne. Rapidly changing alliances of royal family members and nobles meant that war swirled across all of England and Wales, with kings, princes and great magnates being betrayed, exiled, attainted, usurped, killed in battle, executed or simply murdered. There has been a renaissance of interest in this period, much of it fiction, supposition and attribution of motives parading as non-fiction, whereas the truth is, as usual, far more interesting. The wars were an intense power struggle between the rival Plantagenet descendants of two sons of Edward III. Edward had come to the throne aged only fourteen, when his mother Isabella and her lover Roger Mortimer, 1st Earl of March, deposed and disposed of his father, Edward II. Aged seventeen, Edward III and a small party of supporters surprised his guardian Mortimer and executed him. Edward III then reigned from 1327 to 1377 and created the first dukedoms in Britain for his five sons.

Edward unknowingly altered history and destabilised his kingdom by taking widely distributed power from his nobles and concentrating it in the hands of his sons. While the king theoretically held all the land in England, Wales and Ireland (and much of France), vast estates were managed for him by the noble houses. The great magnates, the Marcher Lords on the Scottish borders and the Welsh Marches, had expanded their lands at the expense of the Scots and native Britons, and were virtually buffer subkingdoms, with their own laws. The great lords tried to benefit from intermarriage with the newly created dukes, while Edward III's sons themselves, and their descendants, began to struggle for more power.

These sons, in seniority, became the first dukes of Cornwall, Clarence, Lancaster, York and Gloucester. The eldest son, Edward, known as the Black Prince (1330–1376), was created the first duke in England, becoming Duke of Cornwall in 1337. Since this time, the title now traditionally goes to the first son of the sovereign, as does the title Prince of Wales. Upon the Black Prince's death in 1376, a year before that of his father, the dukedom passed to his nine-year-old son, who succeeded Edward III as Richard II in 1377. Richard II was murdered upon the orders of the Lancastrian Henry Bolingbroke at Pontefract Castle in 1400. Holland's 1603 *Pancharis* gives the following lines to Jasper Tudor describing the deed:

> Richard, Second king by name, at Pomfret slaine by the coward
> Sir Pierce of Exton; who strake him downe, as a butcher
> Striketh an ox on his heade. Woe worth so shameful a monster!
> This trecherus bludy Duke did bring eight tall men in harnesse,
> Each man a bill in his hand, like thieves, to murder his Highnesse;
> Who, with a bill that he got by force, did manfully withstand
> Those Machavile hypocrites (for he killed four men with his own hand)
> Till that he was struck down by the knight; who leapt in a chayer,
> Like cravenous coward, to repose himself from a danger.

Bolingbroke, the son of John of Gaunt, 1st Duke of Lancaster, was proclaimed Henry IV. Aged only twenty-two, Richard II had left no heirs, no Duke of Cornwall. Now the families of the dukes of Clarence, York and Gloucester began to intrigue for the crown, which had been usurped by Henry Bolingbroke of the House of Lancaster.

In 1362, Edward III's second son, Lionel of Antwerp (1338–1368), had been created 1st Duke of Clarence. Clarence's first wife, Elizabeth de Burgh, gave him a single child, Philippa, who married Roger Mortimer, 4th Earl of March (1374–1398). Their son Edmund, 5th Earl of March, had been heir presumptive to Richard II. This was the original Yorkist line to the succession before Henry Bolingbroke had usurped the throne from Richard II, becoming the first Lancastrian king, Henry IV. The uncle of the heir presumptive, another Edmund Mortimer, joined with Owain Glyndŵr and

Henry 'Hotspur' Percy of Northumberland to attempt to put Edmund of March on his rightful throne, but the rising failed in 1403 at Shrewsbury. In 1405, Edmund and his brother Richard were taken from their confinement in the Tower by Edward of Langley, 2nd Duke of York, but were quickly recaptured.

In 1415, Edmund of March's brother-in-law, the Earl of Cambridge, conspired to take Edmund to Wales and to proclaim him king, but this attempt was foiled. Cambridge himself also had a claim to the throne. Cambridge was executed for his part in what is known as the Southampton Plot, but Cambridge's son Richard of York later became the father of Edward IV and Richard III. Edmund Mortimer, 5th Earl of March and the rightful king, died childless of plague in Ireland in 1425.

John of Ghent (now known as John of Gaunt, 1340–1399) was Edward III's third surviving son, and was created Duke of Lancaster in 1362. The founder of the House of Lancaster, John acted as a regent to the young Richard II, and became one of the richest men in the history of the world. However, upon his death, his estates were declared forfeit. Richard II exiled Lancaster's son Henry of Bolingbroke, who later returned from exile and as Duke of Lancaster took Richard II prisoner, having him murdered. This happened in the same year as John of Gaunt's death, 1399. As Henry IV, Bolingbroke reigned until 1413, being succeeded by his son Henry V.

The fourth of Edward III's sons to be made a duke was Edmund of Langley (1341–1402). He was created 1st Duke of York in 1385, becoming the founder of the House of York. His elder son Edward, 2nd Duke of York, died at Agincourt in 1415, and his younger son Richard of Cambridge, a Yorkist claimant to the crown, was executed after taking part in the Southampton Plot. Cambridge was the father of Richard, 3rd Duke of York, and grandfather of Edward IV and Richard III. The Yorkist claim was based upon Philippa Plantagenet being senior to John of Gaunt, Duke of Lancaster. She was the daughter of the Duke of Clarence, Edward III's second son, whereas Lancaster was the third son of the king. However, her claim was weakened through passing through the female line; Salic law, which prohibited female inheritance, was usually followed in England.

Thomas of Woodstock (1355?–1397) was the fifth of the five male heirs of Edward III to survive to adulthood. He was made Duke of Aumale (Normandy) and 1st Duke of Gloucester around 1385, and was also 1st Earl of Essex and 1st Earl of Buckingham. Gloucester became leader of the Lords Appellant, who tried to wrest power from his nephew Richard II. He was murdered in Calais in 1397 on the orders of Richard II, making the king extremely unpopular among his nobles. We can see from this cursory examination of the lives of Edward III's five ducal offspring that there would be different claimants to the English crown.

After this brief background, we can return to the succession of kings. Richard II, the son of the Black Prince, had become king in 1377. He was just ten years old and the grandson of Edward III. The boy king's immediate problem was that he had three powerful surviving uncles: the dukes of

Lancaster, York and Gloucester. In Richard's early years, England was ruled by a series of councils, mainly to prevent the Duke of Lancaster, John of Gaunt, becoming too powerful. Richard II's reign was unstable, with John of Gaunt leaving England because of plots against his person. Another uncle, Thomas of Woodstock, Duke of Gloucester, led a group of nobles including Henry of Bolingbroke, the son of Lancaster, protesting against Richard II's coterie of favourites. At the Battle of Radcot Bridge in 1387, Gloucester's men defeated the royalist army of the Earl of Oxford.

Gloucester's followers, called the 'Lords Appellant', now virtually took control of Richard II's council and court, but later Gloucester was imprisoned in Calais, and murdered upon Richard II's orders in 1397. Richard II had thus killed one uncle, and another, John of Gaunt, Duke of Lancaster, died in 1399. His other uncle, Edmund of Langley, Duke of York, died in 1402, leaving two sons who would be involved in the kingship disputes. Richard now took the huge estates of John of Gaunt's exiled heir, Henry of Lancaster (Bolingbroke). Henry Bolingbroke returned to Wales and captured and deposed Richard there in 1399. Richard II was probably starved to death at Pontefract Castle before February 1400, and from 1399 until the early 1450s the House of Lancaster ruled England in relative peace. Most of the new king Henry IV's reign (1399–1413) was spent dealing with Owain Glyndŵr's War of Independence, where Henry led six unsuccessful invasions into Wales. Glyndŵr was joined by the captured Edmund Mortimer and the war did not end until 1415.

The second king of the House of Lancaster was Henry IV's son Henry of Monmouth (1413–1422). Henry V died of dysentery in France, aged only thirty-five, and his son Henry VI (1422–1461 and 1470–1471) was only a few months old. Henry V's brothers, the dukes of Bedford and Gloucester, thus acted as Henry VI's first regents. Henry VI suffered intermittently from mental and physical inadequacies and had no children, which led to constant intrigue regarding the succession. With relative peace in England under Henry V and in the early years of the young Henry VI's reign, there took place a series of arranged marriages consolidating greater and greater estates into fewer noble families.

These marriages were often contracted between children, and titles could be passed from the female line to their spouses if there were no male heirs. The Mortimer earls of March, who controlled large swathes of Wales and its borders, were descended from Philippa Plantagenet. They intermarried into the Neville family, the earls of Warwick, who possessed huge landholdings in the Midlands, north and north-west. In the east of England, the new duchy of Norfolk had been created by Richard II, and its dukes became firm supporters of the royal family in the east of England. The Stanleys came to control large parts of North Wales and the north-west of England. The Percy family, dukes of Northumberland, had supported Glyndŵr's war against Henry IV and Henry V but still virtually ruled the north-east and much land around the border with Scotland.

Against this background of the immensely powerful Mortimer, Neville,

Norfolk, Stanley and Percy families, Richard Plantagenet, 3rd Duke of York (1411–1460), came to be considered next in line for the throne. York's father, the 3rd Earl of Cambridge, had been beheaded by Henry V in 1415 for his part in the Southampton Plot. However, Richard had received the title of his childless uncle Edward, 2nd Duke of York, who had been killed at Agincourt in the same year. He also received the title and huge estates of another childless uncle, Edmund Mortimer, Earl of March, in 1425. Mortimer had been the heir presumptive to Richard II and was the focus of the Tripartite Alliance, forged between his uncle Edmund, Owain Glyndŵr and the Percys, which aimed to place him on the throne at the expense of the Lancaster heir. Along with his brothers and sisters, Edmund Mortimer, the legitimate king, was for years kept in custody by Henry IV and Henry V.

Richard Plantagenet had claims to the throne through both uncles, and their estates had made him the wealthiest man in England apart from Henry VI. He was 3rd Duke of York, 6th Earl of March, 4th Earl of Cambridge, and 8th Earl of Ulster. However, the House of York had lost political power under the Lancastrian kings. In 1430 York was made Constable of England, and in 1432 he was appointed Guardian of the Coast of Normandy. In 1436 he was made Regent of France, advancing with an army almost to the gates of Paris. In 1437 York was recalled, and in 1440 he was appointed regent to Henry VI again, holding office till 1445.

During his years in France, in virtual exile, Richard of York had spent thousands of pounds of his own money, paying and feeding the garrisons and armed forces, as Henry VI had failed to support him. The Crown owed Richard around £40,000, or at least £30 million in today's money. The income from his estates was also declining. York had been relieved in France by Henry VI's favourite, the Duke of Somerset, a grandson of John of Gaunt. The Lancastrian Somerset, in marked contrast to York, was advanced tens of thousands of pounds for his services to the Crown in France. York was appointed Lieutenant of Ireland in 1449, and in relative exile watched the less competent Somerset surrender lands that had belonged to England for decades. It is thought that Henry VI wished to keep the more popular Duke of York out of England and France, where he might raise armies of loyal troops. After the fall of Rouen to France, the unpopular Somerset returned to England but was fondly welcomed by Henry VI.

However, popular discontent boiled over and in January 1450 Adam Moleyns, Lord Privy Seal and Bishop of Chichester, was lynched by discontented unpaid soldiers at Portsmouth. The bishop was an active supporter of William de la Pole, 1st Duke of Suffolk, a favourite of the king and his chief councillor. Suffolk had spent most of his time fighting the French and was Lord High Admiral. He had negotiated a marriage contract between Henry VI and Margaret of Anjou in 1444, which, in a secret clause, gave Maine and Anjou back to France. When this was discovered Suffolk became deeply unpopular. After losing most of England's remaining possessions in France, Suffolk was sent into exile in Calais. However, he was beheaded aboard ship on his way to exile, probably upon the orders of his rival Richard of York.

A disgruntled House of Commons demanded that Henry VI returned grants of land and money that he had given to his favourites. In the Jack Cade Rebellion, Lord High Treasurer James Fiennes, 1st Baron Saye and Sele, was killed, and in September York landed at Beaumaris Castle in Anglesey and rode for London. He met with the king, but the violence carried on, with the king's favourite Somerset being put in the Tower for a short time for his own safety. However, Somerset was released in 1451 and made Captain of Calais. York realised that he did not have enough support among the nobility to take power, and retired to his favourite seat, Ludlow Castle in the Welsh Marches.

By 1452 York was desperate, and marched with several thousand men to London. At Dartford the road was blocked by the king's army, and York demanded that Somerset be put on trial for his misconduct in the war in France. York also wished to be recognised as Henry's heir apparent. Assured by Henry VI that his wishes would be followed, York disbanded his army, but was placed under arrest for two weeks, after which he swore allegiance to the king at St Paul's Cathedral. In 1453, Henry fined York's tenants, who had supported him at Dartford, and York lost his offices, including that of Lieutenant of Ireland. It seemed to York that he had lost the power struggle for the succession. Queen Margaret was now pregnant, and the marriage of John of Gaunt's direct descendant Margaret Beaufort, to Edmund Tudor, gave another possible Lancastrian line of succession. At the end of 1452, the king appointed his half-brother Edmund Tudor as Earl of Richmond and endowed him at his expense. His other half-brother, Jasper Tudor, was created Earl of Pembroke in the same year.

However, in 1453, Henry VI suffered a complete mental breakdown, possibly brought on by the defeat at Castillon, which drove the English forces from France. Also, on 13 October, his long-awaited son and heir, Edward of Westminster, was born. Because of the king's piety and his physical and mental health, it was rumoured at the time that either Somerset or James Butler, Earl of Wiltshire, was the father of Henry's only child. There may well be truth in the rumour. In this same year, the Neville family, relatives of York, had been in bitter dispute with the Percys in the north of England. We have noted that York's rents and income from land were suffering, as were those of the Nevilles and Percys, which led to some fighting between them.

The great agrarian crisis of the late 1430s had affected their great estates in northern England far more than further south. Poor harvests had led to a permanent fall in rents of up to 15 per cent in the 1440s, and in the early 1450s Richard Neville, Earl of Salisbury, and Henry Percy, Earl of Northumberland, were facing financial losses. Salisbury was protected to some extent by being in royal favour. He managed to keep financially secure by his possession of royal offices and prompt payments from the royal exchequer. However, the infant Northumberland had no prospect of influencing the king. His council spent proportionally more of his income on fees to retainers and had great difficulty in securing royal payment for his garrison at the border town of Berwick. Royal favour was necessary for the earls, their sons and their retainers. The Percys now began a campaign of violence and disorder against the favoured Nevilles. In 1453, their armies had actually faced each other at Sand Hutton before the Archbishop of York mediated.

It was obvious that these two great families, safeguarding the North against the Scots, would take opposing sides in the struggle for royal succession. The Neville alternative to backing York in the power vacuum brought on by the king's illness was to back York's enemy Edmund Beaufort, Duke of Somerset. He was also a Neville kinsman. However, Somerset was in dispute with the Earl of Salisbury's son, another Richard Neville, Earl of Warwick, over parts of the Beauchamp inheritance. York, with little political power among the nobility, made a sensible alliance. Over the winter of 1453/54, the Nevilles decided to back York in his bid to be made Protector of the Realm. York was Salisbury's brother-in-law, married to his youngest sister Cecily Neville, and the Earl of Salisbury wished to remain close to royal favour. The Nevilles next stormed, armed, into Somerset's great council and demanded that the absent York be appointed as Protector of the Realm and Chief Councillor.

York almost immediately had Somerset placed in the Tower, while the Percys began suffering at the hands of the Nevilles. Salisbury and Warwick were now firmly committed to York's cause but in grave danger if Henry VI recovered, which he did at Christmas 1454. Somerset was then released and allied himself with the Percys. York, Salisbury and his son Warwick could no longer command the council or court, and Somerset, Exeter and the Percy earls of Northumberland were restored to favour. The Yorkists were dismissed from their royal offices.

In March 1455, York and his Neville allies, the earls of Salisbury and Warwick, fled from London. Richard Neville, 16th Earl of Warwick, proposed to raise an army in the Midlands and Welsh Marches to give the Yorkist faction the crown. In the war that followed, York and the Nevilles would be known as the Yorkists, while Henry VI, Somerset, the Tudors and the Percys would be called the Lancastrians. The main battles of the Wars of the Roses in the period 1455–1471 demonstrate how unstable England and Wales were at this time, with shifting alliances and an increasingly bitter movement from chivalrous behaviour to battlefield executions of captured nobles. Of the seventeen major battles, the Yorkists won twelve, leading to the House of York taking power for fourteen years from 1471 until the unlikely final victory for Lancaster at Bosworth in 1485. This is the much simplified background to what we now know as the Wars of the Roses.

2

The Genesis of the Tudor Dynasty

To begin to comprehend the Plantagenet civil wars, one has to understand the relationship between England and its unsettled and recently conquered neighbouring country. The House of Gwynedd attempted to unify Wales in the thirteenth century, leading to a direct response from Edward I of England. This led to the killing of Llywelyn II in 1282, and the execution of his brother Prince Dafydd in 1283, which began ensuring English dominance over Wales. By the Statute of Rhuddlan in 1284, Wales was divided into two political and administrative areas. The Principality of Wales was under the king's control and was defended by fourteen substantial royal castles. The Marcher lordships, on the other hand, were a collection of independent authorities, run along semi-lawless lines. This led to the building and rebuilding of over ninety large stone castles on the England–Wales border in the fourteenth century. There were also hundreds of subsidiary fortresses and fortified homes. There were also built a large number of walled towns around castles, essentially copies of the French bastides, within which to settle English, Flemish and other nationalities. The native Welsh were generally proscribed from living in these heavily defended commercial centres.

The new town and its castle became 'symbolical of conquest and the imposition of an alien regime, and the presence within Wales of a privileged burgess element'. There thus grew native resentment of second-class treatment in one's own country, the imposition of a new and alien language, the seizing of land and property, and the killing of the last princes. With a constant undercurrent of rebellion, there were hundreds of prophecies involving a national leader who would free the Welsh. The bards, always a vital part of Welsh communications, culture and identity, continued to tell the people and their lords of the coming of *y mab darogan* – 'the son of prophecy', a national redeemer who would lead the Welsh back to freedom. From at least the sixth century, bards had pleaded for deliverance from the Germanic Saxons and Angles who had taken over England, pressing the Britons back into Wales, and indeed the Welsh words for the English are still derived from Saxon, much like the Scottish Gaelic *sassenach*. In Welsh, the

English people are still *Saeson*, speaking *Saesneg*. With the incredibly fast Norman takeover of England, Wales then faced a new threat, and the new kings and lords who attacked Wales were rightly dismissed as being French in the Welsh language and by the bards – they were French-speaking until around the early fifteenth century. Wales thus saw itself as the repository of the Britons, faced with alien threats, and wanted the return of England to British rule. On the other hand, foreign kings saw Wales, Ireland and Scotland as territories to be assimilated.

One of a line of *meibion darogan* appeared in the fifteenth century. From 1400 to 1421 there was a national war, and unwavering Welsh belief in a man of destiny was crucial in securing support for the cause. Owain Glyndŵr's achievements and radical aspirations 'captured the imagination of succeeding generations of Welshmen'. However, his failure to defeat the English led to the introduction of the Penal Laws of Henry IV. According to Gwyn Alf Williams, 'The ferocious racist penal legislation passed at the height of the Glyn Dŵr rebellion turned the Welsh into unpersons without civic rights.' While the wars added to the continuing decline of Wales both socially and economically, the penal laws left a legacy of real and enduring hate for the English. Anti-English sentiment continued to characterise Welsh prophecies. They were helped by the manner of Owain Glyndŵr's disappearance – he was never betrayed or captured and his death was never confirmed. This added to the expectation that the prophesied deliverer would return some day.

The Penal Laws, prophecies and anti-English sentiment continued throughout the fifteenth century, and the harsh realities forced some ambitious Welshmen to seek advancement within the English sphere. War, plague and economic decline led to depopulation in the bastides and boroughs, enabling some Welshmen to settle in them. However, towns were still perceived as being English and privileged. This period saw the emergence of the *uchelwyr* (high men, or squirearchy) class. They gradually gained office as sheriffs, bailiffs, etc., and were so successful that they were generally the local rulers of Wales by end of the fifteenth century. Although many of them had been rewarded by the English Crown, the *uchelwyr* also actively supported Welsh culture. They worked for English reward but remained Welsh-speaking and Wales-directed, which was vital for the Tudor invasion through Wales.

The Wars of the Roses saw the 'baronage of England let loose in a self-destructive sequence of conflicts and practically every family of substance in Wales was drawn in'. Wales and its Marches played a most prominent part, and there was a fresh and aggressively anti-English outburst which helped reawaken Welsh national feeling. The civil wars eventually gave the unlikely Henry Tudor an opportunity to be king. Jasper and his nephew Henry were well aware that their paternal forebears had been constantly fighting, for over two centuries, in the name of Welsh independence.

From the first king of all England, the Dane Athelstan, through the Saxons, Normans, Plantagenets, Tudors, Stuarts and Hanovers, we can see enough usurpations and 'unrightful' monarchs to make a case that nearly every single person in Britain with non-immigrant grandparents has a genuine claim to the crown. Usurpers and lucky accidents run through the centuries of the ruling monarchs of Britain, and those who are trying to rehabilitate Richard III gloss over his unedifying record, in killing those in his path and declaring his elder brothers and their offspring illegitimate.

It is necessary to state a fact which seems to be neglected or unknown – that the remaining Welsh are the original Britons of the British Isles, and systematic genocide by Germanic and then Norman invaders pushed them, and the threatened British language, into what is now known as Wales. The words 'Wales' and 'Welsh' in fact derive from the Saxon *walsci*, 'foreign', and even now the fewer and fewer native Britons in Wales are often treated as second-class citizens by English incomers, merely for speaking their own language. British history and heritage is not even taught in Wales to any great extent, but in mediaeval times there was still a sense that the British could regain their stolen territories with a *mab darogan*, a son of prophecy. Without this national sense of purpose, the Tudor dynasty could not have happened. The reasons for the end of the Wars of the Roses were very deeply entrenched in Welsh history and expectation.

In 1283, Wales had finally been conquered via treachery, murder, executions and the extermination of its royal family. The country was still restless, as we shall see in the account of Jasper Tudor's ancestors. From 1400 to 1415, English armies packed with foreign mercenaries invaded Wales on six separate occasions in attempts to halt Owain Glyndŵr's War of Independence. Only from around 1420 to 1421, with the final disappearance of Glyndŵr, had there been an uneasy peace in Wales. Welsh rights to citizenship had been taken away by the Lancastrian usurper Henry IV, the country and its churches and documents burned, and children taken into slavery in England. However, the travelling bards still proclaimed hope for the nation. These bards, with their constant promises of a delivery from English slavery, were crucial to the success of the Tudor invasion of England. During the Wars of the Roses, Welsh hopes for freedom interchanged between William Herbert of Raglan and Jasper Tudor, finally coming to rest in Jasper's nephew Henry. Without the bards there would not have been a Tudor dynasty, and they ensured that the pure British ancestry of the chosen 'son of prophecy' was known to nobles, yeomen and commoners, all with a deep sense of injustice. When he assumed the kingship, Henry Tudor commissioned research to prove his bloodline back to Brutus and Aeneas, the supposed forebears of the British race. He did not wish to rely upon his mother's claim through the French Plantagenet John of Gaunt, but upon descent from the original British kings of Britain. Genealogy had been extremely important in Glyndŵr's acceptance by Welsh lords as Prince of Wales, as it was to be in the acceptance of Henry as king.

Jasper Tudor's first important ancestor had been Ednyfed Fychan ap Cynwrig (*c.* 1170–1246), seneschal of Llywelyn the Great and then of his son Prince Dafydd. Even before Ednyfed's time, his family had been great servants of the princes of Gwynedd. Because of their service, all the descendants of Ednyfed's grandfather Iorwerth ap Gwrgan had been granted the concession that they should, in perpetuity, hold their lands throughout Wales free from all dues and services, other than military service in time of war. This special tenure was known as that of *wyrion Eden*, defined by Chapman (2011) as 'a conscious development of a feudal model by the princes of Gwynedd, one which unfortunately opened a competition of lordship which Edward I was in a better position to win'.

Ednyfed was ninth in descent from Marchudd ap Cynan, Lord of Rhos, the Lord Protector of Rhodri Mawr, King of Gwynedd. Thus his family had a lasting link with the rulers of North Wales. Born around 1173, Ednyfed was Lord of Bryn Ffanigl, Cricieth, Cellan, Cwmllanerch, Dinorwig, Erddreiniog, Gwredog, Llanrhystud, Llansadwrn, Penmynydd, Penrhyn Creuddyn and Trecastell. Ednyfed Fychan first came to notice in battle, fighting against the Marcher Lord Ranulf de Blondeville, 6th Earl of Chester and 1st Earl of Lincoln (1170–1232). King John had asked de Blondeville to invade North Wales to attack Llywelyn the Great in 1210, in the Welsh Wars of 1209–1212. De Blondeville's first wife, Constance, Duchess of Brittany (1161–1201), after many vicissitudes had managed to escape his cruelty after being imprisoned by him from 1196 to 1198. She was the mother, by a forced marriage to Geoffrey Plantagenet, of Arthur of Brittany, the real heir to the throne of England, whom King John had murdered in 1203. Ednyfed was said to have cut off the heads of three 'Saxon' lords in battle against de Blondeville and carried them, still bloody, to Prince Llywelyn, who ordered Ednyfed to change his family coat of arms to henceforth display three helms, or armoured heads, in memory of this event.

In 1215, Ednyfed became Llywelyn's *distain*, his seneschal, equivalent to his chief councillor. The same year saw Llywelyn take the castles of Carmarthen (Caerfyrddin), Kidwelly (Cydweli), Llanstephan (Llansteffan), Cardigan (Aberteifi) and Cilgerran. Llywelyn also helped the barons in their forcing King John to sign the *Magna Carta* in 1215. Three of its provisions applied to Wales, and John was forced to surrender Llywelyn's son Gruffydd back to him. In 1216, the other free princes of Wales affirmed their allegiance to Llywelyn at Aberdyfi and he became de facto ruler, as Llywelyn I, of the vast majority of the nation.

In 1218, King John's successor Henry III negotiated directly with Ednyfed Fychan, and confirmed Llywelyn's possessions by the Treaty of Worcester. Ednyfed again represented Llywelyn in a meeting with the King of England in 1232, and helped negotiate the Peace of the Middle in 1234. Now a great landowner across North Wales, Ednyfed seems to have gone on crusade in 1235, and his second wife Gwenllian died in 1236. Llywelyn the Great had a paralytic stroke in 1237, and Ednyfed effectively ran the nation until Llywelyn's death in 1240. Ednyfed continued as seneschal in the service of Llywelyn's son, the Prince of Wales, Dafydd ap Llywelyn.

Although Henry III had formally accepted Prince Dafydd as Llywelyn's successor, there was now constant fighting as Henry reneged upon his agreement and tried to retake Welsh lands. One of Ednyfed's sons was captured and killed by the English in the war of 1245, and it appears that Prince Dafydd may have then been poisoned, dying at his palace at Garth Celyn, Abergwyngregyn, in 1246. Ednyfed also died in this year, still in service, aged seventy-six. He was buried in his private chapel at Llandrillo-yn-Rhos church on the north coast, only a few hundred yards from his great manor of Llys Euryn. His death was recorded in the St Werburgh's Abbey annals in Chester as being an event of great importance, an extremely rare obituary for a Welshman in an English chronicle.

Ednyfed's first marriage was to the flame-haired Efa Brân, also known as Tangwystl Goch ferch Llywarch ap Brân. His children by Efa Brân were Tudur, Llywelyn, Cynfrig, Hywel, Iorwerth, Madog, Angharad and Gwenllian. One son, Sir Tudur ap Ednyfed Fychan, also became Seneschal of Gwynedd, and another, Hywel ap Ednyfed, became Bishop of Llanelwy (St Asaph). Ednyfed's second marriage was to Gwenllian, daughter of the Lord Rhys (1132–1197). The Lord Rhys, Rhys ap Gruffudd, was the Prince of Deheubarth, also known as the Prince of South Wales, who kept much of Wales independent of the invading Normans for all of his reign. To Ednyfed and Gwenllian were born Goronwy, Gruffudd, Rhys and Angharad. Goronwy also became Seneschal of Gwynedd under Prince Llywelyn ap Gruffudd, and the Tudors of Penmynydd in Anglesey were descended from him.

In these times, Wales was a country still mainly tribal in social and administrative organisation. The remarkably equitable tenth-century laws of Hywel Dda were generally followed in both princedoms and Marcher territories, and the Welsh language, with its four distinct dialects, was used throughout Wales and the Marches. The major princes of Gwynedd (North Wales) and Deheubarth (most of South and Mid Wales, less the south-east and south Pembroke) needed an efficient bureaucracy to run their vast and complicated feudal estates, and began to copy the Norman pattern. Families such as that of Ednyfed Fychan, the *wyrion Eden*, became the leaders of such services, and their members were rewarded with substantial gifts of land. Ednyfed and his many descendants spread across much of Wales in their influence and ownership of manors, in return for military, legal and rent-collecting services to their lords. The most distinguished branch of his clan, later known as the Tudors, settled at Penmynydd in Anglesey. The family constantly widened its connections and influence, by intermarriage with the leading families of North Wales and the Marches, such as the Greys, Scudamores and Mortimers.

Goronwy ab Ednyfed Fychan grew up in an atmosphere of royal favour, which allowed his extended family to remain free landholders in their own right. Goronwy would have been trained by his father to serve and administer at the royal palaces of Aberffraw and Llys Rhosyr on Anglesey and at Garth Celyn, which overlooked Anglesey on a crossing point from the mainland. According to the laws, a primary division of the kingdom was the cantref, literally 100 townships. Each cantref was subdivided into two commotes, and each commote was made up of forty-eight townships. The other two townships belonged to the king. One was the 'King's Waste', or the *ffridd*, a desolate and defensive place where castles were eventually built. The other township was the *maerdref*, or royal demesne. This had the best land in the kingdom, and it was here that the *llys*, or royal palace, was built.

The maerdref became the main centre of administration and controlled its own regional issues, such as tax collection and justice. Nowadays, most sites of the royal courts of Gwynedd are virtually unknown, either covered by fields or built upon by later farmsteads or villages after the conquest of Edward I. The component parts of a *llys* and *maerdref* included the *llys* itself, with its royal hall and other buildings, the royal demesne (*tir bwrdd*) worked by bond tenants, and the settlements of the tenants in one or more small hamlets.

The obligations of the king's tenants would include working the fields of the royal desmesne lands and supplying the *llys* with agricultural produce. Other tenants in the commote would be responsible for repair and maintenance of the royal buildings. These duties included, for example at Rhosyr, construction work on the chapel and the *rhaglaw*'s hall and on the lord's privy and stable. The *rhaglaw* was the chief governor, or prefect, of a district. The Welsh laws describe what the king's tenants were expected to provide, such as the hall, chamber, foodhouse, stable, porch, barn, kiln, dormitory, and privy.

It was from these halls or *llysoedd* that Gwynedd was governed. When the king or prince was in attendance at a *llys* he would summon his councillors and other important men from the commote to meet him. Business would be done in the hall during the day, as when Llywelyn the Great signed a charter at Rhosyr in 1237. In the evening, feasting and entertainment would take place around the great open hearth. The centre of Welsh culture lay in the royal courts. The early kings and later princes of Gwynedd would normally have a main preferred palace, while the heart of the kingdom of Gwynedd would always remain at Aberffraw, the location dating back to the Roman period, where the dynasty began.

After Llywelyn II was killed, the *llysoedd* no longer had a role to play, and fell into disuse. Food renders were no longer paid, for which local barns stocked grain and the like for local communities. They were replaced by money taxes, which contributed, along with massive foreign loans, towards the new castles erected by Edward. All the *llysoedd* were demolished and their treasures taken, except for Garth Celyn at Abergwyngregyn, used by Edward I when supervising the building of the 'Iron Ring' of castles. Llys Rhosyr is being excavated and Garth Celyn survives in part on a Roman site, but most have been lost. The duties of Ednyfed and his sons, being virtual Prime Ministers of Gwynedd, would have revolved around perhaps twenty of these *llysoedd*, royal courts.

Along with no less than six of his brothers, Goronwy ab Ednyfed acted as a royal administrator to all these *llysoedd*. He would also have been present with his father and some of his brothers at negotiations with various earls and Marcher Lords, discussing treaties. Goronwy married Morfudd ferch Meurig ab Ithel, daughter of a lord of Gwent. After his father Ednyfed's passing in 1246, Goronwy replaced him as seneschal in 1258, serving Prince Llywelyn ap Gruffydd, Llywelyn II, as his main advisor. Goronwy appears on various occasions as an arbitrator and a witness, and in 1258 he was one of the Welsh leaders who made an agreement with a faction of Scottish lords.

In February 1263, Goronwy, now Lord of Trecastell on Anglesey, led an armed campaign south from Gwynedd to fight the powerful Marcher Lords, who were only allowed to militarily expand their great estates by conquest into Wales. Goronwy led his troops as far as his wife's homeland of Gwent in the south-east. Seeing that Gwynedd was willing to raise a large army outside its region, the English barons held off an invasion. This uneasy standoff meant that the English threat to Gwynedd held off for some years. Goronwy was also at the side of Llywelyn for the signing of the Treaty of Montgomery in September 1267. By this, Henry III officially recognised Llywelyn ap Gruffudd as the rightful ruler of the Principality of Wales, the only time a British leader would be recognised as such by an English monarch. The treaty required Llywelyn to swear homage and fealty to Henry, but also showed the authority that Llywelyn II and his court wielded. Henry's only other choice was continuing an extremely expensive, full-scale war into Wales.

Goronwy died on 17 October 1268, and at least two elegies were written. In one he is acclaimed as the 'rampart of Gwynedd' and the 'wall of the city'. Like his father, he had been a warrior as well as an administrator. Goronwy's brother, Tudur ab Ednyfed, had been was captured during Henry III's inconclusive campaign against Dafydd ap Llywelyn ap Iorwerth in September 1245, being released in May 1247 upon swearing fealty to the king. Tudur had become one of Llywelyn ap Gruffudd's main advisors after 1256, succeeding Goronwy as seneschal until his own death in 1278. Tudur's son Heilyn was held hostage by the king between 1246 and 1263, and submitted finally to Edward I in 1282. The history of Ednyfed Fychan's descendants is complicated, but nearly all fought against the English incursions up to 1282, and in all the subsequent rebellions against English rule.

Of Goronwy's sons, Tudur 'Hen' ap Goronwy ab Ednyfed, born around 1245, followed the previous generations of his family, becoming seneschal to Llywelyn ap Gruffudd. Tudur was responsible for the rebuilding of Bangor Priory. While Tudur Hen was seneschal, the French-speaking Edward I of England determined to finally achieve what his Norman forebears and his Marcher Lords had failed to do. He decided to borrow heavily from foreign bankers and conquer the remaining Britons of Wales. Edward I raised customs duties to help pay for his new wars with Llywelyn ap Gruffudd, and in 1275 negotiated an agreement with the domestic merchant community, which secured a permanent duty on wool. The revenues from the resulting customs duties were handled by the Riccardi, a group of bankers from Lucca in Italy. This was in return for their service as moneylenders to the Crown, which helped finance the Welsh Wars. After this, the Frescobaldi of Florence took over the role as money lenders to the English Crown. In the 1270s, the Frescobaldi had opened an office in London and began financing the wars, eventually supplanting the pioneering Riccardi, who were driven to bankruptcy by unpaid loans made to Edward. With Edward's death in 1307, he left a debt to all creditors that amounted to £30,000. Using today's average earnings, this represents an unpaid bill of £417 million. The Frescobaldi debt was also never repaid, driving them to bankruptcy. Edward's conquest of Wales was thus funded by money literally stolen from the bankers of Lucca and Florence.

Another source of Edward's income was represented by the Jewish community. By 1280, Jews had been exploited to a level at which they were no longer of much financial use to the Crown, but they could still be used in political bargaining. Their moneylending or usury business, a practice forbidden to Christians then, had made many people indebted to them and caused general popular resentment. In 1275 Edward had issued the Statute of the Jewry, which outlawed usury, and in 1279 he arrested all the heads of Jewish households in England and had around 300 of them executed. He formally expelled them from England in 1290. This not only generated revenues through royal appropriation of Jewish loans and property, but it also gave Edward the political capital to negotiate a substantial lay subsidy in the 1290 Parliament. Such is the financial record of 'The Hammer of the Scots' when smashing his tiny neighbour Wales into submission.

A long campaign, with thousands of foreign mercenaries funded by foreign loans and theft from the Jewish communities, was failing when Llywelyn II divided his forces, leaving his main army in Gwynedd to travel south to meet Edmund Mortimer. Mortimer, whose father's life had been spared by Llywelyn, had promised support and wished for a meeting. Near Builth in 1282, Llywelyn was lured into a trap with his small bodyguard and all were killed. His nearby army surrendered upon hearing of their prince's death, and all 3,000 were massacred, in an event hardly recorded in British history. There are no known survivors. Letters from Archbishop Pecham refer to the event, but some have been destroyed, presumably soon after that time to cover up the Mortimer conspiracy and the killings. Llywelyn's brother Dafydd, the new Prince of Wales, was captured in 1283. Before this time the death penalty for 'treason' was hanging, drawing and quartering, but the victim was dead before the drawing of the entrails.

However, Edward I personally invented, supervised and watched a disgusting new form of execution for Prince Dafydd, who was dragged by horses to his place of execution at Shrewsbury. With flayed skin, Dafydd was hung almost to the point of death, then castrated and his genitals burnt before him, before his stomach was slit for his intestines to pour out. The skill of the executioner was to prolong the pain, and Scotland's William Wallace in 1305 faced the same death by the same king. Like Llywelyn's,

Dafydd's body was quartered for display around England, and his head was also spiked for show in London next to his brother's. Edward now took out more massive foreign loans, to pay for the 'Iron Ring' of great castles around Gwynedd, which included Rhuddlan, Denbigh, Caernarfon, Conwy, Beaumaris, Aberystwyth and Harlech.

Almost the entire extended families of Llywelyn and Dafydd were incarcerated for life or killed in order to exterminate the House of Gwynedd. Only the children of one brother of Llywelyn, Rhodri, survived, as he was living in exile. The royal line of Gwynedd, which dated back over 600 years, was finally wiped out when Rhodri's grandson Owain Llawgoch was assassinated upon the orders of the English Crown, in France in 1378, after he had declared himself Prince of Wales.

There had been considerable Welsh support for Edward's Welsh wars from 1257 to 1267 and 1277 to 1283, from nobles jealous of Llywelyn II's hegemony. Gruffudd ap Gwenwynwyn was Lord of Powys Wenwynwyn, also known as Powys Cyfeiliog. This was the southern part of the princedom of Powys and was centred on Welshpool. Gruffudd had actively fought for the English, plotting to kill Llywelyn in 1267, and his son Owain has been implicated in Llywelyn's 1282 murder. Owain altered his family name to 'de la Pole' after his seat at Powys Castle outside Pool. Then known as Y Trallwng (boggy area) in Welsh, and Pool in English, the market town later became called Welshpool.

In Carmarthenshire in 1287, there was a revolt led by Rhys ap Maredudd, a member of the Deheubarth dynasty, unsettled because of lack of rewards for supporting Edward during his wars against Wales. Rhys gained support owing to resistance to new English penalties, restrictions and taxes, and the aggressive stance of new English administrators and tax collectors. The great-grandson of the Lord Rhys, Rhys ap Maredudd had twice sided with England to fight against Llywelyn, the only Deheubarth noble to do so. In gratitude, Edward I had given him some lands, but not returned his ancestral castle and lands at Dinefwr. Rhys was forced to make Dryslwyn Castle, further down the Tywi Valley, his main residence, embarking on a substantial building programme there in the late 1270s and early 1280s. Rhys remained loyal, hoping to regain his lands, but in 1283 Edward for some reason forced him to give up Dryslwyn.

At last, in 1287, Rhys rebelled and this led to his capture of most of the Tywi Valley, the heartland of Deheubarth, including the castles at Dinefwr and Carreg Cennen. The rebellion was quelled by the autumn, but broke out again in November, and was only ended after a ten-day siege of Rhys' final stronghold, Newcastle Emlyn Castle, in January 1288. Rhys went into hiding, but was eventually captured in 1291 and executed for treason at York in 1292. His son, Rhys ap Rhys, was then arrested after his father's execution and was imprisoned in Bristol Castle and then Norwich. He was never released from his incarceration, but is known to have been alive forty-eight years later. Henry IV later followed Edward I's policy of incarcerating Welshmen and their families until their death.

Tudur Hen ap Goronwy, the grandson of Ednyfed Fychan, had fortunately not accompanied Llywelyn to Builth to be wiped out with the rest of his surrendered army. However, he became one of the rebels during the short-lived insurrection of Madog ap Llywelyn, Lord of Meirionydd, in 1294. Madog's rebellion was noted for a document that he drew up in December 1294, entitled the Penmachno Document. Madog signed the document as Prince of Wales, and Tudur ap Goronwy was also a chief signatory, referred to by Madog as 'our Steward', indicating his hereditary importance to the region. Approaching fifty, it is unclear whether or not Tudur fought alongside Madog, who was of a junior branch of the House of the Aberffraw princes of Gwynedd, and a fifth cousin of Llywelyn ap Gruffudd. Madog's father was one of those who had opposed Llywelyn ap Gruffudd at Builth, and had died the next year in exile in England. Madog had returned to Gwynedd after the death of Llywelyn in 1282 and had received some of Llywelyn's lands in Anglesey as a reward from Edward I.

In the autumn of 1294, Madog put himself at the head of a well-planned national revolt in response to the punitive actions of new royal administrators across North and West Wales. Swingeing new taxes had been imposed upon impoverished and war-torn Wales to help pay Edward's unsustainable war debts. Madog was aggrieved by the fact that he had been unable to recover his father's lands, which had been confiscated through the courts despite his father fighting for the English. With unjust land grabs, insensitive officials, the levying of troops in Wales for service in France and the demand for another subsidy from Wales in 1291–1292, insurrection spread across the whole nation.

The Madog uprising quickly spread to South Wales. Caernarfon Castle and town were taken, along with castles at Hawarden, Ruthin and Denbigh, while Madog besieged Cricieth and Harlech castles for months. Morgan ap Maredudd took Morlais Castle in South Wales, while Cynan ap Maredudd besieged Builth Castle. Caerphilly Castle was besieged and Kenfig Castle burnt. Reginald de Lacy, Lord of Denbigh, tried to end the siege of Denbigh Castle but was defeated and his army routed in November. Flint and Rhuddlan were under siege, other castles were taken and bastide towns burnt. In December, Edward led one army to Conwy Castle, where he himself was under siege over the Christmas period, until relieved by his navy in 1295. Harlech was reduced to just thirty-seven defenders and was on the point of collapse when the main Welsh army was ambushed in a night attack by a second English army under the Earl of Warwick in 1295. The Welsh formed 'schiltrons' of pikemen but were decimated by archers, most of whom had been recruited from Wales and the Marches. Madog barely escaped and surrendered around August in Snowdonia.

There was another harsh response from Edward I in the form of even more humiliating and punitive ordinances, restricting the civil rights and economic and social opportunities of the Welsh. Goronwy Fychan, Tudur Hen's brother, was also deeply involved in the Madog war. The brothers, with Madog's capture and death, could either live as outlaws and forfeit their estates, or try to keep the family in power. Both managed to be pardoned. Tudur became a dutiful subject of King Edward, and began serving as a royal official in his clan's heartland of Perfeddwlad, the 'Middle Country' that lies between the rivers Conwy and Dee, between the two traditional kingdoms of Gwynedd and Powys.

However, Edward was still not placated and in 1296 he made a speech to Parliament in which he accused the Welsh of countless 'deceptions and plots'. Tudur Hen was one of a deputation of four leaders which informed Edward I, on behalf of the people of North Wales, that his subjects unreservedly pledged their loyalty to his kingship. Wales could not stand another rapacious invasion. Tudur was also present at Caernarfon in 1301 when it was publically announced that Edward's seven-year-old son was to be the first non-native Prince of Wales, symbolising Wales as a conquered English dominion. In popular folklore, this prince, soon to become the ill-fated Edward II, was born in Caernarfon Castle and presented to his adoring Welsh subjects, while still a babe in arms, as Prince of Wales. The facts are more prosaic. The young prince had a ten-year-old elder brother, Alfonso, still alive at the time of his birth. Alfonso was born at Bayonne in November 1273 and his premature death on 19 August 1284 deprived England of having a king named Alfonso of Bayonne. Prince Edward was born on 25 April 1284, so was never in fact born as heir to the throne or displayed as such. Two other brothers, John and Henry, had died aged five in 1271 and aged six in 1274 respectively. Edward II was a fourth son.

Tudur now paid homage to the first English Prince of Wales, and submitted several petitions to him in 1305. Now known as Tudur 'Hen', the aged, he died on 11 October 1311, being buried in the Dominican friary chapel in Bangor that he had helped rebuild. Because of his low and passive profile since the Madog war of independence, he was enabled to pass on considerable land and wealth to the sons he had with his wife, Angharad ferch Ithel Fychan ab Ithel, the daughter of the lord of the nearby cantref of Tegeingl in Flintshire.

His son Goronwy ap Tudur Hen, Lord of Penmynydd (c. 1285–1331), served the English Crown as a soldier. He was known to be a captain of twenty archers in Aquitaine. Up until this Goronwy, all of the Tudur clan had fought against the English to keep Gwynedd independent. Aged only nine or ten when his father had allied with Madog, Goronwy realised that loyalty to the English king was the only way to ensure that lands, titles and wealth would be secure and safe from attainders. Goronwy remained loyal during Edward II's war with the barons in 1311. The resulting 'Ordinances of 1311' were then enforced on Edward II by the disenfranchised magnates of the realm, and effectively limited the king's authority. Goronwy was also present at Newcastle as leader of some of Edward's Welsh troops and probably saw action at Bannockburn in 1314 during the Wars of Scottish Independence. He served with distinction under the leadership of his distant cousin Sir Gruffydd Llwyd, himself a great-grandson of Ednyfed Fychan. Gruffydd's immediate family had fought upon the side of Edward I during the Welsh wars of 1282–1283 and benefited from confiscated lands.

At this time there was a mainly southern rising in 1316 under Llywelyn Bren, Lord of Senghenydd and Meisgyn in Glamorgan, who later suffered the same grisly fate as Prince Dafydd. His father Gruffydd ap Rhys had sided with Llywelyn II. In 1314 Gilbert de Clare died, and with him the de Clare male line, which had ruled Glamorgan. The lordship of Glamorgan thus passed to a series of Crown 'keepers', men who were new to the area, unfamiliar with its ways and unsympathetic to the Glamorgan Welsh. Resentment once again boiled to the surface. Llywelyn Bren had been a victim of injustice when he had been unfairly relieved of the positions he held under de Clare, and he quickly rallied an army of 10,000 men. They attacked Caerphilly and besieged its castle, leaving a trail of devastation throughout the county. To quash the new rebellion, Edward II sent a massive army to join the local Anglo-Norman lords. Pushing from Cardiff in the south and Brecon in the north, they attacked Bren's forces. A battle took place at Cefn Onn, where Bren's forces were defeated and fled to the uplands of Senghenydd. Here they were cut off by the Anglo-Norman army attacking from the north. Defeat was inevitable and so Bren surrendered on condition that his men were allowed to go home. He was then imprisoned in the Tower of London. For those who fought for Bren, the penalty was high. Heavy fines and ransoms on their lands were just some of the means used to bring men to their knees. To worsen matters, the climate was deteriorating and famine was now widespread. Bren was illegally hanged, drawn and quartered in 1218 by the queen's lover, Hugh Despenser, who was later to suffer the same fate. It is important to show how Wales was never at peace throughout the fourteenth or fifteenth centuries, when it was supposedly 'conquered'.

Meanwhile, in North Wales, Goronwy was appointed Forester of Snowdon for 1318 and 1319, succeeding Sir Gruffydd Llwyd. He was now referred to as a member of the King's Yeomen, typifying his new role within Edward II's jurisdiction in North Wales. A 'forester' was effectively a sheriff used to enforce the law in a specific locality, and the post carried prestige as a valued member of the king's retinue. When an action was brought in 1331 against the former deputy justiciar of North Wales, William de Shaldford, accusing him of having encompassed Edward II's murder, Goronwy and Sir Gruffydd were among de Shaldford's sureties. Goronwy wed Gwerful ferch Madog, the daughter of the baron of Hendwr, and died on 11 December 1331, his body being interred and buried at Bangor Friary. His loyal service to Edward II reinforced his family's place among the most important nobles of the region, and ensured his surviving sons, Hywel ap Goronwy and Tudur Fychan ap Goronwy, received royal favour.

Ednyfed Fychan's great-great-grandson Hywel ap Goronwy (d. 1366?) became a cleric with substantial amount power and prestige in the area. Initially Canon of Bangor, Hywel later became Archdeacon of Anglesey. His brother Tudur took over the family lands and may have served in Edward III's armies in France along with many of his Welsh peers. Both were leading figures in North Wales. An apocryphal tale related how Tudur called himself Sir Tudur. Upon being summoned by Edward III to explain himself, he answered with such spirit that the king immediately knighted him. The story, attributed to the antiquary Robert Vaughan (1592–1667), may have originated in the sixteenth century, the implication being that Tudur foresaw that his descendants would have the power to confer knighthood. Hywel and Tudur were initially law abiding, but both came to prominence in 1344 in a revolt against yet more oppressive laws imposed by both the Marcher Lords and English administrators in North Wales. The bastide town of Rhuddlan in Denbighshire was razed, forcing the resident English population to flee to England. In 1344, an anti-English riot also took place at the fair of Saint Asaph.

Henry de Shalford, burgess of Caernarfon, was appointed as attorney in North Wales by Edward III's eldest son, Edward the 'Black Prince'. Soon after, on 14 February 1345, de Shalford was attacked and killed near the house of Hywel ap Goronwy in Bangor by a band of men led by Hywel's brother Tudur. The result was panic among the English burgesses in North Wales, especially as many seemingly loyal leading Welshmen, such as Madog Gloddaith, appear to have been implicated. The acting sheriff of Merioneth was also killed in 1345, slain while he was holding the county court. Hywel was imprisoned for a time at Launceston in Cornwall, and Tudur in Chester, but they do not seem to have suffered any further punishment. In 1352, they were both known to be back in possession of their ancestral lands in Anglesey.

Perhaps the reputation of their family played a part in their acquittal from any major punishment. The king's administrators probably did not wish to alienate such a powerful family, when it was obvious that Wales still was in a semi-anarchic state. There was a stream of complaints in Parliament about the Welsh; for example, it was claimed that 'unlawful assemblies' were being held at Strata Marcella Abbey 'to excite contentions between the English and the Welsh'. There was despairing correspondence from the burgesses of North Wales in the 1340s when they assumed that the attitude of Welshmen towards Englishmen was one of imminent revenge. Travelling bards were forever reinforcing the Welsh sense of injustice at the Saxons and French invading their lands, promising an imminent day of reckoning.

The last heir of the dynasty of the princes of Gwynedd now made a bid to recover his patrimony. Owain ap Tomas ap Rhodri briefly returned to England after his father's death in 1363 to unsuccessfully claim his inheritance. In 1369, his English lands were confiscated because he led a free company that fought for the French. His grandfather Rhodri, the brother of Llywelyn II, had survived the carnage by remaining on his estates in Surrey and staying loyal to Edward I. Owain became one of the most noted warriors of the Hundred Years' War, being thought of by the French and Bretons as only second in valour to Bertrand du Guesclin. He became known across the Continent as Owain Lawgoch (Owain of the Red Hand) and in France as Yvain de Galles (Owen of Wales). Owain fought across Spain, France, Alsace and Switzerland, and was the only real claimant to the title of Prince of Gwynedd and Prince of Wales. In 1378, while conducting a siege at Mortagne-sur-Mer, he was assassinated on the orders of the English Crown.

The Issue Roll of the Exchequer dated 4 December 1378 records, 'To John Lamb, an esquire from Scotland, because he lately killed Owynn de Gales, a rebel and enemy of the King in France ... £20.' This, of course, was actually the King of England, who claimed the right to the crown of France. John Lamb had joined Owain's men and become his trusted chamberlain, and cut Owain's throat from behind. Owain was the last true Prince of Gwynedd of the House of Aberffraw, and was seen as a threat to any peace in Wales, being regarded as a *mab darogan* who could rescue Wales from its oppression.

The brothers Tudur Fychan and Hywel ap Goronwy had been noted landowners of various Anglesey estates, not least in Penmynydd, which became identified as the family seat. Tudur ap Goronwy also held office across Penrhyn, Trecastell and Dindaethwy, the latter as *rhaglaw*, a position similar to that of a bailiff or sheriff. Goronwy's son Tudur Fychan ap Goronwy was married twice, with his first marriage producing around seven children, but it was his second marriage, to Marged ferch Tomos, that would have the most profound consequences for the descendants of Ednyfed Fychan. Marged was the daughter of the landowner Tomos ap Llywelyn from Ceredigion, the last male survivor of the royal House of Deheubarth. With his second wife Marged, Tudur Fychan (d. 1367) had further children, raising five sons who reached adulthood. Ednyfed, Goronwy, Rhys, Gwilym and Maredudd had the advantage of a noble birth to landowning parents and as such became men of repute in the region, carving out a niche for themselves just like their ancestors had. All except Ednyfed seem to have held positions of administrative responsibility in the royal government of North Wales at the end of the fourteenth century.

The boys' maternal grandfather, Tomos ap Llywelyn, had no boys, but an elder daughter in addition to their mother Marged, called Elen. Marged and Elen were descended from Llywelyn ab Iorwerth on her mother's side and the Plantagenet kings John, Henry III and Edward I on her father's side. Elen was married to Gruffudd Fychan II, Lord of Glyndyfrdwy and claimant to the extinct kingdom of Powys Fadog. Their marriage produced a son, Owain ap Gruffudd, born around 1350. Heir to the lordship of Glyndyfrdwy, Owain would later become better known as Owain Glyndŵr and through his mother was first cousin to the Tudurs of Penmynydd, a relationship that had major ramifications for all the children of Tudur Fychan ap Goronwy.

The eldest son of Tudur Fychan was Goronwy ap Tudur (d. 1382), a soldier and administrator who lived at Penmynydd, the traditional seat of the Tudors, as they can now be called. He was a great-great-great-great-grandson of the line of Ednyfed. Goronwy served in France with Edward, the Black Prince, and in 1368–1369 he was at Northampton in the prince's retinue. He was Forester of Snowdon and steward of the Bishop of Bangor's

Anglesey lands, and in 1382 he was appointed constable of Beaumaris Castle, one of the very few occasions on which a Welshman was appointed to such an office. Just four days later, he died, apparently by drowning, in Kent. His death was mourned by several poets and he was buried in the Franciscan friary at Llanfaes in Anglesey. Goronwy's impressive alabaster tomb was moved to Penmynydd church at the dissolution of Llanfaes. His wife was Myfanwy, the daughter of Iorwerth Ddu of Pengwern, near Llangollen. Their son Tudur was dead by 1400. Their daughter Morfudd married Gwilym ap Gruffudd and his lands therefore passed to the Penrhyn family, although they were eventually to be recovered by Morfudd's descendants, the Tudors of Penmynydd. Ednyfed ap Tudur died around the same time as Goronwy.

The family's close ties of kinship with Owain Glyndŵr and their influential family connections across North Wales ensured that the Tudurs played a central role in the Glyndŵr War of Independence (1400–1420). Three younger sons of Tudur Fychan, namely Rhys, Gwilym and Maredudd ap Tudur, virtually initiated the rising of their kinsman in 1400, taking Conwy Castle in 1401. For more details see *Owain Glyndŵr: The Story of the Last Prince of Wales* (2009 and 2013) by this author. Goronwy, Rhys and Gwilym had a personal relationship with Richard II, being among his esquires of the body, and the latter two brothers fought for Owain Glyndŵr in his war against King Richard's Lancastrian usurper, Henry IV. Rhys ap Tudur had been at times sheriff and escheator of Anglesey, *rhaglaw* (prefect) of Malltraeth and Forester of Snowdon. Both Rhys and Gwilym were excluded along with Glyndŵr from the pardon granted at the end of the first phase of the revolt in 1400. The brothers took Conwy Castle on Good Friday 1401, when the garrison was in church. They withdrew after negotiations and were pardoned, but they seem to have continued in rebellion until near the end. After twelve years of fighting, Rhys ap Tudur was hanged, drawn and quartered at Chester in 1412, and Gwilym ap Tudur was killed around 1413. Their lands passed to their kinsman Gwilym ap Gruffudd. Owain Glyndŵr disappeared around 1415, his brother having been killed and his wife and children taken into captivity, where they soon died.

Maredudd ap Tudur (*fl.* 1388–1404), the youngest of the five sons of Tudur Fychan and Marged, was escheator of Anglesey between 1388 and 1391 and was a burgess of the town of Newborough (Niwbwrch) in the same county. He was *rhaglaw* of the Anglesey commote of Malltraeth in 1387–1391 and 1394–1396. By 1404–1405, Maredudd was an esquire of the Bishop of Bangor. Ricardian propagandists make him out to be an 'alehouse keeper'. He also took part in the Glyndŵr revolt, survived and was pardoned, but most of his family's lands were forfeited to the Crown. Just a remnant of lands at Penmynydd remained in the hands of Goronwy ap Tudur's immediate family. Maredudd married Marged (Margaret), daughter of Dafydd Fychan of Taefeilir, and their son, Owain ap Maredudd, was born around 1400.

Maredudd had few options. Virtually landless and powerless, he was forced to head for London and try to find favour in court. His son's name was later altered from Owain ap Maredudd to Owain Tudor, one of the very first instances where a surname instead of a patronym was used by a Welshman. Had Owain taken his father's name as normal, rather than that of his grandfather, the Tudor dynasty would have been called the Maredudd or Meredith Dynasty. Details of Owain's birth and the family are missing for the period, as the six invasions of Wales during Owain Glyndŵr's war of independence from 1400 to 1420 led to towns, monasteries and abbeys being despoiled and their records destroyed. If not killed in the rebellion itself, members of the Tudur family were stripped of their estates and debarred from holding office, like many other Welshmen. They were replaced by loyalists and English placemen. There was no longer any future in Wales for Maredudd or his son Owain.

In London, Owain Tudor is said to have become the ward of his father Maredudd's second cousin, Lord Rhys. Aged seven, Owain may have been sent to Henry IV's court as a page to the king's steward. Owain is also said to have fought for Henry V at Agincourt in 1415, being promoted to squire, but there are no extant records of the battle. Squire was a status for boys aged around fourteen to fifteen, whereby they were essentially apprentice knights. Squires were assigned to certain knights, bearing their shields, looking after the armour and horses and accompanying the knight on any battles or recesses. After Agincourt, Owain was granted some 'English rights' and permitted to use Welsh arms in England, which possibly indicated his presence in France. During the Glyndŵr Rising, Henry IV had deprived Welshmen of most of their civil rights. In the ode *Owen Tudor to Queen Katherine* (1579), Michael Drayton suggested that Owain had fought at Rhodes with the Crusaders: 'For Christian Rhodes, and our Religious Truth, / To great Achievements first had won my Youth ...'

Owain may have secured patronage at Henry V's court, one source claiming he did so through the influence of his kinsman Maredudd ab Owain, Glyndŵr's only surviving son. Although Glyndŵr disappeared around 1415, the king kept offering surrender terms until 1421. Even after the disappearance of his father, Maredudd ab Owain Glyndŵr had continued to fight and was connected with the Oldcastle plot in 1417. A last pardon was issued to Maredudd on 8 April 1421 and he disappears from view after this date. As yet, his attendance and influence at the king's court is unattested.

The first evidence of Owain in London dates from 13 May 1421, when 'Owen Meredith' was given protection, in order to go abroad in the retinue of Sir Walter Hungerford. Hungerford was a baron who was played a key role as the King's Steward from July 1415 to July 1421 during the wars with the French. This may be another Owain Tudur, but our Owain is also named as 'Owen ap Meredudd' at the time of his imprisonment in Newgate in 1438. If Owain had served with distinction in France, he may have well been rewarded with some official appointment after Agincourt, thus reaching the court and the queen's attention. Sir Walter Hungerford was steward of the king's household again in July 1424. Several historians state that Owain was a keeper, either of the queen's household or of her wardrobe, but there is as yet no evidence. If Owen was Keeper of the Queen's Wardrobe when she was living at Windsor Castle, he would have been in control of the queen's tailors, dressers and anything else relating to her wardrobe room. It was also within his remit to handle all inventories of the dresses and to ensure all clothes that were taken on progress were satisfactorily accounted for when returned. His presence would also ensure that any jewel thieves were discouraged.

In his *Cronicl o Wech Oesoedd* (*Chronicle of the Six Ages of the World*), the 'Soldier of Calais', Elis Gruffudd (1490–1552), states that the 'young squire of Gwynedd' was a servant and sewer to Queen Catherine of Valois, the young widow of Henry V. Catherine (1401–1437) had an older sister, Isabella of France (1389–1409), who had been married as a child to Richard II. Isabella had thus briefly been Queen of England from 1396 to 1399. When Henry IV killed Richard II in 1400, Henry tried to get the widowed Isabella to marry his son, the future Henry V, but she quite reasonably refused. Instead, Catherine was married to Henry V in 1420. Henry V himself had proposed this marriage, while demanding a large dowry and acknowledgement of his right to the throne of France. Even after his victory over the French at Agincourt in 1415, plans for the marriage had proceeded. In a 1420 peace treaty, Charles of France agreed that Henry should be his heir, and Henry married Catherine in June of that year in France. She was crowned in February 1421 at Westminster, and gave birth to Henry, the future Henry VI, in December 1421.

However, Henry V contracted dysentery in France and died in Paris in August 1422 before seeing his only son. Charles VI died a couple of months after Henry V, making the infant Henry VI King of England and English-occupied northern France. The civil wars known as the Wars of the Roses prevented a full English effort to take control of France, and the lands were gradually lost. Catherine was attractive and still only twenty-one, and a wonderful marriage prospect for the upper nobility. It is unknown whether Owain was in her service at this time, or after King Henry's death. Elis Gruffudd related how Catherine first saw Owain on a summer's day when he and his friends were swimming in a river near the court. Intrigued by this handsome man of her own age, she secretly changed roles with her maid and arranged to meet him in disguise. However, Owain attempted to kiss her, and she struggled and received a slight wound on the cheek. On the following day, as Owain served the queen at dinner, he realised her true identity and was ashamed of what he had done. Nevertheless, he was forgiven and the two eventually fell in love and were married.

Another tradition holds that Owain attracted the attention of Catherine at a ball, when he accidentally fell into her lap. Robin Ddu ap Siencyn Bledrydd of Anglesey wrote poems around 1440–1470, including a vaticinatory poem upon Owain's death. In this ode, he states that Owain was no traitor, 'although he once, on a holiday, clapped his ardent humble affection on the daughter of the king of the land of wine'. Michael Drayton (1563–1631) repeated the story:

> When in your presence I was called to dance,
> In lofty Tricks whilst I my self advance,
> And in a Turn, my footing failed by hap,
> Was it not my chance to light into your Lap?
> Who would not judge it Fortunes greatest grace,
> Since he must fall, to fall in such a place?

In 1603, the poet Hugh Holland wrote *Pancharis, containing the first book of the love of Owen Tudor for the Queen*, which again tells us:

> Wherefore, as Owen did his galliard dance
> And graced it with a turn upon the toe;
> (Whether his eyes aside he chanced to glance,
> And, like the lovely God, became so blind,
> Or else, perhaps, it were his happy chance,
> I know not, and record none can I find)
> His knee did hit against her softer thigh.
> I Hope he felt no great hurt by the fall,
> That happy fall which mounted him so high.

After Henry V's death in Paris in 1422, the queen dowager had brought up the future Henry VI, and it is thought that she did not secretly marry Owen Tudor until about 1428 or 1429. Guardians had been appointed to supervise the king's education and training, but because of his infancy, the infant king had been apparently committed to his mother's care by the Protector, Humphrey, Duke of Gloucester, late in 1422. Humphrey was the late Henry V's brother, and thus uncle to the new king. Thomas Beaufort, Duke of Exeter, the young king's great-uncle and guardian, died on 30 December 1426, but no replacement was appointed for eighteen months. On 1 June 1428, Richard Beauchamp, Earl of Warwick, assumed the responsibility.

From this date, the queen seems to have had less contact with her son, as Warwick trained him for kingship, teaching him riding, swordplay and the like. Also, after this date it appears that Catherine and Owen concealed their marriage deliberately, with seemingly few knowing about it until after the queen's death. However, even in the account of Owen's later appearance before the King's Council or in later Yorkist proclamations and manifestoes, there is no question of the validity of the marriage or of the legitimacy of their children. Owain, being in favour in the queen's household, had managed to escape the punitive measures issued against Welshmen in the wake of the Glyndŵr Rising.

The boy king's counsellors had been highly concerned about his young mother remarrying. It seems that a statute or conciliar ordinance was drawn up, forbidding anyone to marry the queen dowager without royal permission. The earliest reference to this appears in *Giles' Chronicle*:

> The lords of the king's Council would not agree to her marrying anyone during the king's minority, because she wished to have the Lord Edmund Beaufort, count of Mortain; but the duke of Gloucester and many other lords objected, ordaining that whoever presumed to marry her, against the Council's letters would be punished in the forfeiture of all goods and in the death penalty as a traitor to the king.

Elis Gruffudd also claims that the council prohibited Queen Catherine from remarrying, adding that she was resentful about the ban. There is no record of any such conciliar as mentioned in *Giles' Chronicle* or by Elis Gruffudd, but many of the King's Council's records for this period have been lost.

In 1428, the queen was twenty-seven years old. Edmund Beaufort was twenty-two, and soon to become the Duke of Somerset. Somerset was to become the great rival of Richard of York and the Earl of Warwick during the forthcoming civil wars. Humphrey, Duke of Gloucester, the fourth son of Henry IV, and his party in the council had needed to prevent this nephew of Henry Beaufort, Bishop of Winchester, the Protector's arch-enemy, from marrying the queen dowager and thereby securing the young king's favour. In October 1425, supporters of the two factions fought at London Bridge, and the bitter Gloucester–Beaufort rivalry was the fulcrum of the following implacable York–Lancaster enmity

There also may have been a legal statute to restrict the queen's choice of a husband, as mentioned in *Hall's Chronicle*, which states that Owain was imprisoned after Catherine's death because he had married her 'contrary to the statute made in the sixth year of the king', *i.e.* in 1428. Like the conciliar decree, such an act does not appear anywhere in print and has possibly been lost. Whatever the truth, it seems that major steps were taken to ensure that the widowed queen did not marry Edmund Beaufort, her late husband's cousin. Edmund Beaufort (1406–1455) was the grandson of John of Gaunt, 1st Duke of Lancaster, and his hatred of Richard Plantagenet, Duke of York (1411–1460) would lead to war.

In the parliament of 1427–1428, a Bill was introduced setting the rules for the remarriage of a queen dowager. The Bill stated that if the queen dowager remarried without the king's consent, the husband would lose his lands and possessions, although any children of the marriage would still be members of the royal family and would not suffer punishment. Another rule stipulated that the king's permission could only be granted once he had reached his majority. At the time the Bill was written, the king was only six years old. The secret marriage of Catherine to Owain Tudor would thus probably have taken place later than the parliament of October 1427 to March 1428. *Giles' Chronicle* states that Catherine deliberately chose a poor commoner for a husband, after the restriction placed upon her remarrying, so that the council 'might not reasonably take vengeance on his life'. News of the surreptitious union only became common knowledge after the queen's death on 3 January 1437.

According to Sir John Wynn of Gwydir,

> Queen Katherin being a French woman borne, knew no difference between the English and Welsh nation until her marriage being published ... but the opposition to her union made her desirous to see some of his kinsmen, hereupon he brought to her presence John ap Meredyth and Howell Llywelin ap Howell his near cousins, men of goodly stature and personage, but wholly destitute of bringing up and nurture, for when the Queen had spoken to them in diverse languages and they were not able to answer her, she said they were the goodliest dumb creatures that she ever saw.

Later Tudor chroniclers like Hall disparagingly refer to the widowed queen as being young and lusty, 'following more her own appetite than friendly counsel, and regarding more her private affection than her open honour'. Owain was described in *Caxton's Chronicle* as 'Owayn, a squyer of Wales, a man of lowe byrthe', but Polydore Vergil described him as 'a gentleman of Wales, adorned with wonderfull giftes of body and minde'.

The previous information is vital to understanding the mindset of both Jasper and Henry Tudor, the descendants of Ednyfed Fychan. Their fathers' fathers had been fighting the English invader for centuries. Jasper Tudor would have known the details of his father Owain, the grandfather Maredudd, and on through the paternal line via Tudur, Goronwy, Tudor, Goronwy, Tudur, Goronwy, Ednyfed, Cynwrig to Iorwerth. He would have known of eleven generations and their exploits through the bards. There were also another seven paternal ancestors to Marchudd ap Cynan, Lord of Rhos and Brynffenigl and head of one of the 'eight noble houses' of Wales. There were yet another twelve paternal ancestors of Marchudd, going back to Llyfeinydd ap Peredur, and ancestors before him. Jasper's had been a lineage of some note, of over thirty generations of Britons.

As A. D. Carr tells us, Jasper and his brother Edmund belonged to 'without a doubt, the most powerful family in thirteenth- and fourteenth-century Wales. They were the leading servants of the princes of Gwynedd and played a key part in the attempt of those princes to create a single Welsh principality. Some were prescient enough to transfer their allegiance to Edward I before 1282; the rest made their peace very soon after and continued to enjoy a significant role in all the royal lands in Wales; at the local level they were often the ones who exercised effective power in the name of the King of England. But there remained an awareness of their Welshness, with its concomitant loyalties, which surfaced from time to time in the fourteenth century and which led them to the side of Owain Glyn Dŵr and to the end of that predominance which had lasted since the early thirteenth century. And it was a descendant of one of those rebels against the English crown who won that crown in 1485.'

While we have seen that some seeds for civil war were sown over the refusal to allow Beaufort to marry Catherine of Valois, it is also necessary to understand the mood of the Welsh nation. English domination was still harsh. Welshmen still had inferior rights to Englishmen in both England and Wales. Royal agents were constantly looking for new sources of income from Wales. For example, they re-let escheated land, which gave them the opportunity to raise rents. Wales had been impoverished, its buildings destroyed and had been denuded of sources of wealth by over a millennium of fighting invasions, and there was little left to extort. Even the abbeys and churches had been despoiled and robbed.

Many restrictions were invoked; for instance, kings and Marcher Lords insisted on sustaining some old Welsh customs such as the virginity fine and *prid* (a four-yearly renewable mortgage of land) because of the better incomes they yielded. Any Welshmen who somehow got to hold office were often subject to harassment or sacking, in that their appointment contravened statutes of Edward I and Henry IV. Welshmen who had lived peacefully for years in towns and villages in England could suddenly be challenged to produce their title for doing so. They might only recover their status as burgesses upon payment of a large fine. Welsh tenants were routinely evicted out of good agricultural land to allow English settlement, for example in Denbigh and across the Marcher and royal lordships. Thomas gives us an instructive fourteenth-century court case in Ruthin:

> A Welshman had married an Englishwoman of some landed means, and upon her death, he claimed the right to continue to hold her English lands. He was debarred on the grounds that he was a Welshman, and the land was given to the dead woman's brother and English heirs ... A shrinking labour supply and trade led to English townsmen and burgesses in Wales seeking to enforce their privileges, which led to a sharpening of the racial structure of the borough community, given that burgesses were English and the labourers Welsh. Expensive military commitments led to demands for heavy taxation.

All in all, resentment simmered continually across the land. The Welsh had nothing to lose by rebellion, and they would be fighting to reclaim what was theirs. The secret children of Owain ap Maredudd ap Tudur ap Goronwy and Henry V's widow would change history.

3

The Early Lives of Edmund and Jasper Tudor, 1430–1454

As queen dowager, Catherine of Valois lived in the king's household and so had been able to directly care for the young King Henry VI. While at the young king's court, the great lords and councillors could keep her under scrutiny. However, at some stage after Henry V's death in 1422, while she was in Windsor Castle, her love affair had begun with her servant Owain Tudor. It may well be that physical relations did not begin until she married Owain around 1429. She became pregnant with Edmund Tudor at Windsor, and at some point stopped living in the king's household. Catherine moved to Hertfordshire to have children, Edmund and Jasper, half-brothers to the king, born around 1430 and 1431. It is not thought that Henry VI, born around nine years earlier in December 1421, was at that time aware of their births.

On 6 November 1429, a month before his eighth birthday and less than four months after the coronation of his rival, the Dauphin, in Reims, the young Henry VI was crowned King of England at Westminster Abbey by his great-uncle, Cardinal Henry Beaufort, Bishop of Winchester. The traditional English rite was modified to incorporate French practices, to demonstrate to all that this was only the first part of a fuller coronation procedure, which could only be completed in France.

The bishop's palace outside the church in Much Hadham in Hertfordshire was probably the birthplace of Edmund Tudor in around 1430. The palace, now Much Hadham House, was originally established as the home of the bishops of London before the Norman Conquest, and had become the home of Owen Tudor and Catherine of Valois. Jasper Tudor was born perhaps a year later at the bishop's palace in Hatfield, also known as Bishop's Hatfield. This was the palace of the Bishop of Ely, Philip Morgan. Morgan had been Bishop of Worcester (1419–1426) and was Bishop of Ely from 1426 until his death in 1435. Ely was the fifth-wealthiest see in England, yet also among the smallest in terms of size or burden. Bishop Morgan must have known the queen, since he had been chancellor of Normandy, was an experienced diplomat and an expert in French affairs. The Welshman had earlier been elected Archbishop of York from 1423 to

1424. He had held Church office in Aberedw, Llanfeugan, Abergwili and Llandegley, and from 1414 onwards was employed extensively on foreign missions and played a prominent part in peace negotiations with France. He would have been able to converse in Welsh with Owain Tudor, and was probably in the confidence of Owain and the widowed queen.

Morgan had been made a Privy Councillor in 1419, and as a bishop he was vigilant in putting down clerical abuses. He died in Bishop's Hatfield, Hertfordshire, on 25 October 1435, and will probably have advised Catherine and Owain, possibly even officiating at their wedding. Until their ennoblement as Earls of Richmond and Pembroke, the brothers were known as Edmund de Hadham and Jasper de Hatfield. The queen spent time at Hertford and her presence there is recorded on 20 February and 6 October 1434, and again on 9 May 1436. Edmund's birthplace of Much Hadham and Jasper's birthplace of Bishop's Hatfield were both ecclesiastical manors, the former the summer palace of the Bishop of London.

Bishop Morgan of Ely and his servants kept quiet about the birth of Jasper, as did the Bishop of London and his household on the earlier birth of Edmund. Owen and Catherine must have known Robert Fitzhugh, who was Bishop of London from 1431 until his death in 1436. Fitzhugh was also a distinguished ambassador, although not so closely connected with France as Bishop Morgan. However, as a civil servant, prelate, councillor and courtier, he must have known the queen, or at least something about her private life. Only one nearly contemporary source has survived to give us information about the queen dowager's movements in this time, *Giles' Chronicle*. It may have been written by one of the masters of St Leonarde's Hospital in York, and Bishop Fitzhugh himself had held that post from 1415 until 1431. Fitzhugh was succeeded by his cousin William Scrope, who was master until 1465.

It seems that the marriage of Owain and Catherine, and the existence of Jasper and Edmund, was secret until the accidental birth at Westminster of another son, Owen. Owain and Catherine had deliberately settled in retreats independent of the main court, and which were run by servants dependent upon their local masters, in this case the two bishops. Loose-fitting clothing would have concealed pregnancy, and was often used to disguise the birth of an illegitimate child. Possibly some of the main councillors knew of Catherine's pregnancies and her morganatic marriage. She would have had to give some excuse for being absent from her ten-year-old son's coronation as King of France in Notre Dame Cathedral on 16 December 1431.

The English claim to the French crown could not be strengthened just by a boy's coronation in Paris. Military intervention was needed to support the existing English presence in France. Loans were raised and, in December 1429, Parliament had voted for subsidies to pay 5,000 men to cross to France in 1430. Three bishops, John Stafford of Bath and Wells, William Alnwick of Norwich and Philip Morgan of Ely, once chancellor of Normandy, accompanied the king. Morgan's palace was now occupied by

Owen and Catherine. On 23 April 1430, the nine-year-old Henry VI sailed from Sandwich to Calais, where he stayed at the castle until July, when he moved to Rouen. Rouen was the administrative centre of the English dominion in France, where his uncle John, Duke of Bedford, Regent of France, resided. Henry stayed for sixteen months in Rouen until November 1431. On 27 May 1431, a large company of guests, including many French and English nobles and important councillors, dined with Bedford and the king, some of them involved in the trial of Joan of Arc, whose death at the stake was to take place three days later in the marketplace only a few hundred yards away.

On 2 December 1431, Henry VI, riding a white horse, entered the French capital for his coronation later that month. With him were the dukes of Bedford and York, the Earl of Warwick and others in a large company. By early February 1432, he was back in England. He had visited his French kingdom for the first and last time. In this period of twenty-one months, from April 1430 to February 1431, Catherine may well have given birth to Edmund and Jasper without her son's knowledge. The king's mother should have attended his coronation, and we can only surmise that she was pregnant. Possibly, she may have been excluded on the grounds of her indiscretion in marrying a Welsh commoner who did not have the rights of an English citizen. The coronation committed England to the military defence of their king's right, but a major reason for Henry VI's unpopularity over the years was the constant loss of French possessions in a never-ending war that drained the country of resources.

Owen and Catherine still kept away from court, and probably had two more children. Their youngest son, Owen, was born at Westminster Abbey in 1432, when the queen dowager was visiting her son Henry VI. Her waters broke prematurely and she was forced to seek the help of the monks at Westminster Abbey. It may be at this point that her marriage and children became common knowledge. Owen, also named as Thomas or Edward Bridgewater, was taken from her and raised by the monks, according to Polydore Vergil. This 'Owen Tudder' became a monk, and was later given a reward of £2 on 30 July 1498 out of his nephew Henry VII's Privy Purse. However, by 1501 he was dead, for in that year the churchwardens of St Margaret's, Westminster, paid 6*d* for 'the knell of Owen Tuder with the bell'. On 18 June 1502, Morgan Kidwelly was paid £3 1*s* 2*d* 'for burying Owen Tudder'.

A daughter of Catherine and Owen, named Jacina, Tacine, Jacinta or Pacina, is supposed to have married Reginald, 7th Baron Grey of Wilton (1421–1493). Grey fought for the Yorkists at Towton and Mortimer's Cross. However, Jacina was an illegitimate daughter, born overseas, of John Beaufort, Duke of Somerset. Beaufort was the father of Margaret Beaufort, mother of Henry VII. There is also mention of a daughter of Catherine and Owen who, Vergil states, became a nun, but little is known of her.

John Ashdown-Hill, in *Royal Marriage Secrets*, believes he has uncovered evidence that Edmund and Jasper Tudor were the sons of Edmund Beaufort,

Duke of Somerset. Richard of York, especially, did not want Somerset to marry such a rich heiress with royal blood. Following the death of her husband Henry V, Catherine of Valois was only twenty-one, and was generally disliked for the simple reason of being French. According to a contemporary rumour Somerset wanted to marry her. She was said to have found it difficult to 'curb fully her carnal passions'. There was passed a statute, which refers to queens generally, but is generally thought to be aimed at Catherine:

> It is ordered and established, by the authority of this parliament for the preservation of the honour of the most noble estate of queens of England, that no man of whatever estate or condition make contract of betrothal or matrimony to marry himself to the queen of England, without the special licence and assent of the king, when the latter is of the age of discretion, and he who acts to the contrary and is duly convicted will forfeit for his whole life all his lands and tenements, even those which are or which will be in his own hands, as well as those which are or which will be in the hands of others to his use, and also all his goods and chattels in whosoever's hands they are, considering that by the disparagement of the queen the estate and honour of the king will be most greatly damaged, and it will give the greatest comfort and example to other ladies of rank who are of the blood royal that they might not be so lightly disparaged.

Ashdown-Hill believes that the coats of arms of Edmund and Jasper, which owe nothing to the arms of Owen Tudor, were derived from the arms of Edmund Beaufort:

> The blue and gold bordures of Edmund and Jasper Tudor were simply versions of the blue and white bordure of Edmund Beaufort ... The whole purpose of medieval heraldry was to show to the world who one was. And the coats of arms of Edmund and Jasper Tudor proclaimed, as clearly as they could, that these two 'Tudor' sons of the queen mother were of English royal blood, while their bordures suggest descent from Edmund Beaufort. The only possible explanation seems to be that Beaufort was their real father.

However, there is also a strong resemblance between the Tudor brothers' arms and that of their half-brother Henry VI. In later years, even Richard III did not dispute that Owen Tudor was the brothers' father. In a proclamation issued in June 1485, Richard described Henry Tudor as 'descended of bastard blood both of father side and of mother side, for the said Owen the grandfather was bastard born, and his mother was daughter unto John, Duke of Somerset, son unto John, Earl of Somerset, son unto Dame Katherine Swynford, and of their double adultery gotten'. There is no mention of Owen and Catherine being unmarried. And would the bishops of London and Ely allow their palaces to be used for producing illegitimate children?

Nowhere did Richard question the legitimacy of Henry Tudor himself, nor of his father Edmund. Instead, he stated that 'the said rebels and traitors have chosen to be their captain one Henry Tydder, son of Edmund Tydder, son of Owen Tydder'. If there were any grounds to impugn the legitimacy of Henry Tudor, his father Edmund or his uncle Jasper, the Yorkists would have used them. Also, we have Owen Tudor's known illegitimate son, Sir David Owen, born in 1459. If Ashdown-Hill's theory was correct, David Owen would have no blood ties to either Edmund or Jasper Tudor. However, in his will, he ordered masses for the souls of 'King Henry VII, Edmund, sometime Earl of Richmond, Jasper Duke of Bedford, my father and mother's souls, my wife's and all Christian souls'. Why would David Owen remember Edmund, who died before David Owen was born, if Edmund was not his uncle?

Henry may have first learned about his new brothers upon his return from France. In May 1432, as 'Oweyn fitz Meredyth', the queen's husband was now granted letters of denizenship. H. T. Evans believed that this was a 'rather lean grant', as Owen was still denied several of the rights of a full citizen, and Evans thought that it 'betokens flagrant insincerity or intriguing suspicion' on the part of the regency government. Henry IV's laws had limited the rights of Welshmen, and it was still illegal for a Welshman to own a property in England or to marry an Englishwoman. Fortunately for Owain Tudor, Catherine was not English.

Denizenship was only granted to high-ranking Welsh subjects who had proved their worth to the Crown during the wars against the French, and Owen was still not granted full rights. He was still barred from becoming a burgess, a freeman or representative of a borough. He was categorically restricted from holding a Crown office in any city, borough or market town in the land. He was, however, given permission to acquire land, bear arms, marry an Englishwoman and run a marital household. Two years later, on 11 March 1434, the queen was able to grant Owen the wardship of the lands and the marriage of the heir of John de Conway of Bodrhyddan in Flintshire. Bodrhyddan Hall, near Dyserth, is still in the hands of the Conway family. In 1436, when Jasper was about five years of age, Catherine was once again expecting a child. It seems that she realised that she was dying, possibly from cancer, and went to Bermondsey Abbey to be nursed by the sisters there. In her will, the queen spoke of her long illness. It may be that she was forced to go there by members of the King's Council, still angered by her marriage. In 1436 (or perhaps 1437), Jasper and Edmund were taken away and placed in the care of the Abbess of Barking for about five years, at which time they were considered old enough for their education to be continued by priests. By 1 January 1437, Catherine had written a will and had given birth to a short-lived daughter, possibly named Margaret. Catherine died on 3 January 1437. She had at least four, and possibly five, children by Owen, so the couple must have been married before the end of 1432, perhaps in 1430. Catherine was laid to rest next to her husband Henry V in the chantry chapel at Westminster Abbey.

The Regency Council under Humphrey of Gloucester and others had mistrusted the Welsh commoner who had impregnated the king's mother, and her death left Owen Tudor without protection. Lacking estates or wealth, he was suddenly at the mercy of the great lords. It seems he decided to escape to Anglesey, and he was at Daventry in Warwickshire when urgently commanded to appear before the king. Deeply suspicious, Owen replied that he 'would not so come without that it were granted and promised him on the king's behalf that he should more freely come and freely go'. A verbal promise of safe conduct from the Duke of Gloucester, on the king's authority, was delivered to him. However, Owen refused to accept its validity, as 'the said grant so made sufficed him not for his surety, less than it were sent him in writing'.

Owen was taken by Lord Beaumont and escorted to London, but went immediately into sanctuary at Westminster, where the monks had brought up his third son, Owen, since 1432. He 'there held him many days, eschewing to come out thereof', although 'divers persons assured him of friendship and fellowship to have come out'. Unsuccessful efforts were made to entrap him by trying to induce him into a tavern nearby. Henry VI was now sixteen, and Owen had discovered that his stepson was 'evilly informed of him' by his councillors. Several weeks passed before Owen decided to leave sanctuary to defend himself before the King's Council. He declared his innocence of any wrongdoing, stating that he was the king's 'true liege man' no matter what any man should say against him. Owen Tudor was released from prison, most probably because of the wishes of his stepson Henry VI, who later provided for his stepfather and his two half-brothers.

Owen, probably still grieving from the loss of Catherine, headed once again back to Wales but was overtaken and arrested by messengers of the council. It was determined to punish him properly, but records are missing as to his alleged crimes. It is generally assumed that his second imprisonment was occasioned by the discovery of his marriage. Council records do not specify any particular reason. However, many may have known of the union during the queen's lifetime, including the lords in Parliament, and it would be extraordinarily difficult to conceal four royal pregnancies and four children. As Monmouth, translating Biondi, stated, 'It is not to be supposed that the court could be hoodwinked in four great bellies.' Biondi added that although the marriage must have been known, yet it was 'winked at by reason of her husband's birth, which though it was not answerable to her present condition, yet to be tolerated in respect of his forefathers, for nobility doth not lose its privileges for want of fortune and want of worth, which he wanted not'. Owen, together with his chaplain and a servant, were committed to Newgate gaol by the Protector, Humphrey, Duke of Gloucester, according to Vergil. All of Owen's possessions were seized. The bard Robin Ddu publicly admonished those responsible for the imprisonment and called Owen 'neither a thief nor a robber, he is the victim of unrighteous wrath. His only fault was to have won the affection of a princess of France.'

The three prisoners escaped from Newgate in January or early February 1438, but were quickly by recaptured by John, 6th Baron Beaumont, with the aid of Thomas Darwent. Thus, on 24 February, Lord Beaumont paid to the Exchequer £80 that he had found on Owen Tudor's priest. Beaumont received £13 6s 8d on 24 March 1438, for his expenses incurred in recapturing Owen. Darwent was very well rewarded, being granted the office of porter at Pontefract Castle for life, with a daily wage of 4d. The three prisoners were placed temporarily into the care of William de la Pole, Earl of Suffolk, at Wallingford Castle, and were back in Newgate in March 1438. Owen's circumstances were probably better when he was transferred to Windsor Castle on 14 July, where he was placed in the custody of the constable, Walter, Lord Hungerford. Walter, 1st Baron Hungerford (1378–1449), had held the office of constable from 1417. He had fought at Agincourt and had been Lord Treasurer of England. However, a week after Owen was sent there, the office of constable was granted to Edmund Beaufort, Duke of Somerset. It seems that Owen's service at Agincourt with Hungerford and his later links in the queen's household with the strong Lancastrian Hungerford was thought dangerous by Yorkists on the council.

Goods and jewels belonging to Owen that had been seized at the time of his arrest were handed into the Treasury on 15 July 1438 by William Milrede of London. The inventory, chiefly of silverware, revealed some Owen's wealth. Perhaps there had been an accusation that this had belonged to the Crown via Henry V's widow. A dozen gilt cups were valued at £32 3s 4d. There was another old gilt cup, a gilt chalice, six enamelled silver salt cellars, a silver ewer, various silver cups and flagons, several candlesticks and basins, two spice plates and 'a paxbrede of silver and gilt with an ymage of Seynt Cristofre'. A 'pax-board' or 'pax-brede' was an *instrumentum pacis*, or 'osculatorium'. This was small plaque of metal, ivory or wood, generally decorated with a pious carving and provided with a handle, which was first brought to the altar for the celebrant to kiss at the proper place in the Mass and then brought to each of the congregation in turn at the altar rails. Again, perhaps these were church items in the possession of Owen when he tried to escape. Several pieces were broken, but the whole collection was assessed at £137 10s 4d.

Owen remained in confinement at Windsor for a year. He was released in July 1439 under a mainprise of £2,000, a massive sum. A writ of mainprise was directed to the sheriff when any man was imprisoned for a bailable offence and bail had been refused, or when the offence or cause of commitment was not properly bailable. It commanded him to take sureties for the prisoner's appearance, commonly called *mainpernors*, and to set him at large. Mainprise was granted, on condition that Owen appeared before the king on the following 11 November and at any other time deemed necessary. This he seems to have done, for on 12 November he was pardoned of all offences committed before 10 October 1439. The mainprise was cancelled on 1 January 1440. Owen had requested to appear before the king, and it appears that his stepson sanctioned his acquittal upon all charges, whatever they were. It certainly seems that the council had wished to punish Owen for the secret marriage to the king's mother. From the 1440s, he had been referred to in various ways: Owen ap Meredith, Owen Meredith, Owen ap Tuder, Owen ap Meredith ap Tudor and so on. It was possibly around this time that Owain ap Maredudd became Owen Tudor, or at least began to be unofficially referred to as this. Otherwise there would have been a Meredith line of kings of England, Ireland and Wales. When his sons had been given into the custody of Catherine de la Pole at Barking from 1437 to 1442, they had been known as Edmund and Jasper ap Meredith ap Tydier.

Henry VI had his own reasons for leniency. He had no parents and no close family. He was just seventeen, and suddenly a stepfather and two step-brothers aged eight and nine came into his life. He now granted Owen by 'especial favour' an annual pension from his own Privy Purse and welcomed Owen to the king's household. While not at the centre of courtly affairs with the great barons, Owen was safe upon its fringes at last. Owen's elder sons, Edmund and Jasper, and possibly an unknown sister, had been placed in the care of the Duke of Suffolk's sister, Katherine de la Pole, Abbess of Barking in Essex, from either when Catherine was sent to Bermondsey, or from the time of Owen's first arrest in 1437. They were certainly at the abbey by 27 July 1437 and remained there until at least 6 March 1442.

The Duke of Suffolk was a great favourite of Henry VI. Katherine de la Pole was to provide Owen Tudor's children with food, clothing and lodging, and both boys were allowed servants to wait upon them as the king's half-brothers. It is not clear whether Henry VI had known of the existence of his half-brothers until his mother told him while she was dying in Bermondsey Abbey. It was after her death that Henry would begin to care for them and eventually raise them to the peerage by giving both brothers earldoms. To a certain extent, the exact Welsh patronymic had already been abandoned, for neither Edmund nor Jasper is noted in the English records as 'son of Owen'. Like him, they are called 'ap Meredith ap Tydier'.

The brothers must have been well treated, for it cost the abbess 13s 4d a week to pay for their food and that of their servants, to which we must add the cost of their clothes and other incidentals. A warrant in the abbess' favour for the sum of £50 was sent to the Exchequer on 14 March 1439 and she was paid on 16 July, but it needed periodic appeals from the abbess to secure further payment of the expenses incurred in bringing them up. Early in November 1440, she had to petition the king for payment of £52 12s 0d which was due to her for the costs of keeping 'Esmond ap Meredith ap Tydir', and his brother Jasper and their servants. A warrant was made out on 5 November 1440, but she was not finally paid until July 1443. Another warrant was sent to the Exchequer on 32 (*sic*) February 1443 for a further payment of £55 13s 4d for their expenses from 1 November 1440 until 6 March 1442. Both warrants, for sums totalling £108 5s 4d, were honoured on 4 July 1443, but thereafter details of the abbess the boys are missing. Their father had been pardoned, and around March 1442 Jasper and Edmund were taken to court by Henry VI.

Owen Tudor had been present with distinguished knights to witness a charter that was signed in the favour of the Duke of Gloucester in July 1440, and was granted some land in Surrey in August 1444. Owen was also given four further substantial grants by the king, in the form of separate £40 gifts, between October 1442 and September 1444. As 'Owen ap Maredudd', he was in the court party that went to France in 1444 to bring back the young Margaret of Anjou, the king's new queen. We know little of Owen's whereabouts over the next fifteen years, and he was probably away from court tending to his estates, possibly in Wales. He had little to do with his sons' upbringing.

Their half-brother Henry VI began to take a special interest in the welfare of Jasper and Edmund. The ascetic Henry arranged for the best priests to educate them intellectually and morally. John Blacman, his confessor and biographer, wrote of Henry VI,

> For before he was married, being as a youth a pupil of chastity, he would keep careful watch through hidden windows of his chamber, lest any foolish impertinence of woman coming into the house should grow to a head, and cause the fall of any of his household. And like pains did he apply in the case of his two half-brothers, the Lords Jasper and Edmund, in their boyhood and youth: providing for them most strict and safe guardianship, putting them under the case of virtuous and worthy priests, both for right living and conversation, lest the untamed practices of youth should grow rank if they lacked any to prune them.

The brothers also received military training, and later were given military positions.

While Edmund and Jasper were growing up, the minority of Henry VI had led to factional struggles among the magnate and gentry classes, and the government of the nation began to deteriorate. Richard, Duke of York, was a direct descendant of Edward III, and the Duke of Exeter also had a claim to the crown. The enmity between York and Somerset eventually led to a series of crises. Throughout the reign of Henry VI, the spectacular gains made in France under the reign of Henry V were slowly lost. English defences were unable to prevent constant attacks by the French. Towards the middle of the fifteenth century, England had lost nearly all of its new lands in France, which led to fury among nobles and commoners alike.

In an attempt to pacify the French, marriage was proposed between Margaret of Anjou, who was a niece of the French king Charles VII, and Henry VI. The notion of a French woman with considerable influence in the running of English affairs angered nobles and commoners alike.

On 23 April 1445, Margaret of Anjou, just fifteen, married the twenty-three-year-old Henry VI at Titchfield in Hampshire. Henry still claimed the Kingdom of France and controlled various parts of northern France. Charles VII agreed to the marriage of his niece to his rival for France, on the condition that he would not have to provide the customary dowry. Instead, he would receive the lands of Maine and Anjou from England. This agreement was kept secret from the English public and, when discovered, was to prove disastrous for the king.

Owen Tudor seems to have been largely living in Wales at this time, but on 15 January 1449 the Chancellor was ordered to authorise the payment of £18 4*s* to Owen for his expenses in France. An Owen or 'Owyn' Meredith was in the royal household between at least 1444 and 1453 and is probably Owen Tudor. Little else is known about Owen, and he now disappears from view until his son Jasper's rise to prominence in the 1450s. Edmund and Jasper were knighted on 15 and 25 December 1449 respectively. Although the king had been married for seven years by 1452, he still had no children, and the death of Duke Humphrey of Gloucester in 1447 had removed his last surviving uncle from the scene. Humphrey was one of Jasper Tudor's predecessors as Earl of Pembroke, and had a severe method of handling land disputes. In 1440, just before his fall from grace, Humphrey was involved in a land dispute with John Whithorne regarding the Isle of Wight. According to Patent Roll 25, Henry VI, 'Humphrey Duke of Gloucester … caused the said John Whithorne … to be brought to Pembroke Castle and there imprisoned in so dark a dungeon and in such misery and lack of food and clothing for seven years and more, that he lost the sight of his eyes and suffered other incurable ills.' According to contemporaries, Humphrey was a cultured and learned man.

Humphrey of Lancaster, 1st Duke of Gloucester, 1st Earl of Pembroke (1390–1447), was 'son, brother and uncle of kings', being the fourth and youngest son of Henry IV by his first wife, brother to Henry V and uncle to Henry VI. Upon the death of Henry V in 1422, Humphrey became Lord Protector to the young Henry VI. He also claimed the right to the regency of England following the death of his elder brother John, Duke of Bedford, who had been regent, which also made Humphrey heir presumptive to the crown. Humphrey's claims were strongly contested by the lords of the King's Council, and in particular his half-uncle, Cardinal Henry Beaufort. Henry V's will, rediscovered at Eton College in 1978, supports Humphrey's claims. Like Jasper, he was Chief Justice of South Wales. However, he annulled his marriage and disinherited his wife to marry his mistress, Eleanor, the daughter of Lord Cobham. Eleanor once consulted astrologers to try to divine the future. The astrologers, Thomas Southwell and Roger Bolingbroke, predicted that Henry VI would suffer a life-threatening illness in July or August 1441.

The king's men arrested Southwell and Bolingbroke on charges of treasonable necromancy. After interrogation, Bolingbroke named Eleanor as the instigator, so she too was arrested and tried, for sorcery and heresy.

The charges against her were possibly exaggerated to curb the ambitions of her husband. She was tried and convicted of practising witchcraft against Henry VI in an attempt to retain power for her husband. Eleanor denied most of the charges but confessed to obtaining potions from Margery Jourdemayne, 'the Witch of Eye', to help her conceive. Bolingbroke was hanged, drawn and quartered, Jourdemayne was burnt at the stake and Southwell died in the Tower, possibly killing himself.

Humphrey's wife had to carry out public penance in London and divorce her husband, and was then condemned to life imprisonment. In 1442, she was imprisoned at Chester Castle, then moved to Kenilworth Castle, then the Isle of Man, finally dying in Beaumaris Castle in 1452. Humphrey's power had thus been broken by his enemies, and he retired from public life in 1441. However, he himself was arrested on a charge of treason in 1447, dying three days later, possibly from poisoning.

With Humphrey's death, the king's immediate family consisted solely of his wife, Margaret of Anjou. The future security of the country seemed to be in jeopardy, and in November 1450 Thomas Young, a Bristol lawyer, MP and protégé of Richard, Duke of York, petitioned for the latter's recognition as heir presumptive, for which he served a term of imprisonment. The Tudor brothers were not thought of as potential heirs to the throne as others, such as York and Exeter, had far better claims.

Here, we must quickly consider the background to the finances of the king. The subject of the king's powers and finances had been a problem since the reign of Henry IV (1399–1413), the Lancastrian usurper who confiscated great estates, especially from leading Yorkists. During his son Henry V's brief reign from 1413 to 1422, his nobles were busy profiteering from plundering France, but under the boy king Henry VI, unrest had grown among nobles and commoners. Many royal lands reverted to the Crown on the deaths of Lionel, Duke of Clarence (1421), John, Duke of Bedford (1435), Queen Catherine of Valois (1437) and Humphrey, Duke of Gloucester (1447). Between 1437 and 1449, Henry VI had granted many estates into the non-royal hands of his favourites, and almost the whole income from what he did retain was enjoyed by members of his household.

In the years preceding the Jack Cade Rebellion of 1450, England suffered from the animosity of the lower classes toward Henry VI. Years of war against France had caused the country to go into debt, and the recent loss of Normandy led to a widespread fear of invasion. Coastal regions of England such as Kent and Sussex were seeing attacks by French armies. Ill equipped by the government, English soldiers took to raiding English towns along the route to France, with their victims receiving no compensation. Henry's call to set warning beacons along the coastline confirmed peoples' suspicions that an attack by the French was possible.

This fear and continuous unrest in the coastal counties inspired some nobles to attempt to force the king to address their problems, or abdicate his throne in favour of someone more competent, such as York. At court, different opinions on how to proceed in the war with France led to party divisions. Henry had wanted peace while his uncle Gloucester and other nobles felt England should continue to fight for England's claim to the French throne. Plotting in court eventually led to the banishment of the king's closest friend and advisor William de la Pole, Duke of Suffolk. Many across the country believed that the king had surrounded himself with advisors who were ineffective and corrupt, especially Suffolk.

Members of the parliament held from 1449 to 1450 in London and Leicester were determined to curtail the king's income and spending. This parliament impeached Suffolk for the failure of his foreign policy and for his insatiable greed, which had impoverished the king. There was hostility towards Suffolk, the king's household in general and, indirectly, the king himself. Suffolk was banished and his headless body washed up on the shores of Dover, probably tossed off a ship after being beheaded following a mock trial. He was said to have been planning a French invasion of England, and to have raped and impregnated a nun the night before he had surrendered to Joan of Arc in 1429. Few missed him except the king.

There was bitter resentment across the nation against those who were enriching themselves from the profits of Crown lands, and thus increasing the need for taxation. The Jack Cade Rebellion, where the Kentish men had risen in arms during the sitting of this parliament, put forward as one of its main grievances a complaint that the king's ministers were preventing the passing of the Act of Resumption for their own selfish ends. Parliament devised a new type of appropriation of money in the hope that it would be less easy to avoid than what had gone before. Individual items from specific farms and fee farms were allocated to the king's household. Direct taxes had been very heavy for a long time, an average of a complete tenth and fifteenth every two years. The demand for a large-scale resumption aroused tremendous opposition in the country at large. Heavy taxation had been accompanied by failure in war, coupled with instability at home and in foreign trade. The London parliament of 1450–1451 was a turning point in the long struggle with the House of Lancaster on the subject of resumption.

Henry VI, urged on by a hated queen, had given away so much of 'the king's own' to favourites that there was almost nothing left for the Treasury. During August 1450, Richard, Duke of York, heir to the throne and the king's most powerful subject, had left his post in Ireland to force his way into the king's presence with an armed escort. He demanded reform. Shortly after this, Parliament first met. With his kinsmen John Mowbray, Duke of Norfolk, and Richard Neville, Earl of Warwick, York then managed to have Edmund Beaufort, Duke of Somerset, taken into 'protective custody'. Parliament was due to resume again on 20 January 1451, and over the Christmas holidays the queen worked to improve the confidence of the king against her Yorkist enemies. Somerset was released from the Tower and, to York's despair, was appointed to the prestigious post of Captain of Calais. Many liberties, privileges and annuities were annulled by this parliament, both on land and on other sources of revenue, such as the customs duties. The very greatest in the land bore their burden as well as the humbler folk.

The massive grants made by the king between 1437 and 1449 were almost entirely undone. However, these reforms did little to rescue the Crown from its debts, which amounted to an incredible £375,000. In current money using the 'economic power' or 'economic cost' indicators, this represents a debt of £121 billion. The kingdom was insolvent.

From August 1450, when Richard of York returned from Ireland, to the First Battle of St Albans in May 1455, when Somerset was killed, the country was dominated by the struggle between these two men. York achieved little in 1451, so by February 1452 issued a manifesto to the people of Shrewsbury, which was an unprecedented attack on the government. He followed this up with an unsuccessful coup at Dartford in Kent. In order to boost their flagging prestige, Henry and Margaret went on royal progress. In the summer they toured the South West and the West Midlands, visiting Southampton, Exeter, Bristol, Gloucester, Hereford, Ludlow, Birmingham and Coventry. Early in winter they visited the southern Midlands and East Anglia, resting at St Albans, Stamford, Peterborough and Cambridge.

When the royal party was at Reading in November 1452, Edmund and Jasper were created earls. Even after the king began to take a personal interest in ruling, from around 1436–1437, he had increasingly alienated public sympathy and support, because he was seen to surround himself with greedy parvenus, desiring speedy enrichment from the king's coffers. This presented a problem around 1452 when the Tudor brothers had both probably reached twenty-one years old. Henry and his advisors had to decide their future role in life, their relationship to the king, the royal family and the magnate class while not alienating the lords or people. The two could not indefinitely remain in the royal family while not formally of it. The descendants of Ednyfed Fychan, *wyrion Eden*, were now to be made the premier earls of England, recognised as the king's uterine brothers, with precedence before all men except dukes.

The pious Henry had carefully supervised the brothers' upbringing since their mother's death, practising the virtues of Christian charity and brotherly love which he held so dear. H. T. Evans suggests that it was the Duke of Somerset who was responsible for the 'flash of Athenian acuteness' during the Christmas holidays in 1452 when the two Tudors were ennobled. However, Henry had already implicitly recognised the boys as his kinsmen by the special provision he made for their upbringing. On 23 November 1452, the Tudor brothers were created earls: Edmund as Earl of Richmond and Jasper as Earl of Pembroke. The brothers now adopted the royal arms, differenced only by a border. They might not be of the blood royal of England, but they were regarded as members of the royal family and therefore entitled to bear the king's arms.

Halsted reports,

King Henry the Sixth, when old enough to assume the reins of government, had not been content with merely releasing, so soon as he could effect it, his father-in-law from imprisonment, but he testified in the most amiable and affectionate manner his kindness and love for his maternal brothers, who were about ten years younger than himself. He had them carefully educated, under the most honest and virtuous ecclesiastics; and when of an age to be removed to court, they are noticed as in attendance on the king and queen. In the year 1452, Margaret of Anjou, who then came to Norwich with the view of raising troops, is particularly stated to have been attended by the king's half-brothers, Edmund of Hadham, and Jasper of Hatfield. It has been already stated how early he interested himself for the former, by endeavouring to secure for his future bride the wealthy heiress of Somerset. The year following their betrothment, he bestowed on him the castle and county of Richmount, or Richmondshire, in the North-Riding of York, creating him at the same time, by letters patent, Earl of Richmond, with this peculiar privilege, that he should take precedence above all earls, and sit in Parliament next to dukes, by reason of his near consanguinity to the reigning monarch.

His brother, Jasper Tudor, in the same year, 1452, he advanced to the dignity of Earl of Pembroke, by which he became possessed of the castle and royal territories in South Wales, appertaining to the title, the earldom having been erected into a county Palatine in 1138; also of the ancient mansion in the metropolis, belonging to the Earldom of Pembroke, a fine building, then denominated Pembroke's Inn, now known as Stationers' Hall. In addition to these honours, the Earl of Richmond shortly afterwards obtained from the monarch, a grant in fee, of the noble mansion called Baynards Castle, situated near Paul's Wharf, on the banks of the Thames; which had recently been enlarged and beautified by Humphrey Duke of Gloucester, the king's uncle; on whose death without issue, it fell to the crown, and was bestowed by Henry upon his brother. Here it is probable the young Earl of Richmond chiefly sojourned, during the interval that elapsed prior to his marriage, this palace of the Saxon kings being usually occupied by some near connection of the crown.

The Tudors were not made dukes, as this would have caused massive resentment at court. They were created earls, as at this time dukedoms were rare, usually only given to the king's sons. Even Henry VI's dead uncles, although created earls when they were quite young, had not become dukes immediately. The procedure of ennoblement consisted of three stages. The king first made an oral or written declaration of creation. This was followed by the ceremony of investiture with the sword of the appropriate county, and then the king would issue a charter, recording and announcing the creation. In the case of the Tudor brothers, the first step in this process took place on 23 November 1452.

The letters patent for Edmund Tudor invested him with the style and dignity of Earl of Richmond, with precedence over all other magnates except dukes, and endowed him with estates of the Honour of Richmond 'in tail male'. This limits the succession to property or title to male descendants only. The first half of the letters patent for Earl Jasper was almost identical. He was granted the style and dignity of Earl of Pembroke and was also to enjoy precedence, after his brother, over all other magnates except dukes. However, whereas the king was able to grant Earl Edmund the estates of the Honour of Richmond, since these had lain in his hands since the death of John, Duke of Bedford, in 1435, the honourial lands of the earldom of Pembroke had been granted to Queen Margaret as part of her dowry in 1447. The Crown had resumed them on 23 July 1451, but the government was probably still arranging alternative sources of income for the queen and may even have considered re-granting the estates to Margaret. Thus, although Jasper enjoyed the style of Earl of Pembroke, he was not yet given the accompanying honourial lands because of conflicting ownerships. Instead, he was granted an annuity of £20 'in tail male' (a fee payable to male descendants) from the fee farm of the City of London and county of Middlesex in order to maintain his newly acquired dignity.

The following two stages of ennoblement were delayed because the king was away and Parliament was not in session, and also because of the special position of the Tudors as the king's half-brothers. Henry would want to elevate them in the most appropriate way, so the second stage of creation, being belted with the sword of the relevant county, had to wait until Christmas was over. Thus the king instructed William Cotton, Keeper of the Great Wardrobe, to provide Edmund and Jasper with a sumptuous wardrobe of velvets, cloth of gold and furs, as well as saddles and other equestrian accoutrements. On Christmas Day 1452, the king and queen were at the manor of Pleasance, near Gravesend, where they watched 'disguisings'. The investitures then took place when the Henry and Margaret returned to London after celebrating Christmas at Greenwich. On 5 January 1453, the brothers were invested in the Tower of London. On the following day, the Feast of Epiphany, the king formally created them earls. As the king's closest kinsmen, they were to be the two leading earls in the kingdom, and the brothers were summoned to Parliament in their new capacity as earls.

The third stage of their creation took place in this parliament, which opened at Reading on 6 March 1453. On this day the Tudors took their seats as premier earls and the House of Commons presented a petition pleading with Henry VI to recognise them as his legitimate uterine brothers. It also asked him to release them from liability under any statute because their ancestors were not English, and to confirm the letters patent which Henry had previously granted to them. The wording of the letters patent of 6 March for Earl Edmund is almost exactly the same as that of 23 November 1452, except that the grant of the earldom of Richmond had to be backdated to Michaelmas 1452. The only other alteration was that the earldom could now extend to Edmund's legitimate male heirs and not simply to the male heirs of his body. The first part of Jasper's patent is almost identical to that of 23 November 1452, by which he was granted the style of Earl of Pembroke and precedence before all peers, except dukes, after his elder brother. The only difference was that, by 6 March

1453, the problems of the honourial lands of the earldom of Pembroke had been settled. Thus Jasper was granted these estates upon the same terms as the grant by which his brother enjoyed the Honour of Richmond, being backdated to 1452 and extended to all his legitimate male heirs. The king assented to the Commons' petition and thereby confirmed their entitlement.

Following their secret births around 1430 and their subsequent hidden childhoods, the Tudor brothers had risen to become the premier earls of England by March 1453. However, despite being the king's half-brothers, they had needed the king to endow them with extensive and profitable lands to maintain their status as earls. Henry's position was still delicate, although relations between his government and its critics had improved somewhat following the successful Act of Resumption of 1450. Henry had recovered many estates but dared not alienate the lords again. Nevertheless, the king had created substantial ownerships for the Tudors, but only at great loss to his own resources. Fortunately the king and Parliament had reached a successful compromise over the Act of Resumption of 1450, and the Crown now had large tracts of land available for fresh alienation, *i.e.* grants.

Against a background of financial difficulties and political intrigue, Henry VI had to be extremely careful in giving estates to his half-brothers. The largest and most valuable block of Edmund's Richmond estates were in Lincolnshire, but the honour also included lands stretching in a narrow arc across England, from Yorkshire in the north to Norfolk in the east. Edmund Tudor took his title from Richmond in Yorkshire, the ancient and once valuable *caput* of the Honour of Richmond. By the fifteenth century, however, the honourial lands in Yorkshire had shrunk to a fraction of their former size and Edmund's estates there were only worth an estimated £40 per annum. However, the king kept adding to the income of his half-brothers. On 23 November 1452, Edmund Tudor was granted two-thirds of the entire Honour of Richmond. The Richmond lands in Lincolnshire had been used to reward royal servants, and there were also Richmond estates in Cambridgeshire and Norfolk. Apart from the Honour of Richmond, the only major estates held by Earl Edmund were the lordships of Kendal in Westmorland and Wyresdale in Lancashire. From November 1452 until July 1453, both earls received regular and substantial grants of land, creating and stabilising their landed wealth. However, after the king's illness in August 1453, grants fell off dramatically.

Apart from ennoblement, it was also necessary to find suitable brides for the new earls and, on 24 March 1453, they were jointly granted the wardship and marriage of one of England's richest and most desirable heiresses, Lady Margaret Beaufort, the only daughter and heiress of John, Duke of Somerset. When Somerset died on 27 May 1444, possibly murdered by Yorkists, his daughter Margaret was a little under a year old, yet she had been married a few years later to John de la Pole, son and heir of the Marquess of Suffolk. On 18 August 1450, the couple had been granted a papal dispensation to remain in matrimony, for the couple had married within the prohibited degrees. The same year witnessed the assassination of Margaret Beaufort's father-in-law, William de la Pole, Duke of Suffolk, and among many charges laid against him was one that he had enriched himself at the king's expense by securing the Beaufort inheritance, estimated at £1,000 per annum. Moreover, Lady Margaret was a rich prize as a bride, not merely because of her wealth but also because of her prominent position in one of the greatest magnate families of England.

Sometime in February or March 1453, the king allowed Margaret Beaufort to divorce John de la Pole. According to her chaplain, John Fisher, she later said that she was given a choice of either formalising her marriage to de la Pole or marrying Edmund. The value of the Somerset inheritance included the 'south parts' of Margaret Beaufort's estates, fifteen manors and twelve fee farms, stretching through twelve English shires but largely concentrated in the South West, especially in Somerset. These manors represented the most valuable portion of the inheritance and nine were in Somerset, two in Devon and two in Hampshire.

As well as enjoying the custody of Margaret Beaufort's inheritance, the new earls of Richmond and Pembroke shared several other estates as a result of royal benevolence. When Margaret and the earls visited Norwich in 1453, the city fathers were at pains to entertain them lavishly, and Edmund and Jasper were each given a gift of £5. Taking all the sources of revenue into account, it appears that Earl Edmund's clear income was not less than £925 per annum. Margaret Beaufort later married Earl Edmund and bore him a son, Henry, on 28 January 1457 at her brother-in-law's castle at Pembroke. As for Jasper's marriage prospects, increasing bitterness and rivalry between the great baronial families of England reduced his opportunities, and between 1461 and 1485 he was more concerned with staying alive than marrying.

The handing of the earldom of Pembroke to Jasper Tudor was less complicated than that of Richmond and Kendal to Edmund. The remarkable unpublished doctoral thesis of R. S. Thomas illustrates the complexities of land ownership for both brothers. John, Lord Beauchamp of Powick, had leased the lands of the earldom, together with the lordships of Trane Clinton, St Clears and Cilgerran, from May 1450 for twelve years, but they were resumed again by the Crown, so the king was able to grant these estates to Jasper and his legitimate male heirs on 6 March 1453. Because of the scattered nature of the honourial estates of Richmond and Pembroke and their other smaller properties, the earls were faced with new and difficult problems of administration, law and finance. However, these problems had been managed by earlier generations of lords and their servants, so seigniorial administration had become quite efficient. Generally, a new lord would retain the vast majority of the former lord's servants, and this seems to have been the case with Edmund and Jasper.

In 1454, there was

confirmation to Jasper, Earl of Pembroke, of divers castles and manors, etc., including the County, Castle, and Lordship of Pembroke with its members and appurtenances, to wit: The hundred and lordship of Castle Martin. The lordship of St Fflorence. The Lordship and Forest of Coydrath. The Castle, Lordship and Town of Tenby. The lordship and bailiwick of West Pembroke and East Pembroke. The Bailwicks of Dongleddy [Daugleddau], Rous [Rhos], and Kemmeys [Cemmaes]. Half the Ferry of Burton. With all their appurtenances, viz., rents of assize and gave rent value yearly £196 3s 7d besides reprisals issues and profits of wind and water mills value yearly £30 13s 4d; profits of coal at Coydrath, 43s 4d; customary tenants in the forest of Coydrath, 52s; the issues and profits of the towns of Pembroke and Tenby £8 3s 7d; the profits of half the ferry of Burton, 16s 10d; profits and perquisites of the Hundred and County Courts held annually, £13 14s 6d; do. escheats, reliefs, and divers, other casual receipts, £26 13s 6d; prises of wines in the ports of Milford and Tenby and elsewhere in the county, £6 13s 6d ...

These were all later confiscated in 1461 and in 1462 given to Richard of Gloucester, the future Richard III.

With the dignity of Earl of Pembroke, Jasper had been given the ancient and valuable lordship of Pembroke, a rich prize and a strategic centre in the west, commanding St George's Channel and the southern route to Ireland. Simultaneously, Jasper received the castle, town and lordship of Cilgerran in north Pembrokeshire; the castle, town and lordship of Llanstephan in Carmarthenshire; and the lordships of Ystlwyf, Trane Clinton and St Clears in south-west Carmarthenshire. When Humphrey, Duke of Gloucester, died in 1447, these lands together had an estimated clear annual value of £363 6s 8d, and by May 1451 their clear value was estimated at £400 2s 8d a year.

The inquisition of 1451 tells us that in the lordship of Pembroke, income from land was the predominant source of revenue, and it was estimated in 1451 that £196 3s 7d (68 per cent) of the clear annual value of the lordship of £287 3s 8d accrued from 'assised' rents of free tenants and from the semi-servile *gafolmen*. Apart from land, Jasper drew upon other sources of valuable income from the lordship of Pembroke. The wind and water mills had an estimated clear value of £30 13s 4d in 1451, or 11 per cent of the total clear value. The sum was drawn partly from the numerous corn mills and partly from fulling mills, which prepared cloth for the local market towns and for shipment from the ports of Milford Haven, Pembroke and Tenby. Apart from income from land and seigniorial rights, Jasper's judicial revenue from Pembroke was considerable. The regalian rights enjoyed by a Marcher Lord meant that, in the sphere of justice the law was his, and he alone enjoyed its profits, not the Crown. In 1451, the judicial profits from the entire lordship of Pembroke were estimated to be worth £40 7s 10d, 14 per cent of the total estimated clear value.

The other estate which Jasper held in Pembrokeshire was the lordship of Cilgerran, with its sub-lordships estimated to be worth £34 7s 3d in clear annual value in 1451. Further east, Jasper held the lordship of

Llanstephan in Carmarthenshire, which was granted to him at the same time as Pembroke and Cilgerran. This rent included the town and castle of Llanstephan, the commote of Penrhyr and the sub-lordships of Ystlwyf, Trane Clinton and St Clears. The clear value of this estate was calculated at £58 1s 7d in 1451. Of this, £26 12s (45.8 per cent) was estimated to accrue from fixed rents, while a further £17 6s 3d came from farms of demesne land and meadows, and from the agistment of animals.

Apart from these lordships, Jasper held a number of other estates in Wales. Across the River Tywi from Llanstephan, the earl was granted in tail male the 'manors' of Cloigyn and Pibwr in the Duchy of Lancaster lordship of Kidwelly on 30 March 1453. At the same time, Jasper received the lordship of Aber in the Caernarfonshire commote of Arllechwedd Uchaf. The third part of the grant of 30 March 1453 was probably the most valuable: the castle and lordship of Cil y Coed, now called Caldicot in modern Monmouthshire, granted to Jasper Tudor in tail male. There is a tradition that Henry Tudor was conceived at Jasper's Caldicot Castle in 1456.

While the Tudor brothers were coming to grips with the details of running councils and widespread estates for the first time, the French were rapidly taking castle after castle in Gascony in 1453, and the Earl of Shrewsbury was killed while leading a relief expedition in July. On 19 October, Bordeaux surrendered and the Hundred Years' War, which began in 1337 with Edward III's invasion, ended in all but name. However, the rivalry between the great northern families of the Percys and the Nevilles led to local warfare in Yorkshire in the summer of 1453.

Other than his Tudor half-brothers, Henry VI had no close blood relatives. His uncles, the dukes of Bedford, Clarence and Gloucester, had all died without legitimate heirs and this left a familial and dynastic void at the court. Henry's government was also still hated as being inefficient and corrupt. His most prominent ministers, especially Wiltshire and Somerset, were scorned by nobles and commoners alike. By 10 August 1453, with the loss of France and domestic problems, Henry VI was reported to have fallen seriously ill, with a complete mental and physical collapse that was to last for more than eighteen months. He fell into imbecility, sitting for days without moving or speaking. The king was unable to speak or even to rise unaided from his chair. Once his attendants had dressed him and placed him in his chair he looked perfectly normal, but when addressed, it was clear that he had no comprehension of what had been said. Incapable of speech, he could give no reply, and seemed unaware of any activity or person in his vicinity. He had to be helped from room to room, and sometimes this required the united efforts of two men. He had to be fed with a spoon, and was lifted from his chair into his bed. He was physically and mentally helpless. There was no question of his being able to discharge his duties properly. He may have suffered from catatonic schizophrenia. It was the first of several bouts of illness which were to leave him permanently feeble. His Valois grandfather, Charles VI of France, had been unstable, and there may have been a hereditary cause. Illness of the body was well understood in the fifteenth century, even if the remedies were usually horrific and generally ineffectual, but this understanding did not extend to mental illness.

In March 1453, Jasper had been granted the forfeited Norfolk estates of York's chamberlain, Sir William Oldhall, which we might think would prejudice the Duke of York against the new earl. Jasper was a newcomer, associated with an unpopular king and even more disliked by queen and court, but York now needed allies. From this time on, Jasper associated with and supported the duke. It was clear that he was a far more capable man than the king, and had wide respect. With the king's illness, immediate steps had to be taken to ensure the survival of the royal government. York was expected to be appointed as regent, and would probably have assumed the kingship, but on 13 October 1453, just six days before the surrender of Bordeaux, Queen Margaret unexpectedly had a son and heir to the crown. It was doubted by the Yorkists that it could have been the king's child, with her favourites Wiltshire and Somerset being posited as fathers. The new Prince of Wales was to be known as Edward of Lancaster, or Edward of Westminster, after his place of birth.

On 21 November 1453, Jasper attended a meeting of the council in the Star Chamber at Westminster, together with a large number of peers. They listened to York's complaint of being deprived of the services of his counsellors, and studied his petition for their restoration. Somerset was the only prominent magnate absent and the council agreed to York's request. Jasper supported York's candidature for regent, but Edmund missed the discussions. Also in November 1453, the Duke of Norfolk presented a Bill of complaint to the council concerning Somerset's administration at home and abroad. The Duke of Somerset was placed in the Tower, for no less than fourteen months, possibly to avert a public trial or for his personal safety.

On 6 December 1453, Jasper was in York's company at a small meeting of the council to consider new means of funding the king's household. As Jasper and Edmund were members of the household, Jasper would have known far more about its inner workings than many other lords. Jasper was under no compulsion to attend this meeting, and the only other three 'lay peers' present were the earls of Warwick and Worcester, and Henry, Lord Bourchier. Bourchier was married to York's only sister, Isabella, and was a member of the duke's council as early as 1449–1450. These were all both kinsmen and associates of the Duke of York. It seems that Jasper was in the centre of the Yorkist faction, and by the end of January 1454, the relationship of both Tudor brothers with York's party was demonstrated in public, and at some possible risk. Writing of their imminent arrival in London, a member of the Paston family noted on 19 January 1454 that 'the earls of Warwyk, Richemond and Pembroke come with the Duke of York, as it is said, every one of them with a goodly fellowship ... And as Geoffrey Pole saith, the Kyng's brethren are like to be arrested at their coming to London if they come.' Geoffrey Pole was one of Earl Jasper's councillors by 1456, so was probably in a position to give such a comment.

The queen and her closest councillors had kept the king's insanity secret as long as they could, and only sometime after the prince's birth was the question of regency raised. A great council was held at Westminster on 12 November to consider it, but York was not invited, although public opinion favoured him. The queen and Somerset, York's main opponent in the land, had been forced to prorogue the parliament until February 1454, hoping that Henry would recover his wits. Thoroughly alarmed at the Yorkist attempt to take over the kingship, Margaret and her supporters tried to jolt the sick king back into sanity. Prince Edward had already been christened by William of Waynflete, Bishop of Winchester, with Somerset, Cardinal John Kemp, and Isabel, Duchess of Buckingham, acting as his godparents. Around New Year's Day 1454, Buckingham presented the three-month-old prince to Henry, and requested the king to give him a father's blessing. The king remained immobile, as he did when Queen Margaret repeated the experiment. Margaret could see that the only hope of the prince's survival lay in the king's recovery, and doctors were urged to try anything to cure him. They put him on different diets, purged him, shaved his head, bled him, rubbed him with embrocation and made him drink fermentations, but to no avail.

York took control of the council, and he and Norfolk managed to get Somerset placed in the Tower while an inquiry was held into his deeds. With her ally Somerset out of the way, Queen Margaret was forced to set up herself as head of the anti-York court party, and in anticipation of the coming session of Parliament she drew up a document asserting her right to the regency. In the February 1454 parliament many peers deliberately stayed away rather than commit themselves to either side, including Edmund Tudor. He may have been ill or away in Wales, but, as in the later English Civil War, we often see brothers taking opposite sides, so that at least one will retain the family estates and honours, or be left in a position to protect his sibling from punishment. Margaret was demanding to be made regent but Jasper seems to have sided with York, whom Parliament chose as Protector in April 1454.

His elder brother, the Earl of Richmond, played a less prominent part in national politics in the three years since his ennoblement, and, although summoned to all great councils and to Parliament, Edmund's presence at a council meeting is only once recorded, on 13 November 1454, when he attested the ordinance reforming the king's household. Similarly, his presence at the great council of July 1454 can only be inferred from the fact that he was not one of the absentee magnates to whom admonitory letters were sent on the 24th of that month. Nevertheless, Edmund, like Jasper, had accompanied York to London in January 1454, with the possible risk of imprisonment facing him.

Despite a possibility of arrest, Jasper was certainly present at the short-lived parliament of February–April 1454, although Edmund was one of the many absentees, and was fined 100 marks for his failure to appear. On 15 March, Jasper attended a meeting of the council at which it was decided that a commission should be issued to three physicians and two surgeons to attend upon the king's person and prescribe remedies for his illness. The archbishops of Canterbury and York, and the bishops of Winchester, Durham, Ely, Worcester, Norwich, Hereford, Lincoln, Coventry and Lichfield, as well as the Prior of St John's, were present. The lay peers present at the same time were the dukes of York and Buckingham, the earls of Warwick, Oxford, Devon, Salisbury, Shrewsbury and Wiltshire, and the lords Graystoke, Fauconberg, Clinton, Stourton, Bourchier, Welles, Scrope of Bolton and Fiennes, and Lord Say. Discounting Jasper, only five of these sixteen were later royalists in Henry VI's faction: Buckingham, Oxford, Wiltshire, Shrewsbury and Lord Welles.

The first month of Parliamentary business was spent in manoeuvring by the queen's court party and the Yorkists, but on 22 March 1454 it was dramatically ended by the sudden death of the Chancellor, Cardinal Kemp. The choice of the nation's regent or Protector now became of extreme importance. Jasper was not among those who visited the sickly king at Windsor with other councillors on 25 March to seek his opinion on the matter of the regency. These councillors found Henry far worse than they had expected, and, on 27 March 1454, Jasper and the other peers agreed that York should become Protector. However, York's appointment was carefully defined and hedged about with several restrictions. The duke's subsequent administration, and the composition and activities of the council during his protectorship, show that his regime was not a factional clique. Jasper and the lords of Parliament next endorsed the creation of Salisbury as Chancellor at Westminster on 2 April, and Jasper attended a council meeting concerned with routine business six days later. York made a genuine attempt to govern well, and to bring some reform, stability and justice to the realm.

Both Tudors were summoned on 29 May 1454 to attend a great council on the following 25 June. However, because of the Percy–Neville feud in the North, the council meeting was postponed until July. The brothers' relations with York may have been more than cordial, for in the July meeting Sir Baldwin Montfort of Coleshill (Warwick) enfeoffed his son Simon and another man with the manor of Coleshill, with remainder to York's eldest son, Edward, Earl of March; Edmund, Earl of Pembroke (*sic*); the Earl of Warwick and his wife; and several others. Whether Richmond or Pembroke was meant is not clear, but the brothers' association with York is clear. It is probably sufficient evidence to demonstrate that Edmund, like Jasper, Buckingham and Shrewsbury, was no committed partisan of Somerset and the queen's party, and was prepared to participate in the attempts made by York to reform the government of England. On 24 July, both brothers were summoned to a second great council to meet on the following 21 October.

We have seen that Jasper was granted the forfeited Norfolk estates of York's chamberlain, Sir William Oldhall, in March 1453, but the earl's receiver-general, John Rogger, attested on 15 October 1454 that the original grant to Jasper had been lost. As regent, it would have been easy for York to restore these Norfolk estates to Oldhall, but although his chamberlain's outlawry was annulled, Jasper still received an exemplification of the original grant to him of these estates upon 15 October. York could not afford to alienate one of the most prominent peers of the realm, one who was both well disposed towards him and a half-brother of the king.

Both Edmund and Jasper were present at a meeting of the great council on 13 November when ordinances were promulgated for the long-awaited reform of the expensive royal household. The lords agreed that it was altogether too large, and 'its numbers of very necessity must be abridged and reduced to a reasonable and a competent fellowship as may worshipfully be found and sustained in the same'. In future, the Tudors were each to have one chaplain, two esquires, two yeomen and two chamberlains to attend them in the household, an establishment only equalled by that of the king's confessor. Both men signed this important document, and their agreement with this reforming measure, which affected them personally as members of the king's household, shows their concern for better government and their sympathy with York's political aims. Neither brother derived any material benefit from their liaison with York, and they seemed to sympathise with the duke's intention to stamp out bad government based on graft and corruption.

On the grounds of economy, the king's household at Windsor had to be reduced. The terrific costs of the royal stables had been addressed. Henry was forced to manage with 428 people, while the queen would have 120 lords and servants in attendance, with a further 38 for the infant Prince Edward. York achieved a great deal in his nine months as Protector, from 27 March 1454 until the last days of the year. However, the king somehow recovered his senses over the Christmas period. York was no longer needed.

4

The Turning Point: The Start of the Wars of the Roses, the Death of Edmund and the Birth of Henry Tudor, 1455–1457

After eighteen months of incapacity, in the last few days of 1454, Henry VI recovered his senses. He now learned for the first time that he had a ten-week-old son and heard of York's actions as Protector of the Realm, and the gains recovered from his favourites. His closest advisors, Somerset and Exeter, were in custody. The queen's party was ecstatic, but York's followers feared the worst, and the end of the duke's far more effective government. William of Waynflete, Bishop of Winchester, and Sir Robert Botyll, Prior of St John, were sent to Windsor to find if the king was really better, or if it was a subterfuge. On 7 January 1455, the men had an audience with Henry and the *Paston Letters* tell us that 'he speke to hem as well as he ever did; and when thei came out thei wept for joye, and he seith he is in charitee with all the world, and so he wold all the Lords were'.

The king's recovery destroyed any prospect of order and good governance being restored, and Richard of York was soon to suffer the revenge of the queen and Somerset. Margaret decided that Henry needed a month's convalescence at Windsor before undertaking his duties properly, and wanted Somerset's release from the Tower to loosen York's grip on government. Somerset was released on bail on 5 February 1455 to the despair of York and his allies. Lancastrian supporters willingly put up bail that Somerset would attend any enquiry, including Buckingham, his half-brother William Bourchier, Lord FitzWaryn, the Earl of Wiltshire and Lord Roos. They knew that when the king resumed power, there was little likelihood of any commission of inquiry into Somerset's actions.

Briefed by Margaret, Somerset complained at a council meeting on 4 March that he had been held for over a year without any charge being preferred against him and asked for his bail to be discharged because there was 'noo lawfull cause proposed ayenst him'. Henry also backed his friend, declaring that Somerset was his 'faithful liegeman', who had done him 'right true … service'. Somerset's bail was discharged and there was never any commission of enquiry. All Yorkist ministers were swiftly dismissed. In March 1455, York's brother-in-law Richard Neville, Earl of Salisbury, was sacked as Chancellor. He was replaced by the Lancastrian Thomas Bourchier, Archbishop of Canterbury. The Yorkist John Tiptoft, Earl of Worcester, was replaced at the Treasury in favour of James Butler, Earl of Wiltshire. York's other great enemy, Henry Holland, Duke of Exeter, was released from Pontefract Castle on 19 March. Exeter had been imprisoned by the Protector since July 1454. Exeter, like the Percys in Northumberland, had been raising men for insurrection. York was stripped of the captaincy of Calais, which was restored to the less capable Somerset.

Queen Margaret was the driving force behind the changes. Her son, Edward of Lancaster, was not yet two years old. She knew that Richard of York wanted a Yorkist dynasty, and that her son's life would be endangered by this. As for York, he had ruled constitutionally, for the greater good of the country. He saw little future with Henry's health restored and his vengeful queen backed by his great enemies Somerset and Exeter. Margaret had effectively restored all of Henry's former friends and advisors to power, in a group headed by Edmund Beaufort, Duke of Somerset and uncle of Margaret Beaufort, Edmund Tudor's young wife.

York, with the earls of Salisbury and Warwick, swiftly withdrew from London. The Tudor brothers had to decide whom to support. The Duke of York was being ousted from all power, but the king's restored advisors had been previously discredited. It seems that Jasper Tudor was one of the main peers who tried to bring the factions together to settle their differences, possibly foreseeing the bloodshed to come. War was not in the interests of either Jasper or Edmund. They had come from nothing into wealth, unlike the great magnates, and had more to lose. Parliament met and measures were again brought to try and improve the king's finances. Most of the grants Henry VI had made since becoming king were cancelled. There were a few grants spared, including those of Edmund and Jasper Tudor. While the brothers were seen as potential allies of the Duke of York, they remained loyal to Henry. Jasper was recorded as now swearing an oath of allegiance to Henry along with other lords. Yet again, Edmund does not appear to be as involved in these proceedings as his brother. From this time, both brothers were now definitely on the Lancastrian side.

In May 1455, a second great council was summoned to meet at Leicester, 'for the purpose of providing for the safety of the king's person against his enemies'. The issue document implied that York and his supporters were 'mistrusted persons' against whom action must be taken. Tellingly, neither York, Salisbury, Warwick nor any other adherent of their cause was invited. Salisbury was York's brother-in-law, and Warwick was Salisbury's son Richard Neville, later to be known as the 'Kingmaker'. The Yorkists had given no excuse for any such proceedings, as they had been living quietly on their estates since their dismissal from office.

However, York, Salisbury and Warwick were now summoned to appear before the Great Council, not as participants but seemingly to be charged with subversion. They obviously feared Somerset's retribution. York was at Sandal Castle, and immediately sent a messenger to his brother-in-law, Salisbury, proposing that they meet. They armed their Yorkshire tenants and marched south, hoping to gather allies, but only the Earl of Warwick and Lord Clinton joined them, forming an army of around 3,000 men, nearly all from Yorkshire. The Duke of Norfolk gathered men from across his lands to join them, but arrived a day too late at St Albans. York's force was travelling too quickly for Norfolk, trying to face the king's army before it was joined by other lords and massively outnumbered the forces mustered by York. By 20 May 1455, York's army was at Royston in Hertfordshire, where the duke issued a manifesto directed to Thomas Bourchier, Archbishop of Canterbury. The letter was also signed by Salisbury and Warwick, all expressing loyalty to Henry. York explained that he had been forced to take arms by the proclamation of enmity summoning him to Leicester and his probable arrest.

York's army had travelled south at a rate of around twenty miles in a day, and, on 21 May, York wrote to the king from Ware, just north of London. He humbly apologised and said that he and his kinsmen were 'coming in grace as true and humble liegemen, to declare and show at large their loyalty', but that they must demand instant admission to his noble presence, so that they could convince him of the 'sinister, fraudulent, and malicious labours and reports of their enemies'. York, Salisbury and Warwick again all signed this letter, and attached a copy of the previous letter sent to the archbishop. Both letters reached London after the departure of the king. The archbishop forwarded them to the king, whose army had begun to march to Leicester. Somehow neither reached him, and it may well be that Somerset intercepted them. He wanted York out of the way forever.

Somerset had directed his Lancastrian allies to march to Leicester, but York had bypassed the East Midlands on his way from York, quickly heading directly for London, where he had great support. Thus Henry's army consisted of only the ordinary retinues of those lords of the council and peers who had happened to be in London at the moment. Jasper and Edmund, the newly ennobled earls of Pembroke and Richmond, had a choice. They were on very good terms with York, Salisbury and Warwick, and had been ennobled at the same time as Warwick. They had supported York at the council meeting when he received the Protectorship during the king's illness. York needed allies among the great lords. Their loyalty lay with their half-brother but his illnesses, inability to lead and inept administrative capabilities and inclination allowed him to be led by favourites such as Somerset. Under Henry VI, the country drifted towards power struggles. However, as Protector, York had displayed true qualities of leadership, offering a more effective, widely based and better government.

The twenty-four-year-old Jasper accompanied the king's army, while Edmund, it seems, did not. This may have been diplomatically agreed between the brothers. Whoever won, one brother would probably keep his lands and title and be able to protect the other from punishment. Certainly,

Jasper was first looked on as a Yorkist, according to the Ordinances of the Privy Council. However, this may have been through Queen Margaret's enmity. Jasper's great Pembroke estates had been assigned to her in the first instance. Jasper had closely cooperated with Richard of York when he was Protector, and probably hoped that there would be no battle. A battle was not expected by the king's party. His lords expected to parley to come to an agreement.

Henry's army had fewer than 3,000 archers and billmen. Although a quarter of the peerage was present, most had only their small London retinues in attendance. Some of their followers had gone directly from their estates to Leicester, following Somerset's call to arms. Edmund Beaufort, 2nd Duke of Somerset, alongside the king, had led the army out of London. He was accompanied by his nineteen-year-old son, the Marquess of Dorset. The veteran warrior Humphrey Stafford, 1st Duke of Buckingham, had his son Lord Humphrey, Earl of Stafford, by his side. Jasper, Earl of Pembroke, the earls of Northumberland, Devon, Wiltshire and the lords Clifford, Dudley and Roos were alongside them. The king's army had left London on its way to Leicester on 21 May, bivouacking overnight at Watford, just reaching St Albans when they were surprised by the news that York's force was nearby, having moved seventeen miles in a day from Ware.

Somerset swiftly took up a defensive position. St Albans was undefended, with no walls or gates, merely a large village that straddled the main road, St Peter's Street. He barricaded all its outlets, and drew the royal army under cover of the line of houses which formed the eastern part of the town. The royal standard was placed in the main street. Seeing York's army slowly advancing from the east, at around seven in the morning Henry sent Buckingham to ask why he had brought an army with him. On 22 May 1455, during a long parley, York answered that he was truly loyal, but demanded that Somerset should be arrested and tried for treason. York said that he could no longer be put off with promises, remembering the oaths sworn to him in 1452, which had never been kept. York sent emissaries to the king assuring him of his loyalty but requesting Henry to deliver 'those who York would accuse'.

Henry VI was never known to show anger, but he had not received York's letters of apology, and he lost his temper when he heard of York's response, shouting, 'By the faith that I owe to St Edward and the crown of England, I will destroy them, every mother's son.' York had not wanted battle, just Somerset to be locked away or executed, the same attitude that Somerset had towards him. York rallied his troops, arguing that the king refused them all reform, would not listen to their petitions, and threatened them with traitors' deaths if they surrendered. His men now knew they had no alternative except to fight for their lives. Somerset's use of narrow barricades meant that York's archers could not be used effectively, but York could not delay an attack. Norfolk had not arrived to give him superiority in numbers, and York feared that more lords would rally towards the king, arriving from their muster point at Leicester. A standoff could also mean that some of his men would defect to the king. York decided to attack, and around midday he formed his men into three columns of infantry. Each attacked the barricades which blocked the three roads that led into St Albans from the east. The attacks failed, with many Yorkists dying to arrows, as the Lancastrians had a clearer field of fire.

Salisbury's son, the twenty-six-year-old Earl of Warwick, noticed that the royalists were successfully defending the barricades. However, they had only few men protecting the long, straggling line of houses which formed the south-eastern part of their front. Warwick found an unguarded dirt track, leading between Sopwell Lane and Shropshire Lane to two inns, the Keye and the Chekkere. Gathering his retainers, he made a decisive thrust through the gardens of Holwell Street and, bursting through the back doors of the houses, ran out into the main thoroughfare of the town. His men thus cut the Lancastrian line in two. Blowing trumpets and shouting 'A Warwick! A Warwick!', they then attacked the Lancastrians from their side of the barricades. The royal force turned around to face this new threat, and could no longer prevent Yorkists pouring over the barricades and attacking them on both sides.

There was ferocious fighting for around thirty minutes, during which Somerset, Northumberland and Clifford were killed. The royal army threw down its weapons and the uninjured were allowed to escape with few losses. However, nobles and knights, weighted with heavy mail and plate armour, were caught and cut down. It seems that Warwick had ordered his men to spare the common soldiers and slaughter the nobles, Somerset being particularly targeted as having to die. It may well be that Warwick, who became increasingly noted for his savagery towards the captured, killed Somerset himself. Some sources state that Salisbury, Warwick's father, restrained the mistreatment of wounded and captured nobles and thus saved their lives. The *Paston Letters* record 'at most slayn vi score [120]'. Of forty-eight bodies buried by the abbot, only twenty-five were those of unknown common soldiers, the others being lords, knights, squires, and officers of the king's household. In this first battle of the Wars of the Roses, there seemed to be no killing of fugitives or prisoners. That horror was yet to begin, after the Battle of Wakefield in 1460.

Wiltshire fled the field early, forever giving him a reputation for cowardice. Sir Philip Wentworth, who bore the royal standard, threw it down and fled. Buckingham, Devon, Dorset, Fauconberg, Roos, Percy and Stafford were all wounded and captured, Stafford lingering in pain from his wounds for two years before dying of plague. The only unwounded prisoner of note was Dudley, who was sent to the Tower. Some captured peers were placed in the custody of known Yorkists, and others were set free on undertaking to acquiesce in York's new regime. The First Battle of St Albans marks the start of the Wars of the Roses, which were to last another thirty-two years. Jasper's fate in the battle is unclear – whether he escaped, or was captured, is unknown. If captured, his former friendship with York and Warwick would have saved him. Henry VI stood passively beneath his standard throughout the battle, and received a very slight wound in the neck from an arrow. York, Salisbury and Warwick knelt before Henry on the dirt floor of a tanner's house where he was having his wound dressed, swearing their allegiance and begging forgiveness. Henry forgave them, although saying, 'Forsothe, forsothe, ye do fouly to smyte a kynge enoynted so.'

The Abbot of St Albans noted the violence: 'Here you saw a man with his brains dashed out, here one with a broken arm, another with his throat cut, a fourth with a pierced chest.' It was Jasper's first experience of battle, and seems to have left him with a lasting wish for peace. He certainly tried, until his own life was at risk, to reconcile the opposing factions, especially seeing the opportunity now that the implacable Somerset was dead.

York was not yet prepared to press his own claims to the throne, preferring to come to an agreement to succeed Henry as king. Besides, he needed much more support from the peerage, and the Tudor earls had showed no animosity towards his plans. York escorted the king to London, pronouncing that the king had been saved from his real enemies. He sent messengers to ask that the citizens should turn out and greet their true king. York proclaimed his personal loyalty to Henry. During 1450, the 1451 parliament, his 1452 rebellion and his protectorate, he had repeatedly stated that all he had ever wanted was the dismissal of the useless Somerset and his corrupt officials. York constantly reinforced his desire for competent and honest persons in government, not the usurping of the king. York and his followers pronounced that they simply wanted a more efficient and fairer form of government.

York replaced the dead Somerset as Constable of England. Archbishop Bourchier remained as Chancellor, while his brother Henry, Viscount Bourchier (married to York's sister Isobel), became Treasurer. Another brother, John Bourchier, became Lord Berners. Salisbury and his son Warwick were confirmed in their appointments, made in December 1453, as guardians of the West March of Scotland for twenty years. Warwick was also made Captain of Calais. Under Henry V, the Percys had been restored to their lands, and eventually, in 1417, to the East March. The West March, however, had become an almost hereditary Neville appointment. Salisbury had first become Warden of the West March in 1420. It was one of the most valuable appointments in England, worth £1,500 in peacetime and four times that if war broke out with Scotland. Although, unlike Calais, it did not require a permanent garrison, the incessant raiding and border skirmishes meant that there would always be a ready supply of trained and experienced soldiers at the warden's command. Humphrey Stafford, Duke of Buckingham, who was still recovering from his wounds, was also asked to help in governing. Buckingham was a staunch Lancastrian and peacemaker, like Jasper Tudor.

Jasper remained associated with the Yorkists despite St Albans. Along with the earls of Buckingham and Shrewsbury he was a moderate, willing to work for either side of government. These three individuals tried to mend bridges between the Lancastrians and Yorkists. Queen Margaret still directed her hatred at the Yorkists, but now departed for Hertford with the king and the baby Prince Edward. The battle had upset Henry's health once more, and he had been advised to recuperate in the countryside. The birth of Prince Edward meant that Richard of York was no longer first in line to succeed Henry VI. The Tudor brothers had been formally recognised as the half-brothers of Henry VI, all of whose uncles and other possible heirs were dead by this time. However, few except the Welsh bards saw the Tudors as potential rulers. The bards wrote that either brother or William Herbert of Raglan might be the chosen one to rescue Wales from the clutches of England.

In May 1455, writs were issued for a parliament to meet at Westminster in the following July, with both Tudor brothers being summoned. The king remained in Hertford, still unwell. Jasper remained in London rather than attend the king's court at Hertford, and on 4 June he and Richard of York, together with York's close supporters Warwick, Bourchier and Fauconberg, attended a council meeting at St Paul's concerned with routine business. Two days later, Buckingham and Worcester renewed their association with York at another council meeting. York was still looking for support from such moderate peers, but it must have been difficult for him to enlarge his following after St Albans.

Parliament opened at Westminster on 9 July 1455 in the presence of Henry. The lords swore allegiance to Henry VI, but measures were yet again undertaken to repair the nation's finances. An Act of Resumption more stringent than any in the preceding five years was passed, although once again a special provision was written into the legislation safeguarding the estates of the earls of Richmond and Pembroke. This was one of the very few provisions appended to the Act. The two brothers were not only members of the royal family, but still valuable associates of York and his allies. As with the exemplification of the grant of Sir William Oldhall's Norfolk estates in October 1454, these provisions were probably seen as necessary for the continued goodwill of such influential peers. Jasper took the oath to the king on 24 July 1455.

As a result of the deaths of men such as Somerset and Northumberland in the battle, several public offices were vacant and, on 2 June 1455, Richard of York was appointed constable of the castles of Aberystwyth, Carmarthen and Carreg Cennen for life, positions formerly held by Somerset. Bourchier became steward in Somerset's place. In the July parliament, a committee consisting of Marcher Lords (*Domini Marchearum*) and the Crown's legal advisers was set up to investigate means of establishing 'restful and sad rule in Wales'. Yet in his dealings with the lawless gentry, especially of West Wales, York demonstrated how futile a distant government's efforts could be. Ensuring public order in Wales was a major problem, soon to be overtaken by civil war and its aftermath. Parliament was prorogued on 31 July 1455, partly to gather in the harvest and partly because of disease in London. It was to be reconvened on the following 12 November. Jasper's attention was shortly to be directed away from the centre of political life at court and Parliament to Wales, a region with which he was to be intimately associated for the next three decades.

Everything looked prosperous for Jasper. As Earl of Pembroke, he had considerable landed interests in South Wales, but his estates were far wider, for he held jointly with his brother the profitable wardship of Margaret Beaufort and valuable properties in the Midlands, as well as several English estates in his own right. On 1 June 1455, he received in tail male the lordships of Whitley and Worplesdon in Surrey. He also took up the farm of the manors of Kingsthorpe in Northamptonshire and Pollestedhall in Norfolk for five years.

Jasper's large and widely separated estates needed effective and efficient administrative machinery. As a great lord, he needed his own household organisation, the most important part of which was his personal council. This was modelled on the Royal Council, which was responsible for all aspects of the king's household and estate management, providing expertise and advice. Jasper and Edmund each maintained a small household within the greater royal household of their half-brother, and it is possible that they normally lived at court with Henry. At the time of the reorganisation of the king's household in November 1454, each earl was allowed to have a chaplain, two esquires, two yeomen and two chamberlains at court. They were the only magnates not holding administrative office in the household, except for Viscount Beaumont, to be allowed this privilege.

Earl Edmund's council is referred to in some financial documents, but its size, composition and duties remain obscure. Members and responsibilities of Jasper's council are better known, and this council is recorded as meeting in London at the King's Head in Cheapside, sometime after Michaelmas 1456. It was probably gathered to deal with the ramifications of the recent death of Edmund, who held many joint properties with Jasper. The fate of Edmund's rich heiress wife, pregnant with Henry Tudor, would also have to be considered. The most important six individuals were named in this meeting, although others would have been present. The councillors present included Sir Henry Wogan, Thomas Vachan (Vaughan), Geoffrey Pole, William Herbert, Walter Gorfen and John Rogger. Wogan, as a knight, appears first on the list. Elsewhere in contemporary documents, Geoffrey Pole and John Rogger are repeatedly referred to as esquires, while Walter Gorfen is always termed a gentleman.

Thomas Vaughan is Thomas ap Robert Vaughan of Monmouth, to be murdered by Richard III in 1483 while in the bodyguard of Edward V. It was customary for magnates, lay and ecclesiastical, to have town houses or inns in London, such as Earl Edmund's establishment at Baynard's Castle, and on 15 November 1456, Earl Jasper and Thomas Vaughan, esquire, one of his councillors, were jointly granted a house in Brook Street, Stepney, called the 'Le Garlek' or 'Garlek-House'. Such a property formed a useful town house for a magnate and his servants, and it probably ended the necessity of meeting in inns like the King's Head. Brook Street was, unusually for London, paved at this time.

Sir Thomas Vaughan is an intriguing character. In June 1450 Vaughan became Master of the King's Ordnance, and between at least 1450 and 1452 he was an esquire of the king's household. As such, Vaughan would have known Edmund and Jasper Tudor before their ennoblement, and may have commended himself to them as a councillor and servant by his work for the king. His prominent position is highlighted by the commission issued to him on 17 November 1456 by Archbishop Bourchier, to administer the goods of the deceased Earl Edmund and to draw up an inventory by the following 28 March. Vaughan was still associated with Jasper in April 1459 as a mainpernor (surety) when the earl farmed estates in Breconshire.

Baronial councils were often dominated by lawyers, but Jasper's known councillors represent a cross section of his administrative officials. Sir Henry Wogan of Wiston in Pembrokeshire and Halsway in Somerset was Jasper's most experienced administrator. His family had played a prominent part in the administration of Pembroke and of the principality of South Wales for decades. Sir Henry was steward of the lordships of Pembroke and Haverfordwest by 1441 and 1442, and in 1449 was also steward of the Bishop of St David's. He was deputy justiciar between 1442 and 1446 when Duke Humphrey of Gloucester held tenure of the earldom of Pembroke, a post Wogan held again in 1455. He sat on numerous commissions, and his pre-eminent position in Pembrokeshire was similar to that of Gruffydd ap Nicholas in Carmarthenshire, with whom he was associated on 7 October 1450 in a commission for defending the coasts of South Wales. By his marriage to Margaret, daughter of Sir William ap Thomas of Raglan and sister of Sir William Herbert, Wogan was related to the most prominent family in South East Wales. His father-in-law was an experienced principality and Marcher official like himself, and his brother-in-law was another experienced administrator, soldier and councillor to Jasper.

Sir William Herbert of Raglan had been granted an annuity of £10 for life by Edmund Tudor on 1 October 1453, and may well have been drawn to Jasper's council as the most prominent magnate in South Wales. Sir William Herbert had been joint captain of Carentan in Normandy when it surrendered to the Duke of Brittany, and he was also present at the Battle of Formigny in April 1450, under the command of Sir Thomas Kyriel. By about 1452 he was knighted, and on 1 October 1453 Earl Edmund granted him a £10 annuity for life from the issues of his manor of Bassingbourne in Cambridgeshire. Herbert was also a servant of the Nevilles as sheriff of their lordship of Glamorgan, and his sister Elizabeth married Henry, son of Sir Edward Stradling of St Donat's in Glamorgan, 'the most able and distinguished of the justiciar chamberlains of South Wales in the early fifteenth century'.

Jasper's choice of both Vaughan and Herbert as his councillors seems odd, as both men became loyal servants of York. William Herbert at first appeared to be on very good terms with both Edmund and his younger brother Jasper, but the Yorkist win at Northampton and his sister's marriage to Walter Devereux later altered his allegiance. Vaughan followed Herbert, a kinsman. A verse from a contemporary poem composed by Lewys Glyn Cothi in 1452 in praise of William Herbert reflects Herbert's early allegiance:

> If Jasper was being pounded,
> he'd [William] pound through a thousand men.
> The nobleman's full of sincerity
> (that will serve him well);
> Gwilym [William] is true and skilled
> for one God before everything else,
> also for the Crown, kindly eagle,
> and above for the earl of Pembroke and his men.

These three men on Jasper's innermost council, Vaughan, Wogan and Herbert, had vast administrative and political experience. Because of their prominent social position in South Wales, linked with each other and with other substantial local families by bonds of marriage, common interest and experience, they could give Jasper valuable information and expertise in local affairs. Their prominence in local society enhanced their effectiveness. However, Jasper's widely scattered estates meant he also needed servants with a more technical training in administration, both of the estates and the household. These duties were generally undertaken by the three remaining councillors present at the meeting in Cheapside. Geoffrey Pole had been an esquire of the king's household for at least ten years from 1442 and, like Thomas Vaughan, may have attracted there the attention of Richmond and of Pembroke. In May 1440, Pole (a corruption of Powell, itself a derivation from ap Hywel) was granted for life the office of marshal of the Great Sessions in the counties of Carmarthenshire and Cardigan. In January 1442, he was appointed steward of the lordship and constable of the castle of Haverfordwest. In January 1443, Pole and Thomas West were granted in survivorship the offices of constable and parker of the lordship of Leeds in Kent, while in October 1451 Pole was appointed serjeant of the king's tents and pavilions.

Like Pole, Walter Gorfen had worked in Wales, and he was perhaps the most highly trained of all Jasper's councillors. From Gorfen in Devon, he began his public career in about 1454 as clerk of the receipt at the Exchequer, and possibly as deputy receiver general of the Duchy of Lancaster. His talents were considerable, as he held a wide variety of offices both in the administration of the Duchy of Lancaster and in the royal government elsewhere. In 1434 he was surveyor of costs in the Monmouth sessions and in 1439 he was ordered to search the records of the lordship of Ogmore. From 1440 to 1461 he was one of the duchy auditors in Wales, and in 1440, 1441, 1445 and 1447 he was an itinerant justice in the duchy estates in South Wales. As royal auditors, Gorfen and William Proctour were appointed to audit the accounts of the royal principality in South

Wales in October 1450, and at the same time Gorfen was commissioned to audit the accounts of the lordships of Pembroke, Cilgerran, Ystlwyf and Trane Clinton, all to be part of Jasper's Pembrokeshire estates in 1455. The earl may have employed Gorfen, like Pole, both for his administrative experience and his local knowledge of Pembrokeshire and South Wales. As two experienced royal servants, they were sufficiently close to be made available to the king's half-brother Jasper.

The remaining councillor was John Rogger, esquire of Leeds in Kent. He was appointed not by one but by both Tudor earls on 6 April 1453 to the unusual office of joint receiver general. It was customary for each magnate to have his own separate administrative machine, quite independent of that of any of his relatives. However, because the brothers had been granted so much land jointly, especially the Beaufort estates, they were probably advised that a joint receiver general would serve their purpose better. One other person who was probably at the council meeting in London, whose appointment may have been arranged there, was Miles Metcalf, whom Pembroke appointed as his attorney general on 1 November 1456. Unlike Earl Jasper's other servants, Metcalf was inexperienced, but during Edward IV's reign he became a prominent official of the Duchy of Lancaster.

Thus Jasper's council was made up of experienced and capable men. However, beyond the central household headed by the councils of the two earls lay their widespread estates, and at the local level Thomas has illustrated the management of these lands. The councillor and official who provided the principal link between the estates and the household was John Rogger, receiver general to both Edmund and Jasper from 1453 to at least 1456. It was his task to supervise the collection of the earls' revenue and to issue receipts, usually indentured acquittances, after he had received any money owed. Much travelling was involved in these operations and even more paperwork in the form of accounts, views of accounts and valors, all of which had to be audited ultimately under his scrutiny.

In January 1454, Rogger, as receiver general and receiver, steward and auditor of the Richmond lands in Lincolnshire, stayed at Boston for nine days in order to audit the local accounts, inspect and allow repairs, fees and wages, and generally scrutinise the financial affairs of the receivership during the preceding year. The same procedure took place in January of the following year, and John Rogger must have done similar work elsewhere for the two earls. Since he continued his association with Earl Jasper, acting as mainpernor for him and his father Owen in 1460, it is believed that he continued to act as receiver general for Jasper after Edmund's death.

As in the Duchy of Lancaster and in other private estates, the earls' major estates were divided into several receiverships, such as those of Kendal, Wyresdale, Lincolnshire and Richmond in Yorkshire. From at least Michaelmas 1453 to 1456, Geoffrey Kidwelly was receiver of the 'south parts' of the Beaufort inheritance, which the two earls held in wardship. The work of the receiver locally was comparable with that of a receiver general, in that he was his lord's chief financial and accounting official in his receivership, primarily concerned with the collection and distribution of revenue, together with certain other executive duties. The various bailiffs and reeves handed the money over to him and received either sealed indentures of receipt or tallies in exchange, which they would then produce at the time of the annual audit in January to ensure their own acquittance. In September 1463, Geoffrey Kidwelly was pardoned by Edward IV as the former receiver general of Earl Edmund and Earl Jasper, but this probably refers to his activities as receiver of the Beaufort inheritance. Similarly, in January 1458, Edmund Blake was appointed receiver general of the lordship, county and honour of Richmond for life, with the customary fees. Although Earl Jasper and the Earl of Shrewsbury leased much of the honour from 5 December 1458, Blake may well have continued in office.

Occasionally, the receiver general, John Rogger, was in the area and money might then be handed directly to him, but he usually forwarded it to the local receiver. The latter then delivered his receipts either to the receiver general or directly to the earl. In addition to collecting the revenue with which he was charged, the receiver was also responsible for authorising and making payments of fees, wages and alms, while any cash owing or which had been spent without proper warrant would either be allowed or, if respited, carried over to the following year. When the receiver and his subordinates in each receivership had drawn up their annual accounts, it was the task of the lord's auditor to examine and audit them. The individual manors and bailiwicks within each receivership were administered by reeves, bailiffs or collectors of revenues, although by the mid-fifteenth century their functions were indistinguishable. Apart from financial organisation, the administration of each receivership had its judicial side, usually in the charge of the chief steward or steward of the lordship, aided by deputy stewards and clerks. The running of the great medieval estates was indeed complicated.

The administration of Jasper's Pembrokeshire estates was somewhat different from that of Edmund's properties in England. Jasper's Welsh lands were Marcher lordships and he therefore enjoyed regalian rights, which gave him a far greater private mastery in his lands there than in other territories. At the head of the lordship of Pembroke's administrative structure stood the chancellor-treasurer, with his own chancery and exchequer. As treasurer, he performed the duties of a receiver in a local receivership. Jasper's exchequer, however, was modelled on that of the king at Westminster, with its own archives and storehouse of memoranda. In May 1450, John Perot, esquire, descendant of an old and distinguished local family based at Haroldston Manor, was appointed treasurer for life and he was still in office in 1459. From at least 1452 he was also chancellor. In July, Perot was ordered to issue writs from the chancery of Pembroke to the mayor and bailiff of Tenby, commanding them to appear before him in chancery to account for recent disturbances in Tenby. Another member of the Perot family, Sir Thomas, was appointed steward of the lordship for life on 19 May 1450, and he was still in office in 1457. The Perots later led men to support Jasper at Mortimer's Cross.

The lordship also had its own sheriff, and in June 1451 John Vernon, esquire, was appointed to the office for life, although by March 1457 Henry Don, esquire, was occupying it. In that year Don was acting as escheator of the lordship, and in October 1457 Don presided over an inquisition post-mortem at Pembroke into the lands late of the Countess of Wiltshire in the county. On the same day as he was appointed to the shrievalty of Pembroke, 25 June 1451, John Vernon was also made constable of the castles of Pembroke and Tenby, and master forester of Coedrath, as well as being appointed to posts in the separate lordships of Cilgerran and Llanstephan. It was thus customary for one man to hold several posts in the lordships simultaneously. The central organ of government at Pembroke was the earl's council there, probably an ad hoc body consisting of the treasurer, steward and other principal officials of the lordship. As for the lordship of Cilgerran and Llanstephan, they appear to have been organised on more conventional lines without a chancery or exchequer. In a surviving account for 1434–1435, it is clear that each lordship had its own receiver and steward, but it was the treasurer of Pembroke who received the income from these lands, and the two lordships did not act independently in sending cash directly to their lord.

The earls of Richmond and Pembroke thus had at their disposal a large and well-organised civil service for the administration of their estates, men who could wear their livery and do their bidding. Only two men appear to have been granted annuities by either brother with no offices attached. The first was Sir William Herbert, as mentioned above, who was granted an annuity of £10 per annum for life on 1 October 1453 by Edmund. The second was Roger Puleston, esquire, who was granted an annuity of 10 marks by Edmund, during pleasure, on 10 September 1455, from the issues of the lordship of Cynllaith Owain in North Wales. The parents of Roger Puleston were John Puleston and Angharad, the daughter of Griffith Hanmer and the granddaughter of Tudur ap Goronwy of Penmynydd. Roger was a staunch Lancastrian and later held Denbigh Castle as deputy constable to his kinsman Jasper during the campaign of 1460–1461. Jasper thus had an efficient bureaucracy working for him, but all was soon to alter.

Both Tudor brothers were absent from the second session of the parliament of 1455–1456, which lasted from 12 November to 13 December 1455. No less than thirty-five lay and thirty spiritual peers also absented themselves, possibly not wishing to discuss new demands that York should once again be appointed Protector. It may well be, however, that Edmund, and possibly Jasper, were busy in Wales. Although summoned to Parliament, the absentees had not taken 'to hert so tenderly ye wele of us as we supposed ye wolde have doo'. They were thus firmly ordered to appear at the third session of this parliament, which was scheduled to open on 14 January 1456.

Just one week after Parliament opened on 12 November 1455, York was again appointed Protector. This had probably been planned in advance, involving York and the Speaker, William Burley, an experienced MP and a member of the duke's council. Led by Burley, the Commons pressed for another protectorate because the alarming increase in local disorder in Wales and the west and north of England required firm handling. It was argued that only York, or someone like him, could undertake the restoration of proper law and order. Wales had never settled, although the Percy–Neville dispute in the North had died down somewhat. However, autumn of 1455 had seen the restart of the bitter Devon–Bonville quarrel in the West Country, with violence in south Devon leading up to Christmas.

Because local disorders throughout Wales were a constantly reoccurring problem, during his second protectorate York decided to conclude the matter once and for all, although he and others had been trying to do so since the fourteenth century. Even before the Glyndŵr war of 1400–1421, Wales had experienced frequent outbursts of local and national violence. With the absentee magnates in the Marcher lordships being private landowners, and those in the Principality of Wales being royal officials, they had given over the administration of their estates to local families, the new wave of *uchelwyr* (high men). As long as they successfully collected incomes, they had been largely allowed to do as they pleased. Absenteeism led to more power in the hands of resident Welshmen, and ancient rivalries flourished. Largely unsupervised, and with a weak central government, many local officials were abusing their powers for their own ends. Thus the quality of both royal and Marcher government in Wales continuously declined.

The most prominent official in West Wales, and the chief problem for the government, was Gruffydd ap Nicholas of Newton and Dinefwr. Gruffydd had accumulated offices and land in Carmarthenshire, and dominated royal government in South Wales. In 1437, 1444–1446 and 1447–1456 he was deputy justiciar of Wales, while from 1443 to 1454 he was deputy chamberlain. His eldest sons, Thomas and Owain ap Gruffydd, were his lieutenants, extending family influence south-west into Pembrokeshire and northwards into Cardiganshire. Gruffydd ap Nicholas's position in West Wales was unrivalled by the time that Jasper Tudor became Earl of Pembroke in 1452, despite attempts to curtail his power. Other Welsh families also dominated their localities, such as the Wogans of Wiston Castle and the Perrots of Haroldston in Pembrokeshire, the Vaughans of Tretower Castle in Breconshire and the Herberts of Raglan in Monmouthshire. York's aims during both protectorships included the restoration of law and order in South Wales, and his lack of success severely dented his prestige.

Gruffydd ap Nicholas, his sons and grandson are integrally important in the story of Edmund, Jasper and Henry Tudor. In 1454, when York was in his first period as Protector, his council ordered Gruffydd ap Nicholas to release Gruffydd ap Dafydd from Carmarthen gaol, but the order was ignored. York had several setbacks in trying to deal with Gruffydd and curb his independence, and this time decided to take severe action. The king's government was not able to rely upon its absent and indifferent chief officers in the principality in South Wales, the justiciar James, Lord Audley, and the chamberlain John, Lord Beauchamp of Powick. York thus seems to have chosen Edmund, Earl of Richmond, to revitalise royal government in South Wales. Although he held no official position in the administration of the royal or Marcher lands of South Wales, from the late autumn of 1455, Edmund intervened to strengthen the weakened control of the central government by direct action. It was previously thought that Edmund was acting for the queen as a counterpoise to York in the region, but he had probably been directed by York.

Apart from one occasion in April 1453 when Edmund and Jasper visited Norwich with the queen, neither of them seems to have been associated with her in any way since their ennoblement. Instead, they were considered members of a loose association of lords focussed around the real centre of power, the Duke of York. In November 1455, when Edmund's presence was first recorded in South Wales, the queen was politically weak and not in a position to confront York's orders, and his second protectorate had not ended. In the second session of the parliament in November 1455, neither Edmund nor Jasper attended as they were probably in Wales to keep the king's peace. The brothers had previously gone on such a mission, possibly because their father was Welsh.

Margaret Beaufort was born, an only child, on 31 May 1443. Her father, John, 1st Duke of Somerset, York's sworn enemy, died shortly after in 1444. A few years later, the wealthy heiress Margaret was married to John de la Pole, the heir of the Duke of Suffolk. Suffolk himself was murdered in 1450 by York's men, beheaded at sea, and in early 1453 the marriage of his son John to Margaret was annulled. William de la Pole, 1st Duke of Suffolk, was a commander in the Hundred Years' War and had been a king's favourite, although he lost many French possessions and York had managed to have him briefly imprisoned for 'treason'. Suffolk was disliked by the people, and from him we get the term 'jackanapes'. At the time it was slang for a monkey, derived from 'Jack of Naples', with 'of Naples' being rendered 'a Napes' in vernacular. Monkeys were one of many exotic goods from Naples exhibited in Britain, and the nickname 'Jack a Napes' acquired the meaning 'upstart person', from its use as Suffolk's nickname. He was one of first nouveau riche nobles, risen from the merchant class and despised by the older houses. His family used a collar and chain on its coat of arms, and as this was more associated with monkey leashes, it led to the insult of 'Jack a Napes' for the duke.

The annulment of the marriage between the infant de la Pole and Margaret may have been requested by Henry VI, who was looking for a good match for Edmund Tudor. Margaret was Suffolk's only child, and the marriage would solve the pressing financial problem of how to let his eldest half-brother live in the style of an earl. The marriage took place on 1 November 1455 at Bletsoe Castle, the birthplace of Margaret. Margaret was around twelve years and five months old, and Edmund probably twenty-five years old. By 30 November 1455, Edmund was staying on the king's business in Wales at Lamphey Palace in Pembrokeshire, a palace of the Bishop of St David's only a few miles east from Jasper's huge castle at Pembroke. It is said that Henry Tudor, the future Henry VII, was conceived here at this time, but Caldicot Castle also claims this. Edmund regularly stayed at Lamphey when on state business in South Wales. The retreat was situated in forest and parkland with fishponds and orchards. Bishop John de la Bere had lent the palace for Edmund's honeymoon and Edmund and Margaret were here again in the spring of 1456. Edmund was signing warrants at Lamphey on 9 March. John de la Bere was almoner of the king's household, from which Edmund must have previously known him. Lamphey (Llandyfai) is south of the bishop's castle at Llawhaden and near the great castles of Pembroke, Carew and Haverfordwest. Llawhaden, like the others, was ordered to be garrisoned by Henry IV in the Glyndŵr war. The bishop's palace at Lamphey was built to be defended, with inner and outer courtyards and battlements. At this time, the palace, one of seven palaces and manor houses maintained by the bishop, was the centre for administration of the whole see of St Davids's. It covered a boundary from Gower to Glascwm on the Hereford border and up to Kerry (Ceri) in Montgomeryshire, then west to the coast at Machynlleth. The total area was around half that of Wales, so Edmund would have had ready access to a large pool of skilled administrators, messengers and legal advisors. There were twenty-seven large rooms noted in a 1536 inventory, with the bishop's chamber, where Edmund and Margaret would have lived, being richly furnished with wall hangings and carpets to the value of £157 7s 10d. There was a great library, along with seven other main chambers for guests and rooms for the servants, which included a cook, porter, barber and brewer.

While Edmund, his new wife and presumably Jasper were concerned with affairs in Wales, by February 1456 the court party, increasingly dominated by Queen Margaret, felt strong enough to move against York. The duke was relieved of his post as Protector. His kinsmen and allies, the Bourchiers, continued to hold the most prominent positions in the royal government, Archbishop Thomas Bourchier as Chancellor and Henry, Viscount Bourchier, as Treasurer, but York's influence and authority was again in decline. Edmund was now asked to re-establish the king's control in South Wales, and had growing success after York had lost official power. At a time when the queen and York were both trying to build a greater power and support base, Edmund's successes enhanced the position and prestige of the royal family and the king's government. York himself had attempted to discipline Gruffydd ap Nicholas during both protectorates, and his attempts had met with total failure.

Because of boundary land disputes across the estates of Jasper and Edmund, around Easter 1456 the king sent the Treasurer and barons of the Exchequer a writ, reminding them of the special provision and emphasising that the two earls were not subject to the terms of the latest Act of Resumption. While Jasper was dealing with issues of estate management,

Edmund was faced with an increasingly hostile situation. Gruffydd ap Nicholas of Dinefwr had not bowed to York, and neither would he acquiesce to Edmund. No peaceful settlement could be arranged, and by June 1456 both were 'at werre gretely in Wales'. Although York had been appointed constable of the castles of Aberystwyth, Carmarthen and Carreg Cennen on 2 June 1455, following Somerset's death at St Albans, Gruffydd ap Nicholas and his sons were still in active control of these fortresses, and preparing to defend them. In 1455–1456, Gruffydd had spent £23 4s on repairs at Carreg Cennen castle and a further £18 12s on garrisoning it with soldiers. Similar preparations were made at Kidwelly castle.

By autumn 1456, the conflict was so bad that it was necessary to send an armed force to escort the auditors of the Duchy of Lancaster across country from Monmouth. Edmund was victorious in the struggle, and by August 1456 he had possession of Carmarthen Castle, being described as its 'custodian' and now occupying the centre of royal government in the principality shires of Carmarthen and Cardigan. However, York was still officially constable of Carmarthen Castle, and he had to move against Edmund or lose even more prestige. York was determined to assert his control over the government by acting as the legitimate constable of the castles of Carmarthen, Aberystwyth and Carreg Cennen, thus neutralising rivals in the principality. If Edmund Tudor attempted to return Carmarthen and its lands to Henry VI rather than the duke, his prospects of power were ended. Edmund was no longer a representative of the duke as Protector. He was now a representative of the king.

In April, York's followers Sir Walter Devereux and his son-in-law Sir William Herbert decided to make their move by gathering a force of about 2,000 men from around Herefordshire. Herbert had been one of Jasper's inner council members. Their force was involved in many local skirmishes, escalating in June when an attempt was made for an invasion on Kenilworth, intending to kill Henry VI. There was no way back now for York's followers. William Herbert, Walter Devereux and members of the Vaughan family joined their forces, stated their intention to fully assert York's authority and headed for West Wales.

On 10 August, their army from Herefordshire and the neighbouring marches set out for Carmarthen Castle, where Edmund was based. The record of indictment of the leading esquires and gentlemen makes it clear that this was a well-armed force of men, led by more than thirty prominent gentlemen and esquires, several of whom were kinsmen or associates of Herbert and Devereux. Together with his younger brother, Richard Herbert, esquire, of Abergavenny, Sir William enjoyed the support of his half-brothers Roger Vaughan, esquire, of Tretower, and Thomas ap Roger Vaughan, esquire, of Hergest. Also involved were Herbert's cousins William and Meredith ap Morgan ap Dafydd Gam, gentlemen, of Raglan and Crickhowell respectively. Similarly, Sir Walter Devereux was accompanied by James Baskerville, esquire, of Eardisley, who was, like Sir William Herbert, a son-in-law of his.

They seized Carmarthen Castle and imprisoned Edmund in its gaol in September 1456. Then they took Aberystwyth, successfully reasserting York's power in western Wales. In both cases, they commandeered the archives of the royal government, as well as the seal of the chamberlain of South Wales. Herbert, Devereux and Thomas Mymme issued commissions to themselves to hold a Great Sessions, which they parodied, it was later alleged, by letting all those indicted go free. From Aberystwyth, they moved through West Wales, re-establishing York's authority.

While Edmund was fighting in Wales, Jasper was in London. Late in April, and for much of May 1456, London was seriously disturbed by anti-alien riots, the Lombards in particular being persecuted. On 30 April 1456, Jasper, together with Exeter and Buckingham and a number of others, was given a commission of oyer and terminer to restore order the city and its suburbs. Oyer and terminer literally means to hear and determine, and is the legal term for one of the commissions by which a judge of assize sat. The judge or judges of assize were commanded to make diligent inquiry into all treasons, felonies and misdemeanours committed in the counties specified in the commission, and to hear and determine the same according to law. On 6 June, Jasper and others were given a similar commission to deal with disturbances in Kent and Sussex, while from January 1457 until 1458 Jasper was appointed a JP for Middlesex. Jasper seems to have spent time in personal attendance upon the king. According to the *Paston Letters*, he was the only lord with Henry at Sheen Palace in Richmond, Surrey, in June 1456. Henry was at Sheen and Windsor palaces in July, but in August he travelled to Coventry to be with his queen.

The task of bringing York's followers to justice was begun in September 1456, when Sir Walter Devereux and Sir William Herbert were successfully summoned before a great council at Coventry in October. It recommended their imprisonment. Back in London, on 5 and 11 October 1456, the queen engineered the dismissal of the remaining Yorkists in power, Lord Treasurer Viscount Bourchier and Chancellor Archbishop Bourchier. They were replaced with the Earl of Shrewsbury and Bishop Waynflete of Winchester. The queen's own chancellor, Lawrence Booth, became Keeper of the Privy Seal, and thus the government was swiftly taken into the hands of the court party.

The West Wales campaign of August 1456 had been the climax of six months of lawlessness on Herbert's part. In March 1456 he had seized control of and terrorised the city of Hereford, and in the following month he attacked and robbed a servant of the Earl of Wiltshire at Cowbridge in Glamorgan. Devereux was imprisoned at Windsor, but Herbert had escaped from Coventry before he could be sent to the Tower of London, taking refuge in Abergavenny Castle. By late October, Herbert had crossed Wales to Aberystwyth Castle. On 25 October 1456, he sent out orders for the men of that lordship, plus men in the lordships of Abergavenny, Usk, Caerleon, Glamorgan and Llandaff in South East Wales, to assemble under arms. Herbert was proclaimed a traitor, and a reward of 500 marks placed on his head. Around the same time, Gruffydd ap Nicholas and his sons, who had fought Edmund, had reached some agreement with Jasper. In autumn 1456, Queen Margaret was travelling throughout the Welsh border areas, on 26 October granting pardon to Gruffydd and his sons Owain and Thomas for all treasons, felonies and other crimes. From this time they were faithful to Jasper and the Lancastrian cause.

The Yorkists drew much of their strength from the vast Mortimer lands that they had inherited. Many of the Yorkist insurgents in Wales and the Marches lived in areas dominated by York, Devereux or Herbert, and a number of them later became trusted servants of Edward IV. John Lyngen, esquire, of Sutton in Herefordshire, was one of those indicted for his part in the campaign, and was committed to the Marshalsea prison. He fought for the Yorkists at Mortimer's Cross in 1461, and was appointed sheriff of Herefordshire in 1465 and 1471. Similarly, three members of the Herefordshire Monnington family fought for York, for which they were later jailed in the Marshalsea – Thomas Monnington, esquire, of Sarnesfield, and Richard and Henry Monnington, gentlemen, of Lawtonshope. Hugh Shirley, gentleman, of Leominster was also indicted and jailed for his part in the West Wales campaign. This insurgent force was a powerful indication of York's support in Herefordshire and the surrounding Marches.

Edmund was possibly released from prison, but apparently contracted an illness, from which he died on 1 November 1456 at Carmarthen. No one was ever accused of directly causing his death and it is possible that he always suffered from ill health. Government records show he was absent from many more meetings than Jasper. Circumstances are obscure – he may have died of plague in prison, of consumption, as a result of injuries, or he may even have been killed. He was buried in a fine tomb at Cwrt y Brodyr, Greyfriars Priory in Carmarthen, but the tomb was moved about 100 years later, after the Dissolution, to St David's Cathedral. Lewys Glyn Cothi wrote an elegy to Edmund, describing his father Owen's great sadness, the desperate loss for Jasper and the consequences of his death for Wales. Edmund was described as a lover of peace, dying in the prime of life. His arms were 'France and England quarterly, a bordure azure charged with fleurs-de-lis and martlets Or.' However, the bard does not blazon Edmund's shield, and says that it was charged with fleurs-de-lis, the three helmets of the line of Ednyfed Fychan, three birds and a bull.

Jasper may have considered York to be a better ruler than his half-brother the king, but Edmund's death confirmed his lifelong support of the House of Lancaster. Jasper had stayed close to the king, but after Edmund's captivity and death he was sent to replace Edmund and to care for his young widow and unborn son. Jasper was at court with the king when he learned of his brother's death, and immediately rode to Wales to take his place. In December, Jasper offered safe refuge for Margaret Beaufort, his brother's widow, in Pembroke Castle.

The death of Edmund had caused Jasper and his officials extensive administrative and legal problems. Edmund Tudor's annual earnings from the Honour of Richmond in 1456 were around £225 from Lincolnshire, £66 from Cambridgeshire, £40 from Yorkshire and £34 from Norfolk. Incomes from his estates at Kendal and Wyresdale brought in £166, Frodsham £16, Hadleigh £14 and Ludgershall £6. The Beaufort inheritance was worth £262. However, all these amounts fluctuated each year. Edmund had held jointly with Jasper Magor, £36; Derbyshire, £32; Solihull and Sheldon, £19; Nottinghamshire, £17; and Hyde, £2. Lands leased from the Crown made £31 and there was £5 from miscellaneous items. Jasper's share of the joint estates with Edmund, as above, made around £106, and his Beaufort inheritance share was worth £262, the same as Edmund's.

Jasper's annual earnings were around the same as his brother's. Pembroke was his main source of income, with £287, while other annual earnings were Llanstephan, £58; Cilgerran, £54; Aber, £26; Kidwelly, £10; and Whitley and Worplesden, £50. The value of the Oldhall lands is unknown. Among Jasper's other estates, Cantrefselyf returned £33 and Kingsthorpe £10. Annuities and fee farms brought in £20 from Pembroke, £11 from Hereford and Builth and £5 from Westley. Like Edmund, Jasper received £5 from miscellaneous items, but also £40 from offices. From these figures, it appears that each Tudor brother had an income of not less than about £925 per annum, but it must be remembered that this sum is merely a general signpost to their actual wealth. As a rule of thumb, the fifty or sixty great lords, or magnates, earned an average of £1,000 a year in the 1440s. There were 200 or so richer knights with an income of perhaps £100, and around 1,000 lesser knights earning about £40 p.a. Also the cream of English society included around 1,200 esquires and 2,000 'gentlemen' of some means, who probably existed on a yearly income of around £20. There was much less reliance on money then than there is now, and many of the daily needs would have been supplied by the estate or farm. A yearly income of £1,000 would have been a vast fortune, while £20 would still have been a comfortable income. Chief Justice Fortescue recorded that many a well-off yeoman was prosperous on an annual income of £5.

After Earl Edmund's death in November 1456, the government now began the process of reorganising the Richmond and Beaufort inheritances. Edmund's wife and his posthumously born son Henry were both minors, which complicated matters. Apart from the estates held jointly by the earls in survivorship, all of Edmund's lands escheated to the Crown, and Henry VI's government quickly put them to profitable use. On 10 December 1456, barely a month after Edmund's death, Duke Henry of Exeter leased the late earl's lands in Cambridgeshire at a farm to be agreed with the Exchequer, while on 15 April 1457 the dowager Countess of Richmond, Margaret, was awarded dower of £200 from part of her late husband's lordships.

On 28 January 1457, Margaret Beaufort gave birth to Henry Tudor, Earl of Richmond, at Jasper's great fortress of Pembroke. A small room in the east end of a tower on the northern wall of the fortress, which in Leland's time contained a 'chymmeney new made with the arms and badges of King Henry VII', is still shown as Henry's birthplace. The outer ward towers were primarily guard chambers, all with three storeys. A guard chamber may seem an unlikely location for a birth and a noble lady's nursery, but the tradition that the room was 'the queen's nursery' was already current in the 1530s. The Henry VII Tower is immediately to the left of the Great Gatehouse and barbican.

After having been a widow for almost three months, thirteen-year-old Margaret Beaufort and her child were lucky to survive the birth. As well as her age, the new mother was also very slender and had a small frame not suited to the rigours of childbirth. By all accounts it was a very difficult pregnancy, and possibly rendered her infertile or incapable of bearing another child. Henry was sickly after his birth and good care by both his mother and the attendant nurses seem to be the reasons for the child surviving. He was probably christened at the thirteenth-century St Mary's, near the castle and inside the town walls, and a stained-glass window by Robert Kempe commemorates the king.

The care of the infant Henry fell to his uncle, Jasper, who was possibly twenty-five when the child was born. Traditionally, Henry was taught by the Benedictine monks at nearby Monkton Priory, across the river from the castle. Monkton Priory church was on the great pilgrimage route to St David's, to which two visits were acknowledged as the equivalent of one to Rome. Jasper soon took up residence at Pembroke Castle and took over the task that had been intended for Edmund, of organising a strong base in South West Wales for the Lancastrian cause. Jasper carried out works on the castle, one of the greatest in Europe, and considerably strengthened the town walls. One length still stretches a thousand paces along the millpond to Barnard's Tower, the most complete of the towers surviving on this straight section. The great cylindrical castle keep is regarded as the finest in Britain, and the castle sits in a tidal loop of a river. Henry and his mother remained for a while in safety at Pembroke Castle, which stood for the House of Lancaster long after the rest of England had submitted to Henry's successor Edward IV.

In January 1457, Jasper was summoned to a great council to be held at Coventry on the following 14 February. Attempts were made to condemn the Devereux–Herbert upheavals on 15 February 1457. Unfortunately, there are no surviving contemporary accounts of this council, only the preface of the 1459 Act of attainder of York and his followers. According to this, the chancellor made many rehearsals to the Duke of York, to which the Duke of Buckingham, on behalf of all the lords present, stated that the Duke of York could only lean on the king's grace. It demanded that York should be punished should there be any repeat, but the preamble does not say of what. The document of the indictments makes no direct accusations of York, which makes it difficult to directly blame him for Edmund's death, even though Herbert and Devereux had to appear before the oyer and terminer sitting at Hereford from 2 to 7 April.

Having dismissed York's allies from the government, the queen needed to get rid of York himself, and the Great Council agreed on 6 March 1457.

York was reappointed Lieutenant of Ireland, to hold the office for ten years, virtually being exiled. During his time in court, Jasper had constantly tried to work with the Duke of York and other nobles in order to try to stop the infighting between the two houses. It was only after the death of his brother that Jasper took over the responsibility of maintaining the Lancastrian ties within Wales and took a stronger line against York. The Great Council closed sometime before 14 March. In March 1457, shortly before the court moved to Hereford, Jasper stayed with Duke Humphrey of Buckingham at Greenfield Manor, in his lordship of Ebbw near Newport, to meet his widowed sister-in-law, Margaret, Countess of Richmond. Quite possibly, he saw his young nephew, Henry Tudor, for the first time. Buckingham and Jasper probably felt an affinity, having been moderates between the two great houses in the preceding years. Duke Humphrey's sheriff of Newport, Morgan ap Jankyn ap Philip, esquire, had travelled to the town of Pembroke with a letter from his master for Jasper, the journeys and negotiations taking nineteen days to complete. It was agreed that Margaret would marry the duke's second son, Henry Stafford, thus helping to consolidate both families' interests. This agreed marriage of the widowed Margaret in 1459 would lessen Jasper's incomes, but later help secure the safety of Jasper's nephew Henry.

Jasper was still travelling on the king's business across South and West Wales, bringing his dead brother's attackers to trial. In the first week of April 1457, a series of indictments was laid against Devereux, Herbert and their various associates, both for their lawlessness in Herefordshire and for their West Wales campaign in the previous year. The king, queen, Buckingham, Shrewsbury and probably Jasper arrived at Hereford to oversee the indictment of Devereux and Herbert. Jasper may have wanted the humiliation of York's associates, in view of the circumstances of his brother Edmund's death. However, the queen's advisers in the court party did not think it wise to humiliate York's followers with heavy fines or terms of imprisonment. Instead, they attempted to divide and conquer, to drive a wedge through the groups of men who had supported Devereux and Herbert by being magnanimous to some and severe to others. On 1 May 1457, it was reported that the Lancastrians had offered Sir William Herbert his life and goods if he would come to Leicester and ask pardon of Henry VI. Thus Herbert was given an amnesty and, coming to the king at Leicester, was granted a general pardon on 7 June 1457. Despite this, the Yorkists were still strong. Herbert was later to be the leading Yorkist, but at this time he was considered to be a Lancastrian.

Herbert's closest associate, Sir Walter Devereux, was gaoled and not given his liberty until acquitted by a trial jury in the King's Bench in February 1458. Similarly, at the same time that Herbert was pardoned, a number of his associates were forgiven their misdemeanours, including his brother Richard Herbert, Roger Vaughan, Thomas ap Roger Vaughan and William ap Morgan ap Dafydd Gam. However, James Baskerville, Thomas Mymme, John Lyngen and Thomas, Richard and Henry Monnington were not pardoned. As part of the programme of wiping out York's success, the constableships of Aberystwyth, Carmarthen and Carreg Cennen castles were transferred to Jasper in April 1457, York to have £40 per annum from alternative sources of income as compensation, but this was a poor exchange for York. Throughout 1457, there was continuing lawlessness in Wales. Some more Yorkists were offered amnesty, and others were jailed, but there were no executions. From this point, Jasper's whereabouts are rarely known, most probably because he was in Wales and played a diminishing role at court and in the government.

On 29 November 1457, Jasper and the other peers were summoned to a great council, to be held at Westminster on the following 27 January. It was the king's intention to achieve reconciliation between the two opposing parties in English political life, the partisans of the queen and those of the Duke of York. A 'love-day' was held on 25 March to mark the alleged new-found affection of one side for the other. However, the queen and York quickly forgot reconciliation and, looking for support from the nobility, prepared for conflict. Meanwhile, Jasper had moved into the inner circle of the court party.

Jasper wished to retrieve the short-lived success of his brother, or at least to prevent further Yorkist inroads. Personal contact with other friendly magnates like Buckingham, who held land in South Wales, was an advantage, but military security could no longer be neglected. On 3 October, the mayor and burgesses, meeting in Tenby's hundred court, had proposed, possibly at Jasper's suggestion, that Tenby's walls were inadequately built and insufficiently maintained. They thus proposed that they should be made at least six feet thick at all points, providing a continuous platform for the defenders, while the town's moat should be cleaned and made thirty feet wide throughout. By his letters patent of 1 December 1457, Jasper granted the walls and moat of Tenby to its mayor, burgesses and freemen forever, empowering them to make the improvements they suggested, and undertook to bear half the cost of all works on the wall himself. The results of refortification are impressive. One additional tower seems to have been built, while existing towers and many of the parapets were raised in height as well. The walls and towers were regularly limewashed for protection against the coastal elements.

Tenby Castle and its walled town were to now act as Jasper's headquarters in Wales, while Margaret Beaufort and the infant Henry Tudor were in Pembroke Castle a few miles west. Despite Jasper's work at Tenby and elsewhere in Wales, England itself was relatively calm, as McFarlane explained: 'For all the military preparedness, the repeated call to arms, the sporadic outbreaks of violence in the provinces, and the frequent likelihood of a major clash, the onset of real warfare was agonizingly slow, because desired by no one'.

It was Jasper's grasp of strategy that allowed the Lancastrian cause to survive. He knew that Harlech Castle needed to be kept in Lancastrian hands, and in his personal domain of Pembrokeshire, he realized what H. T.

Evans calls 'the vast importance of Pembroke and Tenby castles'. Although Pembroke had never fallen to the Welsh, he added to its walls and castle. Tenby had fallen to the Welsh in 1187 and 1260, but had withstood an attack by Glyndŵr's invasion force in 1405. One of Jasper's innovations at Tenby was placing gunports in the walls. He personally seized in April 1459 the surrounding great castles of Carreg Cennen, Carmarthen and Aberystwyth, but it was Tenby and Pembroke that he concentrated upon refortifying. His 'expansive genius' recognised what his predecessors had not. Pembroke and Tenby were a connecting link between England, France, Burgundy, Brittany, Ireland and Scotland. Jasper could now not only escape the country, but also bring in support from other nations.

5

Jasper Tudor and the Wars of the Roses: The Battles of Blore Heath, Ludford Bridge, Denbigh, Northampton and Wakefield, 1458–1460

After the death of Edmund in November 1456, Jasper had spent a great deal of time with his council sorting out his brother's affairs. His brother's lands faced escheat, reversion to the Crown, as his son Henry was only born on 28 January 1457. His brother's wife, Margaret Beaufort, Countess of Richmond, had only just turned fourteen years old. He still held joint wardship of Margaret and her lands with his late brother, and they also had joint ownership of several estates. Jasper was still unmarried and many of the grants to him and Edmund were in fee tail (a type of restriction of land tenure regarding the line of heirs), tail male (where succession to property is limited to male heirs) or in survivorship (where surviving joint tenants take the land). By the spring of 1458, Jasper's failure to marry caused legal problems. It was imperative that he obtained wardship of his nephew Henry to safeguard the Richmond estates, and he made application to his half-brother Henry VI for help in sorting out his affairs.

The Act of Resumption of 1455 had given special provision to Jasper and Edmund, but later the Exchequer had found its phraseology ambiguous. There had been some confusion in the granting of lands, rights and fees to Jasper and Edmund, which Henry had attempted to solve in their favour in Easter 1456. However, the provisions were again misinterpreted by Exchequer officials, and more mandates to clarify Jasper's position had to be issued in 1458. Jasper's problem was that, having no heirs, he was not considered to be exempt from the provisions of the Act. After the disposal of portions of Edmund's lands, the Crown still retained a substantial part of his estate, together with the wardship and marriage of his heir, Henry Tudor, now Earl of Richmond. Owing to Jasper's persistence, on 8 January 1458, Jasper and John Talbot, Earl of Shrewsbury, were granted the wardship of the young Henry and of all his estates in England and Wales, except those in Lincolnshire. (Shrewsbury was to die fighting at Northampton in 1460.) The Lincolnshire estates could be farmed by Henry's tenants, however, for an annual fee to be agreed and paid to the Exchequer. Jasper and Shrewsbury then secured these lands for a rent of around £150 p.a. The agreement was enrolled in the Exchequer in February 1459.

By May 1458, Jasper had approached the king for clarification of the provisions of the Act of Resumption, and on 29 May Henry VI sent a writ of privy seal to the Treasurer and barons of the Exchequer, laying down the course they were to follow. He began by pointing out that he had granted the two earls a variety of estates either in fee tail, tail male or in survivorship, and the two brothers had enjoyed full possession of them. He stated that Jasper was now entitled to the same benefits as when both brothers had lived. Jasper thus became considerably richer as a result of Edmund's death. As well as the joint wardship of Henry Tudor, he now also retained exclusive control over the estates which he and his elder brother had shared. Jasper also acquired complete wardship of Margaret Beaufort, who was still a minor, as well as custody of her dower lands. His personal annual income had been around £925, to which he could now add annual totals from estates formerly held jointly with Edmund (£104), the Beaufort inheritance (£250), half-wardship of Henry Tudor (£85) and the dower land income of Margaret Beaufort (£200). Thus, after 1456, Jasper's income soared and must have approached around £1,565 a year by 1461. To place into context, £1,565 would be worth around £944,000 in 2012 using the Retail Price Index, and £8,900,000 using average earnings. In other words, Jasper was earning about £9 million a year, clear of taxes.

Nine days after Parliament opened, Jasper and fifty-nine other peers swore an oath of allegiance to Henry VI in the Great Council chamber, and he also acted as a trier of petitions from England, Scotland, Wales and Ireland in this session. The chief business transacted was the passing of an Act of Indemnity which absolved York, Salisbury, Warwick and their allies from all responsibility for the events surrounding the Battle of St Albans. Exeter's enemy Ralph, Lord Cromwell, who had conveniently died in 1456, was made one of the scapegoats for the affair.

Jasper was not to enjoy the income from the Margaret Beaufort inheritance. He knew that she would be safer married into a powerful family and following two years of discussions, by 20 July 1459 he and Buckingham had arranged a match between the dowager countess and Sir Henry Stafford, the duke's second son. Buckingham's annual income was calculated at about £3,477 for 1448–1449, making him one of the richest men in England, and Jasper now gained a social and political ally. Buckingham's great wealth had been accumulated over several generations. We must here note Henry VI's generosity to Richmond and Pembroke. Although the nation's premier earls, they had had been endowed with their estates over a period of only five years, at a time when the king faced his own financial difficulties. In 1467–1468, Earl Edmund of Kent, the head of the infamous family of Grey of Ruthin, had an annual net income of about £1,150, but it had taken over a century to reach this figure. Jasper in 1461 was earning about £1,565.

The Russo-English historian Michael Postan suggested that the Wars of the Roses were partially caused by the relative impoverishment of the great lords following poor harvests. This caused them to seek office to gain Crown favour and take the lands of their neighbouring lords. This could be seen on the Scottish Borders, in Wales and its Marches and the West Country. Indeed, the further from London, the more lawless the territory seems in these times. However, in the case of the arriviste Tudors, royal largesse steadily increased their wealth. This fact, together with sharing his mother with the king, explains Jasper's constant loyalty to the House of Lancaster after Edmund's death. Indeed, it was with his brother's death that Jasper first began to display the interest in Wales that he retained throughout his life, often with unfortunate consequences for himself.

Gruffydd ap Nicholas and his sons became close associates of Jasper in these years. In Carmarthenshire, Gruffydd ap Nicholas and his kinsmen had formerly disputed with both Edmund and Jasper but now the family turned towards the Lancastrian cause, having seen their local rivals, the Dwnns (also spelt Don or Dwn), gain favour under York. This change in loyalty was to prove crucial – without it the Tudors would never have gained the throne. Thomas and Owain ap Gruffydd ap Nicholas now proved themselves time and time again loyal supporters of the king and Jasper. On 1 March 1459, a commission was directed to Jasper, his father Owen Tudor, and Thomas and Owain, the sons of Gruffydd ap Nicholas. They were to arrest and bring before the king seven Welshmen, one of whom, John Gruffydd, was described as a servant of John Dwnn. The miscreants were Carmarthenshire men, and John Dwnn was a member of a prominent Kidwelly family which had supported Glyndŵr, and had close ties with Richard, Duke of York. In 1445, John Dwnn's father Gruffydd was an esquire, acting as steward of York's lordship of Usk in Monmouthshire. John Dwnn and his brothers Robert and Henry later became loyal followers of Edward IV, Richard of York's son, with John becoming one of his councillors. The order for the arrest of John Gruffydd and these men was probably an attempt to weaken York's influence in southern Carmarthenshire.

At about the same time, the garrisons of Carreg Cennen and Kidwelly were strengthened on Jasper's orders, after a force of York's retainers, perhaps even led by the duke himself or Sir John Dwnn, had descended on the lordship. Carreg Cennen had been repaired and regarrisoned in 1454–1455 on the orders of Gruffydd ap Nicholas. Jasper had become the commanding figure in Lancastrian Wales, on whom the king and queen relied for aid in that sector. He was undoubtedly a cornerstone of the Lancastrian position, particularly in West Wales, where loyalty to the Crown was strong. Now possibly aged around seventy-six, Gruffydd passed on the baton of leadership to his sons, who were to be prominent Lancastrians.

Gruffydd ap Nicholas had been imprisoned with his brother-in-law Owain Dwnn as followers of Humphrey, Duke of Gloucester, when 'the latter's sun set in 1447', as Garfield Hughes put it. Lewys Dwnn addressed an *Ode to Gruffydd ap Nicolas of Newton*, his mansion near Dynefwr Castle, Carmarthenshire, and an anonymous poet wrote, 'Saith gastell sy i'th gostlaw, A saith lys sy i'th law' – 'Seven castles are maintained at thy expense, and seven palaces are in thy hands.' From his great castle at Dinefwr, Llandeilo, Gruffydd had turned to be a supporter of Henry VI, and had lost some of his offices after the Battle of St Albans in 1455. However, he had resented Edmund Tudor's attempts to bring Wales to hand, and the *Paston Letters* in June 1456 stated that he was 'to be at war greatly' with Edmund. He and his sons, Thomas and Owen, had been granted general pardons on 26 October 1456. Known as the 'Eagle of Carmarthen', his name then disappears from the records, but some genealogies give him as being slain fighting at Wakefield in 1460 or Mortimer's Cross in 1461.

His eldest son, Owain ap Gruffydd, esquire, was born about 1400 and for some time was Governor of Castell Cydweli. Lewys Glyn Cothi addressed an *Ode to Owain ap Gruffudd ap Nicolas on his appointment of Governor of Cydweli Castle*. Owain fought for the House of Lancaster in the coming wars. Another son, Thomas ap Gruffydd ap Nicholas, esquire, was born around 1430, and came to be styled 'the Elder'. Rowland remarks that he was 'one of the most accomplished men of his age and although inclined towards peace, he was owing to the unsettled state of the times engaged in several duels'. He died fighting for the Lancastrians at Pennal in 1468. Without the support of Thomas' son Rhys, Henry Tudor would not have passed through Wales peacefully in 1485.

In the years that followed the fighting at St Albans on 22 May 1455, both sides had jockeyed for position. York was aware of the seriousness of raising arms against the king, and probably lacked enough noble support, although he was popular with the people. He had eliminated some of his major rivals at St Albans, and the Neville father and son, Salisbury and Warwick, were still his main allies. Because of their ongoing hatred of the Nevilles, the great Percy family of Northumberland and the North was always going to stay in the Lancastrian camp. Henry VI, Margaret and her court party recognised the high level of support enjoyed by York. Jasper was even now working to reconcile the sides, but after Edmund's death had moved away from both York's circle and the queen's court party. Jasper himself was an arriviste, with no real power base, no network of great retainers like the Nevilles and Percys. Problems that had caused the original conflict naturally re-emerged. A lack of law and order, especially in London, was blamed by its citizens on the weakness of Henry. A mild and deeply religious man, seemingly still mentally frail, he became increasingly withdrawn. Fearful for her son Prince Edward's future if York once again took over, Margaret again took over active leadership of the government.

York's nephew Richard Neville, 16th Earl of Warwick, the son of the Earl of Salisbury, was Captain of Calais at this time. Like York in Ireland, he was in semi-exile. From late 1458, he led a fleet out of Calais attacking merchant ships from the Hanseatic League port of Lübeck and those of Spain. This enraged the court party, which did not want a Continental war, but ensured Warwick's popularity in London. His attacks removed competitors for the vital English wool trade with Flanders. Warwick was summoned to London to explain his actions before the King's Council, and there was violence between Warwick's retinue and the royal household. Warwick claimed that his life had been threatened, and he swiftly returned to Calais without answering the charges. Margaret quickly took this to be open defiance of Henry's authority.

However, Warwick's popularity and the Londoners' Francophobe hatred of the queen resulted in her moving the royal court to Coventry, in the Lancastrian heartland of the Midlands. She began mustering royal forces, and summoned a council to be held in Coventry on 24 June. York, his brother-in-law Richard Neville, Earl of Salisbury, and Richard Neville, Earl of Warwick, feared that they would be arrested for treason if they went to the Lancastrian court, and refused to attend. They were indicted for rebellion. This was the spark for the main battles of the Wars of the Roses, a name thought to be first applied by Sir Walter Scott in the nineteenth century. A current romantic novelist has tried to rename it 'the Cousins' War', but this term was also applied to the First World War, in reference to the relationship between Queen Victoria's grandsons George V, Wilhelm II and Tsar Nicholas.

While the House of York used the symbol of the white rose quite often, the Lancastrian red rose was possibly introduced only after the victory of Henry Tudor at the Battle of Bosworth, when it was combined with the Yorkist white rose to form the Tudor rose. This was a clever device to symbolise the union of the two houses, and the old *Rosa Mundi*, the pink-and-white *Rosa gallica* var. *officinalis* 'Versicolor', was grown in Tudor gardens to symbolise the harmony.

It does seem, however, that the rose reference far predated Walter Scott's writings. David Hume in 1762 wrote of 'the wars between the two roses', and over a hundred years earlier it was referred to as 'the quarrel of the two roses'. In 1591, in Shakespeare's *Henry VI, Part 1*, Richard of York argues with the Lancastrian leader, Edmund, Duke of Somerset. The two men ask others to show their respective positions by picking a rose – red for Lancaster and white for York. The simple five-petal design of the heraldic rose was inspired by the wild dog rose (*Rosa canina*) that grows in English hedgerows. As a religious symbol it had a long association with the Virgin Mary, who is sometimes called the 'Mystical Rose of Heaven'. Edward I used a golden rose, representing the glory of the Virgin, while his descendants also sometimes used rose badges of different colours, with different religious meanings.

Initially, there seems to be no strong association of the red rose with Lancaster or the white rose with York. The French chronicle *Traison et*

Mort describes how Henry Bolingbroke – the future Henry IV, and first king of the House of Lancaster – had 'rouge fleurs' decorating his pavilion at a joust in 1398. It is not known if these were roses. When the fighting began in 1455, Henry VI preferred a spotted panther, an antelope, ostrich feathers or a silver swan to the red rose. Henry was very proud of the livery of the white swan (or silver swan). He used to grant it not only to his servants, but also, in the course of diplomacy, to eminent foreigners like the Mantuan knights. In England, the swan was originally the device of the Bohuns, coming to the House of Lancaster through Mary Bohun, wife of Henry of Bolingbroke. It seems to have been the favoured Lancastrian device, rather than the red rose.

As far as we know, neither Richard of York nor Richard of Gloucester used the white rose badge. Nobles often had multiple titles, especially the higher barons and lords, so several devices were often used by the companies of men following them. York normally used the 'falcon and fetterlock', while his son Edward IV used the 'sun in splendour', which was later confused with his opponent Oxford's 'streaming star'. However, Edward IV did begin to use the white rose prominently. It was believed to have been the badge of Edward's ancestor, Roger Mortimer. Mortimer was supposedly Richard II's 'true' heir, before his right was 'usurped' by Henry IV. Thus it was a key symbol of the dynastic rights of the House of York, in contrast to Henry IV's 'rouge fleurs'. Henry Tudor used the 'red dragon of Cadwaladr' among his banners, none of which are known to have featured roses, against Richard of Gloucester's 'white boar' at Bosworth.

Also, we must remember that a disproportionate number of men from Wales, and its Marcher counties, fought for the sides of Lancaster and York. The lands and offices attached to the Duchy of Lancaster were mainly in Gloucestershire, North Wales and Cheshire. Both of these border counties had large numbers of Welsh speakers even at this time. The estates and castles of the Duchy of York were spread throughout England, though many were in the Welsh Marches and there were supporters across South East Wales. In the thirty-two years of the forthcoming war, Wales saw some sort of recruiting or action for at least thirty years.

Being indicted for rebellion at Coventry in June, Warwick had nothing to lose. He publicly slandered the unpopular queen and began gaining support. Margaret was alarmed and responded by introducing conscription, an act not used in England, which meant that every town and village in England had to supply suitably equipped men-at-arms to attend a muster in support of the king. Yorkists had realised that their hopes for holding onto any sort of power were being blocked by the queen, while Margaret believed that the Yorkists wanted to take the throne and disinherit, or even kill, her son. The queen toured the northern Midlands raising support, taking with her the five-year-old Prince Edward. She handed out badges of silver swans, the personal badge of Henry VI, to all her noble supporters.

The Yorkists had the problem of Richard of York being based in Ludlow Castle in Shropshire, while Salisbury was at Middleham Castle in Yorkshire. Between them were Lancastrian forces, based in various locations across the Midlands. Warwick was marching north to Warwick Castle with a small army from Calais. There were few recruits from Warwick's Midlands estates, and Warwick narrowly escaped an ambush laid by the Duke of Somerset at Coleshill near Coventry. Warwick's path to his castle, or north to his father, Salisbury, was blocked by larger Lancastrian forces, so he was forced to turn west to join York in Ludlow. By mid-September, Salisbury was quickly moving from Middleham towards Ludlow to join York and Warwick. When their forces met, they planned to march on London, which would probably open its gates to them. Margaret was in Cheshire, and wanted to attack Salisbury's army before it reached Ludlow. She ordered local lords to bring men to the king at Eccleshall Castle, and lords Dudley and Audley were commissioned to raise men and block Salisbury's route. Blore Heath, near Market Drayton in Staffordshire, was the place selected by Audley to halt Salisbury's advance.

Cheshire was a county in which the Lancastrian party could count on securing plenty of fighting men. Prominent among the queen's supporters was Lord Stanley, whose influence in the county was considerable. In 1453, Queen Margaret had come to Chester 'upon progresse with manye greate lords and ladyes with her and was graciously received by the Mayor and citizens'. In 1455 and 1456, she was again a visitor at Chester, entertaining with great hospitality the citizens and gentlemen of the county. In the summers of 1457 and 1458, Margaret and her son had yet again came to Chester, where she kept open house, hoping thereby to draw the county to her party. In 1459, the queen lodged at Eccleshall Castle, the residence of her chaplain, John Halse, Bishop of Chester. As on previous occasions, the queen is said to have kept 'open and royal house' and by her liberality to have gained the support of the gentry.

On 23 September 1459, Lord Audley, Chamberlain of South Wales, carefully stationed his army, recently recruited from Staffordshire and Cheshire. There was probably a large royal army of 12,000–15,000 men, with the Yorkists half as numerous. The young prince, as Earl of Chester, had issued Audley's men with the Lancastrian livery badge of the white, or silver, swan. Margaret rode across the field of battle, exhorting her army, and then went to Eccleston Steeple to watch. Her Lancastrians had dug themselves into an excellent defensive position, while the Yorkists found themselves in battle order with little preparation. Their troops are said to have prepared for death by kissing the ground where they stood, believing that they were now on the spot where they would live or die. We know little of what happened, but there may have been a parley between leaders, a last attempt at peaceful reconciliation. The opening phase of the battle was usually an archery duel, but both armies were out of range of each other and casualties would have been slight.

Salisbury knew that there was no way past Margaret's army. A frontal attack on superior numbers would probably be doomed, but he was aware that the queen probably had other lords coming to assist her, so trying to develop a defensive position was also not an option. He could not retreat and be cut to shreds while in disorder. Salisbury had fought in Scotland and France, so made the tactical decision that his only chance was to feign a retreat from the centre of his position, hoping that the Lancastrians would leave their defences. His plan worked – a section of the Lancastrians saw its opportunity, possibly disobeying orders, and charged across open ground but slowed to cross a stream. At this juncture, the more disciplined Yorkists swung around and attacked. The raw Lancastrian recruits came under a hail of arrows. The more experienced Yorkists attacked and killed hundreds of the advancing Lancastrians, who were floundering with armour and weapons, crossing the muddy slopes of the brook.

After this failed attack, the Lancastrians regrouped and attacked again across the open field. Lord Audley led his well-armoured mounted squires and gentry, crossing the brook to attack Salisbury's men. Arrows poured into his followers, killing many horses and throwing their riders. Archers were instructed to aim at the less well-armoured horses in battle. During this second attack Audley was killed, reputedly by Sir Roger Kynaston of Stocks, near Ellesmere. Kynaston later added Audley's coat of arms to his own to commemorate the event, but switched allegiance to support Henry Tudor after Richard III came to the throne. With Audley's death, command fell to Lord Dudley. Because of the failure of Audley's cavalry, Dudley decided to assault the Yorkists on foot. Around 4,000 Lancastrians marched forward to engage the enemy, and a period of intense hand-to-hand combat ensued for a period of around half an hour. For some reason, the remainder of the Lancastrian forces held back, giving no assistance.

The assault began to fail, a number of the Lancastrians defected to the Yorkist side to save themselves, and the attack collapsed. The Yorkists pressed forward to rout the Lancastrians. The battle itself had lasted all afternoon, but the ensuing rout continued for hours. Lancastrian soldiers retreated towards the south-west, but were pursued and many killed. The death toll at Blore Heath is impossible to ascertain, like most battles in these times, when chroniclers conflated the numbers involved. Probably at least 3,000 men perished, with 2,000 or more of these on the Lancastrian side. Two of Salisbury's sons were taken prisoner. Salisbury still needed to get to Ludlow, knowing that the queen had other troops and that the Lancastrian army had merely been defeated, not exterminated. He was still outnumbered, and immediately led his men on a forced march rather than delay to gather spoils from the battlefield. If his men spent hours stripping armour and weapons and gathering artillery, they would take far longer in carting heavy loads towards safety.

Salisbury cleverly forced a local Augustinian friar to periodically fire a cannon on the battlefield throughout the night. He thought this would dissuade any other Lancastrian forces from quickly approaching the battlefield, giving the impression that the Yorkists were still there. By the time Henry and Margaret returned to Blore Heath the following morning with their Lancastrian army, all they found was a deserted camp, corpses and a frightened friar. Following this qualified success, Salisbury reached Ludlow well in advance of the chasing Lancastrians. Here he was reunited with his son Warwick, who had crossed from Calais with a contingent of experienced soldiers under the command of Andrew Trollope. Other rebel supporters joined, including the untrustworthy Lord Grey of Ruthin and Walter Devereux.

The appearance of the king's personal banners leading the Lancastrians unnerved York. He could convince his men to fight against the French queen and her wicked, corrupt councillors, but fighting against their God-appointed monarch was another matter. Morale in the Yorkist camp slumped, and it was sensed by its leaders. In desperation, York, Salisbury and Warwick issued a manifesto stating their loyalty to the king, much as they had done at St Albans. The Yorkist army then marched south to Worcester and, on 10 October 1459, York, Salisbury and Warwick publicly took an oath of loyalty to the king, but again criticised the 'evil' councillors surrounding him. Henry responded with a pardon to those who would join him within six days. His army had been greatly strengthened by the accession of the heirs of Somerset, Northumberland and Clifford, and other lords killed at St Albans. These young men and their retainers wanted revenge for the deaths of their fathers.

York's army was inferior in numbers, as his Welsh estates had failed to support him. We are still unsure whether York had personally ordered the invasion of South Wales by his marcher retainers in August 1456. This incursion is vital to understanding the ensuing local battles of Ludford Bridge and Mortimer's Cross. York's retainers in 1456 had been led by Sir William Herbert, son of a former steward of the Mortimer lands in Wales, Sir Walter Devereux of Weobley in Herefordshire and his son Walter (the younger). There were also Herbert's Vaughan half-brothers, Roger Vaughan of Tretower and Thomas Vaughan of Eardisley, Thomas Monington of Sarnesfield and John Lingen of Sutton, besides others from Monmouth.

The majority had received a pardon, with Isabella's advisors attempting to drive a wedge between York's supporters. During the lawless action of 1456, when Edmund Tudor died, York's prestige had been lessened in Wales and the Marches, from where he drew half his revenues. The lenient treatment of many of the Herbert–Devereux–Vaughan affinity in the southern Marches had made them now unwilling to support York. The most powerful Yorkist in the area, William Herbert, who controlled much of Monmouthshire and Brecon, did not appear. Indeed, Walter Devereux the younger was the only leader of the 1456 affair definitely known to have come to York's aid at Ludlow. The Yorkists had been skilfully divided by the queen's policy of pardoning the Herberts, Vaughans and others, while punishing the Devereux family, Lingen, Baskerville, Monington and others with recognisances and imprisonment, though they were eventually acquitted.

The Yorkists decided to return to Ludlow, declining battle on the road to Kidderminster and falling back. York hoped that a long and tortuous march would leave the greatly superior royal army trailing well in its wake, or encourage it to break up. The royalists remorselessly followed the retreating Yorkists through Ledbury and Leominster, about a day behind them. The king was later praised in the Coventry Act of attainder for 'not sparing for any impediment or difficulty of way, nor of intemperance of weathers'. During the thirty-day campaign, he 'lodged in bare field sometime two nights together with all your Host in the cold season of the year'. On the last march to Ludlow, there seem to have been floods on the River Lugg, which would have affected the routes from Leominster to Ludlow. The Yorkists took up a position south of Ludlow Castle and its town walls at Ludford Bridge across the River Teme, where they dug a ditch and fortified it with artillery. York probably avoided defending his castle, afraid of being trapped and besieged there.

On 12 October, royal positions were taken up on Ludford meadows, banners displayed and tents pitched. The king probably had with him the dukes of Buckingham, Somerset and Exeter, the earls of Shrewsbury, Devon, Wiltshire, Northumberland and Arundel, Viscount Beaumont, barons Egremont, Fitzhugh, Neville, Ross, Dudley and the new Lord Audley. Jasper Tudor, Earl of Pembroke, seems not to have reached Ludford in time for battle, but possibly was guarding routes to stop other Welsh Yorkists from going to Ludlow.

Buckingham was probably in command at Ludford Bridge, and was to command at Northampton in July 1460. On 12 October the two armies faced each other near Ludford Bridge, but although the Yorkist forces had carefully entrenched themselves, there was hardly any fighting. Not only the banners of the king but also those of the greatest lords were seen that afternoon by the Yorkist vanguard on Ludford meadows. Guns were discharged, seemingly at random, into the gathering dusk, probably to keep up Yorkist morale. To fight against an anointed king in person was treason and sacrilege. Later, the Coventry parliament would be informed that rumours of the king's death were spread in the Yorkist camp and masses said for his soul, to try and convince the soldiers that they were not fighting their king.

However, all was in vain. York's best commander, the veteran Andrew Trollope, captain of the experienced Calais troops, switched sides after accepting the king's pardon. The news spread and that night a significant amount of the Yorkist army deserted, leading to a full-scale retreat the next morning. On hearing this, York, Salisbury and Warwick rode at midnight over Ludford Bridge into York's great castle at Ludlow, ostensibly for refreshment. However, the Yorkist leaders simply abandoned their army and fled. Warwick and Salisbury rode away with York's son Edward, Earl of March. They reached the West Country, where Sir John Dynham loaned them a boat which took them to Calais, where the garrison still supported Warwick.

York, with his second son Edmund, Earl of Rutland, fled from place to place in Wales and, according to *The Historical Collections of a Citizen of London*, 'breke downe the bryggys aftyr hym that the kyngys mayny schulde not come aftyr hym'. It seems that Jasper, with his local knowledge, led a contingent of troops chasing York. York and March managed somehow to take a ship from Wales to Ireland, where he had support from the Fitzgeralds. York had also abandoned his wife Cecily Neville, his two younger sons and his daughter, who were found standing at Ludlow Market Cross when the Lancastrians entered the walled town.

They were placed in the care of the duchess's sister Anne, wife of Buckingham and one of Margaret's supporters. At dawn on 13 October, the leaderless Yorkist troops knelt in submission before Henry, and all were pardoned. Gregory says that many knights and esquires, including Grey of Ruthin and Walter Devereux the younger, came in their shirts, and carrying halters, to submit to the king and were granted their lives. Devereux, however, maintained a long career in Yorkist service until, as Lord Ferrers of Chartley, he fell at Bosworth. Unfortunately, the joyous Lancastrian troops plundered Ludlow, becoming drunk on looted wine and committing outrages. It was reported that the town was cruelly ravaged by the northern army of Margaret: 'And forth with the Kynge rode unto Ludlowe & dyspoiled the towne and castell.' His men had been marching for at least a month, and were going home without fighting. Few towns were more devoted to the Yorkist cause than Ludlow, which belonged to the Duke of York, represented the chief Mortimer powerbase and had Richard's favourite residence for its castle. Here he had mustered the army that melted away in the rout of Ludford Bridge. When Richard's son Edward IV assumed the sovereignty, Ludlow was chosen as the proper seat for the residence of the Prince of Wales.

Before Ludford Bridge, the king had arranged for Parliament to meet at Coventry on 20 November 1458, a month after the battle. Jasper was noted as arriving a fortnight later, on 6 December 1458, 'with a good fellowship'. There is no record of his taking part in the Yorkist rout at Ludford, but it is more than likely that he was present or at least making for the king's forces from Wales. His delay in arriving at the Coventry parliament may well have been caused by pursuit of those in flight like the Duke of York. At this so-called 'Parliament of Devils', each peer promised the king to 'acknowledge You most high and mighty and most Christian Prince, King Henry the VI, to be my most redoubted Sovereign Lord, and rightfully by succession borne to reign upon one and all your liege People'. Stability was supposedly ensured by this oath of loyalty to the king and Prince Edward, sworn and signed by all the peers present, including Jasper. The resulting bill of attainder blamed York for all the political strife of the previous decade. He and sons March and Rutland, together with Salisbury and Warwick, and their chief allies and retainers, men like Sir Walter Devereux and Sir William Oldhall, were attainted and stripped of all their estates.

According to the Yorkist English Chronicler, this meant that York,

Salisbury and his countess Alice, Warwick, March, Rutland, three barons, nine knights and fourteen esquires were attainted. Ludford Bridge was a disaster from which York never really recovered. His eclipse was most serious in the Welsh Marches, his political heartland, which he had failed to defend and which hardly supported him. His son Edward, Earl of March, possibly saw no future in accompanying York to Dublin. In Calais he was able to help Warwick, now the effective leader of the Yorkist party, plan the coup of the following summer, which gave them control of king and government.

At this time, Owen Tudor reappears after years of obscurity. Owen Tudor is noted in the records at a Lancastrian council meeting in 1459 where he, along with Jasper, stood at the king's side and swore loyalty to his sovereign lord and stepson, Henry VI. Both Tudors were issued with new estates, Jasper with one of York's castles and Owen with various manor estates in the Home Counties. Owen himself had also been knighted and was at one time a deputy lord-lieutenant and warden of the forestries. On 19 December 1459, the day before Parliament was dissolved, Owen Tudor was granted a £100 annuity and a lease for six manors in Kent, Sussex and Warwickshire forfeited by John, Lord Clinton. Owen Tudor again features in 1459, having fathered an illegitimate son variously called David Tudor, David Owen, Davy Owen or Dafydd ap Owen. This half-uncle of King Henry VII accompanied Henry through Wales to fight at Bosworth, and was shown the new king's favour in 1485, being knighted.

On 1 March 1459, Jasper headed a commission to arrest Roger Hervey, possibly a burgess of Kidwelly, and others. Alphonso V, King of Aragon and Naples, died in June 1458, and Jasper was elected to his stall as a Knight of the Garter at some time before 23 April 1459. On 2 May 1459, the earl was also granted a tower in the Palace of Westminster, near the entrance to the Exchequer of Receipt, where he could hold his council meetings and keep his legal records and papers. It was to be used, as the letters patent put it, 'for the safe-guard and keeping of the earl's evidences and for the communications and easement of the earl and his council'. Jasper had occupied this tower before by royal licence but was now granted it for life, thereby enjoying the position of a neighbour to the queen, since she held a similar tower nearby in the palace. Increasingly, Jasper seems to have assumed the role of Edmund in Welsh affairs.

Wiltshire, who had been appointed Lieutenant of Ireland in place of York, found it impossible to raise troops to oust York from Ireland, where the duke was popular. Similarly, Somerset was twice beaten back by the garrison of Calais when he tried to reclaim it from Warwick. Although the nobles had united under Henry to give him a much larger army at Ludford Bridge, these setbacks began to cause unpopularity again. The news of his army looting Ludlow, and especially the behaviour of the queen's court party, again caused anger and complaints. Lords and people alike felt that Lancastrian favourites were enriching themselves at the expense of the king and his people. It was as if nothing had changed since York first aired these grievances in the early 1450s. Meanwhile, on 12 February 1460, Earl Jasper was granted, in tail male, the messuage (dwelling) called 'Le Garlek' in Stepney, which he had formerly shared with his now attainted ex-councillor Thomas Vaughan.

According to John Williams, Jasper at this time tried to regain Denbigh Castle from the Yorkists: 'The original town was possibly burnt during the Wars of the Roses.' Leland relates that Edward IV was besieged in the castle, and the town burnt. Other historians relate that Jasper Tudor and a Welsh army only set the suburbs of Denbigh on fire, and in 1459 destroyed that part of the town which lay 'without the walls'. This may relate to a much later siege, however. On 5 January 1460, Jasper was appointed for life to the positions of constable, steward and master forester of the lordship of Denbigh in North Wales, formerly one of York's estates. Jasper had been given control of Denbigh Castle to help block York's avenue of communication between England and Ireland. However, York's supporters had no intention of giving up without a fight, and it was necessary for Jasper to lay siege to the castle. Although the Yorkist leaders had escaped into exile, there were still pockets of resistance, and York's castle was still held for him.

By 16 February 1460, Jasper had informed the king of his requirements, which were fivefold. Firstly, he requested a commission to himself to raise men in Wales to help subdue the castle of Denbigh. Secondly, he asked for the power to pardon the rebels who were prepared to submit. However, those who surrendered but were outlawed or attainted were to be kept in prison until they could give sureties of good behaviour. Thirdly, Jasper asked for authority to execute rebels at his discretion. Fourthly, he petitioned for a grant to himself of all the moveable goods belonging to the men in the castle, so that they could be used to reward his supporters. Finally, he asked for commissions of muster to be directed to three groups of men on whom he could rely to provide him with a besieging force.

One was to be sent to Sir Robert de Vere, Sir William Vernon, Sir Henry Wogan, Sir Thomas Perot, Thomas Wyriot, Thomas Wogan and (another) Thomas Perot, esquires, to assemble men in the lordships of Pembroke, Rhos and Dewisland in Pembrokeshire. A second, for Carmarthenshire and Cardiganshire, was to be sent to Rhys ap Dafydd ap Thomas (a former foe of Gruffydd ap Nicholas), Robert ap Rhys ap Thomas, Ieuan ap Jankyn Llwyd and Peter Baret. A third to be was issued to Philip Mansel, Henry Dwnn the younger, Richard Cradock and Thomas Burghill, esquires, in Gower and Kidwelly.

Sir Robert de Vere, younger brother of John de Vere, the Lancastrian Earl of Oxford, is the most interesting of these men hand-picked by Jasper. He could easily raise men, but seems to have had no connection with West Wales, and there is no record of him being associated with Jasper before this date. However, they must have met at court. De Vere had seen war service in France, and was acting as captain of Caen in Normandy in 1450. He was chamberlain for the Duke of Exeter in the period 1457–1460, and must have been a member of the court party. His nephew John de Vere, second son of the Earl of Oxford, was to become a great ally of Jasper and Henry Tudor, leading the army at Bosworth.

Sir William Vernon of Haddon in Derbyshire, on the other hand, was associated with West Wales. He was MP for Derbyshire in 1442, 1449–1450 and 1450–1451, while from 1451 to 1460 he succeeded his father, Sir Richard Vernon, as treasurer of Calais. Sir Richard himself had landed and administrative interests in Wales; his mother was the daughter of Lord Rhys ap Gruffydd of Llansadwrn. In 1451, William Vernon was acting as one of the deputies of Lord Dudley while the latter was in France, while on 22 May 1450 he was appointed in perpetuity as sheriff of Pembroke, Llanstephan, Ystlwyf and St Clears; constable of Pembroke and Tenby castles; and master forester of Coedrath in Pembrokeshire. Sir William Vernon's tenure of the manor of Stackpole in Pembroke was confirmed to him by arbitrators in 1465. Vernon and his brother John may well have felt a personal animosity towards the Yorkists. Since at least 1453, the Gresley and Blount families of Derbyshire had waged a feud against the Curzon, Longford and Vernon families, the latter three all retained by the Duke of Buckingham while the Blounts were clients of York. The vendetta seriously disrupted life in Derbyshire for a number of years in the 1450s, and Sir William Vernon was close to the centre of the arguments.

The remaining members of the West Wales commission were all servants of Jasper. The capable Sir Henry Wogan was his councillor in 1456, an experienced and senior local official in the principality of South Wales and in Pembrokeshire. Sir Thomas Perot was steward of Pembroke from 1450 until at least 1457. Thomas Wyriot, sheriff of Pembroke in 1442 for Humphrey, Duke of Gloucester, was now acting as Jasper's own esquire, while Thomas Wogan and Thomas Perot, esquires, were both members of the most prominent families in Pembrokeshire. These men were experienced administrative or military officials, bound to Jasper by strong ties of service, political sympathy and loyalty.

The man chosen to raise forces in the principality shires of Cardigan and Carmarthen was Rhys ap Dafydd ap Thomas. He had been bailiff itinerant of Cardiganshire for some time and was beadle of Caerwedros in Cardiganshire from 1432 to 1437, and escheator of that county in 1456–1457. He was also lord of the manor of Lampeter. Ieuan ap Jankyn Llwyd was the second Cardiganshire man, having been beadle of Caerwedros in 1425–1426 and clerk of the Welsh courts in the county from 1426 to 1463. The two Carmarthenshire men mentioned had been similarly used. Robert ap Rhys had been beadle of Catheiniog in 1450–1451, while Peter Baret of Laugharne had been bailiff there in 1440–1443. All these men had years of experience behind them, and in the lordships of Gower and Kidwelly equally prominent local gentlemen had been chosen to raise troops.

In Gower, one of the natural leaders was Philip Mansel, esquire, of Oxwich, holding the lordship of Porteynon and the manors of

Nicholaston, Oxwich, Scurlage Castle, Horton, as well as property in the lordships of Swansea and Kidwelly. Richard Cradock, esquire, was an associate of Mansel on 10 October 1459 when he witnessed the latter's deed entailing land upon the former's sons. Thomas Burghill, esquire, was possibly a kinsman of William Burghill, who had acted as deputy justiciar for Sir Edward Stradling in Cardiganshire in 1430–1455, and both may well have been members of the Burghill family of Angle in Pembrokeshire. Finally, Henry Donn (or Dwnn) the younger, of Picton Castle, Pembrokeshire, had married Margaret, the daughter of Sir Henry Wogan. He was the son of Owain Dwnn of Kidwelly. The Kidwelly branch of the family had been closely linked with York and Sir William Herbert, and Henry Dwnn of Kidwelly married Maud, a daughter of Sir Roger Vaughan of Tretower, Herbert's half-brother. Henry Dwnn of Picton had already served Earl Jasper as escheator and sheriff of the lordship of Pembroke in 1457.

Jasper had sent his petition of requirements to the king by his esquire, Thomas Wyriot. On 16 February 1460, Henry VI wrote urgently to the Chancellor, ordering swift execution of Jasper's requests, sending Wyriot on to him with the detailed proposals, having already alerted the Treasurer about these measures. On 22 February, two letters patent were sealed for the Earl of Pembroke, the first being a commission of array, authorising him to resist York and his associates.

There were two main methods of recruiting men to fight when the necessity arose. The first of these was the indenture, or contract, system. Loyalty of the great magnates to the king had to be ensured. One of their contractual obligations, attached to their holding of their estates, required them to enter into contracts with the monarch for the provision of armed men. Some of these indentures have survived, and show in detail the numbers and type of soldiers the lord had to provide when called on to do so. These major lords entered into similar contracts with those who held lands from them, and this reached down to the lowest scale of the landed classes, so that a landed squire or gentleman might be required to bring two or three men-at-arms or archers, whether mounted or on foot, with him to the mustering point designated by the king.

Towns were put under similar obligations, and also had to provide soldiers when called on to do so. Strict observance of one's contract could be sternly demanded by the mustering officer. Out of this grew the 'affinity' system. Under this, a local magnate might give some guarantee of military protection to his subordinate landholders in return for their obligation to supply him with armed men, but only when he called for them. This bound them to him in other ways than the purely military, and reinforced the bond of pyramidal loyalty on which medieval society depended. Some of these affinities were quite small, while others were very large. William, Lord Hastings, had an affinity of ninety landholders required to supply men in the Midlands, a similar number to that of Thomas, Lord Stanley, in Lancashire.

The other method of military recruitment was a survival of the feudal system, where the king could require his subjects to fight in his army for a period which did not exceed forty days. This period had usually been adequate to deal with an immediate threat, but by the end of the fifteenth century, with extended war, it was sometimes too short. The king would issue a commission of array, addressed to the sheriff of a county or the mayor of a town. This required him to muster all eligible men aged between sixteen and sixty, and specified how many soldiers were required. The subordinates of the sheriff or mayor, the constables, kept a good count of the men in their localities, and knew who would be fit and able to serve. Usually the commissions did not specify a time limit, contrary to the earlier feudal practice, but there was always a natural time limit to the period for which recruits could be kept with the colours.

The second letters patent issued to Jasper allowed him to pardon rebels in Denbigh Castle who were prepared to submit, except for certain outlawed or attainted Welshmen who were to be gaoled until they could provide sureties for their good behaviour. It also allowed him to judge and execute rebels at his discretion, and to muster men in Denbighshire, or in other parts of Wales, in order to reduce Denbigh Castle, additionally fulfilling his petition by granting to him the movables of the rebels within the castle. In February 1460, Jasper thus put Denbigh Castle under siege.

While supervising the attack, on 13 March 1460, Jasper was awarded 1,000 marks (£666) to support the cost of reducing Denbigh and other castles in Wales and the Marches held by Yorkist rebels. He was to take the money from the revenues of York's Marcher lordships. A severely mutilated letter from Jasper to Lord Scales, dated at Ruthin on 29 March, appears to belong to this period. The document is so badly damaged as to be almost unintelligible but seems to be an urgent request to Scales for money, 'seeing the great necessity that I stand in'. Denbigh's surrender took time, but it must have been taken by May, for by 25 May Jasper had left Denbigh and was at Pembroke organising defensive measures there.

Jasper wrote to John Hall, the mayor of Tenby, informing him that he had sent instructions to John White, a burgess of the town, to hand over a ship called *le Mary* to Thomas Wogan, esquire, who could then attack an enemy vessel that lay in Milford Haven. The earl asked the mayor to give Wogan his assistance by providing sailors and men for the expedition. Jasper knew the importance of keeping Milford Sound safe from attack. It is one of the finest natural harbours in the world, with many sheltered inlets providing safe anchorage.

Roger Puleston of Emral, in Flintshire, had been close to Edmund Tudor, and a letter of 19 September 1456 survives from Edmund in which he is granted an annuity of 10 marks for his services. Jasper Tudor, a kinsman of Puleston, worked with Puleston throughout the long wars. Under Jasper, Puleston held important positions in North Wales and played a part in the early battles and sieges. The town of Denbigh changed hands several times between the Yorkists and Lancastrians. When Denbigh was controlled by the Lancastrians, from 1457, Jasper Tudor held the office of captain of Denbigh Castle, while Puleston was its governor. Roger helped Jasper to capture Denbigh Castle from the Yorkists after a three-month siege, probably in May 1460, and held it until he was forced to surrender in 1461. There exists 'a warrant for 200 marks, residue of 1,500 to Burgesses of Denbigh, by Edward IV, towards re-edification of Town burned by certaine rebbels and traytors, 23 Feb., 1st year'. This seems to date from 1461–1462.

After Jasper took Denbigh, he took great pains to secure his rear in the south-west, writing to Puleston from Tenby, urging him not to surrender Denbigh:

> To our Right trusty and well-beloved Roger Puleston, Esq., Keeper of the Castle of Denbigh, – Right trusty and well-beloved – We greet you well, letting you witt that we have received your letters by Hugh, and understand the matter comprised therein; and as touching the keeping of the Castle of Denbigh, we pray you that you will do your faithful diligence for the safeguard of it, as far as in you is, taking the revenue of the lordship there for the victualing of the same, by the hands of Griffith Vychan, receiver there – we have written unto him that he should make purveyance therefore – and that ye will understand the good will and disposition of the people, and that country, towards my Lord Prince [Edward, Prince of Wales] and us, and to send us word as soon as you may, as our trust is in you. Written at my towne of Tenbye, xxiii July. J. Pembroke.

On 5 May 1460, Jasper was granted the farm of York's forfeited lordship of Newbury in Berkshire for seven years, from the preceding Easter, at a rent to be agreed with the Exchequer. This may have been a reward for taking Denbigh. Newbury was the property of Richard of York, and sometime before June 1460 the town was taken by the Earl of Wiltshire, Lord Scales and Robert, 3rd Baron Hungerford. As recorded in the *English Chronicle*, they,

> having the king's commission, went to the town of Newbury, the which longed to the duke of York, and there made inquisition of all them that in any ways had showed any favour or benevolence or friendship to the said duke, or to any of his: whereof some were found guilty, and were drawn, hanged, and quartered, and all other inhabitants of the aforesaid town were spoiled of all their goods.

Henry had sent his lords, Wiltshire being Lord Treasurer, to Newbury in order to discover and punish those who had been in arms against the king, and to collect money. The inhabitants refused to pay, saying they would keep what they had for their lord, the Duke of York. In consequence, some of the townsmen were hanged, drawn and quartered, and all the other inhabitants despoiled of their goods. Newbury suffered the same fate as Grantham and Stamford, which had also been sacked by the followers of Wiltshire. The ravaging of the town played a big role in alienating from Margaret of Anjou those who had formerly sided with the House of Lancaster. Wiltshire and Hungerford were to suffer for their actions at Newbury. Jasper will have made no money from his new leadership or its impoverished citizens.

Queen Margaret was now making preparations to cross the Channel and take Calais. She wanted to capture the dangerous Warwick. Construction began on a transport fleet at Sandwich, and, learning that the transports were completed, Warwick launched a raid on Sandwich and captured the ships. Taking them back to Calais, he and other Yorkist commanders began planning an attack on England. When the Lancastrians renewed their efforts to build a fleet at Sandwich, Warwick attacked and occupied the town in May 1460. Leaving a small Yorkist force in Sandwich, he returned to Calais to prepare his army. On 26 June, Warwick returned to land in Kent with 2,000 men. Marching on London, Warwick was welcomed and the Yorkist ranks quickly swelled to 20,000–30,000 men. The news of Lancastrian indiscipline when taking towns meant that, faced with a choice, citizens would prefer occupation by Yorkists.

Alerted to the new arrival of Warwick, Salisbury and York's son Edward, Earl of March, Henry VI decided to move his army of between 10,000 and 15,000 troops from Coventry to Northampton. Commanded by Buckingham again, the king's army occupied a defensive position along the River Nene. With the river at their back, they dug a water-filled ditch across their front and topped it with pointed stakes. Though the bulk of Henry's army consisted of men-at-arms, he did possess some field artillery. Informed that Henry's army had moved, Warwick moved north from London towards Northampton. While his army was on the march, Warwick despatched a messenger asking to meet with the king. Arriving at Northampton, this messenger was denied access to Henry by Buckingham, being informed that 'the Earl of Warwick shall not come to the king's presence and if he comes he shall die'. Even so, Warwick sent two more messengers before reaching the battlefield. As his army arrived opposite the Lancastrian position, Warwick sent a final message, stating, 'At 2 o'clock I will speak with the King or I will die.' On 10 July 1460, as the hour approached, Warwick formed his soldiers into columns and attacked.

In driving rain, Yorkist troops charged through a shower of arrows. Rain slowed the advance, but also dampened gunpowder and prevented the Lancastrians from effectively using their artillery. Warwick attacked the Lancastrian right, commanded by Lord Grey of Ruthin, who had agreed before the attack to defect. Of all the Welsh Marcher lords, the Greys and Mortimers had a constant history of treachery. Grey had sent a secret message to Edward, Earl of March, saying that he would change sides if the Yorkists would back him in a property dispute with Lord Fanhope. There was probably a promise also of high office, as Grey became Treasurer of

England in 1463. Warwick ordered his men not to harm enemy soldiers wearing the ragged black staff of Lord Grey. Grey's troops simply laid down their weapons and helped the Yorkists over the barricades. With no opposition on his front, Warwick's men swarmed into the Lancastrian camp and turned to roll up Buckingham's line.

Because of the constricted nature of his fortified encampment, Buckingham could not manoeuvre his troops properly to block Warwick's men, and his Lancastrian forces were routed after about thirty minutes of fighting. Henry was in danger of capture, so Buckingham, Egremont and Beaumont fought to the death in an attempt to allow him to escape. However, Yorkist troops quickly seized the confused king from his tent. Yorkist losses at the Battle of Northampton were minimal, but many Lancastrians drowned in the swollen River Nene.

On 10 July 1460, at the time of the Battle of Northampton, the queen was at Eccleshall when she heard the king's capture. Margaret swiftly rode to Coventry with Prince Edward but failed to raise an army. They fled to Wales from Malpas Castle, 'and there hence she removed privily unto the Lord Jasper, lord and earl of Pembroke, for she durst not abide in no place that was open, but in private'. It seems that she was at Chirk Castle for a time before carrying on her escape to Harlech Castle. The new Yorkist government could not tolerate Jasper's continued threat in the west, and, on 9 August 1460, Jasper and Roger Puleston, esquire, his kinsman and deputy constable of Denbigh, were ordered by a Royal Council to hand over Harlech Castle to York's deputy Edward Bourchier, son of Henry, Viscount Bourchier. Jasper refused, and continued to recruit men for Margaret of Anjou. Similar orders were sent by the council to the constables of the Lancastrian castles at Beaumaris, Flint, Conway, Hawarden, Holt, Ruthin and Montgomery. Jasper's troops would not surrender, and on 17 August 1460 Sir Walter Devereux, Sir William Herbert and Roger Vaughan, esquire, were empowered to take all these Lancastrian castles which were 'illegally garrisoned'.

In September 1460, the Duke of York finally returned from Ireland, where he had remained in virtual inactivity. He made a regal progress through the Welsh Marches to London, passing through Shrewsbury, Ludlow and Hereford. According to Jean de Waurin, the gentry of the Ludlow area were joined by the 'seigneurs du pays de Galles', who urged York to take the throne because of his descent from Lionel of Clarence. Waurin does not mention the Mortimer connection, which mattered more to the Welsh, as Mortimer was descended from Welsh princes. Hall wrote that 'the people on the Marches of Wales ... above measure favoured ye lynage of the Lord Mortimer'. Waurin presumably refers to Herbert, Devereux and their associates. Herbert was now fully committed to the Yorkist cause again.

York, along with his wife Cecily Neville, Duchess of York (the aunt of York's ally Warwick), had marched on London, and was received with all the circumstance due a reigning monarch. Parliament was in session when York entered and declared that he was the rightful and legal king, based on primogeniture. There was silence and then uproar in the chamber. York had badly misjudged the mood of the nobles in London, who, along with Londoners, were strongly opposed to York's regal demands. Even Warwick did not support York taking the throne, and Parliament, which agreed that York had the best hereditary claim, did not want to overthrow the king. Warwick had only ever wanted to remove Lancastrian control over the king. The argument was resolved peacefully with an Act of Accord, recognising York as heir to King Henry VI, even though this displaced the six-year-old Edward of Westminster, Prince of Wales.

The Act was passed by Parliament on 25 October 1460, three weeks after York had entered the Council Chamber and laid his hand on the empty throne. Henry VI was to retain the crown for life, but York and his heirs were to succeed. Henry was forced to agree to, or was unable to comprehend, the Act, which was unacceptable to Henry's queen, who saw her son disinherited. There followed a series of negotiations, the result of which was that Henry was to be nominally king until his death, but York was to govern as regent. York now needed to get the young prince, as well as the king, into his possession.

The weakened Henry was now induced to sign a mandate commanding the queen to come to London and bring the prince with her. If the order was not carried out immediately, she was guilty of treason. Officers were immediately despatched to Wales to search for the queen, in order to serve the mandate upon her, but she was nowhere to be found. Margaret and the prince had been fugitives since July, with only eight persons to accompany her in her flight. It was said that her defenceless party was stopped while on its way to Wales, and the queen was robbed of all her jewels and other valuables. While the attackers were busy sorting their plunder, Margaret and her entourage escaped, riding possibly to Chirk and then to Harlech Castle, which was still held for Jasper. Margaret is also said to have joined Jasper at Denbigh, and then Harlech Castle, before possibly reaching Pembroke Castle.

Jasper knew the strategic importance of Milford Haven as the only Welsh harbour equally accessible from France, Brittany, Ireland and Scotland. Pembroke Castle, well sheltered up its river on Milford Haven, was the obvious place for the disembarkation of foreign troops. Margaret and Jasper planned for Jasper to raise and lead a force against the Yorkists in the middle Marches, marching from Pembroke. There is an interesting ode by Lewys Glyn Cothi, bearing the date 1460, and addressed to *Iaspar, Iarll Penfro*, Jasper Earl of Pembroke. It was probably written shortly after the Battle of Northampton, 10 July 1460, likely with the view of inducing the Welsh to rally under the banner of the Earl of Pembroke. Soon Margaret managed to take ship to Scotland, where she had powerful friends, and began raising a new force to help Jasper.

This is the first mention of Harlech in the activities of the wars. A garrison of about a dozen soldiers had been maintained during the reign of Henry V (1413–1423) and Henry VI up to 1444, in which year the garrison was doubled under Edward Hampden. During 1458–1459, the approach to the castle was still being maintained. Various masons, carpenters and other labourers made a new bridge to the fortress using timber, iron and clays at a cost of £10 6s 6d. The castle was also restocked, which shows that it was obviously still a major, ongoing military concern and that it was still worthwhile making use of the houses and buildings within the fortress. The new supplies cost the constable £9 6s 11d. This was the state of Harlech Castle when it began its 'great siege' by the Yorkists in 1460.

The new Yorkist government had been prompt to send orders to the leading Yorkists in the southern Welsh Marches. Sir William Herbert of Raglan had married Anne Devereux, sister of Walter, in 1459–1460, and quickly rejoined the Yorkist party after Northampton. He was now to capture Jasper, assisted by his half-brother Roger Vaughan of Tretower (near Brecon), and several Herefordshire esquires, notably his new brother-in-law Walter Devereux of Weobley, James Baskerville of Eardisley, Henry ap Gruffydd of Vowchurch (described by William Worcester as 'a man of war'), Richard Croft of Croft Castle and Thomas Monington of Sarnesfield. All except Croft had been involved in the Yorkist invasion of South Wales in 1456. However, only Devereux, and possibly Croft, had come to help York at Ludford Bridge. The Yorkists were ordered to arrest people breaking the peace, and specifically two Herefordshire members of the last parliament, Sir John Barre and Thomas Fitzharry, though without success. Fitzharry, who was a lawyer and chamberlain in South Wales, now joined Jasper Tudor. The Yorkist centre of gravity still lay in Herefordshire. Most of the leaders of the 1456 expedition came from there, as did most of Edward's companions at Mortimer's Cross. Although Monington and Baskerville are not in Worcester's list, they are likely to have been there too, particularly Baskerville, whom the Yorkist government had appointed sheriff in 1460.

While these men were pursuing Jasper, the indefatigable Queen Margaret had gathered yet another army, made up of Scots and the remnants of her followers, and crossed the border into England. Northern people seemed to pity her misfortunes, and flocked to her standard; just eight days after the mandate was issued from London commanding her to surrender herself a prisoner, she arrived near the city of York at the head of a large force. York was by far the largest and strongest city in the north of England. Richard of York was astonished to hear the news, and immediately set out with all the troops he could command, marching northwards. York left, as regent and protector, to suppress the Lancastrians in Yorkshire and the north of England. Like Jasper, they could now legally be classed as rebels. He despatched urgent orders to other Yorkist leaders across England to move to the northward as rapidly as possible.

Warwick and Norfolk stayed in London to guard the capital and the imprisoned king, while York's son Edward, Earl of March, moved to Shrewsbury and the Welsh borders to raise men against Jasper. Margaret's plan had been for Jasper to raise troops in Wales and meet her army. Edward and his Marcher councillors such as Herbert and Devereux regarded the Marches as the cornerstone of Yorkist power, and could not risk another disaster like Ludford Bridge. They needed to get rid of Jasper before they could head north to help York. Herbert, Devereux and the other local lords would probably have refused to follow Edward north, exposing their estates to looting, unless Jasper's small force was dealt with. Obviously, Yorkist agents would have alerted the Earl of March to Jasper's movements, operating from the traditional Yorkist strongholds of Ludlow and Wigmore castles. In the far south-west of Wales, at Kidwelly, they also had the Yorkist family of Dwnn.

On 16 December, at the Battle of Worksop in Nottinghamshire, York's vanguard clashed with a Lancastrian contingent from the West Country under Andrew Trollope and was defeated. York then took up a defensive position at his stronghold of Sandal Castle near Wakefield in Yorkshire, and sent a message to his son March to join him. The queen's superior force was near, but York thought he was not strong enough to attack her, and he decided to wait for expected reinforcements. It is said that the queen continually challenged the duke to come out from his walls and fortifications to meet her, and defied and derided him with many taunts and reproaches. Her army was twice as large, so York held his hand.

It may well be that the experienced veteran Andrew Trollope, who had defected to the Lancastrians at Ludford Bridge, had devised a plan to defeat York before his son could join him. It seems that half the Lancastrian army under Somerset and Clifford advanced towards Sandal Castle, over the open space known as Wakefield Green between the castle and the River Calder. The remaining army under Lord Roos and Wiltshire was hidden in the woods surrounding the area. York was probably short of provisions in the castle, and, seeing that the enemy were apparently no stronger than his own army, seized the opportunity to engage them in the open rather than withstand a siege. Somerset, Northumberland, John Neville of Raby Castle, Wiltshire, Roos and Clifford were the Lancastrian leaders. It is believed that as York engaged the Lancastrians to his front, others attacked him from the flank and rear, cutting him off from the castle. In Hall's words, 'when he was in the plain ground between his castle and the town of Wakefield, he was environed on every side, like a fish in a net, or a deer in a buckstall; so that he manfully fighting was within half an hour slain and dead, and his whole army discomfited'.

The Yorkist army was surrounded and destroyed. Of the 5,000 troops the duke had, 2,000 were left dead upon the field. York's twelve-year-old son, Rutland, attempted to escape over Wakefield Bridge, but was overtaken and killed, possibly by Clifford in revenge for his father's death at St Albans. Salisbury's fourth son, Sir Thomas Neville, died in the battle. Salisbury's son-in-law Lord Harington and Harington's father, William Bonville, were captured and executed immediately after the battle. Salisbury escaped the battlefield but was captured during the night, and was taken to the Lancastrian camp. Although the Lancastrian nobles might have allowed Salisbury to ransom himself, it is thought that he was dragged out of Pontefract Castle and beheaded by local commoners, to whom he had been a harsh overlord. It was reported that, when Lord Clifford carried the head of the Duke of York to Margaret on the point of a lance, followed by a crowd of other knights and nobles, he said to her, 'Look, madam! The war is over! Here is the ransom for the king!' After the battle, the heads of York, his son Rutland and brother-in-law Salisbury were displayed over Micklegate Bar at York, Richard of York wearing a paper crown and a sign saying 'Let York overlook the town of York'.

After this point, captured nobles were routinely executed without trial after battle. The displayed heads of the father and brother of Edward of March, and the father of the Earl of Warwick, hardened Yorkist attitudes to any captive lords thereafter. Edward, Earl of March, now became Edward, Duke of York, on his progress towards usurping the crown as Edward IV. Contemporary chroniclers relate that Edward, Earl of March, stayed at a house of friars in Shrewsbury over Christmas 1460. The *Short English Chronicle* claims that he was at Gloucester. At one of these places he heard of the death of his father, Richard of York, and his brother Edmund, Earl of Rutland. He had to avenge his father to the north, and he had to deal with Jasper Tudor to the west. If the Lancastrian forces of the queen and Jasper met, the new Duke of York faced death or exile.

6

1461, the Year of Battles: Mortimer's Cross, the Second Battle of St Albans, Ferrybridge, Towton and Twt Hill

The Act of Accord of 25 October 1460 had made Richard of York heir to Henry VI. Thus his death in battle two months later could be classed as high treason. Under the Act, Edward, now Duke of York, was next in line to the throne on Henry VI's death. Edward did not rush to avenge his father's killing. While his father had marched north to meet the royalist army, Edward had been sent to contain Jasper and the Lancastrians after the Yorkist rout at Ludlow. Edward of York was now informed by his 'scurriers' (mounted scouts who 'scoured' the countryside) that Margaret's successful army was marching south to London.

Edward was also threatened more immediately in the west by Jasper Tudor and the arrival in Pembroke of James Butler, Earl of Wiltshire and Ormond. Wiltshire was to be Jasper's second in command, bringing men from Ireland, France and Brittany. Lewys Glyn Cothi, who was with Jasper around this time, believed that Jasper had also been sent overseas to raise troops, and the *Short English Chronicle* suggests the same. It is more likely that Wiltshire, with experience of the French wars, and estates in Ireland, was responsible for bringing French and Irish support. Wiltshire was a favourite of the queen, owing his English title to her, but there had been doubts about his courage since he had fled from the First Battle of St Albans. As Lord Treasurer, Wiltshire had terrorised Newbury, a town belonging to Richard, Duke of York, who had named him, together with the Earl of Shrewsbury and Viscount Beaumont, as 'oure mortalle and extreme enemyes'. Shrewsbury and Beaumont had fallen at Northampton, from which Wiltshire was absent.

Almost immediately after Newbury's ransacking, Warwick had landed in Kent and entered London, and Wiltshire had swiftly fled to Holland. Perhaps while in Holland he received orders from the queen at Pembroke asking for French and Breton reinforcements, and to arrange for a contingent of his own men and Irish supporters to be ready at Waterford or Wexford. The pro-French Lancastrian regime was more acceptable to France than the more bellicose Yorkists, who were unwilling to abandon the Plantagenet claim to the French throne. This would account for the French, Bretons and Irish whom Wiltshire is reported to have brought via Pembroke to Mortimer's Cross.

Margaret had probably sailed from Pembroke to Scotland around mid-October 1460, accompanied by Exeter. She had entered negotiations with the Scottish queen, Mary of Guelders, widowed since the death of James II at the siege of Roxburgh Castle in August. Scotland then provided troops for Margaret's northern army, in exchange for the cession of the border towns of Roxburgh and the heavily defended Berwick. Queen Margaret ordered Somerset and Devon to bring further reinforcements from the West Country, which had joined her Lancastrian northern army at Hull, early in December 1460. While gathering Scots troops, Margaret heard of York's defeat and death at Wakefield. With her Scots soldiers, Margaret joined the Lancastrian northern army at the start of 1461 and began marching south.

At the same time, in January 1461, Jasper and Wiltshire joined forces in Wales and began to move eastwards. Yorkist intelligence reports of a foreign contingent under Wiltshire arriving at Pembroke may not have been expected, and possibly explain the tradition that Edward was taken by surprise. Jasper's army included Thomas and Owain ap Gruffydd ap Nicholas, Philip Mansel and Sir Thomas Perot, all of whom had fought in his service previously. Also alongside Jasper was his father, Owen Tudor. On 5 February 1461, Owen Tudor had been appointed parker and woodward of the lordship of Denbigh for life. Prior to his creation as a Knight Bachelor, Owen, although excused from duty, had been appointed an Esquire of the Body. An Esquire of the King's Body was one the sovereign's closest attendants and his shield bearer, expected to bear arms and fight close to the king. Years later, in order that he could command a battle of Henry VI's forces at Mortimer's Cross, Owen was made a knight banneret. It is unsure when this was conferred, as it could only be done by the king, and usually on a battlefield. A knight banneret, sometimes known simply as banneret, was 'a commoner of rank' who led a company of troops during time of war under his own banner. His banner was square-shaped, in contrast to the tapering standard or pennon flown by lower-ranking knights, and bannerets were eligible to bear supporters on their heraldic devices. The military rank was higher than that of a knight bachelor, who fought under another's banner, but was lower than an earl or duke.

Jasper's other loyal supporters included Thomas Fitzhenry (or Fitzharry) of Monington and Eton Tregoze in Herefordshire. A lawyer, Fitzhenry had been deputy-justiciar of the principality in South Wales in 1444, 1450–1451, 1453–1454 and 1457–1458. In 1451 he had been retained as a councillor by the Duke of Buckingham, and from 1452–1460 was an apprentice-at-law for the Duchy of Lancaster. In 1460–1461, he was acting as chamberlain of South Wales. Another Herefordshire ally was Sir John Scudamore of Ewyas Lacy and Kentchurch, who was accompanied by his two sons, James and Henry, and a contingent of troops. Sir John Scudamore was also MP for Herefordshire in 1445–1446 and 1449, and the county's sheriff in 1449–1450. Scudamore was several times a JP for Herefordshire, and a prominent official of the Duchy of Lancaster and the principality of South Wales. Sir John had married Maud, daughter of Gruffydd ap Nicholas of Newton, so connected with one of the most prominent families of West Wales. He was also in Jasper's service in September 1461, acting as constable of Pembroke Castle when he surrendered it.

Sir John had served at Agincourt in the retinue of Henry V, as perhaps had his brother Sir William. Sir William Scudamore also brought thirty men to join Jasper's army. Sir James and Sir Henry were sons of Sir John, and these were the four Scudamores of Kentchurch who fought for Jasper, described by Worcester as 'knights in arms in France' and 'knights for Queen Margaret'. There was another Englishman, John Throckmorton of Tewkesbury. A mainpernor of William Herbert in the sedition of 1456, he had been pardoned and had joined the court party. Jasper was also accompanied by Hopkyn ap Rhys of Gower, and, from Carmarthenshire, Lewis ap Rhys, esquire, and Hopcyn Davy, esquire, all of whom served him for some years. The bard Lewys Glyn Cothi also accompanied him. Rheinallt Gwynedd brought troops from Harlech, and others who brought men were Lewis Powys of Powisland and Hopkin Davy of Carmarthen.

Jasper's army contained men speaking five different languages; we know nothing of the numbers, quality or leadership of the foreign troops, except for Wiltshire, who 'fled the field at the start of battle' according to Worcester. Jasper's Welshmen were probably his best troops, but apart from Sir Thomas Perot of Haverfordwest and Owen Tudor, they were led by esquires of Pembroke, Carmarthen and Gower, who seem to have lacked military experience. The army began its march across Wales, presumably from Pembroke. Wiltshire's foreign troops may have been late, delayed by bad weather, which would explain the delay of nearly a month between Jasper's hearing the news of Wakefield (perhaps a week after the event) and the Battle of Mortimer's Cross. The march from Pembroke to Mortimer's Cross is only around 110 miles, around five days' march. It looks as though the invasion force arrived in Wales after the middle of January, and the news should have reached Edward in under a week.

Jasper probably marched through Carmarthen and headed up the Tywi Valley to Llandeilo and Llandovery, then took the road to Brecon in the Usk valley. From Brecon, belonging to the late Buckingham, they followed the Wye past Glasbury into Herefordshire on the Leominster road. One wonders whether Jasper wished to link with the queen's army at Coventry. It was a midwinter march, outside the normal campaigning season, requiring food for thousands of troops and followers and forage for hundreds of horses. In view of the apparent delay, Jasper had every possible reason for haste. Edward's men probably used Croft Castle as an advance base in the final stages of the campaign. Only two miles from Mortimer's Cross, it has outstanding views across north Herefordshire to the Black Mountains.

Edward's main army was possibly stationed around Wigmore Castle, four miles away, and Ludlow, ten miles away. Wigmore had not been maintained since around 1424 and the fall of the Mortimers. The Yorkists would have been mustered when Jasper was within two days' march. The tradition is that they were waiting in ambush, as recounted a century later by the Elizabethan poet Daniel:

Now is young Marche more than a Duke of York,
(For youth, love, grace, and courage make him more)
All which for fortune's favour now do work,
... Now like the Libyan lion when with pain
The weary hunter hath pursued his prey
From rocks to brakes, from thickets to the plain,
And at the point, thereon his hands to lay,
Hard-by his hopes, his eye upon his gain,
Out rushing from his den rapts all away
So comes young Marche their hopes to disappoint
Who now, were grown, so near unto the point.
... His father's death, gives more life unto wrath,
And this last valour, greatest courage hath.
And now, as for his last, his labouring worth
Works on the coast which on fair Severn lies.
Whither, when York set forward for the north,
He sent to levy other fresh supplies:
But hearing now what Wakefield hath brought forth,
Imploring aid against these injuries,
Obtains from Gloucester, Worcester, Shrewsbury,
Important powers to work his remedy;
Which he against Pembroke, and Ormond bends,
Whom Margaret now upon her victory.
With all speed possible from Wakefield sends,
With hope to have surprised him suddenly;
Wherein though she all means, all wit extends,
To the utmost reach of wary policy,
Yet nothing her avail, no plots succeed
To avert those mischiefs which the heavens decreed.
For near the Crosse christened by his own name
He crossed those mighty forces of his foes.
And with a spirit borne to eternal fame,
Their eager fighting army overthrows...

Edward had probably moved south from Shrewsbury, calling for support from the lords of the southern Marches. Among his army were Sir William Herbert, Herbert's brother Sir Richard, his half-brother Roger Vaughan of Tretower, his brother-in-law Sir Walter Devereux, Richard Croft, Henry ap Gruffydd and Sir John Lyngen of Sutton, nearly all of whom had been indicted for their part in the West Wales expedition of 1456, and several of whom had been servants of Richard of York. There were two brothers of Roger Vaughan who were not named as being at the battle (like the Dwnns) but were probably present, Watkin Vaughan of Bredwardine and Thomas Vaughan of Hergest. Edward of York had spent some years with his brother Rutland at Ludlow, so probably knew most of them well. John Milewater of Stoke Edith had been receiver for Richard of York in the Marches, and had been rewarded, like Herbert, for his neutrality at Ludford. Other veterans of the French war were Walter Mytton, of Weston-under-Lizard in Staffordshire, and Philip Vaughan, described by Worcester as captain of Hay and 'the most noble esquire of lances among all the rest'. Lord Grey of Wilton, Herefordshire, Lord Fitzwalter from Norfolk, Lord Audley from Cheshire and Humphrey Stafford of Southwick had probably accompanied Edward from London. Audley, whose father was killed at Blore Heath, and Stafford had become Yorkists recently, after being captured while serving with Somerset in his attempt to take Calais.

The Yorkist army probably contained around 5,000 local troops, a picked force of household retainers mostly raised in Herefordshire and who would naturally fight all the harder for their homes and estates. Jasper's forces seem to have been not as well armed, having little experience of battle but strengthened by foreign mercenaries. Edward, Earl of March, had been assembling men in the border shires and in the Mortimer estates in the Marches, and probably had a larger force than the collection of Welsh, Irish, Breton and French soldiers which Pembroke and Wiltshire had gathered. Members of the Dwnn family of Kidwelly either assisted March in mustering men or were themselves present at the battle, for Jasper blamed them, together with March and the Herberts, for his following defeat.

A Lancastrian attack on Wigmore and Ludlow appears to have been certain, probably after an advance from Brecon. Edward of March was probably based at the great Mortimer castle of Wigmore. The quick defeat of Jasper was the Yorkist priority, and the account in the *Brut Chronicle* records, 'And this time, the earl of March being in Shrewsbury, hearing the death of his father, desired Assistance & Aid of the town for to avenge his father's death; & from thence went to Wales, where, at Candlemass after, he had a battle at Mortimer's Cross against the earls of Pembroke & of Wiltshire.' An appendix to the chronicle refers to 'the bateyle of Wygmore'. The Lancastrians marched towards the Yorkists, meeting about four miles south of Wigmore Castle at Mortimer's Cross. Two valleys meet here at right angles. Yorkist troops, preparing their camp the day before the battle, were frightened by the appearance of three suns. This was a parhelion, appearing when the sun is rising or setting, where the sun shines through ice crystals, creating the effect of a mirror. The troops thus saw the sun twice reflected. Edward provided an explanation to his wary soldiers. The three suns represented the blessing of the Holy Trinity on another trinity, that of himself and his two young brothers, George, later Duke of Clarence (1449–1478) and Richard, later Duke of Gloucester. The 'sun in splendour' was to become Edward's favourite badge, one that showed his men that this tall and strapping eighteen-year-old was a commanding figure blessed by providence.

Shakespeare refers to the parhelion in his play *Henry VI, Part 3*:

Three glorious suns, each one a perfect sun;
Not separated with the racking clouds,
But sever'd in a pale clear-shining sky.
See, see! they join, embrace and seem to kiss,
As if they vow'd some league inviolable:
Now are they but one lamp, one light, one sun.
In this the heaven figures some event.

The battle was possibly fought on 2 February, but was more likely fought on St Blaise's Day, 3 February 1461. The *English Chronicle* tells us that

the iii day of February ... Edward the noble earl of Marche fought with the Walsshmen beside Wygmore in Wales, whose captains were the earl of Penbrook and the earl of Wylshyre, that would finally have destroyed the said earl of Marche ... And the Monday before the day of batayle, that is to say, in the feast of Purification of our blessed Lady about x at clock before noon, were seen iii suns in the firmament shining fully clear, whereof the people had great marvel, and thereof were aghast. The noble earl Edward then comforted and said, 'Be thee of good comfort, and dreadeth not; this is a good sign, for these iii suns betoken the Father, the Son, and the Holy Ghost, and therefore let us have a good heart, and in the name of Almighty God go we against our enemies.' And so by His grace, he had the victory of his enemies, and put the ii earl to flight, and slew of the Walsshemen to the number of four thousand.

There is no clear account of the battle, but it has been suggested that the Yorkists faced south with the River Lugg to their left. Guns could also have been placed here, if any were available after the systematic stripping of Yorkist castles such as Ludlow, which John Judde, Lancastrian Master of Ordnance, had been ordered to carry out after Ludford Bridge. The Yorkist army are believed to have had more archers than the Lancastrian army, and their archers' positions were recommended by Sir Richard Croft of Croft Castle nearby. They would have used the woodland and high valley walls behind them as natural cover, leaving the Lancastrians to attack below. The Yorkists were probably drawn up on foot, between the river and the bank, with their centre near the Battle Oak. We shall never know whether the Lancastrians entered a trap, as indicated by Daniel, but in their advance across open fields they would have received a storm of arrows before close combat,

The Yorkist army consisted mainly of Welshmen and men of Hereford, Edward's own supporters and retainers of the Herbert brothers. The right flank of the Yorkist army was commanded by Walter Devereux, the centre by Edward and the left flank by Sir William Herbert. The Lancastrian left flank, which included the more experienced and professional mercenaries, was under the command of Wiltshire, the centre under Pembroke and the right flank under the joint command of Owen Tudor and Sir John Throckmorton. Wiltshire was said to have begun hostilities by advancing on the York right wing, which was pushed back and scattered. However, Worcester commented that Wiltshire 'fled the field at the start of the battle'. Jasper advanced on the Yorkist centre, commanded by Edward, and both sides fought for some time, before the Yorkists began to gain ground and the Lancastrians broke and scattered westward. Owen Tudor attempted to encircle the Yorkists, but in doing so exposed his left flank to Herbert's forces.

Herbert ordered his men to advance towards Owen's forces, who could offer little resistance. Owen tried to rally his troops, but they broke and scattered. It was clear that, despite possibly losing the early stages of the battle on their right wing, the Yorkists looked set for victory. The Yorkist archers now began shooting volleys of arrows into the Lancastrian cavalry, causing their centre to collapse. Realising the day was lost, Jasper fled the field. Wiltshire had already disappeared. Owen may have staged a fighting retreat to Hereford, where he was taken.

There is a story recounted by Simons that Owen was taken by Edward while leading the 'men of Morgannoc' to the battle. He was imprisoned at Usk Castle. The 'chieftains of his clan', led by John ap Meredydd, a kinsman, came to rescue him, but on their way were attacked in a field beside Caerleon by a greatly superior force. There were but a hundred of them. John ordered one son from each family to the rear, so that at least one member of each should have a chance of escape, but made his own sons charge with him in the front rank. They swept the superior force from the field, and in revenge for this defeat Owen was taken to Hereford marketplace and beheaded. It may be that there was a skirmish at Caerleon before or after the main battle, and the details may be confused.

A story told by Flavell Edmunds in an anonymous guide to Leominster from 1808 is that Jasper sent troops on to Leominster to reinforce a Lancastrian garrison already there. They then drove Yorkist detachments away, but were themselves dislodged while battle was raging at Mortimer's Cross, and were driven back to Kingsland to join the routed main army. It is very doubtful whether Jasper would have divided his army so deep inside hostile country. It is also unlikely there were royalist troops in Leominster, an unwalled monastery town. Blue Mantle Cottage stands next to the battlefield and gives weight to the rumours that Edward's herald, the Bluemantle Pursuivant, was slain during attempts to hold peace talks before the battle.

Local folklore says that the River Lugg ran red with the blood of the massacred Welshmen. Tradition suggests that some fled past Covenhope to the Lugg, only to be pursued and massacred when cornered at a river gorge near Kinsham, where we see the names Slaughterhouse Covert and Bank. Evidence collected by Brooke makes it probable that some sort of last stand was made somewhere near Battle Acre, bearing out the Rowlandson-Edmunds account of a second battle. The battle monument is a mile from the site of the main battle, and uses the words 'near this spot'. This could well have been where Owen Tudor, Throckmorton, Scudamore and other royalist captains may have been taken prisoner. Jasper, Wiltshire, Perot, Sir John, Sir William and Sir James Scudamore all escaped, though James was killed later that year 'at a Herefordshire manor house'. Many of the dead soldiers slain on the battlefields now lie buried in a field just south of Mortimer's Cross known as the Clamp.

In such a murderous struggle, with axe, mace, sword, glaive and brown bill hewing and slashing, the Irish would have suffered particularly badly; according to the Elizabethan poet Michael Drayton, they were in the vanguard:

> The Earl of Ormond ...
> Came in the vanguard with his Irishmen,
> With darts and skains; those of the British blood,
> With shafts and gleaves, them seconding again,
> And as they fall still make their places good,
> That it amaz'd the Marchers to behold
> Men so ill-armed, upon their bowes so bold.

About 4,000 men were killed, mostly Lancastrians. One account is that Yorkists pursued the fleeing Lancastrians all the way to Hereford, where, after a brief skirmish, Owen Tudor and the remaining Lancastrian captains were captured. Owen was held prisoner in the coaching inn that is now the Green Dragon Hotel. He was led to the block in Hereford marketplace by Roger Vaughan of Tretower. Owen was the first person upon whom Edward could avenge his brother Rutland and his father's death. It is said that Owen expected to receive amnesty because of his relationship with the royal family. He apparently was not convinced of his approaching death until his collar was ripped off his doublet by the executioner. Tradition has it that his final words were, 'This head which used to lie in Queen Catherine's lap would now lie in the executioner's basket.' Owen took his approaching death 'meekly' and was beheaded at the marketplace at Hereford on 4 February. According to *Gregory's Chronicle*, a mad woman set his head on top of the market cross, combed his hair, washed away the blood from his face and put more than 100 candles around his head. Owen was buried in the Grey Friars church. The bard Robin Ddu makes a touching allusion to the death of Owen and then turns his hopes to Jasper, whom he styles Owen, and refers to thusly: '*Draig wen ddibarch yn gwarchae, / A draig goch a dyr y cae*' – 'the dishonourable white dragon has triumphed, / But the red dragon will yet win the field'.

Ieuan Gethin (*c.* 1400 – *c.* 1480) of Baglan, Glamorgan, sang the praises of Owen Tudor in a cywydd when Tudor was imprisoned in Newgate between 1437 and 1439. When Tudor was beheaded at Hereford in 1461, Ieuan bitterly lamented the last *mab darogan* to bear the name of Owain, after the assassination of Owain Lawgoch and the disappearance of Owain Glyndŵr. However, he still raised hopes for a future deliverer from the French conquerors:

Er clybod darfod â dur
Newid hoedl Owain Tudur,
Gwilio Siasbar a Harri,
Ei ŵyr a'i fab, yr wyf i

Although it is said that giving up steel
Changed the life of Owen Tudor
To keep watching out for his son and grandson
Jasper and Henry, I will.

Sir John Throckmorton, born around 1414, of Coughton, Warwickshire, was the most notable of between eight and thirteen Lancastrian captains beheaded alongside Owain. David Lloyd and Morgan ap Rhydderch were also executed. Some sources state that Gruffydd ap Nicholas was present with his sons, and that he was killed in battle. It is certain that there escaped several of those whose names are given as having been either beheaded or captured. For instance, Phillip Mansel, Hopkyn ap Rhys of Gower, and Lewis ap Rhys of Strata Florida were in the field again a few years after these events. Sir John Scudamore later held Pembroke Castle against Sir William Herbert, and the two sons of Griffith ap Nicholas also found safety in flight. Philip Mansel was said to have been killed despite surviving, although two of his sons were also killed in the wars, Leonard being killed on 21 May 1471 and John being killed in 1465. Hall, copying Stow, says that David Lloyd and Morgan ap Rhydderch were put to death. David Lloyd was probably the same who, for his services in the French wars, had been made a royal official in the forest of Glyn Cothi, Carmarthenshire, in 1444.

Worcester named none of Edward's companions as having been killed, though he remarks that Philip Vaughan was later killed at the siege of Harlech Castle. The main Yorkist casualty may have been Watkin (Watcyn) Vaughan of Bredwardine, the son of Roger Vaughan and Gwladys, mentioned by the bard Hywel Swrdal. He was killed by an arrow either at Hereford or Mortimer's Cross. He had married Elizabeth, daughter of Sir Henry Wogan, and had at least fifteen children. One of them, William Vaughan of Rhydhelig, the second son, slew the Earl of Warwick, the 'Kingmaker', when the earl was trying to escape from the battle at Barnet in 1471. Vaughan was regarded as the supreme champion on the battlefield after the death of his uncle Thomas ap Roger of Hergest. He was also constable of Aberystwyth castle.

The other notable escapee besides Jasper was James Butler, 5th Earl of Ormonde and Earl of Wiltshire (1420–1461). In 1455 he had been appointed Lord High Treasurer of England, and shortly afterwards fought for the king at St Albans, when, with the Yorkists prevailing, he fled, casting his armour into a ditch. William Gregory's *Chronicle* noted that, after Wiltshire deserted the royal standard at the First Battle of St Albans, 'he fought mainly with his heels for he was called the most handsome knight in the land and was afraid of losing his beauty'. Wiltshire was thereafter known as 'the flying earl'. At Wakefield in December 1460, he had commanded a wing of the army which enclosed and slew the Duke of York. After fleeing Mortimer's Cross, he was taken prisoner having fled Towton, being beheaded at Newcastle on 1 May in the following year.

Mirehouse recounts that

> after the battle of Mortimer's Cross in 1461, Thomas ap Gruffudd, the leader of the Welsh, retired with his younger son Rhys to Burgundy, where young Rhys was brought up and educated; when they returned later to Wales, he was in consequence a soldier and a gentleman, very different from his half-savage brothers, who had never stirred from home. Thomas ap Gruffudd was murdered after his return to Wales, and Rhys ap Thomas became the head of the house. Being a man of sound judgment and broad views, he made friends with the English, and took Carew Castle on mortgage from Sir Edmund Carew, who was going abroad. Lord William Herbert had now become Earl of Huntingdon instead of Pembroke, and Edward IV had granted the latter to his young son. Prince Edward, so there was no one there on the spot to rival Rhys ap Thomas, Lord of Carew. Rhys married Eva, the heiress of Court Henry. After the death of Edward V (Earl of Pembroke), 1483, a boy of thirteen, who only reigned two months, Rhys swore fealty to Richard III, the Hunchback, in 1484.

Rhys was to switch allegiance the following year to Henry Tudor.

After their victory, the Yorkists spent over two weeks at Hereford. Patrols chased the enemy into Wales, probably looking for Jasper and Wiltshire. Lewys Glyn Cothi addressed an ode to Jasper Tudor, when the bard was in concealment: *I Maredydd Amharedydd o Drefeglwys, Pan Oedd y Barrd as Herw o Achaws Siasper Iarll Penvro*. The poem, addressed to Meredith son of Meredith, of Trefeglwys in Montgomeryshire, was probably written shortly after Jasper was defeated at Mortimer's Cross. The bard, like his master Jasper, was obliged to live in concealment, flying from place to place, hiding himself in mountains and forests. In the poem he gives a vivid description of the places of his concealment, and how he finally arrived at Maredydd's mansion, where he met both a welcome reception and a kind protector. Lewys was not only in hiding with Jasper, but also with Owen ap Gruffudd ap Nicholas, the brother of Thomas, who escaped to Burgundy.

This was the first victory for Edward, and showed the Lancastrians that the new Duke of York was a man to be feared. Jasper had escaped from the field in disguise, and shortly afterwards is found writing letters from Tenby in an attempt to rally resistance in North Wales. Fresh troops were raised by York, and other preparations made for his advance to London. Soon after the battle Edward was given a commission by the Privy Council to raise fresh levies in Warwick, Bristol and the border counties, having in the meantime moved on to Gloucester. On 12 February 1460, Warwick wished York to array the men of all the shires from Stafford to Dorset. Warwick knew that Jasper's army was beaten, freeing York to raise fresh forces, and he feared Margaret's fast advance on London. Warwick himself raised an army from London, Kent and East Anglia and headed north to face the Lancastrians. It was on the day of Edward's commission that Warwick moved from London to St Albans. Warwick took with him the king, hearing that the northern army was nearing London. Margaret had begun her southward march before news of Jasper's defeat had reached her.

At St Albans, Warwick blocked roads and built an elaborate series of fortifications, caltrops and pavises. A caltrop is literally a foot trap, made up of two or more sharp nails or spines arranged in such a manner that one of them always points upward from a stable base. They served to slow the advance of both horses and troops, as stepping on one could incapacitate its victim. Pavises are heavy oblong shields, not carried but set up to protect the whole body. He assumed personal command of the centre, and Norfolk and Warwick's brother John Neville, later Lord Montagu, led the right and left battles, what we would call divisions today. A contingent of archers was directed to hold the town. Warwick attempted to cover as much ground as possible and his line extended over four miles. Lacking sufficient men for a front this long, he intended for each part of his army to hold back any attack until the other two wings could join the fighting.

Queen Margaret was aided by Sir Andrew Trollope, and they were greatly assisted by information from a Yorkist captured at Wakefield, Sir Henry Lovelace. He had been released to rejoin Warwick upon the promise that he would both provide intelligence and switch allegiance at the appropriate time. He may have been promised the earldom of Kent. Knowing Warwick's strategy, the Lancastrians headed west and took Dunstable on 16 February 1461. Trollope then advised Margaret that the army should march south-east in the night, to turn Warwick's position at St Albans. The Lancastrians completed their unexpected night march with minimal confusion, and Trollope led advance units forward against St Albans the following morning. Pressing up Fishpool Street, they were forced to retreat due to a hail of arrows from the Yorkist archers. After a subsequent attack failed, Trollope, recognising that the Yorkist archers were unsupported, led a force around to the north-west and cut them off from the rest of Warwick's army. Throughout the rest of the morning the Lancastrians fought house-to-house, beginning to overwhelm the Yorkists. As the fighting raged, Montagu did not support his brother as he believed the Lancastrian attacks to be mere diversions in support of a major enemy effort from the north. At last realising the severity of the situation, he turned his battle south and prepared to fight the Lancastrians.

Around noon, Trollope and Somerset began assaults on Montagu's position on Bernards Heath. Under severe pressure, Montagu's men held their position as their commander sent desperate messages to Warwick calling for aid. However, Warwick himself was not convinced that this was a main attack, held his position and withheld reinforcements. Thus the forces of both Warwick and Montagu were worn down by superior numbers as each failed to support his brother. As the afternoon passed, Warwick finally understood Montagu's position and directed his men to move down the Sandridge Road to assist Montagu. He was met with resistance from his commanders as some felt that the army had already been defeated and further fighting was meaningless. Others, such as Sir Henry Lovelace, the steward of Warwick's own household, were possibly intent on more treachery. On Bernards Heath, the Lancastrians finally succeeded in breaking the Yorkist lines, causing Montagu's men to flee. Pressing south, Warwick's men engaged the advancing enemy but Lovelace's Kentish contingent may have then defected. However, Lovelace's 'defection' may have been an excuse given by Warwick for his defeat, as Lovelace was never attainted by Edward IV. With dusk, Warwick realised the fight was lost and ordered a retreat towards Chipping Norton. Exhausted from the night march and a day of fighting, the Lancastrians decided not to pursue.

While casualties for the Second Battle of St Albans are not known, it is estimated that the Lancastrians suffered around 2,000 losses while the Yorkists incurred around 4,000. The most prominent casualty was the Lancastrian John Grey of Groby, whose widow, Elizabeth Woodville, was to marry Edward IV. Following the battle, Henry VI was recovered and his guards, including Lord Bonville and Sir Thomas Kyriel, were captured and executed despite his protestations. The two lords had kept guard over the king during the battle to see that he came to no harm, and in return for their gallantry the king promised the two men immunity. However, Queen Margaret, who was present at the battle, remembered that Lord Bonville had been one of the men who had held Henry in custody after Northampton in July 1460, and wanted revenge. Disregarding the king's promise of immunity, she gave orders for the beheading of Bonville and Kyriel the next day, 18 February 1461. It is alleged that she put the men on trial and had her seven-year-old son, Prince Edward of Westminster, presiding as judge. The boy allegedly said that they were to have their heads cut off. The Lancastrian commander Andrew Trollope, who had been injured by stepping on a caltrop, was knighted by Prince Edward, a month after the seemingly decisive Lancastrian victory. This delay can only have been due to his humble birth, for he was described by the near-contemporary Burgundian Jean de Waurin as '*un très soubtil homme de guerre*' and by another chronicler as '*Magno capitaneo et quasi ductore belli*', highly positive comments. Trollope joked with the little prince that, because he had been immobilised by a wound, he did not deserve to be knighted 'for I slew but fifteen men, for I stood still in one place and they came unto me, but they still bode with me'. His importance to the Lancastrian cause can be seen by the fact that in March 1461, the newly proclaimed Edward IV offered a £100 reward to anyone who killed 'certain named enemies of the House of York', a list which included Trollope.

The queen now marched towards London to repudiate the political settlement of the parliament of 1460. However, as Abbott explains, the Lancastrian army was refused admission owing to the citizens' well-founded fears of looting and ultimately withdrew north:

> A large meeting of the city refused her entry and she withdrew to Yorkshire, while the gates of London were thrown open to March and Warwick … in order to obtain money to defray the expenses of her army and to provide them with food, she made requisitions upon the towns through which she passed, and otherwise harassed the people of the country by fines and confiscations. The people were at length so exasperated by these high-handed proceedings, and by the furious and vindictive spirit which Margaret manifested in all that she did, that the current turned altogether in favour of the young Duke of York. The scattered forces of his party were reassembled. They began soon to assume so formidable an appearance that Margaret found it would be best for her to retire toward the north again. She of course took with her the king and the Prince of Wales.

The queen had London at her mercy, but hesitated mainly because the king did not wish to attack it. As Henry was unwilling to enter London by force, negotiations began between Margaret and the council. Apart from the extremely hostile attitude of the Londoners, the difficulty in keeping discipline in her Scottish soldiers and the news that Edward and Warwick were marching towards London, Margaret now learned that Edward had defeated Jasper and was uniting with the remnants of Warwick's army. Concerned about this threat, the Lancastrians began withdrawing northwards to a defensible line along the River Aire in Yorkshire. From here they could await reinforcements from the north.

Warwick, having escaped westwards with the remnants of his army, met Edward five days later on 22 February at Chipping Norton, or at Burford, in Oxfordshire. Edward was accompanied by William Hastings and John Wenlok, who possibly joined him after the battle at Mortimer's Cross, as they are not reported to have been fighting there. Edward of York's absence from St Albans is curious. Edward had possibly received information of Margaret's approach on 28 January, the day on which commissions were issued in the king's name to noblemen and sheriffs to raise troops. Margaret reached St Albans before Edward had left the Marches, so it seems that Edward delayed marching to Warwick's assistance. He could easily have reached London, where there was much support for the House of York. Instead he spent nine days in Hereford after victory on 3 February, moving to Gloucester on 12 February. Edward delayed yet another week at Gloucester, where, around 18 February, he learned of Warwick's defeat at St Albans on the previous day. Three days later, Edward had only reached the outskirts of Oxfordshire, meeting the defeated Warwick on 22 February. It may well be that he wanted Warwick out of the way. Warwick had stood in the way of Edward's father, Richard of York, taking the crown, and Edward's victory at Mortimer's Cross wiped out the defeats at Wakefield and St Albans, giving him a significant sense of destiny. Ten years later, before Tewkesbury, Edward covered forty miles a day. To help Warwick he had covered less than forty miles in three weeks.

Edward reached London on 26 February 1461, where the citizens' enthusiasm for 'thys fayre whyte ros and herbe, the Erle of Marche' was unbounded. Many joined Edward's mainly Welsh army in St John's Fields, Clerkenwell, and, under the guidance of the chancellor, George Neville, the people and army proclaimed Edward king upon 1 March. Two days later, the Yorkist leaders met at Baynard's Castle and formally offered Edward the crown. He was next proclaimed king on 4 March before the Chancellor, George Neville; Archbishop Bourchier; the Bishop of Salisbury; the Duke of Norfolk; Warwick; Lord Fitzwalter (Sir John Ratcliffe); Walter Devereux (Lord Ferrers of Chartley); and Sir William Herbert. It is noticeable that special reference was made to Herbert as one of the 'chosen and faithful' of Edward. He had certainly replaced Warwick as Edward's right-hand man and chief advisor, and Warwick began to grow disenchanted with the many favours granted to Herbert.

Warwick had wanted an end to the queen's court party and the king's favourites, not for the House of York to claim the throne. Warwick did not want a change of regime, but a better regime. Edward had told Warwick of his appreciation of the services of his friends from the Marches. On meeting with Warwick in Oxfordshire, he had referred to them as men who had come 'at their own cost'. Edward's defeat of Jasper gave him the confidence to take the kingship, following the triple-sun omen of divine favour, 'for which cause, men imagined, that he gave the sun in his full brightness for his cognisance or badge'. He no longer needed Warwick – he had Herbert and Devereux.

Jasper Tudor had probably ridden to Pembroke Castle and then Tenby Castle, and on 25 February 1461, three weeks after Mortimer's Cross, he wrote to his men Pulestor and Eyton at Denbigh Castle, exhorting them to be faithful and to prepare to avenge the beheading of Jasper's father, Owen. The letter was written from Tenby (spelling modernised):

To the right-trusty and well-beloved Roger à Puleston, and to John Eyton, and to either of them. Right-trusty and well-beloved Cousins and friends, we greet you well. And suppose that ye have well in your remembrance the great dishonour and rebuke that we and ye now late have by traitors March, Herbert, and Dunns, with their affinities, as well in letting us of our Journey to the King, as in putting my father your Kinsman to the death, and their traitorously demeaning, we purpose with the might of our Lord, and assistance of you and other our kinsmen & friends, within short time to avenge. Trusting verily that ye will be well-willed and put your hands unto the same, and of your disposition, with your good advice therein we pray you to ascertain us in all hast possible, as our especial trust is in you. Written at our town of Tenbye the xxvth of February. PEMBROKE.

Sir John ap Elis Eyton was later rewarded for fighting at Bosworth with estates around Rhiwabon (Ruabon), and his monumental effigy, one of the best in Wales, can be seen in St Mary's church. His collar is marked 'SS' to signify his bravery, and Henry VII awarded him an annuity of ten marks 'in consideration of the time and faithful service performed for us ... in the course of our triumphal victory'.

The letter shows that Jasper blamed the Herberts, Dunns (Dwnns) and their kinsmen, like the Vaughans, for his defeat. Similar letters or personal messengers would have been sent to Jasper's allies and associates across Wales in an attempt to avenge his loss. He would want to discover the extent and consolidate the strength of Lancastrian support, to hopefully bring down the new usurper king. Jasper's great servant Roger Puleston served him faithfully through the wars, and before had served Edmund; on 19 September 1456, Edmund had written him a letter (in abbreviated mediaeval Latin) granting an annuity of 10 marks for his services. Another letter from Jasper Tudor commits Flint Castle to Puleston's custody, probably a few days after Mortimer's Cross.

As soon as he was crowned, Edward made preparations to head north and crush the Lancastrian army, leaving London upon 11 March. His army was made up of three groups, under Warwick, Warwick's uncle William Neville, Lord Fauconberg, and the king. In addition, John Mowbray, Duke of Norfolk, was sent to the eastern counties to raise more men. As the Yorkists approached, Henry Beaufort, Duke of Somerset, left Henry VI, Margaret and Prince Edward at York and deployed his Lancastrian army between the villages of Saxton and Towton. On 27 March, Warwick's vanguard forced a crossing of the river at Ferrybridge, using planks to fill the gaps in a bridge that the Lancastrians had destroyed. Warwick lost many men in the freezing winter water and to the frequent hail of arrows coming from a small Lancastrian force on the other bank. Once the crossing was managed, the Lancastrians retreated. Warwick now had his men properly repair the bridge, while camp was established on the north side of the River Aire.

Very early the next morning, this Yorkist vanguard was ambushed by 500 Lancastrians under John Neville and Lord Clifford. Completely surprised and confused, Warwick's forces suffered many casualties. Lord Fitzwalter, Warwick's second in command at camp, was mortally wounded while trying to rally his men, dying in agony a week later. Warwick was himself injured by an arrow in the leg, and his half-brother 'the Bastard of Salisbury' was killed while retreating. Perhaps 3,000 men died in the fighting. Hearing news of the battle, Edward arrived with his main army and found the bridge again ruined. Edward organised a counterattack, asking Warwick to attack Ferrybridge. To support Warwick's advance, Fauconberg was ordered to cross the river four miles upstream at Castleford, from where he advanced and attacked Lord Clifford's right flank. While Warwick's assault was largely held, Clifford was forced to fall back when Fauconberg arrived. In a running fight, the Lancastrians were defeated and Clifford was killed near Dinting Dale, in sight of the main Lancastrian army. Clifford was killed by an arrow in the throat, having removed the piece of armour that should have protected this area of his body. It seems that he needed to drink from the stream during a lull in the fighting. Warwick's reputation suffered again in Edward's eyes.

Edward's army had been relatively small leaving London, but was said to be huge upon arrival a few weeks later at Towton, near Ferrybridge. As a recognised, officially crowned king, Edward could now recruit under commissions of array. To refuse his call to the king's standard was a treasonable offence, punishable by death. Recruitment was rigorously enforced, from the great barons and magnates down to local Crown officials. The official 'Crown down' feudal system had also been distorted by defensive baronial alliances into 'bastard feudalism', a system of retainers which encouraged the raising of armed men by the nobility and gentry. It was enforced by captains riding across the country to call in subordinates, who themselves recruited on a 'pyramid' basis on large estates that crossed county barriers. It was one's duty to take up arms, or one's lands and offices could be confiscated and one's life put at risk. It was a difficult time for allegiances. Two competing kings were now recruiting, and men had to quickly make difficult choices. The numbers recruited on both sides for Towton were massive, because each side made an extra effort to be seen as the 'real' king's party.

Edward advanced across the River Aire the morning after Ferrybridge, although Norfolk's army had not arrived. The Welsh foot soldiers who had triumphed at Mortimer's Cross, reinforced by the levies of Kent, constituted the nucleus of the Yorkist army. Waurin states that the Lancastrian army comprised a large body of Welshmen who, led by Andrew Trollope, displayed great bravery in a blinding snowstorm. However, there would actually have been few Lancastrian Welshmen, as Jasper's army had been smashed at Mortimer's Cross only a few weeks previously. If any Welshmen were arrayed against Edward at Towton, they may have been raised either by Margaret, when she sought refuge in Wales after Northampton, or by Exeter and others as they passed from the West Country along the borders of Wales towards Wakefield.

The Lancastrians intended to hold up an exhausted and starving Yorkist army on the River Aire, about eight miles to the south of York, their intended target, and protected their rear from an outflanking manoeuvre by destroying the bridges over the River Cock north-west of Towton and over the River Wharfe at Tadcaster. Somerset deployed the Lancastrians on a high plateau, with its right protected by the stream of the Cock Beck. He had a strong position and a numerical advantage, but there was an extremely strong facing wind. A blizzard blew snow into his soldiers' eyes, hampering visibility. Edward IV's maternal uncle, William Neville, Lord Fauconberg (*c.* 1410–1463), ordered his archers to fire continuously into the opposing ranks, while their blinded opponents shot volley after volley short of the enemy. Lancastrian arrows were picked up from the ground by the intended victims and shot back again. Assisted by the fierce wind, Yorkist arrows caused thousands of casualties, giving a greater range of up to fifty yards. The Anglo-Welsh archers, so successful at Crécy (1346) and Agincourt (1415), were devastatingly effective against these 'naked men', so called because of their lack of effective defensive equipment. With men falling all around him, Somerset was forced to leave his defensive position on the hill and ordered his men to attack, crying 'King Henry!' The Lancastrians, by force of numbers, slowly began pushing the Yorkists back. On the Lancastrian right, its cavalry succeeded in driving off the Yorkist cavalry, but Edward quickly shifted troops to block the advance. Edward, a giant of a man, raced around the battlefield urging on his men at this crucial juncture. As the battle raged, the blizzard worsened, with several impromptu truces called to clear the dead and wounded from between the lines. Edward was probably going to be defeated and killed, but Norfolk's army arrived soon after noon. Joining Edward's right, his army slowly began to turn the battle.

Now dangerously outflanked, Somerset shifted men from his right and centre to meet the threat, but Norfolk's fresh troops began to push back the Lancastrian right as the soldiers were becoming exhausted. Finally the line broke, Norfolk's men poured through and the entire Lancastrian army collapsed into full retreat. Men fled north in an attempt to cross the Cock Beck. At the river a small timber bridge quickly collapsed, and men stumbled across on a bridge of bodies. Urging his cavalry forward, Edward pursued the Lancastrian remnants as they retreated to York. Somerset, Exeter, Devonshire, Wiltshire, Beaumont, Hungerford and Fitzhugh, with many Lancastrian knights, escaped on horseback, while their foot soldiers were cut down. The chase continued all night and for part of the next day. Defeated foot soldiers were normally left alone in these wars, with the nobility targeted instead, but in this battle there may have been a sea change in strategy. It's possible that the loss at Ferrybridge, combined with Warwick's desire for revenge and known bloodlust, contributed to the death toll. The head of Warwick's father, and the heads of Edward's father and brother, were on display nearby at York, which again may have led to increased violence from the Yorkists. The Croyland Chronicler related that the blood of the slain lay caked with snow, which then covered the ground, and that afterwards, when the snow melted, the blood flowed along the furrows and ditches for a distance of two or three miles.

Sir Andrew Trollope was killed – 'a damaging blow' as he was a superb tactician for the Lancastrians – and was posthumously attainted. His son, Sir David Trollope, also died in battle. The Earl of Northumberland, a first cousin of Edward, was killed and buried in the north choir of St Denys's church at York, probably with his brother Sir Richard Percy. The body of Lord Welles was taken to Methley, and buried in the Waterton Chapel. Lord Dacre was buried, with his horse, in Saxton churchyard, where there is a monument to his memory. The dead soldiers were at first buried in five great pits on the battlefield, and in separate graves in the valley.

Casualties are not known, although some sources indicate they may have been as high as 28,000. Others estimate losses around 20,000, with 15,000 for Somerset and 5,000 for Edward. The largest battle fought in Britain, Towton was a decisive victory for Edward and effectively secured his crown. Hall stated that no quarter was given, but some Lancastrians were wounded or made prisoners, and Polydore Vergil says that some were cured and some died. The death count seems to indicate that killings continued after defeat. A chronicler was in no doubt about Edward's intentions of giving 'no quarter': 'He made proclamation that no prisoner should be taken, nor one enemy saved.' The vendettas resulting from six bloody battles in the previous eighteen months explain the merciless treatment of the Lancastrian knights and nobles at Towton, but do not account for the brutality of the predominantly Southern Yorkist soldiery against their Northern Lancastrian opponents. There must have been a central order – surviving troops would have been exhausted and would have preferred to rest, get warm and celebrate than spend hours chasing fellow countrymen.

For 75,000 men to fight and 28,000 to die on one day demonstrates the brutality of the 'biggest, longest, bloodiest battle on English soil'. Chroniclers agreed that the battle was fought from early morning to late afternoon, followed by a pursuit and rout off the battlefield from Towton to Tadcaster and ten more miles to York, lasting through the night. The devastation of the opening arrow storm was joined in the engagement itself by the ferocious power of the weapons of the trained men-at-arms, such as the hand-and-a-half sword and the poleaxe. In the rout, the mace and well-named 'horseman's hammer' were used on the unprotected heads and backs of men trying to run for their lives.

Escaping Lancastrian nobles only had time to ride through York, stopping to quickly mount Henry, Margaret and Prince Edward. They then rode out of Bootham Gate and through forests and over moors to take refuge in Scotland. Margaret, along with the king and child and a small retinue of attendants, stopped a short time at Alnwick Castle. However, upon finding that her enemies were gathering strength and advancing, and that the country was becoming more disposed to yield allegiance to the new king, she crossed the frontier into Scotland. The queen was again a fugitive and an exile, apparently with no hope of ever being able to enter England again. However, the indefatigable Margaret later left Henry and her young son in Scotland to again seek aid in France and Burgundy.

1. Jasper Tudor and his wife from stained-glass windows in Cardiff Castle.

2, 3 & 4. The coats of arms of Owen Tudor, Edmund Tudor and Jasper Tudor respectively. Jasper and Edmund were given the arms of England, quartered lions and lilies, by Henry VI with the augmentation of a border. Though very similar, on closer viewing the coats of arms of Jasper and Edmund are different – to distinguish the brothers, while Jasper's arms had the addition of *a bordure azure with martlets or* (a blue border featuring golden martlets), for Edmund the martlets were alternated with the lilies of France in honour of the firstborn of Catherine of Valois. The martlets were a device used by their father, Owen Tudor.

Opposite: 5. Jasper Tudor's mother, Catherine of Valois (1401–1437), the daughter of Charles VI of France. Here she is marrying her first husband, Henry V (1386–1422), on 2 June 1420. He died young, never seeing his infant son, Henry VI. Catherine later married Jasper's father, Owen Tudor.

Here shewes howe kyng Henry the vth was solempnely maried
to Dame kathn the kynge doughter of ffraunce

6. Pembroke town walls and castle were repaired by Jasper Tudor. The walls run almost two miles around a narrow peninsula in which the town lies, with the castle at its tip. Remains include four of the six flanking towers and one of the three gatehouses. Barnard's Tower is the most complete survivor, overlooking the great mill pond.

7. Pembroke Castle from the air. The double-towered Great Gatehouse is on the left, with the Henry VII Tower the first guard tower on the left of it. The domed, circular Great Keep is seventy-five feet high, with walls twenty feet thick at its base. The castle and its earldom were granted to Jasper Tudor in 1452.

8. Caldicot Castle, Castell Cil-y-Coed, one of Jasper's castles and the place where Henry VII was said to have been conceived. It was held by the House of Lancaster and Katherine of Valois, Jasper's mother, before being taken over by the Herberts when Jasper was in exile.

9. Reconstruction of Henry Tudor's birth in the guard tower on 28 January 1457 at Pembroke Castle. This is a small room in the east end of a guard tower in the outer wall, which in Leland's time contained a 'chymmeney new made with the arms and badges of King Henry VII'. It is known as the 'Queen's Nursery' in the Henry VII Tower.

10. This painting by Edwin Austin Abbey depicts a scene from Shakespeare's *Richard III*, where the hump-backed villain brazenly tries to woo the Lady Anne Neville, the widow of Prince Edward, who he killed.

11. Henry VII and his queen, Elizabeth of York, in stained glass at Cardiff Castle.

12. Margaret Beaufort was Jasper Tudor's sister-in-law.

13. Castell Carreg Cennen was the site of several battles in the Wars of the Roses, between Edmund and Jasper and their Yorkist enemies. It was surrendered by Thomas and Owain, the sons of Gruffydd ap Nicholas, in May 1462 to Richard Herbert and Roger Vaughan. Slighted, it is still an imposing ruin.

14. Henry VI was Jasper Tudor's half-brother, responsible for Jasper's accession to the earldom of Pembroke. Jasper was to fight for his cause from 1455 until the king's murder in 1471.

15. Ludlow Castle was the centre of Yorkist power and the administrative centre for the Welsh Marches. It was from here that Jasper supervised the Marches and Wales during the infancy of Arthur, Prince of Wales.

16. Tenby Walls – in December 1457 Jasper granted the walls and moat of Tenby to its mayor, burgesses and freemen forever, empowering them to make the improvements they suggested, and undertook to bear half the cost of all works on the wall himself. The walls were thus widened to at least six feet thick at all points, providing a continuous platform for the defenders, while the town's moat was cleaned and made thirty feet wide throughout. One additional tower was built, while existing towers and many of the parapets were raised in height as well.

17. Ludford Bridge led to the Broad Gate, the only survivor of Ludlow's seven medieval gateways. The thirteenth-century drum towers and the portcullis arch survive. In 1459, the Yorkist army surrendered after its leaders fled.

18. View in the morning mist from Wigmore Castle, the great stronghold of the Mortimers in the Marches, where Edward IV stayed before the Battle of Mortimer's Cross in 1461.

19. Battlefield site at Mortimer's Cross, taken from the bridge over the Lugg. The Lancastrians did not wish to fight but were forced to as they wished to cross the river and join Margaret's northern army. Some 4,000 out of 9,000 men who fought are said to have died.

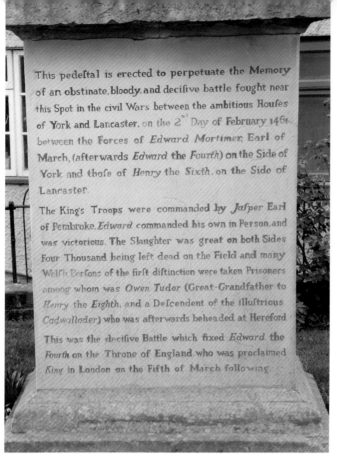

This pedeftal is erected to perpetuate the Memory of an obftinate, bloody, and decifive battle fought near this Spot in the civil Wars between the ambitious Houfes of York and Lancaster, on the 2ⁿᵈ Day of February 1461 between the Forces of *Edward Mortimer*, Earl of March, (afterwards *Edward the Fourth*) on the Side of York and thofe of *Henry* the *Sixth*, on the Side of Lancaster.

The King's Troops were commanded by *Jafper* Earl of Pembroke, *Edward* commanded his own in Person, and was victorious. The Slaughter was great on both Sides Four Thousand being left dead on the Field and many Welfh Perfons of the firft diftinction were taken Prisoners among whom was *Owen Tudor* (Great-Grandfather to *Henry* the *Eighth*, and a Defcendent of the illuftrious *Cadwallader*) who was afterwards beheaded at Hereford

This was the decifive Battle which fixed *Edward* the *Fourth* on the Throne of England who was proclaimed *King* in London on the Fifth of March following.

20. Memorial monument at Mortimer's Cross, near the battlefield, erected in 1799. The battle was fought in the River Lugg's water meadows between here and Kingsland.

21. Harlech Castle, one of Edward I's 'Iron Ring of Castles'. The World Heritage Site, which was then lapped by the sea, held out for seven years against various sieges and attacks from 1461 to 1468.

22. Twt Hill in 1461 was the scene of the defeat of Jasper in 1468. It is a small hill, the site of a previous battle outside the walls of Caernarfon Castle, where Glyndŵr unfurled his golden lion flag for the first time in 1401.

23. Chepstow Castle, showing the lower bailey from Marten's Tower. After hearing of the defeat at Tewkesbury in 1471, Jasper returned here. In the lower bailey he may have beheaded Sir Roger Vaughan, who had been sent to kill him.

24. Tretower Court Main Hall – this fortified manor house alongside Tretower Castle was renovated and extended by Sir Roger Vaughan, when granted to him by William Herbert.

25. Tomb of Thomas and John White. In St Mary's Church, Tenby, lie the effigies of father and son Thomas and John White, both merchant and mayor. Thomas was mayor in 1471 and is said to have hidden Henry and Jasper in his house in that year. Each man lies with a peacock at his head and a hart at his feet. Their wives and children are depicted on the sides of the alabaster tombs, coffins denoting those that died in infancy.

26. Underground medieval passage from the demolished White's House, next to the church of St Mary's in Tenby, leading under Upper Frog Street to Jasperley House, now Boots the Chemist.

27. Engraving by Charles Norris in 1812 of the ruins of White's House next to the medieval church of St Mary in the walled town of Tenby.

28. Cellar under Mayor White's House, Tenby, where Jasper and Henry hid for three days while waiting for a boat and favourable winds and tide to take them to France.

29. Tenby Harbour – a tunnel led from Jasperley House to the harbour to allow the easy escape of Henry and Jasper. Tenby was an important deep-sea port in the Middle Ages, with regular commerce to the Continent.

2708. - ELVEN (Morbihan). - Forteresse de Largoët
L'Étang et les Tours

En 1487, les Français ayant envahi la Bretagne, incendièrent le château. Les murs seuls restèrent intacts; la restauration du château fut commencée en 1491, après la réception de l'indemnité allouée par la Duchesse Anne.

30. Les Tours d'Elven, also known as the Chateau l'Argoët, before restoration. Henry Tudor was kept in the great octagonal keep, and the Duke of Brittany was housed in the circular Tour de Connétable de Richemont when he visited. The castle was burnt in the French invasion of 1487.

31. Mill Bay where Henry landed near Dale, Pembroke. Brunt Farm, just seen at the top of the hill, is supposed to be named thus because the steep climb disembarking and hauling up equipment caused Henry to exclaim that it was 'brunt', or burdensome work.

32. The bridge over River Teifi, leading to Cardigan walled town, port and castle. If Henry was not allowed to cross here, he would have to head inland to try and cross near the heavily defended Cilgerran Castle.

33. Sudeley Castle near Cheltenham, Gloucester, was improved by Richard III. It became a favoured residence of Jasper Tudor after Bosworth, and Catherine Parr is buried there. Henry VIII, Lady Jane Grey and Anne Boleyn all stayed here.

34. Henry Tudor House, in the medieval walled city of Shrewsbury. Built in the early 1400s and originally a collection of shops, houses and a brewing inn, it has been known by various names such as the Lion Tap and the Trotting Horse. It has now assumed its earlier name as Henry was supposed to have lodged here en route to Bosworth.

35. The Jasper Tower, Llandaff Cathedral. The Jasper Tower is on the left. In front are the ruins of the thirteenth-century bell tower it replaced. The gift of Jasper Tudor, it was built of blue lias on an older foundation, housing a ring of thirteen bells.

36. To commemorate the triumphs of the Tudor dynasty, Henry VIII commissioned Hans Holbein for a wall painting at Whitehall Palace in 1537. This is the preparatory drawing (cartoon) of half of the mural, showing Henry and his father Henry VII. The painting was destroyed by fire in 1698, and the other half of the cartoon, showing Jane Seymour and Elizabeth of York, is lost.

Edward advanced to York on 30 March 1461, where he was received with great solemnity by the mayor and commons of the city, in procession. They had obtained the king's grace through the intercession of Lords Montagu and Berners. The heads of the Duke of York, the Earl of Rutland and the Earl of Salisbury were removed from the gates of York and placed with their bodies at Pontefract, then known as Pomfret, prior to magnificent funerals at Fotheringhay and Bisham Abbey. Only four executions took place at York, of the Earl of Devonshire, Sir Baldwin Fulford, Sir William Talboys and Sir William Hill. The 'flying earl' of Wiltshire was captured by William Salkeld at Cockermouth a month after the battle, presumably while trying to take a ship to Scotland. Wiltshire had fled early from the First Battle of St Albans in 1455; fought at Wakefield in 1460, with his personal battle possibly causing the death of York; fled early from Mortimer's Cross; and fled with other lords from Towton. He was beheaded at Newcastle on 1 May 1461 for his role in beheading Edward's father and brother after Wakefield. Although some fighting continued for the next decade, Edward IV now ruled in relative peace for some years, until the readeption of Henry VI in 1470.

However, after Towton, Jasper continued to hold the Welsh fortresses of Pembroke, Denbigh, and Harlech for his half-brother, Henry VI. The defeated Jasper was now unaided and largely without resources in Wales to face the triumphant new king. All the other Lancastrian leaders were in exile. Edward IV now had only one problem in securing his throne – Jasper Tudor. The records of the principality shires in South Wales for the years 1459–1461 are scarce, possibly because the administration was severely disrupted. It is clear, however, that civil disorder was upsetting the smooth running of royal government. We know that Jasper's close associate Thomas Fitzhenry deliberately destroyed the records of the county courts and petty sessions of Cardiganshire for 1460–1461 in order to embarrass the new government.

Jasper had been reported taken at Mortimer's Cross in February, but seems to have joined Margaret of Anjou. Perhaps he sailed from Pembroke, Tenby or Harlech to join her. His activities in the spring and summer of 1461 are not recorded, but he probably continued to maintain Lancastrian resistance. He does not appear to have been present at the Siege of Pembroke, possibly because he believed that this great fortress could be relied upon to put up strong resistance, like Harlech, if subject to attack. Later in 1461 he shifted his sphere of operations to North Wales, where he was aided by the Duke of Exeter, who had escaped from Towton, and Thomas Fitzhenry, the recently dismissed chamberlain of South Wales.

Edward IV now determined to replace the existing administrative hierarchy in Wales with new men upon whose loyalty he could count. Thus the Herbert, Devereux, Vaughan and Dwnn families were singled out for royal favour. On 8 May, William Herbert was appointed justiciar and chamberlain of South Wales for life, constable of Dinefwr Castle, and steward of Carmarthenshire and Cardiganshire. On 9 and 10 May, the new governor of South Wales, along with his brothers Thomas and John Herbert and Hugh Huntley of Dixton in Monmouthshire, was commissioned to seize the county and lordship of Pembroke and all the lands of Jasper Tudor in England and Wales, as well as Dunster Castle in Somerset. They were also to take the estates of Sir James Luttrell and certain estates of John, Earl of Shrewsbury, in the Marches.

Also in May 1461, John Neville, the brother of Warwick, was made a Knight of the Garter and given the title of Baron Montagu. He had been wounded at Blore Heath in 1459 and captured with his brother Thomas, being held at Chester Castle for almost a year. The brothers were released after the Battle of Northampton and he fought at the Second Battle of St Albans in 1461. Neville was again captured, but released the day after Towton. From York, Edward headed south for his coronation and ordered Montagu to move north to lift the Siege of Carlisle by Scots and Lancastrians, which he did in June. In July, Montagu took Naworth and in November besieged Bamburgh, which surrendered on Christmas Day.

On 28 June, Edward was formally crowned king at Westminster. With Herbert's active participation, Edward IV had been proclaimed king on 4 March 1461. The new government's attempts to crush the remaining Lancastrian opposition in Wales had gathered momentum in the spring, with the appointment of new officers in the principality. At the coronation, Warwick was not made a duke as had been confidently expected by his supporters. This disappointment and the 'favouritism' now shown to Herbert hurt deeply, distancing Warwick from Edward. Immediately after the coronation, another considerable redistribution of power took place in Wales. Lord Hastings was made chamberlain of North Wales. Richard Grey, Lord Powys, became steward of Ceri, Cedewain, and Montgomery. John Tiptoft, Earl of Worcester, became Justice of North Wales. Jasper's enemy John Dwnn was made constable of Aberystwyth and Carmarthen, and sheriff of Carmarthenshire and Cardiganshire, 'with all profits of pasture of Aberystwyth', and the custom called 'prysemayse'. (Prysemayse is mainprize, a writ directed to the sheriff, when the offence or cause of commitment is not properly bailable, commanding him to take sureties for the prisoner's appearance, commonly called mainpernors, and to set him at large.)

On 8 July 1461, the escheator of Surrey and Sussex was ordered to seize Earl Jasper's possessions in those counties. All other possessions had already been taken. Also on 8 July, Herbert and Devereux were empowered to array all able-bodied men in the counties of Hereford, Gloucester and Shropshire. Early in August they were appointed to inquire into all treasons, insurrections and rebellions in South Wales and to pardon all who submitted, except Jasper Tudor, John Skydmore, Thomas Cornwall and Thomas Fitzhenry. With the two lords on this commission were Lord Herbert's brother Thomas Herbert, a half-brother named William Herbert and John Dwnn. In July, the Duke of Exeter joined Jasper Tudor in North Wales. He had escaped after Towton to Scotland and then joined Margaret in Burgundy.

From July 1461, there was little or no Lancastrian menace in the north of England, or from Scotland, and both sides now concentrated upon Wales. The Lancastrians wished to reinforce Jasper, and Edward wanted to exterminate him. Edward needed to take over the remaining Lancastrian castles, which Jasper had manned and provisioned. A Lancastrian embassy led by Hungerford went from Scotland to Charles VI in France to secure 20,000 crowns and 2,000 men to support Jasper in Wales. However, the king died as they were en route, and his pro-Yorkist son Louis thwarted their plans. Hungerford and Whittingham were arrested in Dieppe, Somerset imprisoned near Dieppe, and their letters to Margaret of Anjou were intercepted. The urgency of Edward's invasion of Wales was alleviated by the arrests in France.

On a previous occasion the Yorkists had held Denbigh, giving Jasper great difficulty in taking it. Now Lancastrians held it, and another letter from Jasper to Roger Puleston on 24 July requested him to safeguard Denbigh Castle and to collect as much money as he could:

> To our Right trusty and well-beloved Roger Puleston, Esq., Keeper of the Castle of Denbigh. Right trusty and well-beloved – We greet you well, letting you wit that we have received your letters by Hugh, and understand the matter comprised therein; and as touching the keeping of the Castle of Denbigh, we pray you that you will do your faithful diligence for the safeguard of hit, as far as in you is, taking the revenue of the lordship there for the vittaling of the same, by the hands of Griffith Vychan, receiver there – we have written unto him that he should make pureyance therefore – and that ye will understand the goodwill and disposition of the people, and that country, towards my Lord Prince [*i.e.* Edward, Prince of Wales, eldest son of King Henry VI] and us, and to send us word as soon as you may, as our trust is in you. Written at my town of Tenby, the xxiiij of July. J. PEMBROKE.

However, Edward had already tried to make peace with the Pulestons and Griffith Vaughan. Early in July, he had enrolled them on a commission in Chirkland with a number of other former royalists of North Wales. However, they did not surrender the castle, so could not have accepted his commission.

The new king had given his most loyal supporters political and administrative power, and now rewarded them with peerages. From 26 July 1461, Sir William Herbert and Sir Walter Devereux were summoned to Parliament as Lord Herbert of Raglan, Chepstow and Gower and Lord Ferrers of Chartley. With new titles and wide powers, the king's lieutenants in Wales prepared for the seizure of the remaining Lancastrian areas. A second commission, like that given to Herbert on 9 May, was now given to Herbert and his associates on 10 August 1461, ordering them to finally seize Jasper's estates and those of other Lancastrians. The Patent Roll records this:

Commission to William Herbert, knight, lord Herbert, Thomas Herbert, esquire of the body, John Herbert and Hugh Huntley, to take into the king's hands the county and lordship of Pembroke with its appurtenances in England and Wales and the marches of Wales and all castles, lordships, manors, lands and possessions late of Jasper, earl of Pembroke, a rebel with power to appoint stewards, constables, receivers, auditors and other bailiffs.

Herbert's men achieved this task, and were held accountable for the revenues (the issues) of these lands from 10 August 1461 to 23 January 1462. On 3 February 1462, Edward IV granted Jasper Tudor's lands to Herbert, and on 21 February ordered the Treasurer and barons of the Exchequer not to pursue him for payment of the earlier incomes.

Parliament was not to meet until November, and Edward decided to spend a considerable portion of the interval in the Marches to keep in close touch with the attacks against Jasper, whose movements appear to have attracted considerable attention. On 12 August 1461, Roger Kynaston and a number of others were commissioned to urge the king's subjects of Shropshire to array a force at their own expense for the defence of the county and the adjoining parts of Wales. Kynaston was sheriff of Merionethshire. Separate commissions to act against Jasper Tudor were also issued on that day to Thomas, John, and Richard Herbert. The general muster was to be at Hereford.

The king had reached the borders before the end of August. On 4 September he was at Bristol, where he was 'most royally received'. A letter written in Bristol on 9 September relates, 'As for any grete doing in Wales I trust God we shal not doubte. The Lord Herbert and the Lord Ferrers of Chartley with divers many other gentilmen ben gone afore to clense the coimtreye afore us.' On 9 September he left for Gloucester, from where he moved to Ross, Hereford and Ludlow. Edward arrived with his army at Hereford on 17 September, eight days after his forces were told to muster there. He left the actual campaigning to his chief Welsh lieutenants, Sir William Herbert, Henry Bourchier of Essex and Walter Devereux, Lord Ferrers. Edward stayed in Ludlow Castle from 18 to 26 September, but abandoned his march as it was reported that Ferrers and Herbert had been successful across Wales. King Edward returned to London for the opening of his first parliament on 4 November.

Lord Herbert's influence had increased rapidly. On 7 September 1461, he received the custody of the Welsh estates of the Duke of Buckingham during the minority of Henry, the heir. It included the lordship of Brecknock, Newport and certain other parts of Gwent. By another grant he became steward of the royal lordships of Clifford, Glasbury and Wynforton in the Marches. His brothers, Thomas and Richard, and Lord Ferrers were associated with him in gaining more commissions and offices.

From 9 September, the Yorkists had only two important strongholds to deal with besides Denbigh. Harlech Castle was held by David ap Einion and some English Lancastrian refugees, notably Tunstall, while Pembroke Castle was held for Jasper by Sir John Skydmore. Herbert first attacked the formidable Pembroke, Jasper's main seat. A fleet was sent to cooperate in the attack, so that no assistance might reach the castle from the sea. Philip Castle of Pembroke and Thomas Mansel were empowered to man some ships for the purpose, and the *Paston Letters* record on 30 August that Edward had sent his navy to support a siege. The ship for which Castle and Thomas Mansel were called upon to provide mariners was the *Trinity* of Minehead. The Yorkists marched west. Oystermouth Castle, near Swansea, one of the gateways of Gower, was already in the hands of a local Yorkist, Sir Hugh ap John. Like many Welshmen he had fought in France, and he had been one of the council of Robert Norreys. He was now constable of the castle, and reeve of the lordship of Gower.

Tenby probably offered no resistance, although Jasper had spent money on its castle and town walls. Pembroke Castle had been 'victualled, manned, and apparelled for a long time after' by Jasper, but his deputy Sir John Skydmore (Scudamore), when summoned by Herbert to surrender, gave in 'without any war or resistance' on 30 September. Perhaps Jasper had told him to surrender it, to save its ruination. Scudamore received a written pledge from Herbert and Ferrers that his life would be spared, and that his lands would not be confiscated. Both promised to intercede with the king on his behalf. Despite this guarantee, when Parliament met, a Bill of attainder was brought against him. Herbert was present in the parliament in which the attainder was moved and it was rejected. The lords had promised that 'he should have better than his livelihood, and he was then admitted unto the king's good grace as he hath ready to show in writing under the seal of the said Lord Herbert'. However, at the latter end of the parliament, Scudamore's estates were forfeited by royal ordinance: 'after many lords and knights had departed, by marvellous private labour', a Bill personally signed by Edward was brought to the Commons containing an ordinance that Scudamore should forfeit his livelihood, saving his life and goods. At the time he was at home 'trusting to the promise of Lords Herbert and Ferrers'. The king later changed his mind, on 30 September, and Scudamore was restored 'to the king's grace', showing Herbert's new influence. Sir John Scudamore had fought for Jasper earlier in the year at Mortimer's Cross. Prolonging the fight against the new Yorkist regime must have seemed a futile exercise to men like Scudamore, for the chances of the defeated and scattered Lancastrian forces rallying with much hope of success were becoming increasingly slight.

With his taking of Pembroke Castle, Herbert gained its most important inmate, the four-year-old Henry Tudor, Earl of Richmond, who spent the next decade in Herbert's care as his ward. As William Herbert was awarded Jasper's lands by Edward IV, Henry came into his custody. Because Henry was a member of the Lancastrian royal family, Herbert paid £1,000 for his wardship. Furthermore, he was given control over the boy's future marriage. At some point, Herbert sought to marry the young earl to his daughter Maud, as mentioned in his will. According to Polydore Vergil, young Henry Tudor was 'kept as prysoner, but honourably browght up with the wyfe of William Herbert'.

Herbert's wife, Anne Devereux, took care of Henry at Raglan Castle. Henry was still addressed as the Earl of Richmond, even though the actual estates of the earldom were given to George, Duke of Clarence, brother of Edward IV. Henry regarded Anne Devereux with affection, even after becoming king twenty-five years later, as she had effectively replaced his mother in his childhood years. He grew up with her children, a vital factor on his road to Bosworth Field. Anne was particularly kind to the child, and when he triumphed in 1485, Henry Tudor sent for her to come to London. While with the Herberts, Henry was educated by two Oxford graduates. Master Edward Haseley, Dean of Warwick, taught him grammar. His other tutor was Andrew Scot (Andreas Scotus), and both were remembered favourably by Henry after he became king. Other instruction was provided by Sir Hugh ap John, mentioned above as holding Oystermouth Castle. Hugh was also remembered with a gift by Henry when he was king.

It is interesting to know about the feelings of Anne Devereux. Her father was Sir Walter Devereux of Bodenham, Herefordshire, Lord Chancellor of Ireland from 1449 to 1451. A very prominent supporter of Richard of York, he had served him in France and remained his supporter throughout the War of the Roses. In 1452, for taking part in York's march on London, Devereux was attainted for treason by Parliament. At this time, Devereux began holding the great Wigmore Castle in Hereford for the Yorkists. Devereux fought against the king at St Albans in 1455, where the king was captured and York restored to complete power.

Shortly after the victory, Parliament pardoned Walter Devereux. As the Lancaster party manoeuvred to reverse their losses, outbursts of lawlessness grew in the Welsh Marches. Walter Devereux, as constable of Wigmore Castle, descended on Hereford with the castle's garrison and captured the mayor and justices in the summer of 1456. Devereux then brought before the justices several local men whom the justices were obliged to condemn to death, and they were subsequently hanged. Devereux followed this by mustering a force of 2,000 archers from Gwent, and marched on the castles at Carmarthen and Aberystwyth, which he took by assault. Afterwards, he declared a commission of oyer and terminer to judge and condemn more people whom he believed hostile to York. Among his prisoners captured at Carmarthen were Edmund Tudor, half-brother of the king and father of young Henry, and Robert Rees, Keeper of the Welsh Seal. Edmund died in unexplained circumstances in Devereux' custody. Knowing that her father was responsible for Henry's father's death must have placed a debt of obligation upon Anne Devereux. And there was more. Her brother was Walter Devereux the younger, Jasper's inveterate enemy, who had just been created Baron Ferrers of Chartley by Edward IV. Henry Tudor's mother, Margaret Beaufort, was not given care of her son. She and her husband, Henry Stafford, lived at Bourne (Lincolnshire) and Woking (Surrey).

However, Margaret was still allowed to correspond with her son and visited him at Raglan Castle at least once.

On 4 October 1461, Henry Wyndsoure reported that

> all the castles and holds both in South Wales and in North Wales are given and yielded up into the king's hand; and the Duke of Exeter and the Earl of Pembroke are fled and taken to the mountains, and diverse lords with great puissance are after them. And most part of gentlemen and men of worship are come in to the king, and grace of all Wales.

However, Denbigh still held out until around January 1462, Carreg Cennen until May 1462 and Harlech until 1468.

The Yorkists had captured Pembroke Castle on 30 September, after which Herbert led the bulk of the royal army into North Wales to pursue Jasper, who was thought to be hiding in the mountains of Snowdon with Henry Holland, Duke of Exeter. Exeter may have brought reinforcements from Scotland to Jasper by sea, for the Lancastrian leaders were able to put a force in the field and meet Herbert in battle at Twt Hill (or Tuthill), outside the walls of Caernarfon in north-west Wales. This took place on 16 October, and Jasper, Exeter and Thomas Fitzharry of Hereford were beaten off, probably while attempting to take the walled and towered bastide town and castle by surprise.

The only specific reference to this battle occurs in a list of persons attainted for treason at the November parliament, which states that

> Henry Duke of Exeter, Jasper Earl of Pembroke and Thomas Fitzhenry late of Hereford, esquire, at a place called Twthill (Tutehill) beside the town of Caernarfon in Wales, on the Friday after the feast of the translation of St Edward last [16 October 1461] raised war against our same sovereign, intending then and there to proceed to his destruction by treacherous and cruel violence, against their faith and allegiance.

Twt Hill was a complete victory for Herbert, who destroyed the last Lancastrian field force in Wales. Jasper, Fitzhenry and Exeter escaped, most probably to Scotland, possibly first going to Ireland. On three subsequent occasions before his last exile in Brittany, Jasper returned to Wales and made abortive efforts to revive opposition to Edward IV, on the first two occasions making his escape by way of the coast near Harlech, where he appears to have had friends among the local gentry. His defeat isolated the remaining Lancastrian castles. Most Welsh Lancastrians ended active resistance by mid-1462, but Harlech Castle, which could be resupplied by sea and would require a costly and difficult effort to reduce, continued in Lancastrian hands until 1468. There is a Watergate at Harlech Castle, now half a mile from any high tides. Eighteenth-century paintings of the castle still show the sea lapping its walls. However, all Wales still remained vulnerable to seaborne invasion should Margaret receive French assistance.

On 4 November 1461, on the very first day of Edward IV's first parliament, Jasper was formally attainted for his support of Henry VI. Another early Act of the new king's reign attainted the young Henry Tudor, probably induced by the active part his uncle Jasper took against the king. Edward stripped the young Henry Tudor of his territorial possessions and gave them to his brother George, Duke of Clarence, but did not grant George the dignity of Earl of Richmond. At the same time, the chief supporters of the deposed Henry VI were attainted and their estates forfeited. According to this Act, Henry VI, his queen, Earl Jasper and a large number of other loyalists, 'divers times since the fourth day of March last past, stirred, laboured and provoked the Enemies of our said Sovereign Lord King Edward the fourth, of outward Lands to enter into his said Realm with great battle, to reap war against his Estate within the said Realm', planning to conquer it, depose Edward IV and destroy him and his subjects. Moreover, Earl Jasper, the Duke of Exeter and Thomas Fitzharry had, in particular, 'reaped war' at Twt Hill near Caernarfon in North Wales 'against their faith and allegiance, and so they were attainted and their estates forfeited'.

7

Plotting, Exile and Return to Power: The Battles of Hedgeley Moor, Hexham and Banbury, 1462–1469

Edward IV's priority after assuming the kingship was to avoid antagonising his aristocratic allies while also providing a strong regime that would re-establish order and loyalty in a traditional setting. This was provided by William Herbert, the son of Sir William ap Thomas, 'the Blue Knight of Gwent', and Gwladys Ddu, daughter of the famous Welsh commander Dafydd Gam, who was killed in Henry V's service at Agincourt. With Jasper's seeming eclipse, the Welsh-speaking Herbert's upbringing came to inspire devotion from the bards. From around his orbit came kinsmen and friends who formed a core of loyal officers in Edward IV's service. In the nine months leading up to February 1462, Herbert gathered into his and his relatives' hands the southern counties of the principality and practically all the southern Marcher lordships apart from Glamorgan, Abergavenny and the earldom of March. By 1468, there were few areas in Wales (Glamorgan being the major exception) of which he was not either lord, custodian or principal official. One Welsh poet called him 'King Edward's master-lock'. Edward actually created two new independent lordships for Herbert: Crickhowell and Tretower were detached from the earldom of March in June 1463 and made a full-fledged Marcher lordship, and so was Raglan (formerly part of the lordship of Usk) in March 1465. Herbert's personal control over all the lordships that came into the king's hands was unique. He had replaced Jasper at the centre of hopes for Welsh revival, and bards flocked to his sumptuous Welsh-speaking court at the tremendous castle of Raglan.

Warkworth's Chronicle reported around February 1462 that 'Kynge Edward was possessed of alle Englonde, excepte a castelle in Northe Wales called Harlake, whiche Sere Richard Tunstall kepte, the whiche was gotone afterwarde by the Lorde Harberde'. Denbigh had fallen in January 1462. Its castle must have suffered considerable damage during these years, with a substantial grant having been made to repair the disastrous effects of the earlier Lancastrian siege. Early in 1462, Edward IV advanced a sum to enable the burgesses to rebuild their houses, 'brent by certain rebells and traytors'. While Harlech Castle, which could be resupplied by sea and thus required a costly and difficult effort to reduce, continued in Lancastrian hands, Wales remained vulnerable to seaborne invasion and to the ongoing intrigues of Jasper. After Twt Hill, Jasper is thought to have spent the next year in Ireland, Scotland and France trying to raise funds and men for the cause. The remote garrison at Harlech Castle kept North Wales in a state of war for several years while the rest of England and Wales was relatively peaceful. The defendants were offered a free pardon to surrender, and refused several times between 1461 and 1468. In Edward's first parliament, which had begun in November 1461, there was around 4 March 1462 a petition complaining about the depredations from Harlech:

Shown unto your great wisdoms, the poor tenants and commons of the ground of North Wales. Where many and divers of them been daily taken prisoners and put to fine and ransom as it were in land of war; and many and divers of them daily robbed and spoiled of their goods and cattle contrary to the law, by David ap Ieuan ap Eynon, Griffith Vaughan ap Griffith ap Eynon, Jenkyn ap Iorwerth ap Eynon, Thomas ap Ieuan ap Eynon, Griffith ap Ieuan ap Eynon, John ap Ieuan ap Eynon, John Hanmer, Morys ap David ap Griffith, David ap Ieuan ap Owen, David ap Einon ap Ieuan, Grommys ap Ieuan ap Eynon ap Ieuan, Grommys ap Howel ap Morgan, Edward ap Morgan, John Tother, clerk, Griffith ap Ieuan ap Iorwerth, and Rheinallt ap Griffith ap Bleddyn, and Morys Robert; and over more the said David ap Eynon calleth himself by the name of Constable of Harlech, and that keepeth to the use and behove of him that he calleth his sovereign lord King Henry VI, saying as well by his mouth as by his writing that the said castle was committed to him by his sovereign lord aforesaid and by his sovereign lady Queen Margaret and his right and gracious lord Prince Edward, and sworn to keep it to their use and will not deliver it to no other person saving to such as one of them will assign, notwithstanding the King's commandment is the contrary.

And daily the said David and all the aforesaid other misdoers take and repute in all their demeanour the said late king for their sovereign lord and not the king our sovereign lord that now is as their duty is. And moreover all the said misdoers taketh oxen, sheep, wheat, and victuals of the said poor tenants for stuff of the said castle with strong hand and will not deliver it to no such person as the late King hath deputed to be his constable there ... pray the king by the advice of his lords ... in parliament assembled ... but if so be that the said David ab Ieuan ab Einion, deliver the said castle to such person ... as the king has committed the keeping thereof, before the feast of the purification of our Lady next coming; and also as well the said David, and also the foresaid misdoers, come into the king's town of Caernarfon in peitible wise, and there before the king's justice or chamberlain of North Wales, or their deputies, find sufficient surety of their good baring, before the said feast; that else they and each of them, be attained of high treason, and repute and take for traitors, and that to be proclaimed in the counties of Meirionydd and Caernarfon. And that they and everyone of them, forfeit all their lands and tenements to the king, that they or any of them have or han, or any other person or persons have or han to their use, or any of them. Petition answered: Let them have what they desire ...

While Jasper was losing his estates and power, his chief opponent in Wales and the Marches, William Herbert of Raglan, was being showered with the former offices of Jasper, Wiltshire and other enemies of the new king. On 3 February 1462, Herbert was officially granted a baronetcy and the new title of Lord Herbert of Gower, with substantial properties:

> Grant to William Herbert, king's knight, lately raised to the state of baron, and the heirs of his body, for his good services against Henry VI. Henry duke of Exeter, Jasper earl of Pembroke, James earl of Wilts, and other rebels, of the castle, town and lordship of Pembroke, the hundred and lordship of Castlemartin, the lordship of St. Florence; the lordship and forest of Coydrath, the castle, lordship and town of Tenby, the lordship and bailiwick of West Pembroke and East Pembroke, the bailiwick of Daugleddau, Rhos and Kemeys, a moiety of the passage of Burton, the castle, town and lordship of Kilgerran, the lordships and manors of Emlyn, Maenordeifi, Diffymbriam, the forest of Kevendryn, the castle, lordship and town of Lanstephan, the lordship and manor of Penrys and la Verie with the lordships and manors of Osterlowe, Trayne Clynton and St. Clear, the lordships and manors of Magor and Redwick, the castle, manor, town and lordship of Caldicot with appurtenances in South Wales and the marches, the castle and manor of Goodrich and the lordship and manor of Archenfield with appurtenances in the march of Wales and the county of Hereford, and the manor and lordship of Walwyn's Castell in South Wales, late of James, earl of Wilts, and in the king's hand by reason of an act of forfeiture in Parliament at Westminster, 4 November, with all royal rights, franchises, liberties, courts, counties, hamlets, views of frank-pledge, cantreds, commotes, hundreds, fairs, markets, parks, warrens, knights fees, advowsons, wreck at sea and other profits, with all issues from 4 March last.

On 12 February 1462, Herbert was also given a grant, in return for £1,000, of the custody and marriage of Henry Tudor, son and heir of Edmund, Earl of Richmond. That same day, Herbert was appointed to the custody and lordship of Swansea, Gower and Kilvey, and all manors of the deceased John, Duke of Norfolk, at the rent of 1,000 marks (£666). He took over the valuable Welsh estates of James Butler, Earl of Wiltshire, on 12 June 1262. He now held the castle and manor of the lordship of Crickhowell and Tretower and the king's castle and lordship of Dinas and Blaenlleveny. This property was to be held by the service of one knight's fee, which is probably why his kinsman Sir Roger Vaughan was enabled by Herbert to live at Tretower Castle and rebuild Tretower Court. In 1462, Herbert was also installed as a Knight of the Garter. In 1463, William Herbert was given the manor and castle of Dunster, the manors of Minehead, Carhampton, Culveton, East Quantock, Iveton and lands in Somerset, the manors of Chilton and Blancombe in Devon, and the manors of Stonehall and Woodhall in Suffolk, and other lands of the late Sir James Lutterrell. Some of the estates granted to Herbert had been expected to go to Warwick, who increasingly resented the king's favouritism of Herbert. Herbert was now lauded by many of the bards he encouraged at his court at Raglan as the new deliverer of Wales, but they were also inspired by the example of Harlech, and its lone survival gave the Lancastrians some hope to renew their efforts.

Jasper had been attainted and eventually found his way to Margaret of Anjou's small court in Scotland, then Brittany and later to Bar in Burgundy. The queen must have been delighted that her constant supporter was still alive, but Edward now realised the threat of foreign invasion with French backing. He therefore needed to exterminate the few small pockets of Lancastrian resistance at home. Denbigh Castle had finally surrendered to the Yorkists by January 1462, seeing no hope of being relieved by Jasper. It seems that, in the early part of this year, Jasper was in Ireland causing trouble. A 1462 letter to John Paston from John Russe alludes to Jasper trying to raise a force in Ireland: 'For these three weeks came there neither ship nor boat out of Ireland to bring no tidings, and so it seemeth there is much to do there by the Earl of Pembroke ...' He had probably escaped from Twt Hill to Harlech, then sailed to Ireland and Scotland, and then to Brittany in the course of the year before returning to the north of England and Scotland.

In exile in Scotland, Margaret of Anjou had found it difficult to raise any more support. It seemed that Lancastrian hopes were dead. Therefore she tried to arrange a marriage between the seven-year-old Prince Edward and a Scottish princess. She succeeded conditionally, but still could not raise troops for a second invasion of England. Desperate, Margaret had sent three noblemen as her messengers to her uncle Charles VII of France to seek help. However, he was dying in agony, passing away on 22 July. Sometime after this, she received a letter from two of her messengers at Dieppe. The letter began by saying that they had already written to Margaret three times before – once by the return of the vessel called the *Carvel*, in which they went to France, and twice from Dieppe, where they then were – but all the letters were substantially to communicate the same bad news, that the king was dead, and that her cousin Louis had succeeded to the throne. Margaret knew that the previous letters must have been intercepted by Edward's agents. The new king had no favourable opinion of her cause, and his officers at Dieppe had seized all the messengers' papers to take to the king, who had shut up Somerset, one of the messengers, in the castle of Arques, near Dieppe. Louis had apparently been prevented from imprisoning the other two, lords Whittingham and Hungerford, by their having been granted safe conduct.

Edward IV was possibly the first English king to fully understand that it was an absolute necessity to use insert spies into sources of enmity. To a great extent, his political and personal survival depended on counterespionage. Anthony Spinelly was used as a factor and spy first by Edward IV and then by Richard III, Henry VII and Henry VIII. Such was Spinelly's notoriety that, in 1513, Louis XII blamed the Anglo-French war upon him, yet Louis' successor, François I, called him his good friend. In 1462, Edward IV's agents picked up 'oon callit Jon Worby of Mortland a spye'. Under torture, Worby confessed the whereabouts of Margaret of Anjou and her party, and then informed them of a proposed Lancastrian invasion of England.

Worby had been captured by Lord Southwell, and was a servant of Sir John Russell. He confessed that

> King Henry, late King of England in deed but not in truth, and she that was queen Margaret his wife, and Edward her son, the duke of Britain, Edward the duke of Burgoyn, Sir William Taylbos, the lord Roos, Sir Richard Tunstall, Thomas Ormond, Sir W. Catesby, Thomas Fykeharry. These lords and knights be in Scotland with the Scots. The duke of Exeter, earl of Pembroke, the baron of Burford, Jon Ayne. These shall land at Beaumaris by the appointment of Robert Gold, captain of the duke of Burgoyn. Duke Henry of Calabria [Queen Margaret's brother], the lord Hungerford, the lord Morton [Dr John Morton], the duke of Somerset with 60,000 of men of Spain. These shall land in the coast of Norfolk and Suffolk. The lord Louis, the duke of Spain, Henry the dauphin of France, Sir John Fortescue, Sir Jon Russell of Worcester, Sir Thomas Burtayn, the earl's brother of Denschyr, Sir Thomas Cornwaylys. These lords and knights shall land at Sandwich by appointment. Then coming after these lords and knights before written to assist them with all the power possible they may make: the King of France with 100,000 men, the King of Denmark with 20,000, the King of Aragon 1,000, the King of Navern with 20,000, the King of Cesyl [Castile] with 25,000, the King of Portugal with 10,000; the which would be appointed to enter the realm of England.

Thus three armies, including one led by Margaret's father, René of Anjou, would invade with nearly a quarter of a million men. The details of Worby's 'confession' undoubtedly were expanded by him in an attempt to save his life, and the plot was said to have been hatched by the garrison of Harlech Castle to try and bring Jasper back into Wales. They needed Jasper to coordinate and lead Lancastrian attacks there and in England. Jasper was to be helped at Beaumaris 'by the appointment of Robert Gold, captain of the duke of Burgundy'. Harlech had been a point of entry and exit for Lancastrians for seven years, for messengers and refugees to pass to Scotland and Ireland. Apart from the rumoured landings by Jasper in Wales, Somerset in East Anglia and a Franco-Spanish force in Kent, it was claimed that the Earl of Oxford was behind a series of attacks launched against English coasts by Lancastrian raiders operating out of France. Oxford was also thought to be conspiring to lead a party of armed retainers, supposedly raised on the king's behalf, to intercept and kill Edward as he rode north to meet Lancastrian attackers from Scotland. Yorkist agents had intercepted letters passing between Oxford and Queen Margaret. There were possibly two plots, but both are known as the Oxford plot, or Oxford conspiracy, as its focal point appears to be John de Vere, 12th Earl of Oxford.

Only as late as 1459 had Oxford committed himself to Queen Margaret's cause against York. In May 1460, his eldest son, Aubrey, had married Buckingham's daughter. Oxford was ill, possibly wounded, after the Battle of Northampton in 1460, and was exempted from attending king, council or parliamentary sessions. However, in February 1462, Oxford was arrested together with his son Aubrey and others and convicted of high treason before the Constable of England, John Tiptoft, 1st Earl of Worcester. Tiptoft presided over many trials that led to the attainders and executions of Lancastrians, an office which he carried out with exceptional cruelty. Some of his victims were impaled, and he was known as 'the Butcher of England'. On 20 and 26 February 1462, Oxford and his son Aubrey were executed on Tower Hill. Oxford was beheaded, but some report that Aubrey and others were hanged, drawn and quartered. Oxford was succeeded by his second son, the twenty-year-old John de Vere, who was allowed to assume his father's title and estates in 1464. This 13th Earl of Oxford was later, along with Jasper, the focal point for Lancastrians and led Henry Tudor's army at Bosworth. Oxford had married Margaret Neville, whose brother was Warwick 'the Kingmaker'.

Antonio della Torre tells us that Edward set out in March 1462 for Northumberland to deal with the threat of invasion by the Scots and Lancastrians. He states that a plot by Oxford to assassinate Edward had been discovered eleven days previously. Oxford had intended to follow Edward northwards. The king had 1,000 horsemen and Oxford would have 2,000 men in his retinue following, supposedly to assist the king but in reality to attack. Meanwhile, Somerset would sail from Bruges to England, Henry would cross the border with the Scots and Jasper would come from Brittany. Somerset and Hungerford sailed from Flanders to Scotland in March, but Margaret, by now despairing of Scottish support, was to sail for Brittany with her husband's commission to treat with Louis XI.

To prepare for the planned attack in aid of the Oxford plot in 1462, Jasper Tudor was already in Brittany. Antonio della Torre, Edward IV's envoy to Francesco Sforza, Duke of Milan, reported that Earl Jasper had arrived in Brittany by 25 March 1462 and it was from here that he was to invade Wales at the time of the alleged plot.

Margaret remained in Scotland through the winter, but in Spring 1462 she had determined to go herself to France and see her cousin the king, in hopes that, by her presence at the court, and her personal influence over the king, something might be done. The king had been her playmate in their childhood. He was the son of Marie, her father René's sister. She sailed on a French merchant ship from Kirkcudbright, on the western coast of Scotland, and so passed down through the Irish Sea and St George's Channel, thus avoiding the Straits of Dover, where she would have risked being intercepted by English men-of-war. She took Prince Edward with her and left Henry VI behind. She found that Somerset, Hungerford and Whittingham, the noblemen whom she had sent to France the summer before, had left France and gone to Scotland to seek her. They had provided themselves with a vessel, in which they intended to take the queen away from Scotland and convey her to some place of safety, not knowing that she herself had embarked for France.

On 16 April, Queen Margaret arrived in Brittany, where she was received by Jasper. Desperate for funds, she borrowed money off the Duke of Brittany for her small party to travel further. With Jasper, she moved on to Angers to see her relatively penniless father, René of Anjou, King of Naples, and waited for King Louis' arrival from the south of France. The Oxford plot being exposed, they needed the French king to offer support. They met Louis, who initially agreed to an alliance with the Lancastrians. Jasper had been constantly travelling between Ireland, Wales, Scotland, Brittany and France on behalf of the cause. However, Louis soon reneged upon his initial promises to fund the invasion of England, leaving the responsibility to Margaret's friend Pierre de Brézé (1410–1465). De Brézé was a high-ranking officer in the government of Normandy, and had been one of the commissioners on the French side to negotiate, with Suffolk and the others, the terms of Margaret's marriage. He had played a very prominent part in the tournaments and other celebrations that took place in honour of the wedding before Margaret left to marry Henry VI.

In May 1461, Jasper's enemy William Herbert of Raglan had been made chief justice and chamberlain of South Wales. On 1 March 1462, Sir William and his brother Thomas, Esquire of the Body, were given a commission by the king to take vessels and ships within the port of Bristol, and other parts of the west, towards Wales and ports in Wales to resist the king's enemies. Lancastrian ships were to be cleared out. On the same day, Lord Herbert and Walter Devereux, Lord Ferrers, were commanded to array all able-bodied men in South Wales and the Marches, as it appears that the king's agents had informed him that Jasper was to land once more. Two castles also still held out and were to be attacked.

Carreg Cennen was manned by Thomas and Owain ap Gruffydd ap Nicholas. A force of 200 men was despatched from Raglan under Lord Herbert's younger brother, Sir Richard, and their kinsman, Sir Roger Vaughan of Tretower, to take the great fortress, which capitulated on 1 May 1462. Some 500 men were then employed to despoil the great Welsh castle on its crag in the Tywi Valley. Its complete slighting took some three months. It has a cave running into an internal water supply, and was almost impregnable, so its destruction was necessary.

In the meantime, Earl Jasper seems to have left Margaret in France to visit Henry VI at Edinburgh. He left Scotland early in June 1462 with Sir John Fortescue, now the exiled king's chancellor, arrived in Flanders and reached

Rouen in Normandy on 13 June, carrying letters of credence from Henry VI to King Louis. Here they discovered that, because of misuse, a licence which Louis had earlier granted to all adherents of Henry VI to travel freely in his lands had been revoked. Safe conducts were now required from all travellers who wished to enter France. Fortunately, Charles the Bold, Count of Charolais (and later Duke of Burgundy), was sympathetic to Jasper's appeal for assistance. Charles provided them with letters to King Louis' officers, which enabled them to complete their journey.

Jasper seems to have left Fortescue behind at Rouen, for he had arrived without him at Chinon in Touraine probably by 24 June 1462, and certainly by 28 June. Meanwhile, since 5 June, Queen Margaret and King Louis had again been deeply engrossed in secret negotiations at the magnificent château at Chinon. Jasper arrived as these talks were being successfully concluded. On 24 June, a secret agreement was concluded whereby Louis agreed to lend Queen Margaret £20,000 *tournois*. Margaret now basically gave Calais as collateral for a loan from the King of France. In return for the loan, she was to convey to Louis the port and town of Calais, which was still held by the English, or else pay back double the money she borrowed. Thus it was not an absolute sale of Calais, but only a mortgage of it. Nevertheless, as soon as this transaction was made known in England, it excited great anger and seriously injured the queen's cause.

The loan was made on condition that, if Henry VI ever recovered Calais from the Yorkists, either Earl Jasper or the Gascon noble Jean de Foix, Earl of Kendal, should be made captain of it. The new captain would then swear an oath to deliver Calais to the King of France within a year or else repay the French loan. In return, Louis promised to pay Henry VI 40,000 crowns if ever Calais actually came into his possession in this way. De Foix was expelled from the Order of the Garter in 1462 for entering Louis' service. From Chinon the negotiators moved to Tours on the Loire, and on 28 June 1462 a formal public treaty was issued, declaring a hundred-year truce between Henry VI and Louis XI. Each king promised not to aid the enemies of the other, Margaret signing on behalf of her husband, who was still in Scotland with his son. Jasper Tudor was one of the signatories of this Treaty of Tours and now the Lancastrians appeared to enjoy the full diplomatic support and financial backing of England's greatest enemy. Jasper began planning another invasion.

From Tours Margaret moved to Rouen and then Boulogne, setting sail for Scotland late in October. Jasper had gone on before and was with Henry VI at Berwick, waiting for the arrival of Margaret of Anjou with French troops. Unfortunately, the forces she took with her were quite inadequate, since Louis XI was reconsidering his new alliance in the face of diplomatic pressure and military threats from Edward IV. The Lancastrian party returned to Scotland and from there sailed south to Northumberland on 25 October. Fortunately for Margaret, Bamburgh Castle was in the hands of Sir William Tunstall, brother of Sir Richard Tunstall, formerly chamberlain to Henry VI, and was surrendered immediately. Her army marched to

Alnwick, laying a successful siege to the castle, which soon succumbed. Her 2,000-strong French army then quickly took over Bamburgh, Dunstanburgh, Warkworth and Alnwick Castles, but Scottish supporting forces only joined briefly, and alienated the English by their plunder before returning home. Probably the Lancastrians should have delayed the invasion of England until 1463, by which time Jasper may have recruited substantial Welsh support.

In Wales, Jasper knew that Lancastrian cause was still alive and that the new king's administration was once again facing a fairly obstructive population. Because of this, the Great Sessions had not been held in Carmarthenshire or Cardiganshire in 1461, while in 1462 the administration ensured that it spent £44 on repairs to Cardigan and Carmarthen castles. Both counties had experienced a financial relapse in 1460–1461, and in the more northerly areas of Cardiganshire it was almost impossible to find men who were prepared to act as royal officers. In spite of Herbert's energetic efforts, the government was still unpopular in Wales, and the sons of Gruffydd ap Nicholas, recently dispossessed of Carreg Cennen, were still committed to Jasper's cause.

Warwick was commissioned to lead a counter-attack in the North, while Edward organised heavy ordinance to be brought from London to retake the castles. Early in November 1462, Edward headed north with thirty-nine peers – the greatest number of peers assembled in a later medieval army – equipped to lay siege. On hearing of Edward IV's approaching army, Henry VI, the queen and most of their French force fled back to Scotland, only to be battered by fierce winter storms that drove some of their ships onto the rocks or onto a hostile English coastline. Edward suffered with measles at Durham, so Warwick took charge of operations. Somerset, Roos and a Yorkist deserter, Sir Ralph Percy, were in Bamburgh Castle with about 300 men. Sir Richard Tunstall and Lord Finderne possessed Dunstanburgh with another 300 Lancastrians, and Hungerford and Whittingham, Margaret's former messengers to France, held Alnwick with around 120 French mercenaries. Warwick rode daily from Warkworth Castle to supervise operations at each castle.

Montagu, Arundel and Worcester besieged Somerset at Bamburgh. Jasper was unable to raise the Yorkist sieges of the castles held by Lancastrians, but somehow managed to enter Bamburgh Castle to join Somerset. In Gairdner's *Three Chronicles* we read, 'The Wednesday by fore Cristmasse, Anno Domini mccccclxii. In Castello de Banburw sunt dux de Somerset, comes de Penbrok, dominus de Roos et Radulfus Percy, cum ccc. hominibus. At the seege of Hem sunt comes de Wyceter, comes de Arundel, dominus de Ogyl et dominus de Muntegew cum x ml.' Jasper, Somerset, and the lords Roos and Percy, with 300 men, were besieged by Worcester's army of 10,000 men. They were attacked by lords John Neville and Ogle. The Lancastrian defenders left in Bamburgh vainly hoped for Scottish aid, but this did not materialise and on Christmas Eve the castle surrendered. Somerset and Sir Ralph Percy accepted pardon and swore fealty to

Edward IV, but Jasper and Lord Roos, although offered pardon, could get no assurance that their forfeited estates would be restored to them. They therefore accepted safe conducts that allowed them to withdraw to Scotland. In any case, it seems most unlikely that Jasper Tudor, Henry VI's half-brother, would have accepted any terms offered by King Edward. Shortly afterwards, a Scottish relieving army did invade England, but it was too late to save what little had been gained by the queen's expedition. Jasper and Thomas, Baron Roos, were escorted to Scotland in January 1463, to again join the exiled king and queen.

Sources state that Bamburgh and Dunstanburgh were formally handed over on 26 and 27 of December 1462. Sir Richard Tunstall left Dunstanburgh but later reappears defending Harlech Castle in the same year. Edward offered good terms because his army was cold in the incessant rain, and he sensed the mood of his men. He also did not wish to damage by heavy bombardment these powerful Northern castles, which were a great defence against the Scots. However, the main reason was that he believed that a Scottish army was preparing to invade.

Notably, one of the Yorkists who accompanied Lord Scales and Asteley on their sieges of the Lancastrian castles of Alnwick and Bamburgh during the Northumbrian campaign was a lawless misfit, Sir Thomas Malory (*c.* 1416 – *c.* 1471). He had been released from ten years of captivity under Lancastrian rule for various breaches of the peace. During a later period of imprisonment for felony in 1469–1470, Malory used the various Arthurian romances known as the *Vulgate* cycle, to write the *Morte d'Arthur*.

Around June 1462, Queen Margaret, with her son Prince Edward, Exeter, Lord Rougemont-Grey, Sir Humphrey Dacre, Sir Edmund Hampden, Sir Robert Whittingham, Sir Henry Bellingham and the redoubtable Sir Robert Tunstall, left Scotland to besiege Carlisle Castle and burnt its suburbs. Warwick's brother Lord Montagu arrived in June and beat off the besiegers, who headed west. In July 1462, Montagu lifted the Scottish-Lancastrian siege of Carlisle, forcing Humphrey Dacre to hand over his ancestral castle at Naworth, as the Yorkists concentrated on the few remaining Lancastrian castles.

On 6 January 1463, George Douglas, Earl of Angus and Warden of the Marches, with de Brézé, commander of the French, appeared outside Alnwick Castle. The Yorkist besiegers retreated, allowing the French garrison, with Hungerford and Whittingham, to escape to Scotland. De Brézé stayed to assist the Lancastrian cause, and in March 1463 Sir Ralph Percy turned back to support the Lancastrians and handed over Bamburgh and Dunstanburgh to Henry VI. In May 1463, Hungerford and the French again took Alnwick after the besieged Yorkists were betrayed by Sir Ralph Grey.

Following the failure of the Northumbrian expedition of 1462, Queen Margaret and her followers set about the task of inducing Louis XI to give them further assistance and of preventing any improvement in his relations with Edward IV. Sometime between 18 April and 1 May 1463, Jasper, the

Duke of Exeter, Sir John Fortescue and other Lancastrian leaders sailed from Scotland to Sluys in Flanders, where the count of Charolais and Philip the Good, Duke of Burgundy, assisted them in their journey to see Louis XI via Lille and Tournai. A combined Scottish and Lancastrian army, which included Mary of Scotland, the young James III, Henry VI, Margaret and de Brézé, laid siege to Norham Castle, an important English border castle on the Tweed, to the west of Berwick, from 15 July 1463. Warwick and his brother Montagu responded by gathering an army and advancing towards Norham in July 1463. They arrived in July, eighteen days after the start of the siege. The Scottish-Lancastrian army fled in panic. Queen Margaret and her son, with de Brézé, Fortescue, the French force and other councillors, escaped to Berwick, from where they sailed to Flanders. Henry VI remained in Scotland, where he was protected by Bishop Kennedy of St Andrews. Henry and Margaret would never meet again. Margaret had promised to deliver Berwick and Carlisle to Scotland, but these plans came to nothing permanent beyond the temporary handover of Berwick for twenty years, with a failed joint Scottish and Lancastrian siege of Carlisle.

Henry VI was in another Lancastrian force which tried to take Durham, supported by Sir Edmund Montfort, later a great servant of Jasper. The lords Roos, Rougemont Grey, Dacre and Sir William Tailboys were also in the force. The Lancastrian attempt was seen off by Warwick and Sir Ralph Percy, whose brother had been killed at Towton and who had turned to support the Yorkists, holding Dunstanburgh Castle for Edward IV. Margaret of Anjou travelled again to France to try to prevent Louis from reconciling with Edward IV, but failed. The Neville brothers raided southern Scotland, reaching sixty-three miles across the border before a lack of supplies forced them to retire. Power in Scotland was mainly in the hands of the regent, Queen Mary of Guelders, mother of the twelve-year-old James III. With Margaret and de Brézé gone, Mary negotiated a ten-month truce which began in December 1463. The effective Scottish contribution to the Lancastrian cause was over.

Back in Wales, Harlech Castle was one of the massive fortresses built by Edward I in the late thirteenth century to dominate Gwynedd, today the UNESCO World Heritage Site of the 'Iron Ring' of castles. Beginning with Rhuddlan and ending with Flint, they included Conwy, Caernarfon, Harlech, Beaumaris, Cricieth, Cardigan, Builth and Aberystwyth. Like Edward's other Welsh strongholds, Harlech was designed and built to be supplied by sea. Recent research by Paul Remfrey has conclusively proved that Harlech was not built *ab initio* by Edward, as believed by historians, but was a native Welsh castle like Cricieth and Cardigan, improved by Edward's master builder, James of St George d'Esperanche. By the end of 1462, Herbert had captured all the Lancastrian strongholds in Wales except Harlech Castle, which remained in the hands of a garrison commanded by the Welshman David ap Einion and included such prominent English Lancastrians as Sir Richard Tunstall.

It is important to note here Sir Richard Tunstall's part in the wars. He was knighted in 1451, becoming part of Henry VI's household, taking part in the battles of Wakefield in 1460 and St Albans and Towton in 1461. After Towton, he fled to Scotland with the Lancastrian royal family and was attainted. Campaigning in Northumberland, he had been captured in July 1462, but escaped to serve in the Lancastrian garrisons at Alnwick and Dunstanburgh castles. He was in Wales at Harlech in 1463, but by early 1464 he was back in Northumberland, fighting with Somerset at the battles of Hedgeley Moor and Hexham. After the Lancastrian defeats in Northumberland, Tunstall personally escorted Henry VI into Lancashire, where the king was hidden for over a year. Tunstall returned to Harlech, and he finally fell into Yorkist hands when the castle fell in August 1468. His story is one of great courage, and he served with Henry Tudor at Bosworth in 1485.

Jasper probably accompanied Margaret to France and briefly joined her small court in exile in the Duchy of Bar, part of her father's lands. Jasper now spent most of the 1460s travelling between Wales, Scotland, England, Flanders, Burgundy, France and Brittany on diplomatic missions for Queen Margaret. If caught, there is little doubt that he would have been executed. In 1463, Jasper's follower Roger Puleston took part in an unsuccessful plot to dethrone Edward IV, as a result of which he was arrested. However, he was soon pardoned by Edward and allowed to return to Emral. The king even appointed Puleston and others to a commission in Chirkland, but Puleston nevertheless secretly maintained his contacts with Jasper Tudor and other Lancastrians. Jasper was known to be in Brittany and France in 1464.

The most important Lancastrians in exile were Somerset, Exeter and Jasper. Somerset and Exeter spent most of their time away from Margaret's court, while Jasper Tudor lived mainly abroad until 1470, possibly only attending the small court at Bar once, and then spent fourteen more years in exile with his nephew, Henry Tudor. There were between 50 and 200 of Margaret's longstanding intimates around her, including three knights who steadfastly supported her until they lost their lives at Tewkesbury in 1471. Edmund Hampden had served as queen's carver, while William Vaux and Robert Whittingham had both married ladies of Margaret's household. By 1464, there were some new arrivals to bolster her cause. George Ashby, formerly keeper of Margaret's signet, and Edmund Beaufort, 3rd Duke of Somerset, the brother and successor of Henry Beaufort, who had been executed after Hexham, had both been fortunately released and joined her.

The noted prelate John Morton, later a cardinal, had been taken, freed and captured again while trying to reach Scotland. He finally escaped from the Tower of London and made his way to St Mihiel in Bar, where he became Keeper of the Privy Seal. However, the queen's court housed only thirteen men of knightly status or above. The only ecclesiastic of note was Thomas Bird, Bishop of St Asaph, possibly now styled Archbishop of Canterbury. The queen could not offer a magnificent court. According to her chancellor, Sir John Fortescue, she did everything possible for her followers, but from her parental pension of 6,000 crowns she could only sustain them in the necessities of food and drink. Jasper was hardly there, preferring to work for Henry VI and his son in Britain.

Throughout the summer of 1463, Margaret tried to prevent reconciliation between England and France. Her efforts were in vain, for at Hesdin in the Pas-de-Calais on 8 October 1463 a truce was signed by Louis XI, Edward IV's ambassadors and the dukes of Brittany and Burgundy. It ensured the cessation of all hostilities on land for one year, and instructed the parties to the truce not to assist each other's enemies in any way. The treaty was a major blow to the Lancastrians. It left only Scotland as a refuge and source of support, although that too might soon become hostile as a result of the increasing threats of the English king. Edward wanted Jasper Tudor, and Louis managed to rid himself of Jasper in 1463, giving him a mere £500 *tournois* to leave the country. The earl was no longer of any use to him. French sources state that Earl Jasper was given the money in order to '*retourner en Angleterre*'. However, that would have been a death sentence. Instead Jasper returned to Scotland, without the queen, in December 1463. Margaret could no longer stay in Burgundy after the treaty was agreed, and went to live with her impecunious father René, Duke of Anjou. He had been the second son of the King of Sicily, and his other titles included Count of Provence, Count of Piedmont, Duke of Car, Duke of Lorraine, King of Naples, King of Aragon and King of Jerusalem. His sister Marie had married Charles VII, becoming Queen of France, so he was an uncle of Louis of France.

Lancastrians continued to work for Edward IV's overthrow and the rupture of the four-country truce of 1463. Jasper's return to Scotland coincided with the arrival of the Duke of Somerset, who had rejoined Henry VI there following a brief venture into supporting Edward IV. Somerset now assured Henry that there were many ready to support him. Somerset's treachery towards Edward IV was equalled by that of Sir Ralph Percy, who, like Somerset, had accepted Edward's pardon but handed over Bamburgh and Dunstanburgh castles to the Lancastrians in March 1463. At the end of the year, Guillaume Cousinot de Montreuil (1410–1484) arrived at Bamburgh, where Henry VI was then staying. He was the envoy of Duke François II of Brittany, having been France's diplomatic representative in England between 1444 and 1449. The duke seemed to be more than sympathetic to Henry's plight. On 22 February 1464, Cousinot returned to France with messages from Henry VI to his wife, her parents, the Duke of Brittany and probably also to the Count of Charolais and Louis XI.

To Duke François, Cousinot now explained Henry's great popularity in England, and asked for immediate help. Brittany was in effect largely run by its pro-French chancellor, Guillaume Chauvin, at this time. Henry declared himself to be in danger and requested that the duke should send men to his aid directly, or to Earl Jasper in Wales. Jasper must have followed Cousinot from Bamburgh soon after, for in March he had arrived in Brittany, with letters of recommendation from Louis XI requesting that François assist him with troops and supplies in returning to Wales. Upon 26 March 1464, Chauvin and François II of Brittany provided Jasper and his followers with a *congé d'aller* for England, and gave them the protection of a fleet of ships from St Malo and the estuary of the Rance. They were placed under the command of the vice-admiral, Alain de la Motte. Jasper would be in frequent contact with the duke for the next twenty years. Although Louis XI had originally commended Jasper's scheme to the Duke of Brittany, diplomatic considerations required yet another turnaround by 19 June 1464, when the king wrote to the duke criticising the assistance he had given to Earl Jasper.

On 7 July, François replied, stating that by assisting Jasper he had done no more than carry out the king's original wishes, which he diplomatically stated were always uppermost in his mind. In the meantime, Lancastrian loyalists in England and Wales had started minor insurrections in East Anglia, Cheshire, Lancashire and Gloucestershire in the first two months of 1464. These had little effect and were ruthlessly suppressed. At the same time, in North Wales, Jasper's men Roger Puleston, John and William Hanmer and Edward ap Madog had been engaged in treasonable activities and were hunted down by the Duke of Norfolk. On 1 March, the younger John Paston wrote his father that Norfolk 'hath great labour and cost here in Wales for to take divers gentlemen here who were consenting and helping on to the Duke of Somerset's going; and they were appealed of other certain points of treason, and this matter'. At about the same time, in Carmarthenshire, Philip Mansel of Gower, Hopkyn ap Rhys of Llangyfelach and Lewis ap Rhydderch ap Rhys, a monk of Strata Florida were ringleaders in a minor and obscure insurrection centred on Dryslwyn Castle in the Tywi Valley, which was suppressed by Sir John Dwnn, sheriff of Carmarthenshire and Cardiganshire.

Philip Mansel had been closely associated with Jasper in the last few years of Henry VI's reign, and the link between them still held. Nearly a month after Edward IV's accession, Mansel was still dating documents by the regnal year of the deposed Henry VI, probably an indication of his unwillingness to accept the new regime. He was a brother-in-law of Thomas and Owain ap Gruffydd ap Nicholas, great supporters of Jasper and the House of Lancaster. Hopkyn ap Rhys had fought with Jasper at Mortimer's Cross three years previously, and both Philip Mansel and Hopkyn ap Rhys were attainted in 1464 and had their lands granted to Roger Vaughan, a kinsman of Lord Herbert.

Thus, in March 1464, we read of Philip Mansel's treachery and the problem of Harlech:

And where Philip Mauncell, late of Oxenwich in Gowersland in South Wales, squire … have against their faith and allegiance the 4th day of March, the first year of the reign of our said sovereign lord, and diverse times since, at a place called Dryffryn [Dryslwyn] in Carmarthenshire in south Wales, stirred, laboured and provoked, Margaret late called queen of England, Edward her son late called prince of Wales, and Jasper late earl of Pembroke, rebels and enemies unto our said sovereign lord, to enter into his realm of England, with great battle to arrear war against his estate within this said realm, to conquer the same from the possession and obedience of our said sovereign lord, and to depose him of his royal estate, crown and dignity and to destroy his most noble person and subjects. And also where the king is lawfully and rightfully entitled to the castle of Hardlough [Harlech] in the shire of Meirionydd in North Wales, and to have the possession, rule and governance thereof, as parcel of his principality of Wales; David ab Ieuan ab Einion, late of Hardlough aforesaid gentleman, and Reynold ap Gruffydd ap Pletheu gentleman, have with great might, continually since the said 4th day of March 1461 (the said first year), hitherto traitorously kept the said castle out of his possession, to the intent that the said Henry late called King Henry the sixth, the king's great enemy and rebel and the said Margaret late called queen of England and Edward her son late called prince, and other the king's enemies, rebels and traitors, should there have their entry into this realm, to subdue it out of the king's possession, rule and governance, and to destroy his most royal person; and to the same effect, have not only there since the said 4th day of March, made commotions and gatherings against his estate, crown and dignity, but also traitorously received, kept and supported, Thomas Danyell, squire, and John Dowbegyng gentleman, attainted of high treason, and laboured, provoked and stirred the said Henry, Margaret and Edward, and other the king's enemies and traitors, to have entered into the said realm.

And furthermore it is ordained ... that a writ of proclamation be made and directed to the mayor and sheriffs of the city of Chester, commanding them by the same, to make in the same city open proclamation, three several days together, afore the said Easter fortnight, that the said Dafydd and Reginald, before the feast of Ascension of our Lord next ensuing the said 21st day of January, submit themselves to the good grace of our said sovereign lord, and become sown his true faithful liegemen; and afore the same feast of Ascension, peaceably deliver unto him, or to such as his highness shall appoint, the said castle. And if they submit not themselves, and become not sworn to our said sovereign lord, and deliver the said castle as is aforesaid; then they, and he of them that so doe not, stand and be convicted and attainted of high treason, and forfeit unto our said sovereign lord, all the manors, lands, tenements, possessions and inheritances, that they, or he of them so making default, and not appearing and doing as is aforesaid, or any other to their of his use now has, or had the said first day of October in England, Wales and Marches thereof.

It does not appear that Harlech surrendered following this ultimatum, but on 26 October 1464, William Herbert was appointed constable of Harlech for life. Herbert was again appointed constable on 28 August 1467. The status of Harlech is mentioned in another chronicle, which was seen by Leland but no longer survives. This states that, in 1464, 'thus Edward possessed all England and Wales, save Harlake that Sir Richard Tunstal kept, but after gotten by the Lord Herbert'.

There is no record of Jasper's actual landing in Wales from Brittany in 1464, nor of his activities when he got there. He may have remained in Brittany, but the Mostyn family believes that he was in Wales at this time. Ieuan Fychan ap Ieuan ap Adda of Pengwern and Mostyn was a second cousin, on the maternal side, to Jasper. In 1415, he had been an esquire in the retinue of Thomas Fitzalan, Earl of Arundel and Surrey and Lord of Chirk. Ieuan's son, Hywel ap Ieuan Fychan, followed the fortunes of the House of Lancaster, and it is said that Jasper sought refuge at Mostyn Hall with Hywel ap Ieuan in 1464. Hywel's son Richard ap Hywel fought for the Tudors at Bosworth.

Back in the northern Marches, by Spring 1464 the Scots had agreed to treat for peace, and Montagu, Warwick and their brother the Bishop of Exeter arranged to meet the Scottish ambassador in York. Montagu rode with a small force towards Scotland to escort the Scottish ambassador from the border to York. The Duke of Somerset tried to ambush Montagu near Newcastle but the latter was warned by his scouts and able to evade this attempt. Somerset, his brother in law Sir Henry Fitzlewis and Sir Nicholas Latimer had all been attainted in 1461 and all three were in Dunstanburgh when the fortress was surrendered on 27 December 1462. They had been freed by Edward, but all three returned to the Lancastrian camp.

Montagu continued his journey northwards gathering troops as he went. When Montagu reached Hedgeley Moor on 25 April, he had an army of 5,000–6,000 men. There he met a Lancastrian army of 5,000 men commanded by Somerset, Roos, Hungerford, Sir Ralph Grey and Sir Ralph Percy. Percy had already changed sides several times during the war. Before even striking a blow, the whole of the Lancastrian left or rearward division, commanded by Hungerford and Roos, dissolved in a total rout, leaving the centre, under Somerset, Bellingham and Grey, together with the right or vanward, under Percy, horribly exposed. Montagu ordered the advance to contact. The Lancastrian centre soon joined their fellows on the left in flight, Somerset and his officers swept along, unable to stop the rot. Percy by now was virtually surrounded, and he sustained mortal wounds seeking to break the encircling ring. 'I have saved the bird in my bosom,' he is said to have uttered as his mount stumbled. Despite his humiliation on the field, Somerset was able to rally many of the Lancastrians and retreat in reasonably good order.

Montagu then marched north, but Somerset led the remaining Lancastrian army south to Hexham. Somerset had fetched Henry VI with him, but placed him eight miles from the battle as he did not wish to risk the king being captured for a fourth time. As the Lancastrians were taking up their positions on 15 May 1464, the Yorkists charged from their positions on higher ground. The right detachment of the

Lancastrian army, commanded by Lord Roos, again turned and fled across the Devil's Water and into Hexham before a single blow had been struck. The remnants of Somerset's force were hemmed in and unable to manoeuvre. Lancastrian morale collapsed, and after some token resistance the remains of Somerset's army was pushed into the Devil's Water by the Yorkist infantry. A rout followed, and Montagu had thirty leading Lancastrians executed in Hexham on the evening following the battle, including Somerset and Lord Roos. Sir William Tailboys was captured and executed shortly after as he tried to flee north with £2,000 of Henry's war chest. On the loss of its leadership, Lancastrian resistance in the north of England collapsed. Henry VI escaped into Northumberland, but his later capture at Clitheroe in Lancashire meant the rebellion was effectively over. John Neville, Lord Montagu, was now made Earl of Northumberland. Next, he led the royal artillery to take Alnwick Castle on 24 June and Dunstanburgh Castle on that day or the day after. Bamburgh Castle was taken by heavy bombardment. (In 1470, Neville was forced to relinquish the earldom of Northumberland and in recompense made Marquess of Montagu, an honour between that of a duke and an earl, so we will keep referring to him as Montagu.)

In Autumn 1464, Herbert was given £2,000 to cover his costs by Edward IV, and 'divers habilments of war' by the Master of the King's Ordinance. He was ordered to take Harlech, the only castle left in Lancastrian hands. *Gregory's Chronicle* noted that Harlech Castle was 'so strong that men find it impossible to get it'. It was to no avail. In 1464, Parliament called on Harlech to submit and Edward IV gave the garrison until 1 January 1465 to surrender. The offer was yet again ignored, like that of 1461. In March 1465, yet more possessions had been granted by Edward IV to his faithful lieutenant William Herbert. He received lands taken out of the lordships of Usk and Monmouth, which, together with the castle and lands of Raglan, were formed into 'one united royal lordship', with royal privileges similar to those of the Lord of Abergavenny: 'And the said William and his heirs and assigns shall have within the said limits all royal rights, prerogatives, and customs belonging to royal lordships, and all royal courts and other jurisdictions, powers, and authorities as in any other royal lordship in Wales or in the marches of Wales etc., etc.' In effect, Herbert, as mentioned in the document, was given the same rights as 'Richard, Earl of Warwick, and Anne his wife have in the manor of Bergavenny, or the lord of any other lordship in Wales; and no justices, stewards, escheators, coroners, ringilds, or other officers or ministers of the King shall interfere'. To go with this unparalleled power for a Welshman under English jurisdiction, in September 1468, Herbert was made Chief Justice of South Wales and steward of many of the king's lordships across Wales from the Cardigan coast to Clifford in the Marches. Many of his family were also given power and estates by Edward IV.

Herbert was known as Gwilym Ddu, William the Black, and was being praised by the bards at this time as being the man who could deliver Wales from the English, most notably by Lewis Glyn Cothi, who called him 'the greatest man, the gem of the crown ... a Welsh hero for Wales in Gwent'. William Herbert, Earl of Pembroke, was the first Welshman to be raised to the dignity of an earl, and it was largely owing to his influence that so many Welshmen gravitated to Edward's court. He was the first of his family to bear the surname Herbert, or any surname at all, as his forebears kept the usual Welsh patronymic style. Edward IV, upon raising him to the earldom, instructed William and his brother 'to forego the British manner'. Thus William (Gwilym) ap William (Gwilym) ap Thomas (Tomas) ap Jenkyn (Siencyn) ab Adam became William Herbert after an alleged Norman forebear named Herbert Fitzroy.

In 1464–1465, £34 17s 10d was spent on repairing the walls of Carmarthen Castle, while from April 1465 the deputy chamberlain, Hugh Hunteley, visited the castles of Cardigan and Aberystwyth to inspect the garrison. In 1464–1465 and 1466–1468, it was decided to employ three guards on full night watch throughout the year at Caernarfon because of the activities of Lancastrian rebels. In 1464–1465, William Lathom and other men were paid £3 for riding with William Laken, deputy justiciar of North Wales, and with the royal auditors from Caernarfon to Oswestry. There was still lawlessness in Wales, so Jasper had a chance of launching a successful invasion if he could bring sufficient forces with him and was supported by the Lancastrians in England. In 1464–1465, it was necessary to employ agents to provide Herbert with information about the situation at Harlech Castle, and John Gruffydd in 1466 and John ap Maredudd in 1467 were each sent there to discover the strength of the Lancastrian garrison. Because of the Harlech rebels and their frequent incursions across northern villages and towns, the north was even more troubled than the south of Wales, and as late as November 1467 the garrisons at Beaumaris, Caernarfon, Conwy and Montgomery were strengthened, 'considering our Rebelles been daily in the said country'.

Warwick had been negotiating with France for Edward IV to marry Louis XI's sister-in-law Bona, daughter of Louis, Duke of Savoy. However, Warwick was infuriated when, in September 1464, Edward revealed that he was already married, to Elizabeth Woodville. Warwick's plans had been sabotaged by the secret marriage, contracted on 1 May of the same year. He had been unknowingly deceiving the French into believing that Edward was serious about the marriage proposal. In the long run, Edward was seeking to build the Woodville family into a powerhouse independent of Warwick's influence. From this point on Warwick increasingly stayed away from court, although the promotion of Warwick's brother George Neville to Archbishop of York shows that the earl was still in favour with the king. In July 1465, when Henry VI was once more captured, in Lancashire, it was Warwick who escorted the fallen king to his fourth period of captivity in the Tower.

In the spring of 1466, Warwick was sent to the Continent to carry out more negotiations with the French and Burgundians, proposing a marriage involving Edward's sister Margaret. Warwick increasingly came to favour French diplomatic connections. However, Edward's new father-in-law, Richard Woodville, Earl Rivers, who was now Treasurer of England, was in favour of a Burgundian alliance. There was rivalry within the English court, not alleviated by the fact that Edward had signed a secret treaty in October with Burgundy while Warwick was unknowingly forced to yet again carry on sham negotiations with the French. George Neville was later dismissed as chancellor, while Edward refused to allow a marriage between Warwick's oldest daughter, Isabel, and Edward's brother Clarence. It became increasingly clear that Warwick's position of dominance at court had been taken over by Earl Rivers, and his military role by his brother Montagu and William Herbert.

During 1466, the Earl of Worcester led a campaign into North Wales, apparently in reply to the garrison of Harlech raiding Wrexham, seventy miles away. Sir Richard Tunstall, one of the castle's defenders, had been able to mount a raiding expedition across North Wales and even threatened Shrewsbury on the English border. Town and castle garrisons were again strengthened. Worcester's campaign did not seem to result in any arrears of revenue from Caernarfonshire and Anglesey being paid. There is also no evidence that the earl ever managed to reach Harlech. The Calendar of Patent Rolls for 5 February 1467 records a

> grant for life to Walter Devereux, knight, lord Ferrers, of the office of captain or constable of the king's castle of Aberystwyth in South Wales with all profits of the town of Aberystwyth and nil [*sic*] meadows, feedings, pastures and customs called Prysemayse in Aberystwyth, receiving the accustomed fees from the issue of the king's castle, lordship and manor of Aberystwyth at the hands of the chamberlain of South Wales and also the accustomed daily wages for one armed man and 12 archers from the same.

In September 1467, Margaret Beaufort managed to see her son Henry, visiting him at Raglan Castle when staying in the West Country. She spent a week there with her husband Henry Stafford, and it seems that she was pleased with the Herberts' care and upbringing of the ten-year-old Henry.

Around October 1467, Harlech was involved when a chronicler recorded that some letters from Queen Margaret had been captured from a messenger trying to enter Harlech Castle. They were taken by Lord Herbert to the king. They implicated many, including the Earl of Warwick, in treason and suggested their sympathy to the Lancastrian cause, but the king accepted Warwick's written denial, despite his refusal to come to court to answer the charges. The messenger's confession was simply dismissed, and he was sent directly to Warwick to repeat the charge to his face.

During later 1467, international relations at last began to favour the House of Lancaster. In early 1468, Edward IV made alliances with the dukes of Brittany and Burgundy, contravening the previous four-nation treaty of non-aggression. Louis had to stop the three nations from harming the interests of France. In mid-June 1468, agents of Edward IV in Kent arrested a tailor (or shoemaker) named John Cornelius, at the port of Queenborough. The courier was caught carrying letters from Lancastrian exiles in France to secret Lancastrian sympathisers in England. He was a servant of the Lancastrian Sir Robert Whittingham. Attainted in 1461, Whittingham still supported Henry VI, and in 1463 had accompanied Margaret of Anjou to Burgundy. After the defeat of the Northern Lancastrian army, in 1464 he escorted her to Koeur Castle at St Mihiel, in the Duchy of Bar. By the summer of 1468 Whittingham had returned, being in the last remaining Lancastrian garrison at Harlech. Cornelius had been employed by Margaret as an emissary to her supporters in England and Wales and upon his arrest was probably returning to France. Cornelius was taken to the Tower and had hot irons applied to his feet to obtain information from him. Edward IV authorised the use of torture to extract from the prisoner the names of the intended letter recipients. The Cornelius case may be the only known example of officially sanctioned torture in England before the time of Henry VIII, and its authorisation demonstrates that the government was still not at ease with the Lancastrian threat.

As Cornelius was tortured, he implicated the guilty and innocent alike, anything necessary to alleviate the pain. He implicated those from whom he had brought letters, including John Hawkins, a servant of Lord Wenlock. Hawkins in turn then made accusations against Sir Thomas Cook. Cook was a draper and merchant who had risen to be Mayor of London and was a main creditor of Edward IV. Lord Wenlock was a former Lancastrian, then serving Edward IV as a trusted diplomat. Hawkins implicated several others and was executed, but suspicions about Wenlock were suppressed so that he could conduct the king's sister, Margaret of York, to Burgundy for her wedding to Duke Charles. (Unhappy with the Burgundian alliance that the marriage cemented, Wenlock later abandoned Edward and, with Cook, supported Richard Neville, Earl of Warwick, in securing the temporary restoration of Henry VI in 1470.) Wenlock escaped with the surrender of a small quantity of land, but Cook was convicted and suffered crippling fines. Probably Sir Thomas Malory was also implicated. Malory was later specifically exempted from a 1468 pardon along with several other men known to have been involved in the Cornelius plot. The first of several Lancastrian plots uncovered in 1468, the conspiracy revealed a general dissatisfaction with Edward IV and his government, which helped oust the king from his throne in 1470.

In 1468, events had at last begun to turn in favour of Jasper and the Lancastrian cause. Ignoring Warwick's advice, Edward IV and his influential Woodville supporters had arranged alliances with the dukes of Burgundy and Brittany in the spring of 1468. Louis XI of France was left vulnerable to attack on three fronts, and looked for some way to harm Edward's plans. The Yorkists still wanted control of France. Jasper Tudor was in France and

Louis once again took him up as his protégé. Louis needed to stop Edward helping Burgundy, and the Lancastrian cause at last gained an ally. As early as 12 September 1467, a Milanese observer in Paris had forwarded the news to Milan that there was considerable discontent in England, and that the Welsh had taken up arms against Edward IV. He added that Jasper was going to Wales and Queen Margaret was sending with him some of her Lancastrian lords in exile. On 10 June 1467, the community of Flintshire had agreed to pay the king a subsidy of 1,000 marks. However, because of poverty, which was the result of the depredations of the Lancastrian rebels under Jasper, they were unable to pay it. As late as 9 April 1472, the matter was still not settled.

Despite promising news of discontent in England, Louis XI, known as 'the Spider' for his diplomatic wiles, took some time to authorise assistance for Jasper. Only on 1 June 1468 did he sign the necessary order authorising Antoine Roguiet, his treasurer of war, to provide Jasper with three ships and £293 5s 5d for his expedition to Wales. This was not enough for a serious military expedition, but Louis probably merely wished to threaten Edward IV rather than start a costly war. On 28 June, Jasper landed in Wales with three ships, 'fifty men and a few pennies'. Jasper would have known that there was not enough French support, financial or military, but took the opportunity to do as much damage as possible. He probably landed at Tŷ Gwyn, Barmouth or on the Dyfi estuary near Harlech. If Jasper could not give the garrison any fresh supplies or additional men, he could certainly strengthen its resolve. Harlech was probably not under siege when he landed, but it certainly became besieged while he was ravaging Denbighshire. Referring to Harlech, one contemporary declared that 'that castylle ys so stronge that men sayde that hyt was impossybylle unto any man to gete hyt'.

A strong Lancastrian supporter was Gruffydd Fychan, Gruffydd ap Gruffydd ab Einion (*c.* 1430–1468) of Cors y Gedol, Llanddwywe, Merionethshire, about six miles from Tŷ Gwyn. Gruffydd Fychan was one of the three captains that held Harlech Castle against Edward IV. Gruffyd Fychan is said to have built Tŷ Gwyn to allow easy landing for a secret rendezvous with supporters and a quick escape to sea should the need arise. Gruffydd Fychan was a patron of the renowned poet Tudur Penllyn, who wrote about Tŷ Gwyn and described it as a fine 'house built half in the waves'. It was said by Penllyn that Gruffydd knew just when to expect the arrival of Jasper, the 'black eagle' flying in from Anglesey or the Isle of Man. A tradition is that Jasper lay concealed in the building with his ward, the future King Henry VII, when plotting the downfall of Richard at the Battle of Bosworth. Tŷ Gwyn can still be seen on the quay in Barmouth, and has a fine Tudor ceiling.

Men flocked to Jasper's banner on hearing of his arrival, and he quickly formed an army of 2,000 men, marching sixty miles over the moors to Denbigh, which was raided and burned. According to the sixteenth-century Welsh Chronicler Elis Gruffydd, in 1468–1469 there was antagonism between the counties of Caernarfonshire and Merionethshire, which supported Henry VI, and Denbighshire, which supported Edward IV, hence Jasper's concentration on Denbigh: 'The old Lord Jasper and some time Earl of Pembroke ... rode over the country and held many sessions and cases in King Harry's name'. This was the same tactic employed by Herbert and Ferrers in 1456 when they seized the castles of Carmarthen and Aberystwyth in the Duke of York's name. Jasper wanted to show that Henry VI was the true king of England and the centre of justice. Having seized Denbigh, Jasper burned it so that 'the new towne ... was clere defacid With fier by hostilitie'. Denbigh had already suffered in Jasper's siege of 1460, and the second onslaught was probably a major cause of the decay of the old town. Williams noted that there was 'a Warrant for 200 marks, residue of 1,500 to Burgesses of Denbigh, by Edward IV, towards re-edification of Town burned by certaine rebbels and traytors, 23 Feb., 1st year'. This seems to represent 1461–1462. However, 1468 is named by Pennant as being when Jasper Tudor, with 2,000 Welsh, burnt the town, so the '1st year' possibly refers to 1471–1472, after the final overthrow of Henry VI in April 1471. According to the sixteenth-century antiquarian Sir John Wynn of Gwydir, his great-great-grandfather, Ieuan ap Robert ap Maredudd, of Eifionydd in Caernarfonshire, was a Lancastrian partisan who assisted in the ravaging of Denbigh as one of Jasper's captains. Sir John adds that Lord Herbert granted his ancestor safe conduct on 4 November 1468 so that he and his followers might parley.

Williams writes,

Sir John Wynne, in his *History of the Gwydir Family*, mentions an ancestor of his, a Lancastrian, who invaded the Duke of York's estate in Denbighland, and wasted, with fire and sword, the suburbs of Denbigh. But according to others, it was Jasper Tudor who returned to the charge and headed the second attack. This proves that there was even then a town without the walls.

'In revenge for this,' adds Sir John, 'Edward IV sent William, Earl of Pembroke, with a great armie to waste the counties of Caernarfon and Merioneth, and to take the castel of Harddlech (held by Henrie, Earl of Richmond,) which earl performed his charges to the full, as witnesseth this Welsh rime: '*Mlarddlech a D'mbech, pob dor–yn cynneu, / Nan'eonwy yn farwor, Mil pedwar cant oediant Idr, A thri'gain ac wyth rhagor.*' Which maybe literally translated, 'In Harlech and Denbigh every door flaming; the Vale of Conway reduced to embers, in the year of our Lord 1468.' Sir John adds, 'the whole country was reduced to cold coals' – to cinders. So great was the desolation, that those who had mortgaged their lands did not think them worth redeeming. Denbighland was then one immense forest, the 'woods climbing to the top of Snowdon'. The country was very thinly peopled.' Sir John tells us further that the marks of the war were seen in his day.

Camden, speaking of Denbigh, observes, 'We read that out of malice to King Edward IV., who was of that house (York), this town suffer' d much by those of the family of Lancaster.'

In his 1836 history of Denbigh, Williams relates that, eight years after being dispossessed of the walled town of Denbigh, Jasper returned in 1468 and burned the town in revenge rather than trying to conquer it. The castle was strong and would have needed cannon to take it, but it was a great Yorkist symbol of power near the English border. The campaign spurred Edward IV into action and he sent orders to Herbert to raise a force and attack the Lancastrian-held Harlech Castle. On 3 July 1468, the Lords Herbert and Ferrers were commissioned to array men in Gloucestershire, Herefordshire, Shropshire and the Marches to combat the rebels in Wales, and they quickly gathered a substantial army, variously estimated at between 7,000 and 10,000 men.

Lord Herbert sent half of his army under his brother Richard Herbert to devastate the coast and hinterland north of the castle, preventing it being easily supplied with food. This force moved along the North Wales coast and then up the valley of the Conway and, according to Sir John Wynn, Lord Herbert so 'wasted with fyre and sworde all Nanconwy and all the countrey lyinge between Conwey and Dovy' that it had not fully recovered a century later. Jasper marched to try and relieve the last Lancastrian stronghold, Harlech Castle, under siege by William Herbert, who had marched north from Pembroke. The northern army of Richard Herbert defeated Jasper's small force and scattered his army. The Herbert brothers captured and beheaded twenty of Jasper's men. William of Worcester recorded that Herbert hanged seven brothers in Anglesey, despite their mother's pleas to spare one of them. He records that she fell to her knees and cursed him, 'which curse fell on him at Banbury'.

The siege of Harlech castle was conducted under the direction of sir Richard Herbert, whilst his brother William (afterwards earl of Pembroke) was engaged in subduing the Lancastrians among the Snowdonian recesses, and in the isle of Anglesea. The earl, it is said, committed great ravages on this occasion; and, among other acts of cruelty, he caused every mansion which belonged to a Lancastrian to be burnt to the ground. Now, although it would be with out the province of a note to enter more largely into the history of the two brothers; yet the following anecdote, preserved in the family of lord Herbert of Chirbury, of a conversation which took place between them just before the battle of Banbury, may not be irrelevant here. The earl, in reviewing his army, came up to his brother, and found him, with a grave countenance, leaning upon his poleaxe. And he said to him, 'What makes thee assume that position, and that forlorn visage? Art thou fatigued? or art thou afraid?' Sir Richard replied, 'I am not afraid, brother; and that you will see anon; but I cannot help thinking of the old woman in Anglesey, who, in counting her woollen beads, cursed you for every bead she counted, because you refused to spare the life of one of her seven sons condemned to the gibbet for being Lancastrians.

William Worcester recounted:

> Truly the said Lord Herbert made a continuous siege powerfully around Harlech castle up to 14 August. On which day Dafydd ab Einion, the captain of the castle, restored the castle to the will of the Lord Herbert and the mercy of the king. And thus in that place handed over and captured from the besieged were Richard Tunstale, Henry Bellingham, William Stoke, knights, and Whittington, Thomas Elwyke, the said Dafydd ab Einion, Trublode and other to the number of fifty people. Truly the said Lord Herbert led the said people to London to the Tower, from which Thomas Elwick and Trublode by the Earl Rivers, constable of England, were condemned and beheaded in the moat of the Tower. Truly on 8 September Lord William was created earl of Pembroke by the lord king on account of his conspicuous capture of the aforesaid castle.

The siege of Harlech was described by the bard Hywel Dafi, who wrote of men being 'shattered by the sound of the guns'. A little-known fact is that a cannonball or shell passing by a man can kill him, much as wind generator blades kill passing bats. It is a phenomenon known as 'wind of ball'. This injury occurred when a cannonball, in flight, passed close to any part of the body. It was considered most dangerous when passing close to the stomach, leaving no obvious marks but often causing almost instantaneous death. Remarkably, it was also noted that 'wind of ball' was never fatal if the ball passed close to the head. Dafi also wrote of 'seven thousand men shooting from every port, their bows made from every yew tree'.

After Jasper's nearby defeat, this final siege lasted only a month. According to Worcester, only one man, Philip Vaughan, an esquire of Hay in Breconshire, was killed at the siege. Dafydd ab Ieuan ab Einion, the constable, was one of the fifty prisoners taken to London by Herbert, along with Sir Richard Tunstall, Sir Henry Bellingham, Sir Robert Whittingham and Sir William Stoke. Despite their stubbornness, the defenders of Harlech were treated with leniency and only two obscure Lancastrians were executed. Dafydd ap Ieuan and Gruffydd Fychan did not suffer upon surrender, thanks to Herbert influence. Tunstall, Bellingham and Stokes were later pardoned, while Whittingham must also have been shown mercy for he survived, like Tunstall, to rejoin Henry VI at his readeption in 1470–1471. As for Jasper, he outwitted his enemies yet again, leaving them empty-handed:

> The Lord Herbert got the castle of Hardelowe in Wales; that castle is so strong that men said that it was impossible unto any man to get it, but poyntment it was gotten. And some of the petty captains were beheaded on Tower Hill at London, for that castle was fortified and vitailed by

shuch at Lord King Harry; one of the men was called John Treublode. Also that year, a little before the siege of that castle, the old lord Jasper and sometime earl of Pembroke was in Wales; and he rode over the country and held many sessions and cysys in King Harry's name. Men wern that he was not owte of walys whenn that the Lord Herberde come with hys oste; but favyr at sum tyme dothe grate ese, as hit ys prevyd by the hydynge of that lorde sure tyme Erle of Pambroket.

One story, preserved by the sixteenth-century Welsh Chronicler Elis Gruffydd, relates that Jasper was hidden by a gentleman of Mostyn in Flintshire, possibly his kinsman, Hywel ab Ieuan Fyehan of Pengwern and Mostyn. It was said that, in order to make his escape by sea, the earl was forced to carry a load of pea straw on his back like a peasant as he made his way to the ship moored nearby at Picton pool. From there he is supposed to have sailed for Brittany, more by his own skill, it was said, than by that of those with him. The last Lancastrian stronghold had fallen after eight years, a feat that inspired the song 'Men of Harlech', while Jasper Tudor managed once again to avoid being captured. So spectacular had been Jasper's *chevauchée* across North Wales that the news spread across Europe and on 2 July 1468 the Milanese ambassador in Paris was able to report the events, adding that Queen Margaret was coming from Lorraine to see Louis XI in an attempt to persuade him to give Jasper further assistance.

In 1468, following Jasper's defeat at Harlech, the Yorkists waged a punitive campaign across north-west Wales. A century later, John Wynn of Gwydir recorded that Herbert 'wasted with fire and sword all Nanconwy and all the land lying between Conway and Dovy ... the whole borough of Llanrwst and all the vale of Conway besides carried yet the colour of the fire'. For his capture of Harlech, Lord Herbert was given Jasper's earldom of Pembroke on 8 September 1468. In November 1468, Edward paid Herbert £5,521 for his services in Wales. The cost of subduing North Wales and finally capturing Harlech had been considerable, a sum of £7,177 being allocated to Lord Herbert to meet his expenses, so he was probably never paid in full. On the recovery of the fortress in 1468, King Edward IV placed a garrison of twenty-four men within the walls at the Crown's cost. This number had dropped to twenty by the time he was succeeded by Richard III in 1483, but was then raised to sixty by the end of his reign. Thomas Guto'r Glyn warned Herbert not to do any more harm to the Welsh Lancastrians in North Wales:

Tax not Anglesey beyond what it can bear.
Let not the Saxon rule in Gwynedd and Flint.
Confer no office upon the descendants of Horsa.

In November 1468 occurred the executions of Henry Courtenay and Sir Thomas Hungerford, heirs of Lancastrian partisans, and of John

Poynings and William Alford, squires accused because they 'had familiar conversation with the Duke of Somerset and his accomplices' while in Bruges for the wedding of Margaret of York and Charles of Burgundy. Edward's agents must have been responsible for the arrests. These men were guilty of communication with the Lancastrian exiles, probably to increase their opportunities of better fortune if Henry VI was restored.

After his father and brother had been executed, for several years, John de Vere, Earl of Oxford, went about his business on his estates, occasionally hunting and dining with his mother's cousin, John Howard, who would later become the Duke of Norfolk. In November 1468, however, the twenty-year-old Oxford was arrested and imprisoned in the Tower for treason. Supposedly he made a confession, saving his own head but resulting in the executions of two other men. By January 1469, Oxford was released from the Tower, where he is said to have been kept in irons, and received a royal pardon that April. Oxford soon joined the Lancastrian exiles overseas, realising that he was under constant threat in England. Oxford's treatment had long-term consequences for the House of York.

Warwick's power was waning fast. The Woodville family of Edward's queen was in the ascendant. Warwick had been made to look a fool when Edward chose Elizabeth over his own choice of a French princess as queen. Then Lord Rivers, Richard Woodville, was made an earl and his son Anthony made Lord Scales. They were given key government posts and all twelve surviving Woodville children were married into the gentry, while Warwick's own daughters had been banned from marrying. Warwick became close to Edward's disaffected nineteen-year-old brother. Warwick the 'Kingmaker', responsible for Edward's usurpation to power, now thought that George, Duke of Clarence, could become king. In April 1469, a rebellion in Yorkshire, probably inspired by Warwick, was led by a 'Robin of Redesdale' but quickly dissipated. As it ended, another started, again in Yorkshire, led by Robin Hildyard, or Robin of Holderness, who seems to have been protesting about Corn Tax. The protestors marched on York to be met by Northumberland. After a skirmish outside Walmgate Bar at York, Hildyard was captured and executed. The rest of the rebels fled. Both leaders had connections to Warwick. There were unsuccessful risings in 1469 in South Wales, but the Yorkist government, led by the capable and energetic Herbert, was able to consolidate its position in the following years. The finances of Carmarthenshire and Cardiganshire rallied and the collection of revenue became more efficient and successful. Nevertheless, there was a continuous undercurrent of tension, which was visible in precautionary measures taken by Herbert and the government.

Around 21 June, Warwick was in open rebellion and sent out orders to stir up the people 'for the time to be busy was now at hand'. In June 1469, Oxford joined Warwick and Edward's brother the Duke of Clarence. On 29 June, Warwick wrote to his supporters announcing the marriage of his daughter to Clarence, which the king had banned. On 4 July, Warwick, his brother-in-law Oxford, Clarence and George Neville sailed for Calais without the king's knowledge. Around the same time, Robin of Redesdale emerged leading a third revolt in the North. 'Robin' was a supporter of Warwick. His identity is uncertain but he was probably either Sir John Conyers of Hornby (d. 1490) or his brother Sir William Conyers of Marske (d. 1469). Edward was riding to tour the North before going to East Anglia. He was at Fotheringhay Castle to meet the Dukes of Norfolk and Suffolk on 4 July, and appeared to be unaware of the growing threat. On 7 July 1469, Edward was at Grantham, intending to continue his progress north with his Woodville family, but the rebel army of Robin of Redesdale was marching south from Yorkshire. In Nottingham Edward finally realised the seriousness of the situation, urgently requesting 100 archers from Coventry.

Vastly outnumbered by the rebels, Edward turned south, sending the Woodvilles into Norfolk for safety while Earl Rivers and his son John returned to their manor at Grafton Regis in Northamptonshire. Edward sent an urgent summons to William Herbert, the new Earl of Pembroke, and Humphrey Stafford, Earl of Devon, to march north as quickly as possible, collecting all the men they could. Unusually, Pembroke brought very few archers, most of whom were provided by Devon's force. Clarence married Warwick's daughter Isabel in Calais on 11 July 1469, potentially giving Warwick's Neville family a hold in a new line of kings. In a joint letter of 12 July, Warwick and Clarence complained about Edward's confidence in his ambitious and newly created lords, especially the Woodvilles, trying to gain support among the great barons: 'The king estranges great lords from his council and takes about him others not of their blood inclining only to their counsel.'

Upon 15 July 1469, Warwick landed at Sandwich and marched towards London via Canterbury, gathering the men of Kent. Edward was still at Nottingham. On 16 July Warwick was at Canterbury, where he found those who wished to assist him 'arrayed for war'. More supporters gathered in the Midlands, including Thomas Wake, sheriff of Northampton, Thomas Stafford of Middleton and Sir Edward Grey of Astley. Redesdale's Northern rebels continued to march south. Warwick was welcomed in London by 20 July, and headed directly north along Watling Street. One chronicler says that he had 20,000 men with him. The rebels bypassed Edward at Nottingham and continued south. Herbert and Devon met at Cirencester and began marching north to join the king. On 22 July, the Northern rebels left the Great North Road at Stamford, moving through Northampton towards Daventry. Edward and his small force remained in heavily defended Nottingham Castle for some time. Herbert and Devon continued marching north towards Chipping Norton.

The rebels reached the area around Daventry around 24 July, possibly heading towards Coventry. Herbert and Devon approached Banbury and sent an advance guard of around 2,000 cavalry towards Daventry. The Yorkist cavalry came across the rearguard of the rebels possibly on the Banbury Lane or near Daventry and charged, but were beaten off. The rebels turned towards the royal army of Herbert and Devon. On 25 July,

William Herbert, Earl of Pembroke, reached Banbury but an argument broke out with Devon. One source claims that this was over a Banbury barmaid, both wanting to spend the night with her, and that Herbert won as the senior earl. It is more likely that Herbert's army reached Banbury first and took all the available lodgings for his men. Devon, with his 6,000 archers, left Banbury and camped around twelve miles away. Cavalry under Lord Latimer clashed with Herbert's men near Edgcote. Either Latimer or his son Sir Henry Neville was captured and executed by Herbert.

On 26 July 1469, the Battle of Edgecote Moor, sometimes called Banbury, was fought on the Northamptonshire–Oxfordshire border, six miles from Banbury. At some point in the morning, Herbert, with around 7,000–10,000 men, formed up on Wardon Hill on the northern side of Danesmoor, on the northern side of Trafford Bridge. Around 10,000–15,000 rebels were on Edgcote Hill on the southern side of Danesmoor. It is also possible that the two sides were arrayed the other way round. The rebels crossed the river to attack Wardon Hill, firing thousands of arrows into Herbert's men. A trained archer could fire twelve arrows a minute. Lacking Devon's archers, Herbert suffered great losses, so was forced to leave the hill and attack the rebels. Herbert's forces began winning, and Sir Richard Herbert, the Earl of Pembroke's brother, is recorded as twice cutting his way through the rebel lines and back with his poleaxe. It is likely that the rebels retreated back over Trafford Bridge, and Robin of Redesdale, probably the Warwick supporter Sir William Conyers, was killed at this point. His younger brother Sir John took over command, and seems to have acted as 'Robin' in future.

Just when Herbert's royalists were about to win, a new force was seen arriving to the east on the top of Culworth Hill, shouting 'a Warwick! a Warwick!', and carrying Warwick's bear-and-ragged-staff banner. Herbert's army believed that the whole of Warwick's army was coming and their lines started to collapse, as fresh troops assaulted their flank. A rout followed. However, Warwick's 'army' was a force of only 500 men, described as the 'rascals of the towne of Northampton and other villages about', led by John Clapham. Warwick's main army had only just reached Northampton.

The Yorkist army was slaughtered, and among the dead were at least 168 of the flower of Welsh nobility. It is recorded that around 1,500 rebels were killed at the same time. Both Herbert and his brother were captured. One account says that they were taken to Banbury, but others say they were taken to Warwick and Clarence at Northampton, where they were executed at Queen Eleanor's Cross, the site of Warwick's greatest victory nine years earlier. The bards were distraught. Many moved between the noble houses. One, Ieuan Deulwyn, accused another, Bedo Brwynllys, of speaking with a forked tongue to the Yorkist Richard Herbert of Coldbrook and Jasper Tudor in order to deceive both of them. Bedo wrote an elegy for Richard. Ieuan, however, wrote poems in praise of both William and Richard Herbert, his principal patron, and a great elegy upon Richard's death. Ieuan's wife's cousin was Rhys ap Thomas, whom he also praised in poetry.

Also at the battle was the young ward of William Herbert, Henry Tudor. After watching the carnage, he was led to safety by one of Herbert's men, Sir Richard Corbet. Corbet took him to the house of Herbert's brother-in-law, Walter Devereux, Lord Ferrers, at Weobley in Herefordshire. The Yorkist Corbet (1448–1492) of Moreton Corbet, Shropshire, was later to fight for Henry's Lancastrians at Bosworth. Indeed, as early as July 1470, Corbet joined Jasper Tudor in France.

'Black William' Herbert had married Anne Devereux, the sister of Walter Devereux, Lord Ferrers. The *Oxford Dictionary of National Biography* states that Henry Tudor was with Herbert at Edgcote/Banbury in 1469, when Henry would have been twelve years and six months old. Anne Herbert also went to Weobley after her husband's execution. This is known from a quote from a petition of Sir Richard Corbet of Morton Corbet to Henry VII that, after the death of Lord Herbert, 'he was one of them that brought yr grace out of the danger of yr enemies and conveyed yr grace to ye town of Hereford unto Jasper now duke of Bedford'. However, a nineteenth-century history of the Devereux family claims that Walter Devereux, Lord Ferrers, rescued Henry from the field at Edgcote. Sir Richard Corbet of Morton was Ferrer's son-in-law, but fought against him at Bosworth, taking men to fight for Henry. Lord Ferrers was a committed Yorkist who fought at Towton, Barnet and Tewkesbury and died fighting for Richard III at Bosworth. Henry's mother Margaret Beaufort had panicked upon hearing of the defeat, and sent a messenger to Raglan Castle to check upon her son's safety. Not for some days did she find that he had been taken to safety in Weobley, and she sent expenses for his keep, and twenty shillings for him to buy a bow and arrows for practising archery.

The Battle of Edgecote Moor was almost a national disaster for Wales, so many were the Welsh gentry who were killed on the field or executed afterwards with their leader, William Herbert of Raglan. One Welsh bard even called on Jasper Tudor to avenge the death of William Herbert, although they fought on opposite sides. But when Henry Tudor became a claimant to the throne, all Wales rallied to his support. That it did so was largely due to the work of the bards. The Welsh bards were also by tradition seers, endowed with prophetic vision. The vaticinatory verses of no less than thirty-five bards writing at this time have been preserved. Many spoke of the young prince beyond the seas in terms of Arthur, who would rise to rescue the Welsh from Saxon oppression, or of Owain Glyndŵr, whose mysterious disappearance led some to believe that he would again return. Of all such bards, the most prolific was Dafydd Llwyd ap Llywelyn of Mathafam near Machynlleth. Their work kept the Welsh people in a ferment of expectation.

The king had not heard of Herbert's defeat and death, and left Nottingham on 29 July, three days after the battle, to rendezvous at Northampton. Nearing Northampton, his small force received the disastrous news and almost immediately disintegrated. Warwick had sent his brother Archbishop

Neville to capture the king, which he did at Olney on the road to London. Edward was taken to Warwick Castle and then Middleham Castle in Yorkshire. Lord Scales escaped and claimed sanctuary. Earl Rivers and his son Sir John Woodville were taken at Chepstow Castle and brought to Kenilworth for execution on 12 August. There was no pretence at any legal trial for the queen's father and brother. Sir Thomas Herbert was beheaded in Bristol, and, on 17 August, Devon, who had not taken part in the battle, was captured by a mob and lynched at Bridgwater in Somerset. Warwick suddenly controlled the country. Edward IV had quickly lost public support – his wife's family were seen as greedy newcomers, wrongly influencing him. However, while Warwick was popular with the public, he had little support among the great barons.

Warwick gave himself Herbert's offices of chief justice and chamberlain of South Wales, and tried to win over his brother-in-law, Edward's best friend William, Lord Hastings, by making him chamberlain of North Wales. On 10 August, Warwick sent out writs for a parliament to be held at York on 22 September, near the Neville seat of power rather than in London. Warwick may have wished to replace Edward with Clarence in this parliament, because on 8 August the Milanese ambassador in France reported that Warwick intended having Edward pronounced a bastard and to give the crown to Clarence. There was always a suspicion that Edward was not the son of Richard of York. Edward was around six feet four inches, while his father York and brothers Clarence, Rutland and Gloucester were of small stature.

There was now rioting in London and fighting in Norfolk, Gloucestershire, Lancashire and Yorkshire. Agents again reported that a Lancastrian invasion under Jasper was thought to be imminent in South Wales. There was a short-lived revolt on the border with Scotland. Edward was by now in Middleham Castle, and the troubles across the land forced Warwick to free him by 10 September. He first compelled the king to sign pardons for all who had been engaged in the late insurrection, including himself and Clarence. With Edward's help, he could then raise a force to crush the Northern revolt, with Humphrey and Clarence Neville being executed at York on 29 September in Edward's presence. Edward now called his brother Richard of Gloucester, his brother-in-law Suffolk, the earls of Arundel and Northumberland, along with lords Hastings, Essex, Mountjoy and other council members, to join him. He then felt strong enough to ride to London and retook power. Warwick was now in a quandary and had to hope that Edward would not punish him unduly.

In September 1469, the council decided to send Lord Ferrers to South Wales 'for the sueretie and defence thereof and resistence and repressing of the Kinges enemyes and rebelles in cas they wolde presume or take upon thaim to arrive there'. On 13 September, Ferrers was commissioned to summon aid from the sheriffs of Gloucestershire, Herefordshire and Worcestershire. Several Welshmen seized this fresh opportunity to create disorder out of the Yorkist regime's disunity, and late in 1469 the elder sons of Thomas ap Gruffydd ap Nicholas, Morgan and Henry, seized the castles of Carmarthen and Cardigan. This necessitated a commission to Richard, Duke of Gloucester, on 16 December 1469 to contain the outburst.

There was seemingly a reconciliation of Edward with Warwick and Clarence. A modus vivendi was achieved for some months, but the restoration of Henry Percy to Warwick's brother Montagu's earldom of Northumberland upset the Nevilles greatly. A major problem for Edward was the loss of Herbert in controlling Wales. Edward's youngest brother, Richard of Gloucester, now appears as his right-hand man, being appointed Constable of England for life on 17 October, and in November becoming Chief Justice of North Wales and chief steward and surveyor of the Principality of Wales and the earldom of March. As for Jasper, he was recorded as being in the service of Louis XI at the royal court from October 1469 to September 1470.

8

Losecoat Field, the Readeption of Henry VI, Jasper's Return to Power and the Battles of Barnet and Tewkesbury, 1470–1471

On 6 January 1470, Edward's youngest brother, Richard of Gloucester, received another commission to act against rebels in South Wales, working with the dead Herbert's former supporters. On 7 February, Gloucester replaced Warwick as justiciar and chamberlain of South Wales and steward of Cantrefmawr and Cardiganshire. By February 1470, all the major Welsh offices taken by Warwick had been given to Richard. On 16 February, Warwick was replaced as constable of Cardigan Castle by Sir Roger Vaughan of Talgarth. By a letter dated 26 February 1470 and written from Tenby, Jasper, acting on behalf of the deposed Henry VI, appointed Roger Puleston as governor of Denbigh Castle. What he had been doing is unknown, but by July he was back in France.

After the defeat of his forces at Edgcote Moor, Edward IV had patiently waited for an opportunity to consolidate his power again. Warwick and Clarence were still unsettled despite Edward's attempts to reconcile with them. A rebellion arose in Lincolnshire under Richard, Lord Welles. Lord Welles and his son Robert had previously taken part in the insurrection of Warwick and Clarence. In March 1470, Lord Welles attacked the house of Sir Thomas Burgh, the king's Master of the Horse, wrecking it. Edward summoned Welles and his brother-in-law Sir Thomas Dymock to London. Welles pleaded illness, and instead claimed sanctuary at Westminster. He left sanctuary on promise of a pardon, and now Edward made him write to his son, telling him to give up Warwick's cause. Edward threatened Robert Welles with the execution of his father unless he submitted. Robert pulled back his troops but did not submit to Edward, so the king ignored his pledge and beheaded Lord Welles and Dymock at Huntingdon. Edward was determined to quickly stamp out rebellion. He had relied upon Warwick and Herbert to do so in the past, but Herbert was dead and it seems he could not trust Warwick with armed followers, at least for the time being.

Edward quickly marched north to Stamford and found that the rebels were camped at Horn Field, near Empingham in Rutland, under Sir Robert Welles. Welles was probably awaiting reinforcements from Warwick and Clarence, so Edward IV attacked immediately on 12 March 1470. The rebels, in fleeing, 'cast off their country's coats to haste their speed away and hence gave to the place its name of Losecoat Field'. Sir Robert Welles was captured and beheaded a week later, after making a confession implicating both Warwick and Clarence in the rebellion. Both Lord Welles and Sir Robert were attainted in the parliament of 1475 and their lands taken by the Crown. The Welles attainders were reversed in Henry VII's first parliament. It is worth mentioning here that virtually all of the Plantagenet land gains, both legal and illegal, under Edward IV and Richard III were reversed by Henry VII, ensuring support among previously disaffected noble families and their gentry followings.

In April 1470, Sir John Clapham, one of Warwick's squires, was captured in the Channel by Sir John Howard. Clapham's actions had won the Battle of Edgecote Moor for Warwick against Herbert. Later in April, Clapham was tried at Southampton and beheaded. Thomas Mortimer reported that

of these acts none gave so much horror as the execution of Sir John Clapham, one of Warwick's officers, and about, twenty other gentlemen of Henry's party, who, being taken on board a ship at Southampton, were, by the earl of Worcester (Tiptoft), lately made high-constable of England, ordered to be hanged, then fixed to the gallows by their legs, and afterwards impaled upon the highways. These instances of barbarity, instead of filling the spectators with fear and apprehension, inspired them with the most implacable hatred and indignation against the authors of the horrid scene. Numbers of reputable personages of the Lancastrian party fled over to France, among whom was John de Vere, earl of Oxford, who giving Warwick an account of the temper and state of the nation, and the certainty of his being strongly supported on his arrival, that nobleman drew the most favourable omen of success to his expedition: but he was for some time prevented from sailing by the proceedings of the duke of Burgundy. This prince, as we have elsewhere remarked, espoused the interests of Edward ...

Fearing for their lives after being implicated in the Lincolnshire rebellion, Losecoat Field and Clapham's activities, Warwick and Clarence had fled to France, arriving on 1 May 1470. Clarence's wife lost a child, Warwick's grandchild, giving birth on the ship to Calais. They were welcomed by Jasper, in the service of Louis, at the royal court. Oxford had soon joined them there. At the French court, Jasper and Louis now attempted a rapprochement between the Yorkist 'Kingmaker' and the Lancastrian queen. From October 1469 until September 1470, Jasper Tudor had been in the company and service of Louis XI, who was paying him a pension of £100 a month. Louis was known by contemporaries as 'the Universal

Spider', and 'the Cunning' as he had constantly plotted from Burgundy against his father Charles VII of France. However, during his reign of 1461–1483, Louis also acquired the epithet 'the Prudent', as his careful scheming meant that France stayed out of major wars while acquiring states such as Burgundy and Picardy. His fiscal prudence also meant that France built up its commercial and trading strength. Louis did not wish to become involved in the English civil wars, but equally wished England to be weakened so that there would be no threat of any more invasions into France.

Jasper had served Margaret faithfully. They were almost the same age, and he had known her well for twenty-four years, since her coronation in 1445, sometimes accompanying her on progresses. Although he obviously had doubts about her husband's capabilities, Jasper was working tirelessly to ensure that Edward of Westminster, now aged eleven, would succeed Henry VI. The deposed and inept king had been captured for a fourth time in 1465, and his son was the only future for the House of Lancaster. Warwick was around three years older than Jasper and the queen, and Jasper had known him at court and also collaborated with his father Salisbury before St Albans in 1455. Jasper thus knew Warwick and Margaret very well, and probably talked to his kinsman King Louis to effect their reconciliation. Unless Warwick came to the queen's side, and unless Margaret accepted conciliation with her hated enemy, the chance of Edward of Westminster succeeding to the throne was almost non-existent. Lancastrian armies had been regularly trounced in battle, and most of their leading nobles had been killed or executed.

Mainly through Louis' diplomacy, Warwick and Margaret of Anjou conspired to regain the throne for Henry VI. Louis' chief aim in his relations with England was to stimulate trouble there and prevent any Anglo-Burgundian alliance hostile to France. Warwick realised that he could never regain a dominant position in England while Edward remained king, nor could he rely on the feckless Duke of Clarence, whose unpopularity precluded his choice as king. Thus, Warwick and Louis XI determined to work for the restoration of Henry VI and for a marriage between Warwick's daughter, Lady Anne Neville, and the young Edward of Westminster, Prince of Wales. Not surprisingly, these suggestions were received with disdain by Queen Margaret, who had no reason to trust Warwick in view of the part he had played in deposing her husband. Oxford, however, had received a gracious welcome from the queen, who said that he had 'suffered much thing for King Henry'. That July, Jasper had returned to the French court to be present when the Warwick spent fifteen minutes on his knees begging for Margaret of Anjou's forgiveness.

Louis XI had also been persistent and persuasive, and Margaret eventually relented in the face of the attractive arguments put forward by Jasper, Oxford and others. On 25 July 1470, the Prince of Wales was betrothed to Lady Anne at Angers in the Loire Valley, and agreement was reached about the means by which to restore Henry VI. Warwick and Jasper Tudor were to sail to England, to be followed at a safe interval by the queen, her son and his Neville bride. Clarence had also to be satisfied, and was recognised as next in line to the throne after the infant Prince of Wales, Edward of Westminster, justifying the exclusion of Edward IV either by attainder for his treason against Henry, or on the grounds of his alleged illegitimacy.

In an accord between Louis XI, Queen Margaret and himself, Warwick agreed to restore Henry VI in return for French support for a military invasion of England. On 28 July, the Florentine diplomat Sforza di Bettini, Milanese ambassador to Louis XI, reported to his master that Wales would be the destination of the Lancastrian force because of its continued loyalty to Henry VI, recently demonstrated by the support that Jasper Tudor had been able to command in the north of the country. On 29 July 1470, Jasper went from Amboise to the coast with Warwick.

After gathering men, on 9 September, Jasper, Warwick, Clarence and Oxford set sail for England from La Hogue in Normandy. Jasper was appointed joint lieutenant for Henry VI, and the earldom of Pembroke was nominally restored to him. On 13 September, in sixty French ships under the direction of the Admiral of France, the Lancastrian army had disembarked after nightfall at Dartmouth and Plymouth. On the following day Jasper rode toward Wales to raise troops. Warwick set off towards London with the main army. A mock rising in the North was planned to lure Edward away from London. The king thus heard of the landing when he was in Yorkshire and thus was never going to be able to reach London before the Earl of Warwick.

Edward IV was forced to flee on 2 October when he learned that Warwick's brother, John Neville, 1st Marquess Montagu, had also switched to the Lancastrian side, making the king's military position untenable. When Warwick and Clarence were plotting against Edward IV, they had tricked him into giving them a commission of array. Edward, supposing that the troops so raised would support him, duly gave it, only to find out at a later date that their real purpose was to bring about his downfall. Also in 1470, John Neville, Marquess Montagu, raised soldiers in West Yorkshire, ostensibly to fight for King Edward IV against Warwick and Clarence in the South. At the last moment, Edward IV found that he was about to be arrested by these same soldiers and had to flee into exile. Edward and his youngest brother, Richard, Duke of Gloucester, took refuge in Burgundy. Burgundy was ruled by Edward's brother-in-law Charles, Duke of Burgundy, and Edward's sister Margaret of York.

Warwick entered London unopposed, freed the king from the Tower and restored him to the throne on 3 October. At Louis XI's insistence, Warwick now followed the French king's wishes and declared war on Burgundy. Oxford was made steward of the king's household and Constable of England, and he carried the sword of state when Henry was re-crowned. However, by this point Henry was too feeble to rule unaided. He had to be led by the hand when paraded through London. Just two days later, Oxford ordered the execution of the Earl of Worcester, the man who had ordered the execution of Oxford's own father and brother. The execution methods Worcester had used on some of Warwick's supporters, impaling bodies after hanging them, had repulsed even his contemporaries, so his own execution was well attended and applauded.

Henry Tudor was now thirteen years old, old enough to understand the danger he had been in after the battle at Edgcote. Since his guardian had been killed by Warwick, he was under the sole protection of William Herbert's widow, Anne Devereux. She had taken Henry and her Herbert children to her family's home in Herefordshire. Henry's mother tried to regain custody of her son after Herbert's death, but events had moved too quickly.

On 27 October, Reginald Bray paid three pence for a barge to take Henry Tudor from London to Westminster for an audience with Henry VI. Henry VI was said to have told the boy that he would one day sit on the throne of England. However, Henry VI had a son to succeed him, although the boy was still in France with his mother. After the meeting, Henry Tudor, his mother Margaret Beaufort, her husband Stafford and Jasper dined with the royal chamberlain Sir Richard Tunstall. Henry reunited with his mother, and they stayed together for over a week at the Beaufort residence at Woking in November 1470. After that they parted, and Henry left to rejoin Jasper. It is probable that the next time Henry saw his mother was after the Battle of Bosworth Field, when he had become King Henry VII.

Henry VI's restoration immeasurably increased Jasper Tudor's wealth and prestige, and he was again rewarded with lands, monies and grants, but Henry Tudor was not made the Earl of Richmond. The title had been given to Edward IV's brother Clarence, and Clarence would not give back the holdings of the Richmond estates. Since Clarence was an ally of Warwick, there was nothing Jasper or Margaret could do. Jasper, having spent ten years in exile and with little money or prestige, now kept his nephew with him. With the Prince of Wales himself still a minor in France, Jasper himself exercised Prince Edward's authority as *locumtenens generalis*. It was in this capacity, for example, that, at Monmouth on 16 December 1470, Jasper appointed Roger Puleston, esquire, as sheriff of Flint during pleasure. The Welsh poet Lewis Glyn Cothi described Sir Roger Puleston in one of his poems as a powerful warrior who possessed great wealth, a noble mansion and an extensive territory.

On 14 November 1470, Jasper received the farm of the estates in Wales and the Marches of the late William Herbert, Earl of Pembroke, to hold for seven years at a rent to be agreed with the Exchequer. On 7 December, he was granted the free disposition of the advowson of the parish church of Meifod, in the diocese of St Asaph. From 20 December 1470, Jasper was appointed a JP and on commissions of array for Gloucestershire and Herefordshire. On 16 January 1471, Jasper and a number of men from this area, including Thomas Fitzhenry, were given a commission of oyer and terminer there. On 14 February, Jasper was appointed constable of Gloucester Castle for life. While Jasper was busy settling Wales and the border shires, in London the new government was summoned, sitting from 26 November until Christmas. The legislation of 1461 – and indeed all that of Edward IV's reign – was dismantled, and Edward and his allies were proscribed. Thus, Jasper was automatically restored to the title of Earl of Pembroke and to any estates, offices or privileges he had held before 1461. However, since Lord Herbert had also been created Earl of Pembroke on 8 September 1468 and had never been attainted, his son inherited the title. Hence, until 1471, when Earl Jasper was attainted for a second time, there were technically two earls of Pembroke, although Jasper had the stronger title. As well as having his former estates restored to him, Jasper was richly rewarded with new lands.

Meanwhile, Edward was searching for fresh allies. A letter by Edward IV was sent from St Pol to François II, Duke of Brittany, on 9 January 1471. In it, Edward IV prayed François would assist him in the recovery of his kingdom and give credence on his behalf to his uncle, Jacques de Luxembourg. The letter, in a secretary's hand, with autograph signature, was written during Edward's stay at the court of Charles, Duke of Burgundy, at St Pol.

Jasper's greatest new windfalls came on 14 February 1471, when he was granted three more substantial estates. He received the lands formerly of Richard Grey, Lord Powis, during the minority of his son John, together with the boy's wardship and marriage. Grey's chief landed interests lay in Welshpool (Montgomeryshire) and the castle there, the manors of Pontesbury and Charlton (Salop), Whissendine (Rutland), Deeping (Lincolnshire) and Kersey and Layham (Suffolk). The second lease, to Jasper and Warwick jointly, was of the castle and town of Bronllys, the lordships of Pencelli and Cantref Selyf, the manors of Llangoed and Alexanderston, and a third part of the barony of Pencelli (all in Breconshire, and all previously farmed by Earl Jasper); they were to hold these properties so long as they were in the king's hands and at a farm to be agreed with the Exchequer. Finally, Jasper and Warwick were leased the castles and lordships of Brecon, Hay and Huntington, which were in the king's hands because of the death of Humphrey, Duke of Buckingham, and the minority of his son Henry.

The chief Herbert estates that went to Jasper were extensive, for not only did the late earl hold the castle and lordship of Raglan, but he had also been granted either in fee or at farm the lands of Sir James Luttrell centred on the castle and lordship of Dunster in Somerset; the Shrewsbury lordships of Goodrich and Archenfield in Herefordshire; the lordships of Walwyn's Castle and Haverfordwest in Pembrokeshire; Gower, Loughor, Kilvey and Swansea in Glamorgan; Crickhowell and Tretower in Breconshire; and one-third of the lordship of St Briavels and the entire lordships of Chepstow in Monmouthshire and Tudenham in Gloucestershire. These grants to Jasper, together with the restoration of his former estates, immeasurably increased his wealth, territorial power and prestige. He now dominated a great triangle of land with its apex at Welshpool in the north and its corners at Pembroke in the west and Tudenham in the east. After ten years of danger as a political exile, the king's half-brother had every expectation of continued royal generosity. On 22 February, Jasper was granted the goods of the persons within Denbigh Castle, for his services during the siege. He was also commissioned to raise men in Wales to resist Edward and others.

Charles the Bold of Burgundy had initially been unwilling to help Edward, but Warwick's declaration of Anglo-French unity prompted Charles to aid the exiled Edward. From Burgundy, Edward thus raised an army and a fleet to win back his kingdom. When Edward sailed from Flushing, landing at Ravenspur in Yorkshire with a relatively small force on 11 March 1471, he only just avoided capture. The forces of Oxford's younger brother Thomas had discouraged the ex-king from landing on the Norfolk coast. Montagu tried to raise troops in the Pontefract area to fight King Edward IV after his return from Flanders, but local lords answered that they were Percy followers, and without a call from Henry Percy, a traditional enemy of the Nevilles, they could not turn out to fight. They asked to see Neville's commission of array, as they knew he did not have one. Viscount Beaumont opposed Edward's landing at Ravenspur and joined forces with Exeter, but they were too weak and were forced to stand aside at Newark and allow Edward to march south to London.

The devious Clarence now deserted Warwick, realising that the marriage of Warwick's daughter Anne Neville to Edward of Westminster would probably end his own hopes of kingship. He reunited with Edward, believing that his fortunes would be better off as brother to a king than under Henry VI's uncertain rule. York only opened its gates to Edward after he promised that he had only come to reclaim his dukedom, just as Henry Bolingbroke had lied seventy years earlier. As he marched southwards, Edward began to gather support.

On 25 March 1471, Jasper was on a commission to raise men in Herefordshire against Edward. On the same date, we read of Warwick's fear for success in the urgent lines he had addressed to his old comrade Sir Henry Vernon:

Right trusty and Well beloved – We grete you well and desire and heartily pray you that inasmuch as yonder man Edward, the King our soverain lord's great enemy, rebel and traitor, is now arrived in the north parts of this land, and coming fast on South, accompanied with Flemings, Easterlings [from the Baltic states], and Danes, not exceeding the number of two thousand persons, nor the country as he Cometh not falling to him, ye will therefore, incontinent and forthwith after the sight hereof, dispose you to make toward me to Coventry with as many people defensibly arranged as ye can readily make, and that ye be with me in all haste possible, as my veray singular heart is in you, and as I may do thing to your weal or worship hereafter. And may GOD keep you – Written at Warwick on March 25th.

A postscript was added in Warwick's own handwriting appealing to his personal friendship: 'Henry, I pray you ffayle me not now, as ever I may do for you.'

In this period, of course, England had two kings, both of whom are accorded two official reigns. Edward entered London unopposed on 11 April, where he took Henry VI prisoner yet again. The period of Henry VI regaining his crown, the 'readeption', is from 3 October 1470 to 11 April 1471. However, Oxford was busy raising a Lancastrian army against Edward IV. The result was the Battle of Barnet on 14 April 1471, where Oxford commanded the right division. Under cover of darkness, the Yorkists moved close to Warwick's Lancastrians, and clashed in thick fog at dawn. With the main armies engaged under Warwick and Edward contesting the centre, Oxford and his troops routed the Yorkists' left wing under Lord Hastings, chasing them as far as London and causing rumours of a Lancastrian victory to spread. They began pillaging, but Oxford managed to round his men up and return to the field. There followed disaster as Montagu's troops mistook Oxford's men for troops of Edward IV, and began to fire on them. Oxford and Beaumont had lost their way in the fog, suddenly emerging to confront their own army, who mistook Oxford's heraldic star device for Edward's 'sun in splendour'. The Lancastrians unleashed a hail of arrows on Oxford's men. In the confusion, Oxford's troops, raising a cry of treason, fled the field. Montagu was then killed, and, while retreating, the dismounted Warwick was also killed by Yorkist soldiers. Oxford fled to Scotland, finding time on the way to write a letter to his wife, whom he would not see again until 1485. He asked her to send him money, men and horses and, optimistically, advised her to 'be of good cheer and take no thought'.

Mortimer reports that

> it is said, Edward, who in all his other battles was accustomed to order that the common soldiers should be spared, and the officers put to the sword, had ordered now that no quarter should be given. The earl of Oxford and the duke of Somerset fled into Wales, to the earl of Pembroke [Jasper], who was levying troops for the earl of Warwick; the duke of Exeter was wounded, stripped, and left for dead in the field, where he lay till the evening, when, coming to himself, he made a shift to crawl to the house of one Rutland, where his wounds were cured; but he was afterwards seized, and committed to the Tower. This battle was no sooner over than Edward posted to London, and entering into St. Paul's at evening service, with his royal captive, he there offered his own and his enemies standards; and, to prevent any doubt of the death of the earl of Warwick and his brother, he caused their naked bodies to be exposed to public view for three days successively, in the cathedral of St Paul, after which they were carried to Bisham, in Berkshire, to be interred, in the priory founded by their ancestors of the house of Montacute.

Edward imagined, that by the death of the earl of Warwick he had established his throne on a solid foundation; but he soon received fresh proofs that the war was far from being ended with this battle: for, on Tuesday in Easter-week, queen Margaret, the brand of the war, and no less terrible to Edward than Warwick, had landed at Weymouth, in Dorsetshire, attended by her son the prince of Wales, the countess of Warwick, the prior of St John of Jerusalem, the lord Wenlock, many other persons of distinction, and a body of French troops, in several ships.

Because of foul weather, Margaret of Anjou had been delayed leaving France. It was not until 24 March that it was possible to leave the port. Although the weather was by no means settled, the queen determined to wait no longer. The Countess of Warwick, who had been left in France when her husband went to England, sailed from Harfleur at the same time with the queen, though in a different vessel. Believing it to be safe to come to England, Queen Margaret and her son, Prince Edward, crossed the Channel with John, Lord Wenlock; John Beaufort, Marquess of Dorset; and the brother of Edmund Beaufort, Duke of Somerset, all landing at Weymouth. She was readying her troops to join Warwick when she heard the news of Warwick's defeat. She was welcomed on the quayside by Somerset himself; John Courtenay, Earl of Devon; Sir John Langstrother; Chief Justice John Fortescue; and Doctor John Morton. She had been out of the country for eight years, and the party journeyed to Cerne Abbey. There, on 15 April, they first heard of the terrible disaster at Barnet. Jasper had ridden to join Margaret of Anjou at Cerne Abbey, and was with her when she was told of the loss.

Margaret announced she would return to France immediately and remove her son from the dangers which the Yorkist victory posed to him. Jasper, as much as anyone, now convinced her that she must fight for her son rather than leave the country for a further period of relative poverty at Koeur-La-Petite. Jasper Tudor said he would have little difficulty in raising a substantial force from the many Lancastrian sympathisers who lived in Wales. Cheshire, also strongly Lancastrian, would undoubtedly support her. The North could always be counted on for substantial numbers of followers. Margaret's West Country lords assured her that strong forces would be recruited from Devon, Cornwall, Somerset, Dorset and Wiltshire. Her son, now aged seventeen, wanted to fight. Margaret assented, and men went out to muster a large army of men from the West Country.

Heartened, despite her husband's fresh captivity, Margaret next met the Countess of Warwick and they took quarters at Beaulieu Abbey in Hampshire. In total area, Beaulieu was the largest Cistercian church in England and was responsible for three royal daughter houses: Netley, Hailes and St Mary Graces in London. Jasper left to gather his men in Wales, and on 3 May 1471 was waiting near Chepstow for Margaret's army to join his. The defeated Lancastrian forces from Barnet, led by Somerset, joined with the fresh West Country troops and marched toward the Welsh border in order to recruit more troops and also meet up with Jasper's men. However, alerted by his agents, Edward IV moved at all speed with his 5,000-strong army towards the Welsh border. He needed to intercept the Lancastrians before the forces led by Margaret and Somerset could meet up with Jasper Tudor's Welsh army.

However, Edward was unsure whether Margaret intended to march upon London, so it was not until 29 April that he reached Cirencester, a day's march from the city of Gloucester's crossing on the Severn. A force from Somerset's army had feinted to march away from the Severn to Malmesbury, but the main army had been welcomed at Bristol, where it was reprovisioned and took on more men. Somerset seemed as if he was preparing for battle at Chipping Sodbury, but in fact he had just sent advance patrols there while his army headed west to Gloucester at all speed to cross the Severn. Edward arrived at Chipping Sodbury to find no opposing force. Having been outmanoeuvred, Edward despatched riders to tell Gloucester's governor to hold the city at all costs, as he was marching to support him. The Lancastrians had marched thirty-six miles through the night, but found the city's gates locked. Somerset's exhausted men were in no fit state to lay siege, where they would possibly be caught between Gloucester's force and Edward's oncoming Yorkists. They now marched another twenty-four miles to Tewkesbury, hoping for another crossing of the Severn.

It is amazing how quickly medieval armies could move about the countryside, carting provisions, weapons and sometimes artillery, despite there being no paved roads. Most troops were on foot, and they did not possess the excellent boots, specially designed for the purpose, worn by Roman soldiers and the armies of today. They were often carrying their own weapons and armour. A Roman legion on the line of march was expected to march 40 Roman miles a day. A Roman mile is 1,000 paces, or about 4,850 feet, so this would equate to around 37 miles a day with lighter armour, in good footwear on good roads. Foreign observers attending the manoeuvres of the Imperial German army just before the First World War noted that the troops regularly marched 35 miles a day. During the Second World War, Commando and Parachute Regiment training required 40 miles in nine hours, and today the Royal Marines aim to cover 30 miles in seven hours. Compared with these times, the standard march of 20–30 miles a day by a fifteenth-century army, on a poor and intermittent diet, compares favourably. The one-day march of Edward IV's army in 1471, from Sodbury Hill to the battlefield of Tewkesbury, covering some 36 miles in high summer temperatures, was one of the greatest recorded marches in history, as was Somerset's night march to Gloucester. His men must have been absolutely shattered prior to battle.

The Severn was in full spate, and the next crossing point was Tewkesbury, but Somerset now found that Edward's army was so close behind that he had to stand and fight rather than cross to meet with Jasper's troops. Somerset quickly took up a strong defensive position. Margaret rode among the troops to encourage them before the fighting, and stayed at Paynés Manor during the battle. Edward reached Tewkesbury on 4 May and immediately engaged the 7,000-strong enemy. He could not allow his tired troops to rest. Somerset believed he saw a weakness in the Yorkist centre and attacked. The Yorkists under Edward IV and Richard, Duke of Gloucester, held off the attack, then counter-attacked and routed the Lancastrians. Both Somerset's younger brother, the Marquess of Dorset, and the Earl of Devon died on the field.

Edward of Westminster, Prince of Wales, was found wounded in a grove by some of Clarence's men and taken to Edward IV. Hutton tells us that 'by the best accounts ever submitted to the world, there were only four persons in the room with Edward the Fourth, when Sir Richard Crofts brought in the prince; Clarence; Dorset; Gloucester, and Hastings'. The Prince of Wales was summarily executed, despite pleading for his life to Clarence, who had sworn allegiance to him in France barely a year before. Other versions state that Edward IV killed him, or that Edward, Clarence and Richard of Gloucester, the three brothers, jointly despatched the rightful heir. Whatever the case, he was murdered after being found. Many Lancastrian nobles and knights sought sanctuary in Tewkesbury Abbey, but, two days after the battle, Somerset and other leaders were dragged out of the abbey, and were ordered by Richard of Gloucester and the Duke of Norfolk to be put to death after perfunctory trials. Among them was another brother of the Earl of Devon. This was the eighteen-year-old Richard of Gloucester's second engagement in the wars. The future Richard III had also fought at Barnet.

An exciting account of the battle, with a different ending for the Prince of Wales, is found in Mortimer, who says that Margaret

left her sanctuary, and, putting herself and son at the head of the few troops she had with her, began her march, passing through the counties of Devon and Somerset, where her troops were continually increased by the coming in of the inhabitants, until they amounted to a very considerable army. At length she reached Tewkesbury, in Gloucestershire, on the twenty-ninth of April, having that day performed an incredible march of thirty-six miles, through very bad roads: here Margaret proposed to rest her wearied troops for a few days, and then proceed towards Wales, to join the earl of Pembroke, who had gotten together a considerable body of archers from the counties of Chester and Lancaster, famous for breeding that kind of soldiers, and was on the march to meet her.

In the meantime Edward, who, on the first notice of the queen's landing, had proscribed her and all her adherents by proclamation, immediately set out at the head of his army, in order to attack her before she could join the earl of Pembroke; but as he had with him a great train of artillery, it was impossible for him to march with so much expedition as the Lancastrians; he however made greater dispatch than could be expected, and, after a very painful and fatiguing march, he, on the third of May, encamped within three miles of the enemy.

The queen and her generals hereupon held a council of war, to deliberate what measures were the most proper to be taken. Their first intention was to have passed the Severn about Gloucester; but that city having refused to open its gates, she could not cross the river from her present situation, without exposing her rear to certain ruin; it was therefore determined that the queen's forces should entrench themselves in a park adjoining to the town of Tewkesbury, where they were flanked on both sides with hollow ways, ditches, hedges, and almost impassable grounds, with the town and abbey behind, and a strong entrenchment was to be thrown up in their front, and in this position, which, if fully effected, would have been impregnable, they were to wait the coming up of the earl of Pembroke with his forces.

But the execution of this scheme was prevented by the vigilance, courage, and activity of Edward, who determined to attack them in their entrenchments before they could farther fortify them. With this view, he, the next day, May 4, drew forth his army in two lines, one conducted by his brother, the duke of Gloucester, while himself, with his other brother, Clarence, assisted by the lord Hastings, commanded the second. On the side of the Lancastrians, the duke of Somerset, with his brother, lord John Beaufort, commanded the first line; the lord Wenlock, under the prince of Wales, who was considered as the commander in chief, the second; and Courtney, earl of Devonshire, the third.

The attack was begun by the duke of Gloucester with great fury, but Somerset's men, who guarded the front of the entrenchments, stood their ground with great bravery, and it is more than probable that Edward would have been baffled in his attempt this day, had not one of those accidents so frequent in engagements turned the scale of victory: it seems the duke of Gloucester before the battle, had received instructions from Edward to use all possible means to draw the duke of Somerset's division out of the trenches; Gloucester pursued these instructions with equal punctuality and success. Finding himself so warmly received by the van of the Lancastrian forces, he began a sham retreat, in such seeming hurry and confusion that the duke of Somerset, naturally of an impetuous disposition, imagining they fled, ordered the second and third lines to support him, and began his march in pursuit of the runaways, through the defiles which led out of the trenches, and a desperate fight ensued; for the Yorkists facing suddenly about, recovered their former ranks, and fell upon the Lancastrians with the utmost fury; at the same time a detachment of two hundred horse, sent off by Edward, attacked Somerset's division in flank, and disordered him so much, that he was obliged to fall back through the defiles to his former station; but in doing this he was so hotly pursued, that most of his line were cut in pieces. The duke of Somerset, amazed at his not being supported by the lord Wenlock, found that nobleman coolly standing at the head of his division, without having advanced a single step to sustain the first line: the fiery duke was so enraged at this treachery as he thought it, that, riding up, he clove the lord Wenlock through the brains with his battle-ax.

By this time the duke of Gloucester had followed the enemy so close that he was actually within their entrenchments, and was soon followed by his royal brother, with the second line. Everything in the queen's camp was now in confusion, the first division of her army was already defeated with great slaughter, and the second and third lines betook themselves to flight after a very faint resistance. In short, Edward gained the most complete victory perhaps that any history recounts, for, though not above three thousand of the Lancastrians fell in the fight, yet scarce a man of note of the queen's party escaped death or captivity. Among the slain were the earl of Devonshire, the lord John Beaufort, the duke of Somerset's brother, sir John Delves, sir Edward Hamden, sir Robert Whittingham, and sir John Luckner. The duke of Somerset, the great prior of St. John, and about twenty other gentlemen, took refuge in the abbey church, as a place of sanctuary; but they soon found themselves deceived, for they were taken thence the next day, and executed.

Margaret of Anjou herself was discovered, with her son, in another religious house, to which they had fled for shelter, and were brought to Edward, who ordered the queen to close custody in the Tower, where she continued four years, till the king of France thought proper to ransom her for the sum of fifty thousand crowns. But a more pitiable fate awaited the young prince, for, being brought into Edward's presence, and that king asking him 'how he durst presume to invade his kingdom, with banners displayed?' the noble youth replied with an unseasonable vivacity, 'that he came to recover his father's crown, and his own natural inheritance:' a reply which so stung Edward, that he struck the prince on the face with his gauntlet; this served as a signal to the king's remorseless friends, Hastings and the lord Thomas Grey (afterwards Marquess of Dorset), who forth with dragged the gallant youth out of the apartment, and plunged their daggers in his breast. The battle of Tewkesbury, fought eighteen days after that of Barnet, was the twelfth since the beginning of the quarrel between the two houses of York and Lancaster; but it was not the last, though followed by no other during this reign: and though the event of this field seemed to have extinguished the hopes of the house of Lancaster, yet there was still a small army in the field, under the command of the earl of Pembroke; but this dispersed of its own accord, on hearing of Edward's late victory, and the earl, leaving the defence of Pembroke to sir John Scudamore, fled into Brittany, taking with him his nephew Henry ...

With both Henry VI and Queen Margaret in captivity and the heir to the throne dead, the House of Lancaster was leaderless, and Edward IV in a position of unassailable strength. Jasper had been recruiting in South Wales, and was marching from Chepstow Castle, but he was unable to reach Queen Margaret in time to prevent her defeat. Because of its scale, Jasper realised that 'matters were past all recovery' and returned to Chepstow. Here, according to Vergil, he lamented the 'headiness, which is always blind and improvident' that led to Somerset's defeat. He was not to know that Somerset had been trapped by state of the river and Edward's incredibly fast march.

According to Edward Hall,

Kyng Edward at this season, not beynge out of feare of the erle of Pembroke, sent prively in too Wales, Roger Vaughan, a man there bothe stronge of people and of frendes, to the entent of some gyle or engyne sodaynly to trap and surprise the erle: but he having intelligence of certayne frendes, how that watche was privilie leyed for him, sodainly in the some towne [Chepstow] toke Roger Vaughan ...

This was Roger Vaughan, esquire, of Tretower in Breconshire, who had been responsible for the execution of Owen Tudor after the Battle of Mortimer's Cross ten years before. In the first days of May 1471, Jasper captured and beheaded Roger Vaughan, who had been sent to capture him: 'When Vehan, desired hym [Jasper Tudor] to be good to hym, he answerid that he should have such Favour as he shewid to Owene his Father, and so caussid his hedde to be smitten of.' Around 1450, Herbert had settled Sir Roger Vaughan at Tretower, where he built its great hall – a magnet for poets – and the battlemented courtyard. With fine wines and food, it was 'a court of royal style, the maintenance of 100 men'.

Jasper's nephew Henry Tudor was now the only adult Lancastrian heir left – except Exeter – who was not in custody or dead. Jasper Tudor understood the danger, and hastened to take the fourteen-year-old Henry from the Welsh Marches. Realising that all was lost and that it would be futile to advance and fight unaided, Earl Jasper fled with Henry on 4 May to Pembroke Castle after his act of personal revenge. The pair rode urgently from Chepstow towards Jasper's estates in West Wales, where he still had support and where there could be temporary protection before the Yorkists came for them. Edward sent Morgan ap Thomas to capture him. Jasper probably sent his followers home, knowing that their deaths in battle would be futile. His priority was to protect his nephew from the king. Pembroke was thought impregnable, but Jasper will have had no illusions about trying to defend it with no force left to raise any siege. A spiral staircase leads down to a great cavern, 'the Wogan', measuring around eighty by thirty feet, in which boats were stored. He could slip away by boat when the tide was in, to take a larger ship. However, he was soon besieged and the Yorkists were obviously aware of this escape route.

Knowing that he could not take the castle by force, Morgan, a grandson of Gruffydd ap Nicholas, built ditches and entrenchments on the landward side, intending to starve the earls into surrender. After eight days, Dafydd ap Thomas, Morgan's own brother, arrived with 2,000 followers, described as 'a ragged regiment, with hooks, prongs, and glaives, and other rustic weapons', and began to raise the siege. From the *Thomas Book* we read,

Thomas ap Gruffydd's two elder sons, Morgan and David became, on their father's decease, warm partisans, on opposite sides, of the houses of York and Lancaster. When Jasper, Earl of Pembroke, after the overthrow of Queen Margaret at Tewkesbury, retired to Pembroke, accompanied by his nephew, Henry, Earl of Richmond, Morgan ap Thomas invested the castle, in order to prevent them escaping out of the country. Upon this David ap Thomas hastily collected about two thousand men, armed any way, felon the besiegers by surprise, obliged them to retire, and gave the earl and his young charge an opportunity to escape to Tenby ... both are said to have lost their lives in the Wars of the Roses.

The biographer in the *Cambrian Register* noted that 'Morgan and David were home-bred men, Morgan was the better man; David the better soldier. Morgan I had rather have for my friend; David I would more fear as an enemy. Morgan had more virtue in him, the other more strength and force.' A poem by Lewys Glyn Cothi also notes that Dafydd, alarmed at the perilous situation of the Lancastrian earls when besieged by Morgan at Pembroke, collected his retainers, raised the siege and shipped both the earls at Tenby.

Some believe that because of the consistent loyalty of the Dinefwr family to Lancaster this story is untrue. More likely is the fact that there seemed absolutely no hope for the Lancastrians, but the family wished to hedge its bets and bore no ill will whatsoever to Jasper. Thus, as throughout history in civil wars across the world, brothers fought on opposite sides to ensure the family estates held intact. The brothers could easily have arranged the whole charade. It does seem that both brothers died before Bosworth, and their younger brother Rhys ap Thomas and his two younger brothers David (the second David) and John all fought at Bosworth.

We must here mention the interlocking loyalties of families across the region. Gruffydd ap Nicholas, the most powerful man in the south-west of Wales, had married Mabel ferch Meredith ap Henry Donne (Dwnn) of Kidwelly Castle. Their son was Thomas ap Gruffydd. By his second marriage, Gruffydd married a daughter of Sir John Perrot of Haroldstone Manor, Pembroke. Their daughter married Sir John Scudamore of Kentchurch. His third marriage was to the daughter of Jenkin ap Rhys of Gilfach Wen, who married Philip Mansel. The Mansels and Scudamores were prominent Lancastrians, while the Donnes were Yorkists until the early 1480s. A younger son of Gruffydd, Owain, married the heiress to Henry Maliphant of Upton Castle, Pembrokeshire. Owain was active in the civil wars, flying with Jasper and Lewys Glyn Cothi to Snowdonia after Mortimer's Cross.

However, Thomas ap Gruffydd, the eldest son, escaped from the fighting to go to the court of Burgundy. When his wife Elizabeth Griffiths died, Thomas seems to have attracted a lady of whom the Count of Charolais was enamoured. The count, the future Charles the Bold of Burgundy, enforced Thomas' expulsion back to Wales. In Wales, Thomas was noted for duelling to settle feuds rather than risk clan retainers moving to war.

In 1468, at Pennal in Merioneth, he fought and killed the Yorkist David Gough, then removed his armour to rest. He was run through by one of Gough's men.

In the notes to the poems of Lewys Glyn Cothi we read,

David Gough, having made himself master of the castle of Llanvihangel, commonly called Castell y Bere, situated on the western skirt of Cader Idris, had frequent opportunities afforded him, of which he, together with his followers, availed himself, of sallying forth from this fortress to annoy the Yorkists. The latter were at last compelled to apply for aid. To check therefore 'Coch of Pennant' (as the hero of the poem by Lewys Glyn Cothi was called) in his marauding excursions, Herbert, earl of Pembroke, sent a select troop of his men from South Wales, under the command of Thomas ab Griffith ab Nicholas, who was esteemed a most expert manager of steed, sword, and lance, having in his youth exercised himself in the use of them, in the service, and at the court of Philip the Good, duke of Burgundy. The two rival chieftains met near the village of Pennal, in Merionethshire. The spot where they met is called, in history, 'Pennal Field'/ The chiefs soon singled each other out; and after a dreadful struggle, David Gough fell before Thomas ab Griffith. On the fall of their leader the followers of David Gough dispersed. And Thomas ab Griffith, fatigued by the conflict, retired to an adjoining field: and while he laid himself on his face on the grass to breathe, he was killed by the spear of a Lancastrian, who followed him. His corpse was conveyed to Aberdovey, and from thence by sea to Bardsey island, where he was buried among the 'eleven thousand saints'. On the field, where he expired, a cenotaph consisting of stones and sods was erected, which is still extant covered with stunted oaks. It is in the next field but one, on the right hand, after passing Pennal bridge on the road towards Aberdovey. The field next to this, situated towards the west, and containing about nine acres of land, was the field of battle. Opposite, on the south of the road, is another tumulus, larger and more ancient, composed of artificial ground, and now covered with full grown Scotch pine. Of this tumulus nothing is known. They are both on the Talgarth estate.

Thomas had been first married to Elizabeth Griffiths, the heiress of Sir John Griffiths of Abermarlais. His second marriage seems to have been to Elizabeth, the daughter of James de Bourgogne, an illegitimate son of Philip of Burgundy. The second marriage produced many illustrious descendants, but his first marriage gave him Morgan, David, Rhys, another David and John. His daughter Margaret married the great Lord Richard Herbert of Coldbrook, who died at Edgcote, and another daughter married a son of Lord William Herbert of Raglan.

Henry and Jasper managed to break through the encircling troops, and rode eleven miles east, seeking refuge in the walled town and port of Tenby. They hid in a basement in the centre of town, and escaped towards the harbour in underground tunnels. Under cover of darkness, they shipped aboard a waiting barque at Tenby Harbour. The Elizabethan topographer and antiquarian George Owen of Henllys records that the two earls were assisted in their flight by a member of the White family of Tenby, 'which the good prince not forgettinge at his comeinge to the Crowne rewarded Mr ... White, with a lease of all the kinges Landes aboute the saied Towne of Tenby a good recompence done to one man, for a goode deede to the whole Realme'. Owen failed to give White's Christian name and later writers have suggested that it was probably either Thomas White, several times mayor of the town between 1457 and 1472, or his son John or Jenkyn White.

Just outside the great St Mary's church stood White's House, now demolished although the entrance to its cellar can be seen in a drawing by Charles Norris from around 1810. There are hundreds of sketches and watercolours of Tenby by the Norris brothers in Tenby Museum. One can still access this cellar under the road from the cellar in Jasperley House, now a Boots chemist, in the High Street. Other tunnels, now bricked up, led from the intriguingly named Jasperley House. It said to be from the cellar of White's House, where there are the remains of a fireplace, that Jasper and Henry Tudor passed through to Jasperley House, and then via another tunnel to Tenby Harbour to escape. Tenby was perhaps the busiest port in Wales at this time, and a boat leaving at high tide would have raised little suspicion. There were no harbour walls for mooring in deep water at this time at any port in Britain. Ships would anchor in the sheltered 'roads' off a harbour, while waiting for favourable conditions, then come into harbour to be beached for loading and unloading at low water or use small rowing boats.

This author has been fortunate to explore the 'secret tunnel', one of many in Tenby. Within the walls, its Georgian buildings are nearly all built on Tudor cores, with cellars, many interlinked, possibly for smuggling. From the basement of Jasperley House (Boots chemist) there is a brick-roofed passageway twenty paces long, almost six feet high and three feet wide. Passing beneath the road from just under the front door of the shop, it comes to the cellar of the demolished White's House, now under the present churchyard. The cellar has three blocked roof openings of which two had spiral staircases. The chamber is around eight feet high, lined with dressed stone blocks, and around seven paces long and five paces across (dimensions from a plan by A. J. Stubbs, dated 7 February 1983). In one corner there is a quadrant-shaped structure with a vertical flue, similar to a fireplace with a chimney.

Laws and Hewlett-Edwards inform us that the important townsman Thomas White died in 1842:

John or Jenkin le White, the father of Thomas, served as Mayor of Tenby 18 times ... Thomas White had done good service to the Tudors during his Mayorality (1457) for with his assistance Jasper Tudor, uncle to King Henry VII, rebuilt the walls of Tenby. When in 1471 the Earl and his nephew escaped from their castle of Pembroke after the battle of Tewkesbury, it was Thomas White, Mayor of Tenby, who conveyed them safely to Brittany in his own ship which the good prince (says John Owen) not forgetting at his coming to the crown, rewarded Mr White, then Mayor of Tenby, for his good service with a lease of all the King's lands about the said town of Tenby, a good recompense to one man for a good deed to the whole realm. The Whites are said to have been wine merchants. They had two houses in Tenby, one in what is now the churchyard, and an older one on the other side of the street (this older house ran back to Crackwell Street and was sketched by Norris, the picture is in the Free Library, Cardiff). They were connected by an underground passage. The White's monuments are the most important in Tenby Church.

However, the grant of demesne lands was made to Thomas White's son John in 1483, therefore it cannot have been made by Henry. Griffiths, in *Mediaeval Boroughs of Wales*, suggests that the Tudors may have financed the church spire and west porch in gratitude.

On 2 June, the Tudors, with 'certain other friends and servants', sailed out of Tenby. They knew that William Herbert and Walter Devereux had been sent to crush all resistance in Wales. The Tudors had wished to land in France, where Jasper had already established diplomatic relations and where they could expect a welcome at court from his kinsman Louis XI, but were blown off course. They may have landed temporarily in Jersey because of bad weather, and were then forced to land at Le Conquet in the extreme west of the Duchy of Brittany, then an independent nation and in almost constant conflict with France. They were taken to François II, Duke of Brittany, in his capital of Nantes. After a short stay in Vannes, the Tudors were granted asylum as privileged prisoners, but at the mercy of political manoeuvrings between England, France and Brittany. The young Henry was fourteen years and seven months old in 1471 when Jasper had smuggled him out of Wales, and would remain in exile for almost another fourteen years. The bloody disposal of leading Lancastrians who had survived the battles of Barnet and Tewkesbury in 1471 had left Henry exposed to Edward's dynastic 'tidying-up' process, and he and Jasper now became targets of Edward's diplomatic policy.

Back in England, Thomas, the illegitimate son of Sir William Neville, Baron Fauconberg and Earl of Kent, had taken part in setting Edward IV on the throne in 1461. Known as the 'Bastard of Fauconberg', or more usually as simply 'Thomas the Bastard', in 1471 he served Warwick, and helped him reinstate Henry VI. The Bastard was appointed the captain of Warwick's navy, and cruised the English Channel between Dover and Calais to intercept assistance coming to Edward. Around the time of Tewkesbury, Warwick gave him orders to raise the county of Kent on behalf of Warwick and Henry VI. He marched through Kent and Essex, and collected a large number of men. On 14 May, the Bastard appeared at

Aldgate and demanded admission to the City of London. This was refused, and the Bastard set fire to the eastern suburbs. The garrison of the Tower of London, led by Earl Rivers, the queen's brother, who had been injured at Barnet, repulsed them. (Rivers had inherited the title from his recently executed father.) The citizens of London also defended vigorously, and pursued the Bastard and his army as far as Stratford and Blackwall.

The Bastard now made his way west to Kingston-upon-Thames, intending to capture or kill Edward IV. However, Rivers had held London for Edward, and cleverly sent word to the Bastard that Edward IV was leaving England, inducing the Bastard to return to Blackheath. However, on hearing that Edward's army was approaching, Fauconberg journeyed with 600 horsemen to Rochester and then returned to his fleet at Sandwich. Only there he learned that the Lancastrian cause was lost, and Edward sent Richard of Gloucester for Fauconberg's submission, and to take custody of his thirteen ships and most of his immediate followers. The Bastard's main captain, Spysyng, was beheaded, and many of the rebels were hanged. Edward IV rode into Kent and also beheaded the mayor of Canterbury, who had helped raise men for the Bastard. Edward also fined the counties of Kent and Essex. The Bastard was pardoned upon 10 June, and was sent to serve Richard of Gloucester in the North, but on 22 September 1471 Fauconberg was taken to the castle of Middleham, Yorkshire, and was beheaded upon Gloucester's orders. No reason is known and there was no trial.

Together with exiled Lancastrians and mercenaries from several countries, Fauconberg's army may have numbered as many as 16,000 men in total. If the Bastard had taken London, he could also have captured Edward's wife, Elizabeth Woodville, and their children and released Henry from the Tower. Edward IV realised that Henry VI could no longer be allowed to live, and within a few days of the rebels' assault on London Henry VI had been murdered. As his son and heir, Edward of Westminster, had also been murdered, there were no real rivals left in England to pose a threat to the Yorkist king. On 21 May, while on his way to suppress Fauconberg and the Kentish rebels, Edward had passed through London in triumph with the captive Queen Margaret of Anjou beside him in a chariot. She was placed in the Tower of London, and Henry VI died in the Tower that same night, at the hands of, or by the order of, Richard of Gloucester, according to several contemporary accounts. Gloucester was Constable of the Tower. In the old ballad *The Wandering Jew's Chronicle* this event is described:

I saw the white and red rose fight,
And Warwick gret in armour bright,
In the Sixth Henries reign;
And present was that very hour,
When Henry was in London Tower,
By Crookt-backt Richard slain.

The Milanese ambassador in France reported, 'King Edward caused King Henry to be secretly assassinated ... he has, in short, chosen to crush the seed.' It was announced in public that the king had died 'of pure displeasure and melancholy', but few believed this. Hutton and others state that Henry was murdered on Ascension Eve, which is always a Thursday, but 'eve' may indicate that he was killed on the previous day. Others believe that he was killed in the early morning of 22 May. Dafydd Llwyd of Mathafarn and others believed that Henry was killed on Thursday 23 May. Henry's body was displayed in its coffin as if he had died naturally but it is said that he was stabbed. Margaret of Anjou remained in the Tower, subsequently being taken to Windsor and Wallingford before being returned to her father's estates in Anjou in 1475. From Tewkesbury on 4 May 1471 to the death of Fauconberg on 22 September, Gloucester was named by contemporary sources as having murdered both the Prince of Wales and Henry VI, and Fauconberg was known to have been executed by him without trial.

The House of York now was secure in ruling England and Wales. The king's brother Gloucester later married Anne Neville, the widow of Prince Edward and the younger daughter of Warwick. The Wars of the Roses appeared to be over, and there were to be fourteen years of relative peace. With the deaths of Somerset and his younger brother, distant cousins of Henry VI and possessing a remote claim to succeed him, the House of Beaufort had been almost exterminated. Only the female line of Somerset's uncle, the 1st Duke of Somerset, remained, represented by Lady Margaret Beaufort and her son Henry Tudor. Henry remained in exile in Brittany for the rest of Edward IV's reign. However, the year after the Battle of Tewkesbury, Henry Tudor's mother, Lady Margaret Beaufort, married Lord Stanley, one of Edward IV's most powerful supporters. This event probably caused the powerful Stanley family to turn against Edward IV's brother Richard of Gloucester when he became king as Richard III, and was instrumental in giving Henry Tudor the kingship.

9

Exile in Brittany and France, 1471–1484

John de Vere, 13th Earl of Oxford, had fought heroically at Barnet and escaped into Wales, probably aiming to join Jasper's men. He was around eleven years younger than Jasper, aged twenty-eight and in his prime as a warrior. Oxford had succeeded to the title, although now attainted, on the execution of his Lancastrian father and brother. It is unsure, but either or both may have been hanged, drawn and quartered by the Earl of Worcester rather than beheaded as peers. Oxford was now the only major adult Lancastrian noble surviving to assist Jasper in his efforts. He was probably with Jasper's army near Gloucester or Chepstow, for he did not fight at Tewkesbury. Oxford and Jasper suddenly realised that, with the killing of Henry VI and his only son Edward of Westminster, the fourteen-year-old Henry Tudor now had a valid claim to the crown. Henry's claim was the last chance for Lancastrians to see their attainders reversed, lands restored and families secured. Henry's sudden importance was crucially understood by Edward IV. Oxford probably left Chepstow with Jasper and Henry in May 1471 to head for Pembroke Castle. From Pembroke or Tenby, Oxford sailed to France to carry on the Lancastrian fight, this time for Henry Tudor. Jasper and Henry would have intended to meet him there, but had been shipwrecked and were not allowed to leave Brittany. There was no way that Oxford could have any longer come to any accommodation with the Yorkists, and their treatment of his father and brother would have severe consequences for their cause.

The political situation on the Continent was unsettled, and similar to England and Wales, with regional and familial allegiances often being stronger than those owed to the Crown. France was still not one country, with two different major languages, Occitan in the south and what we now know as the French language in the north. For instance, René of Anjou, Good King René, was known as *Rainièr d'Anjau* and *Rai Rainièr lo Bòn* in Occitan but *René d'Anjou and le Bon Roi René* in French. There was also Breton, similar to Welsh, taken there by British refugees from the Germanic invasions of England. Brittany was still an independent duchy. Different royal Valois and Bourbon families owned huge swathes of what is now France, and Burgundy was run virtually as an independent state. Great feudal magnates ruled across the land, trying to increase their territories by military excursions, marriages and political alliances. They only supported Louis XI of France when it was to their advantage, and his central monarchy was often impoverished. Some titular heads, like René of Anjou, of the House of Valois-Anjou, Queen Margaret's father, were almost penniless. This was despite René ostensibly being ruler of the French duchies of Anjou, Provence, Lorraine and Bar (the area next to Lorraine); Naples and Piedmont (10,000 square miles of territory based around Turin) in modern Italy; Jerusalem; and Aragon in Spain, which then included the Italian, French and Spanish islands of Sicily, Corsica and Majorca.

By now, increasing trade had meant that commercial classes dominated life in most cities, controlling the greater part of France's liquid assets. However, merchants endured constant trade disruption caused by aristocratic rivalries which continued after the end of the Hundred Years' War. They generally supported a strong central government and peace. Louis XI was now aged thirty-eight, and after ten years as king he felt strong enough to try and control no less than fourteen regional royal princes and barons who owed him feudal obligations. At this time, the royal writ was valid in only around half of France, much as some Marcher Lords in England ran their own lands as personal fiefdoms, collecting their own taxes. However, Louis was extremely concerned that it seemed that the latest English civil wars had ended after a quarter of a century. Louis knew that Edward IV wished to revive his claim to the throne of France, dormant since 1453. The remaining great magnates would also want war with France, with the concomitant hopes of vast plunder. Louis was well aware that Edward's agents and diplomats were looking for support from disaffected lords across France, Brittany and Burgundy to overthrow the French king.

Equally, Jasper knew that his kinsman Louis needed support against Edward, and had known the French king for years. He knew that Louis would help him against Edward, which would distract Edward from attacking a weakened France. However, while sailing for France to effect these plans with Oxford, Jasper and Henry had been forced to land in Brittany. Duke François II of Brittany was the same age as Louis, thirty-eight in 1471, and also knew Jasper, who was now aged around forty. These three similarly aged men, Louis, François and Jasper, were to decide the future of the English monarchy. François ruled one of the richest dukedoms in Europe but he had no legitimate children at this time, a single daughter surviving infancy in 1477. She is known to history as Anne of Brittany. François thus desperately needed alliances to ensure Brittany's survival as an independent state, with around seven other rulers having a direct interest in his lands.

Brittany, with no male succession, was a target not just for Louis XI of France, but also for Charles the Bold, Duke of Burgundy; Edward IV of England; and Maximilian I of Austria. Maximilian (1459–1519) was King of the Romans and later Holy Roman Emperor. Other threats came from

Jean IV, Prince of Orange (1443–1502), and Louis II, Duke of Orléans (1462–1515), who later became Louis XII of France. The pressing priority for François was to stop Louis XI, who needed Brittany for its income, from making it part of an enlarged French state. François realised that Henry of Richmond, the latest contender for the English crown, could be handed over to Edward IV, in return for support against France. Equally, Henry could be kept as an insurance policy to discourage friendship between England and France. Henry and Jasper could also possibly attract Lancastrians to help fight against France in the case of an invasion. François suddenly had an important bargaining counter in his desperate attempt to keep his nation independent. Henry and Jasper were well aware of their precarious situation.

Tradition says that Jasper and Henry hid for three days in the cellars and tunnels of Tenby, before embarking for France via a tunnel to the harbour. They were shipwrecked or stranded at either Camaret or Le Conquet, little fishing ports in north-west Finistère, near Brest. They had then probably been conducted under guard to the Château de l'Hermine at Vannes, Duke François II's palace, where Jasper 'submitted himself and his nephew to his protection'. Vergil, Commines and other authorities say that François 'received them willingly, and with such honour, courtesy, and favour entertained them as though they had been his brothers, promising them upon his honour that within his dominion they should be from thenceforth far from injury, and pass as their pleasure to and fro without danger'. The phrase 'within his dominion' could be interpreted as a threat to the Tudor earls, as he did not promise to protect them once he had given them up.

News of Jasper's arrival in Brittany reached London by 28 September 1471, when Sir John Paston reported that 'men say that the Kynge shall have delivered of him hastely, and some say that the Kynge of France would see him safe, and shall set him at liberty again'. Thus it was well known that Edward wanted Jasper – and, by proxy, Henry – returned quickly. Equally, however, Paston related the value of the Tudors to Louis XI, who also wanted the earls in his hands.

As soon as Edward IV knew that the Tudors were in Brittany, he pressed Duke François for their extradition. The latter replied, according to Polydore Vergil, that he had given them his word that they could enjoy his protection. However, the duke promised Edward that 'he would for his cause keep them so sure as there should be none occasion for him [Edward IV] to suspect that they should ever procure his harm any manner of way'. It was a promise François kept, although it never satisfied Edward, who had to console himself with the duke's promise that the earls were safely in his protective custody. The Tudors were first kept in the Château de l'Hermine at Vannes, but it was susceptible to attack from the sea. Fearing that the earls would be snatched by the English or the French, they were moved to Suscinio, one of François' country residences near Sarzeau on the gulf of Morbihan. Edward IV's ambassadors now demanded that the Tudors must be treated more as prisoners than guests. At the same time, French envoys also insisted that earls were put under far stricter control, to stop them being captured by any English force. François II was forced to accept these terms and the prisoners' movements and privileges were curtailed. We know that Jasper's personal servants were sent home, and that they were given Breton soldiers 'to wait upon them and to guard them'. At least one of Jasper's servants was to meet him at Mill Bay fourteen years later.

Edward IV and Louis XI continued to demand the handing over of the Tudor hostages. Louis XI was also the first cousin of Jasper Tudor. His father, Charles VII, had been the brother of Jasper's mother, Catherine of Valois, the dowager Queen of England. Louis thus believed that he had the right to the guardianship of his kinsmen Jasper and Henry and could use them to threaten Edward. Edward simply wanted them dead. François II therefore decided to separate Henry and Jasper, lessening the chance that both would be captured together. Around October 1473, the earls were taken from Suscinio to the duke's palace at Nantes, then the capital of Brittany, and soon after separated, being moved to the castles of Josselin and Largoët under the command of the de Rieux family. This may have been because of the possible danger of kidnap, or because of plotting by the earls to escape to France.

Jasper was taken to the mighty fortress of Josselin in central Brittany in late 1473 or early 1474. Josselin, which had been temporarily abandoned by the de Rohan family, was about twenty-five miles north-east of Vannes. The three remaining connected towers at Josselin demonstrate the immense fortress that it once was, and only four towers of its nine remain after its slighting. The château is situated in the heart of the town, overlooking the River Oust. Henry was taken to the Château de Largoët at Elven in 1474, ten miles south-east of the port of Vannes. Henry stayed in one of the famous Tours d'Elven with the de Rieux family, who had children of a similar age. An intriguing footnote, to the little-known story about the foreign invasion of England by Glyndŵr and a French army in 1405, is that the invasion fleet and army was commanded by Jean II de Rieux. This Breton lord and Marshall of France had brought 2,800 knights and men-at-arms to march into England, but unfortunately many warhorses died on the crossing, depleting his effectiveness. The invasion petered out at Worcester, owing to lack of supplies and provisions. The grandson of Jean II was Jean IV de Rieux (1447–1518), Marshal of Brittany, who was honoured to have Henry Tudor as his guest, and who later ruled Brittany as the regent of Anne of Brittany. Earl Jasper and his nephew were still being well treated, despite their separation and sterner confinement. The Duke of Brittany was fully aware of the value of his two guests as diplomatic pawns, and neither Edward IV nor Louis XI was able to get possession of them. As long as England and Burgundy threatened France, Henry and Jasper could expect asylum and some measure of support from Louis.

The Earl of Oxford was in France with Sir William Beaumont. Viscount Beaumont fought at Northampton, was captured at Towton and fought under Oxford at Barnet, probably escaping with him to Wales and France, and later landed with Henry Tudor and fought at Bosworth. By 1473, Oxford had collected twelve small ships at Dieppe. He had been given a small amount of assistance from Louis XI's to harass Edward. At this time, Oxford may well have been plotting with his surviving brother-in-law, George Neville, Archbishop of York, and perhaps with the discontented Clarence as well. Oxford carried out raids on Calais before landing with his fleet, on 28 May 1473, at St Osyth in Essex, but he was quickly repelled. On 30 September, with about eighty other men, including his brothers George and Thomas de Vere, he seized the castle on St Michael's Mount, a tidal island off Cornwall. On 27 October, Edward issued a commission to the sheriff of Cornwall, Sir John Arundell of Trerice, along with Sir John Coleshill, Sir Henry Bodrugan and others, to take the castle. From November 1473, Oxford was besieged in St Michael's Mount. However, in a sally by the castle's defenders, Arundell was slain on the sands.

Oxford was somehow acquiring provisions, so the siege's new leader, Sir John Fortescue, tried negotiating. Oxford's men were ultimately lured away with promises of royal pardons. After a siege by an army of 6,000 men, lasting twenty-six weeks, Oxford and Beaumont were finally forced to surrender in June 1474, and Oxford was attainted the following year. His life was saved probably at the intercession of the Howards, although on condition of enduring perpetual imprisonment in the castle of Hammes outside Calais. Beaumont was imprisoned with him. Hammes was one of the two great fortifications, along with Guisnes Castle, that defended Calais. Oxford's only child was said to have been sent to the Tower, where he died. His wife, Margaret Neville, the sister of Warwick the 'Kingmaker', was reduced to earning a livelihood by her needlework. Oxford and Beaumont remained in prison for ten years until freed in 1484, when they joined Jasper and Henry at Paris.

Duke François had consigned Henry Tudor to the custody of the twenty-four-year-old Jean IV de Rieux, who was Marshal of Brittany, the wealthiest and most powerful of the duke's subjects. He served as both military commander and diplomat, and was the owner of several strategic castles and estates. As François' right-hand man, de Rieux became the tutor to the infant Anne of Brittany. Young, talented and energetic, he seems to have been an excellent companion and role model for Henry, now apart from Jasper.

His castles and great estates were in the southern part of the duchy, stretching from Pontivy to the fortresses of Ancenis and Rieux guarding the eastern border. As Henry was kept guarded within the marshal's entourage, Henry will have become familiar with his other residences. In the Château de Largoët, about halfway between Suscinio and Josselin, Henry stayed in the Tour d'Elven. The great seven-story octagonal keep of the castle is the highest keep, or donjon, in France, and there is a chamber which is still labelled '*pièce ou fut enfermé le comte de Richemont*'. The tower is 144 feet tall, with 177 steps in total, being built to include views out to sea around 15 miles away. It had only been constructed around a decade earlier, and

Henry was probably housed in a small, narrow room on the second floor, although he could have been on the sixth floor. It may well be that Henry stayed in both the tall donjon, and the other, smaller Tour d'Elven, called La Tour de Connétable du Richemonde. The Duke of Brittany, by a curious coincidence, had also borne the British title of the Duke of Richmond.

He was allowed to exercise, which probably included hunting with de Rieux in Elven's 50,000-hectare park, and also probably participated in tiltyard contests with squires and men-at-arms. He had plenty of time to improve his archery here, his skills at which were noted when he was king. Henry became a fixture of the refined Breton court, as de Rieux spent most of his time in attendance on the duke, and observers commented on the elegant manners, piety and mastery of French of this tall and slender young man with fair hair. The Lord of Rieux became a friend and ally of Henry, being honoured to guard the 'comte of Richemonte'. Both Tudors will have been treated well, although restricted in their movements.

Moving in the upper echelons of the court, Henry will have learned of diplomatic complexities and ramifications for the first time. He will have learned of his kinsman Louis' strengths and weaknesses, and could probably converse in Breton as well as French with his hosts. He had had a Welsh-language upbringing in Pembroke, Harlech and Raglan, and Breton is almost identical to Welsh. Having been brought up in these major fortresses, he will have also realised their relative impregnability if he led any invasion of England and Wales. The Tour d'Elven stood on high ground overlooking the wide, flat, eastward expanse bordering the River Vilaine. Louis' armies would come this way, across Anjou or Poitou, if they attempted to conquer Brittany. Its strategic significance was similar to that of Chepstow, guarding the lowest crossing of the Wye into England. Chepstow was another castle Henry knew well, having been there with Jasper after Tewkesbury. More than anything, Henry and Jasper knew that they were still never safe, whether in the hands of Louis, François, Charles the Bold or Edward. They must have decided that their eventual invasion would not head east towards London, which would require taking the huge Pembroke, Swansea, Cardiff, Newport and Chepstow castles and many other fortresses, but head north on a much more circuitous route.

However, Louis, with his limited finances, had come to prefer negotiation and manipulation to military measures. He did not have the resources for a war with Brittany, which in any case would leave his nation unguarded against attack by England or Burgundy. Louis had a major problem with Charles the Bold, Duke of Burgundy from 1467 to 1477. Charles governed estates from Burgundy to the Netherlands, encircling northern France, and wished to become king of a unified state by expansion. In 1465, he had organised dukes and nobles inside and outside France into the League of the Public Weal, to resist Louis' centralising policies. In 1474, the conflict heightened with Charles' new strategy of a dual attack on Louis. His army pushed east into Alsace and he made a treaty with his brother-in-law Edward IV and François of Brittany. Now Louis was threatened by England to the north, Burgundy to the east and Brittany to the west, as well as by powerful nobles from the Languedoc region of the south. Charles now pledged to Edward and François that he would conquer Normandy, with Edward's assistance. Europe was on the brink of major warfare, and Jasper and Henry were fortunate to be peripheral to events at this time.

As part of the agreement, Edward, who had just murdered Henry VI, grandson of Charles VI and claimant to the French throne, was to be crowned at Reims. During Henry's reign, England's substantial holdings in France had been reduced to the Pale, the area around Calais. The Yorkist king wanted to reverse this humiliation, and, with England at peace, invaded France in June 1475. Louis was too weak to fight against England and Burgundy while also keeping his frontier secure against Brittany. With massive loans, Louis financed an excellent Swiss mercenary army to mobilise against Charles in the east of France. He similarly bought troops to deal with the English attack, using mercenaries to delay any advance. Edward was also virtually bankrupt. Charles was pinned down by the Swiss, fighting in Alsace, so could not assist Edward. François and others of Charles' declared allies now did not join in, preferring to see how the war developed. Edward led a massive army of 16,000 troops through Burgundian territories towards Reims, but Charles would not allow him to enter his towns, fearing pillage.

With autumn approaching in 1475, the campaigning season was coming to an end, with worsening weather for moving troops. Supplies were running short. Edward did not wish to start campaigning over the winter period, but to return empty-handed to England would be regarded as a disgrace and harm his prestige across Europe. Louis had prudently kept his army away from battle, not wishing to escalate matters. Richard of Gloucester argued to begin fighting a path into France, but, as Philippe de Commines wrote, Edward was now more inclined to the pleasures of the flesh than battle, as the king 'strongly loved ease and pleasure'. Edward's exploits with Lord Hastings among the opposite sex will have been well known to Louis, who offered the English king 75,000 crowns for peace, plus a pension of 50,000 crowns, under the terms of the Treaty of Picquigny. This was signed near Amiens on 29 August. Louis backed it up with generous financial inducements to the main English commanders. Hastings was the chief advocate of the treaty, and received 2,000 crowns a year. Lords Howard and Montgomery took 1,200 crowns each per annum, Chancellor Thomas Rotherham 1,000 crowns a year, and John Morton 600 crowns annually. Louis XI helped pay by creating a devalued variant of the *écu à la couronne*, the French crown, called an *écu au soleil*, because the sun now appeared above the shield.

Louis de Bretaylle, English envoy to Spain, stated that this great bribe took away the honour of all Edward's previous military victories. There was to be a seven-year truce, and Edward would not pursue his claims to the French throne. Louis was allowed to ransom Margaret of Anjou from Edward's custody, on payment of 50,000 crowns. Louis reputedly said, referring to the hospitality he lavished on Edward, that the invasion was ended by 'pâté, good wines and venison pasties'. Lesser nobles and men, who would have expected to share booty after battles, were furious at having to leave France. Lords and people alike back in England despaired that the king had taken money not to fight. Louis had bought off England for the foreseeable future. The 1475 treaty marked the true end of the Hundred Years' War.

In revenge for their support for Louis, Charles invaded Switzerland. On 2 March 1476, the Swiss attacked and defeated the Burgundians at Grandson in Switzerland, and on 5 January 1477 Charles was killed at the Battle of Nancy, ending the Burgundian Wars. Now Louis had succeeded in destroying his sworn enemy, so began forcing other French lords who still favoured the feudal system to give in to his central authority. Some, like the Duke of Nemours, were simply executed. The lands belonging to the Duchy of Burgundy, drawn up by Louis' great-great-grandfather John II for the benefit of his son Philip the Bold, reverted to the Crown of France. Louis was now only left with the problem of Brittany to consider.

From 1475, after Picquigny, Jasper and Henry became increasingly important as diplomatic pawns. From 1471, they had been under the explicit protection of François II, who had rejected constant English and French demands, keeping his word to grant the earls asylum. Edward IV's envoys constantly mixed promises with bribes to try to take the Tudors, but now altered their position. François II had hoped for a full-scale war between France on one side and England and Burgundy on the other while he concentrated upon strengthening his duchy. However, he viewed the conclusion with some trepidation. England was at peace with France, and France was far stronger now that Burgundy had been taken over. Importantly, Louis XI promised Edward, by the Treaty of Picquigny, that he would not start a war against François of Brittany. Edward believed that this would induce Duke François to hand over Jasper and Henry. Edward thus started negotiations with Brittany to negotiate the renewal of the Anglo-Breton treaty, and to finally deal with the problem of the Tudor earls.

Negotiations were slow until the autumn of 1476, when Edward despatched a high-powered embassy to Brittany, led by Robert Stillington, Bishop of Bath and Wells. Vergil tells us that Edward wanted Henry taken back to England to marry one of the king's daughters, thus uniting the houses of York and Lancaster. Not even François believed this change of tack, but he was a sick man, worn down by ill health, the English ambassadors and his own courtiers, who were receiving gold and promises from Stillington. The ambassadors promised to escort Henry back to England, saying that he would not be harmed. Henry would be granted his full Beaufort inheritance, and would be married to a prominent Yorkist woman to further ensure his safety. It was even rumoured that Edward IV wished to marry Henry to his own daughter Elizabeth of York to integrate Henry and the House of Lancaster into the Yorkist line. By marrying Henry into his family, he would neutralise this last Lancastrian threat. Henry refused adamantly to go back with the envoys in 1476. Probably Jasper had advised him by messenger never to trust the king, and especially his brother Richard of Gloucester. Henry Tudor's father had died in Yorkist custody before he had been born, and nearly all of his nineteen years had been spent in care, custody or exile. Henry had become a pragmatist, even separated from his beloved uncle.

The French diplomat Philippe de Commines met Henry in both Brittany and France, and wrote of him that he was 'without power, without money, without right ... and without any reputation but what his person and deportment excited; for he had suffered much, been in distress all the days of his life, and particularly a prisoner in Bretagne to Duke François from the eighteenth year of his age who treated him as kindly as the necessity of his imprisonment would permit'. Commines recorded that, as a young man, the Earl of Richmond claimed that 'from the time he was five years old he had been always a fugitive or a prisoner'. François was anxious to make some gesture that would rescue his reputation in England, needing England as an ally against France, and Vergil says that the duke was 'worried with prayer and vanquished with price'. In late 1476, after five years of pressure from both France and England, and having succumbed temporarily to illness, François gave in and consented to send Henry to England. Edward IV had also promised to reward many courtiers at the Breton court when Henry returned to English soil, so there was little opposition to the refugees being sent home. Henry's friends and English supporters rushed to the Breton court and urged the duke to allow Henry to stay.

In November 1476, Henry was reluctantly escorted to Vannes and given to the English envoys. He was then escorted north overland to St Malo, where ships were berthed ready to take him back to England. The nineteen-year-old exile found himself under an English military guard waiting for favourable winds and tides. One of the duke's chief advisers, du Quélennec, had been away from court. He had enjoyed the earls' company under supervision in his household at Suscinio. Admiral of Brittany since 1432, Jean du Quélennec, Vicomte du Faou, was one of the duke's most trusted councillors. He was vehemently against the proposal, but was away from court when the duke reached his decision. The admiral rode quickly to court, pleading for Henry's cause, saying, 'Most noble Duke, this paleness of countenance is unto me a messenger of death.' François asked what was wrong and the admiral replied that his duke had forgotten his promise and delivered instead 'that most innocent imp, to be torn in pieces by bloody butchers, to be miserably tormented, and finally to be slain'. Duke François protested, but the Vicomte du Faou insisted: 'Henry is almost lost already, whom if you shall permit to step one foot out of your jurisdiction, all the world shall not after that be able to save his life.'

Pierre Landais, François' chief counsellor, was despatched to St Malo in order to try to retrieve the situation. Henry had either developed, or pretended, an illness, hereby missing tides and delaying the departure of the ships to England. He must have suspected duplicity on Edward's part or have been counselled by his uncle, and was playing for time, looking for a means to escape. Landais arrived just as the English were due to sail, and entered into a lengthy discussion with the envoys, saying that François now wanted Henry back in his own protective custody. During the argument, Henry somehow fled and was chased through the narrow streets to St Vincent's Cathedral, where he claimed sanctuary. The citizens of St Malo then crowded around, and refused to allow the English to break sanctuary tradition by entering the cathedral armed. The angered envoys were forced to sail home without Henry, having held Henry for three days, and Henry returned to court with Landais. Thus is history changed forever – we may not have seen the Elizabethan Age, the English Empire or England as a Protestant nation if Henry Tudor had slipped on his dash to the cathedral.

It is unknown whether Jasper was to board with Henry. Histories at this time were written about the eventual king, not his uncle, but it is known that both Jasper and Henry were now returned to the Breton court at the Château de l'Hermine at Vannes. François apologised profusely to the earls, reassuring the 'comte de Richemont' that he was now safe, but also tried to appease Edward IV by making Henry's imprisonment more secure. He now kept his original promise to Edward IV; in October and November 1476, both Henry and Jasper were placed in custody as prisoners. Henry was escorted from the Tour d'Elven by Vincent de la Landelle, and Jasper from Josselin by Bertrand du Parc. These Bretons were made separately responsible for the custody of the earls, who may have been kept separate for some time. With this increased security, Edward should have been satisfied, but again sent delegates in 1477 to try and bring the earls to England.

In the spring or summer of 1478, the despairing Oxford attempted to escape Hammes Castle by jumping from the walls into its moat. He may have been attempting suicide, and the *Paston Letters* state that 'some say to steal away, and some think he would have drowned himself'. The Duke of Clarence had just been executed by his own brother, Edward IV, and it may be that Oxford believed that Clarence's death was his last hope of freedom extinguished.

The next few years saw Jasper and Henry in relative obscurity. The death of Charles the Bold at the Battle of Nancy in January 1477 had left opposition to King Louis across France leaderless, and he was concentrating on consolidating his power. Henry must have watched the process with interest, as he was himself to allow no over-mighty nobles to threaten the realm. By 1480, mainly by non-military means, Louis had almost completed the piecemeal unification of France, the only remaining obstacle being Brittany. Louis lacked the military might to confront the network of Breton castles, and consolidated his territorial gains by political and economic initiatives. Louis improved the central taxation system and instituted a system of royal post horses, enabling his agents to travel the realm, looking into ancient rights, land holdings and possible evasion of feudal dues. His financial exactions deliberately fell more heavily on the landed nobility than the commoners or merchants. To strengthen the Crown against any aristocratic backlash he won the support of the major cities by granting urban privileges and encouraging the growth of trade and industry. He took into his councils members of the mercantile class, as what was good for trade was good for France and his central power. Louis employed civil lawyers to draw up a huge volume of edicts governing farming, land reclamation, commercial regulations, the restriction of hunting estates, etc. During his reign Louis more than quadrupled royal income and could claim that enriching the Crown was allied with enriching those upon whom the prosperity of France rested.

However, Louis XI still saw some value in holding Henry and Jasper, and applied more pressure in 1477 and in 1482, when envoys were sent with large sums of money to try and secure their release into France. Henry was still in captivity at the Château de l'Hermine in Vannes, where he had been joined from Josselin by his uncle Jasper. Bretons involved in closely guarding the exiles included Bertrand du Parc, Jehan de Guillemet, Vincent de la Landette (or Landelle) and Louis de Kermené. Vannes was an important seaport in the Morbihan, situated not far from both of the great ducal courts at Rennes and Nantes. Today the Château de l'Hermine is a rebuilt town hall, but the town walls and small parapet towers still stand, as does the fifteenth-century layout of the Old Town. Envoys from both France and England continued to pressurise the duke and it may have seemed at times that he had no option but to capitulate. In 1481–1482, Henry was still at Vannes, where his custodians, Jean Guillemet and Louis de Kermené, were paid expenses of £2,000 *tournois*, while Jasper's watchdog, Bertrand du Parc, was paid £607 10s *tournois*. In 1482 they were given into the hands of Jean de Robihan (Robien).

In February 1482, Edward promised Duke François 4,000 archers to defend his borders, a major condition being the surrender of Jasper and Henry. These military negotiations were fortunately not concluded because of Edward's death in the following year. In June 1482, Edward reconfirmed his alleged desire to 'welcome' Henry Tudor back into his kingdom as a treasured member of his inner court. He again claimed that he wanted Henry married into a strong Yorkist family, and again his own daughter Elizabeth of York seemed to have been used as a lure. Edward stated that should Henry acquiesce to this request then he would treated as a loyal and valued courtier and not only would he receive his Beaufort inheritance upon his mother's death, but he would also receive much more. Should Henry continue with his exile, he would lose everything. It is thought that Margaret Beaufort herself, a Lancastrian by birth who had married into the Yorkist regime, supported such a move.

However, Edward IV died unexpectedly on 3 April 1483. With Edward dead, Henry and Jasper were now given greater freedom in their movements. François was free of his promise to the English king to keep the earls in secure custody. Events moved quickly in England. The king's brother

Richard of Gloucester imprisoned the boy king Edward V and seized the throne. Edward's wife, Elizabeth Woodville, fled with her daughters and remaining son, Richard, to sanctuary at Westminster. Henry and Jasper knew that Richard was a more aggressive character than his brother. The Earl of Richmond would now become the focus for all those who thought that Gloucester was an unworthy king guilty of murdering his nephews Edward V and Richard of Cornwall. As a result of Richard III's ruthless behaviour, he quickly became unpopular and Henry became the only real alternative.

Richard of Gloucester was crowned Richard III on 6 July 1483. Just a week later, on 13 July 1483, Dr Thomas Hutton, an eminent cleric, was commissioned to negotiate with Duke François about matters of common interest to England and Brittany. It is clear from the Breton response to this diplomatic initiative that the fate of Henry and Jasper was the chief point of discussion. Hutton had returned to England by around 26 August, for on that day François' envoy, Georges de Mainbier, was given his instructions for negotiations with Richard III. Protesting his friendship and affection in conventional diplomatic terms, François declared that Louis XI of France had requested delivery of Richmond several times since Edward IV's death and was currently threatening the duke with war unless he acquiesced.

Brittany, it was alleged, could not long hold out against King Louis unless she received English support. If it was not forthcoming, the duke might be forced to hand Henry and Jasper over to the French. François' threat was clear; Louis could support the Tudors in an invasion of England, and de Mainbier outlined his terms for being bought off. Richard would have to provide François with 4,000 archers, as previously promised by Edward, at his own expense and at a month's notice. If necessary, another 2,000–3,000 men, at the Duke of Brittany's expense, must be sent to deal with the French threat. The demands were so high that it was extremely difficult for Richard to meet them, and this was probably intentional, for at the very time of these negotiations in July–August 1483, François was probably organising the invasion fleet that would be ready to put to sea under Henry and Jasper by 1 September. Although François was reluctant to defy Richard III openly, he constantly evaded his requests for the earls' surrender. Henry was in great favour with the duke, and there were rumours of negotiations for his marriage with the duke's daughter and heiress, Anne.

Edward's best friend, Lord Hastings, had been crucial in advising Richard to take the protectorship and preventing the pair of them being sidelined by the queen's Woodville family. However, it is clear that Richard's subsequent deposition, imprisonment and probable murder of Edward V and his brother alienated Hastings. He had been Edward IV's friend and advisor for many years, and to see the king's children 'vanishing' obviously more than disturbed him. Richard had Hastings executed on a trumped-up charge without trial. Richard had already illegally murdered the honourable Yorkist loyalist Sir Thomas Vaughan, the chamberlain to the young Edward, who had previously served Jasper Tudor and shared 'Le

Garlek' in Stepney with him. Richard also killed Queen Elizabeth's brother Lord Rivers and the queen's son Lord Grey. The three men had been riding from Ludlow to London as Edward V's bodyguard when tricked and captured by Richard on 30 April. They were executed without trial in late June. Other members of the queen's Woodville family began to flee the country if they could, some joining Henry.

The usurper king's main supporter among the great nobles was the Duke of Buckingham. Many Yorkist peers had begun distancing themselves from Richard in the first weeks of his reign. Whether Buckingham now wished to replace Richard or wanted Henry Tudor on the throne is unclear. Perhaps he was afraid, after the deaths of the rightful king Edward V and his brother, and of Hastings, Vaughan and Rivers, that he would also be victim to the new king's ambition. Buckingham himself had a claim to the crown. He took his leave of the king after some argument at Gloucester late in July 1483. It may well be that he discovered the murder of the Princes in the Tower, and communicated the fact to Elizabeth Woodville, who had fled with her daughters to sanctuary at Westminster. Using high churchmen, Richard had lured out her other son, Prince Richard by saying that Richard was needed for his brother's coronation. The princes were heard playing together a few days later, and then they vanished. They were declared illegitimate so that Gloucester could take the crown as Richard III.

Buckingham rode to his castle at Brecon, to which Richard had compulsorily retired John Morton, Bishop of Ely. Throughout the first part of Edward IV's reign, Morton had remained loyal to Henry VI and thus suffered the life of an émigré in Scotland and France. He submitted to Edward only in 1471, after the terrible Battle of Tewkesbury. Morton knew Jasper Tudor well, for they had been in exile together. Sir Thomas More relates that, at Brecon, Morton discovered Buckingham's great weakness: his ambition. Morton thus began to convert Buckingham's discontent into a desire for rebellion. Buckingham enjoyed descent from Edward III through three of his four grandparents, and this may have played a part in his allying with his cousin Henry Tudor in 1483 to attempt to overthrow Richard III. It would seem that Buckingham was attempting to put Henry on the throne but it may be that he was using Tudor as a pawn to achieve his own ends. Gladys Temperley recounted:

> The story goes that the duke had quite forgotten the superior claims of the Countess of Richmond and her son, until, riding between Worcester and Bridgnorth, he met the former, and it flashed into his mind that 'she and her son, the Earl of Richmond, be bothe bulwarcke and portecolice betwene me and the gate to entre into the majestic royall and gettynge of the crowne'.

Along parallel lines, Henry Tudor's mother, Margaret Beaufort, Countess of Richmond, had also begun plotting Richard III's downfall. She knew that her only child was in grave danger with Richard in power. She was now married to one of the most powerful barons, Thomas, Lord Stanley. According to Vergil, she knew of the death of the Princes in the Tower before Buckingham's rebellion erupted at the end of October 1483. Margaret used her physician, later to be Henry VII's doctor, to pass messages. Dr Lewis of Caerleon was also Queen Elizabeth Woodville's doctor, and through him the countess suggested to the queen that Henry might marry either the queen's elder daughter, Elizabeth, or the younger girl, Cecily. With the aid of the queen and her followers, Henry could then defeat Richard, become king and give security to the Woodvilles. The queen would never have agreed unless she knew that her sons were dead. Lewis of Caerleon was a Cambridge-trained mathematician, theologian, astronomer, doctor of medicine and teacher at Oxford. As physician to the women, Caerleon was able to travel openly between Lord Stanley's London house and Elizabeth's sanctuary at Westminster.

Margaret Beaufort put her life on the line for Henry in the 1483 plot. The surviving correspondence of mother and son is described by Starkey as 'more like the letters of two lovers'. Margaret signs off one letter to Henry on his birthday: 'My dearest and only desired joy in the world ... at Calais town, this day of St Agnes, that I did bring into the world my good and gracious prince, king and only beloved son.' Another of Margaret Beaufort's agents in the affair was Sir Reginald Bray, who had been her steward and receiver general since 1465. Margaret's third husband, after her infant marriage and her subsequent marriage to Edmund Tudor, had been Sir Henry Stafford, the younger son of Humphrey, Duke of Buckingham. She married him in 1458–1459 and he died in 1471. Bray was very well known to the Stafford family, and his seat in Parliament as MP for Newcastle in 1478 was controlled by the Staffords. Morton and Buckingham decided to seek allies in their plot, using Bray to seek Margaret's support. Bray himself was deeply implicated in the Beaufort–Woodville plot, as the discussions between Margaret and the queen were later called. Margaret used him 'to draw unto her party, as secretly as might be, some such noble or worshipful men as were wise, faithful, and active, who were able to make help in the cause'. Bray quickly gained the support of Sir John Guildford of Kent and his son Sir Richard, Sir John Cheyney of Wiltshire and his brothers Robert and Humphrey, and Sir Giles Daubeney of Somerset.

The queen's son Thomas Grey, Marquess of Dorset, the son of her first marriage to John Grey, Lord Ferrers of Groby, managed to escape from sanctuary at Westminster, and he also was involved. Thus two major conspiracies to overthrow Richard III were formed in the first weeks of his reign. One involved a general uprising all across the south of England, led by many local Yorkist lords. The other was meant to be led by Buckingham from Wales. However, it was a very untidy confederation of many separate plots, badly organised, with Lancastrians such as Margaret and Morton wanting Henry as king, 'Edwardian' Yorkists who believed that Edward IV's children were still alive, others impelled by revenge for the princes' deaths, and some who aimed to reverse land grabs. And, of course, Buckingham may have wanted the throne of England for himself. Having contacted Elizabeth Woodville and prepared the ground for a marriage between Henry Tudor and Princess Elizabeth of York, Margaret Beaufort got in touch with her son. She chose as her courier Christopher Urswick, a clerk and Cambridge graduate, whom she had given the rectory of Puttenham, Hertfordshire, in December 1482.

Lady Margaret 'gave Christopher in charge to go unto erle Henry into Brittany, and to signyfy unto him all that was doone with the quene'. Not until the last minute, according to Polydore Vergil, had Margaret discovered the existence of the Buckingham–Morton plot, 'which whan she knew she alteryd hir intent, staying Christopher at home, and sent Hugh Conwey into Bryttane unto him soon Henry with a good great sum of money, commanding him to utter all thinges, and exhort hys returns, and especyally to advyse him to arryve in Wales, wher he should fynde ayd in readiness'. No explanation is given for the change of messengers but it may be that Margaret preferred to employ Urswick to negotiate with Bishop Morton, whom Urswick is next recorded as visiting in Flanders after Morton's flight there. (Morton fled after the failure of the Buckingham plot.) The man who actually visited Henry, Hugh Conway, was the son of John Conway 'Aer Hen' of Botryddan, Flintshire, and may well have been a Stanley retainer. Hugh Conway and Thomas Ramme were sent by different routes to seek Henry. Conway and Ramme were to supply him with funds, and advise him to return as soon as possible and land in Wales, 'where he shoulde not doubte to fynde both aide and comforte and frendes'. The messengers arrived in Brittany on the same day, and the news they brought was the turning point in the young earl's career.

Richard had officially seized the throne on 26 June. Richard III's claims were tenuous and there would be other claimants. Richard had immediately asked for the closing of French and Breton ports to English exiles, notably Elizabeth Woodville's brother, who had a large part of the fleet. It is also important to remember that Buckingham, Richard III and Henry Tudor were the only surviving adult male heirs to the House of Plantagenet. Later historians, especially Polydore Vergil, would later claim Buckingham really intended to defeat Richard and place Henry Tudor on the throne. There were uprisings against Richard III just days after his coronation, which highlighted popular dissatisfaction. Margaret sent a large sum of money to her son, raised from loans in London. She advised him to come to Wales as soon as possible, since he would receive support in Wales, particularly from Buckingham. Buckingham wrote a letter to Henry on 24 September 1483 which stated that he would support the rebellion against Richard, even though his and Henry's interests may not be perfectly compatible. It is fairly certain that Buckingham suspected his own life was in danger with Richard III in power. Buckingham told Henry the rebellion would begin on 18 October, thus giving Henry only three weeks' notice. He did not mention acknowledging Henry as king, nor Henry's marriage to Elizabeth of York.

Henry's landing in Wales was to coincide with risings in all the Southern counties from Kent to Devon.

Heartened by the news of plotting against Richard, Henry and Jasper saw François and asked for help. Vergil says that Henry 'conferryd all thinges with the duk, spewing that he had concealyd an assured hope of obtanyng the realme of England, and prayd therfor that the same might be browght about both by his good help and assent, whiche whan so ever habylytie should serve he wold not fale to requyte'. The duke agreed and was generous with his support. Unfortunately, popular discontent in England, which may have been due to the murder of the Princes in the Tower becoming known around this date, led to a premature rising in Kent, early in October. Richard was taken completely by surprise, but his measures were prompt and effective. He does not seem to have suspected Buckingham of rebellion initially, and had no large army assembled. However, such a massively planned uprising could not remain secret and Richard was informed on 11 October that a vast rebellion would occur in a week.

Richard had heard vague descriptions of a plan a few weeks before and had summoned Buckingham to him. The duke feigned a stomach ache and was sent a command to come to the king, but again refused. The rebellion was less than a week away when Richard was informed of Buckingham's involvement and the extent of the rebellion. On 15 October a proclamation was issued against Buckingham, and troops were immediately raised. Three days later, according to the plan, Henry's adherents in the Southern counties rose, and on the same day Buckingham raised his standard at Brecon. However, the haughty Buckingham was disliked by major Welsh leaders like Rhys ap Thomas, who did not support him, and a violent storm made the Severn impassable, preventing his joining Henry's Devonshire supporters. Buckingham, having coerced very few of his Welsh tenants into supporting him, was chased by the Yorkist Thomas Vaughan of Tretower. Serious floods in the Severn Valley were said to have lasted for ten days, and for a century after these were called the Great Water, or Buckingham's Water. Many of his hungry and cold Welsh force deserted, having been impressed into action by their new lord against their wishes. Buckingham fled from his troops, but was betrayed to Richard and beheaded at Salisbury on 2 November. Other risings across the rest of southern England fizzled out. Richard attempted to prevent a mass exodus of rebels but failed, with many joining Henry in Brittany.

In Wales, Richard III was using some of Jasper's former servants. There was an order of the King's Council in 1283 to Henry Wogan, Treasurer of Pembroke, to deliver out of the first revenues of his office £100 to be employed for the 'stuff' of Pembroke Castle, and also 20 marks for other small things necessary to be purveyed there. There was also a warrant to Richard Mynours, chamberlain of Carmarthen, to pay £113 14s 6d to Richard Newton for the expenses incurred by him on the castle of Pembroke. Buckingham's rebellion demonstrated the weaknesses inherent in Richard III's regime. Edward IV had successfully deposed Henry VI in 1461 because he had strong support in London and the South. He had the support of the Church, including the papal legate, and he had a justified grievance against Henry VI, who had broken the Act of Accord and waged war on, and killed, Edward's father. Richard III's main support was in the less populated, less wealthy and less influential North. The Church was divided in its view of him and the bishops of Ely, Exeter and Salisbury (a brother of Elizabeth Woodville), along with the Archbishop of York, all directly opposed him.

By 1 September 1483, the Duke of Brittany had assembled a small fleet of five ships and 324 men who were to be put at the disposal of Henry and Jasper for a month. In addition, on 30 October, François made Henry a cash loan of 10,000 crowns, intended for immediate expenditure on Henry's arrival in England. He never needed the money. Henry sailed, probably from Paimpol, on 30 October, and in support of him Duke François said he was willing to commit 5,000 Breton troops. The fleet was prepared at Brest and was commanded by Jean du Quélennec. The weather was as bad at sea as it had been for Buckingham on land, and a violent storm scattered the fleets. Henry did not reach Poole in Dorset until around 12 November, with only two ships. Discovering the local population to be hostile, he sailed on to Plymouth, where he perhaps learned of the collapse of the rising, and the presence of the victorious Richard nearby at Exeter. Royal troops tried to convince a landing party that they were Buckingham's men and his plot had succeeded, but Henry would not land, and some of his Breton troops were captured and ransomed. Henry's only course was to return to Brittany, although he landed near Valognes in Normandy, again perhaps because of storms and unfavourable winds. While at Exeter, Richard summarily beheaded Sir Thomas St Leger and Thomas Rameney. In London, Sir George Browne and seven of Edward IV's yeomen of the Crown were tried and executed. In mid-December 1983, commissions were sent to every county from Yorkshire southwards, to investigate the risings and confiscate property for the king.

On his arrival in France, Henry immediately sent messengers to the French court requesting leave to cross into Brittany. This was granted and, in addition, an esquire of the French royal household, Henri Carbonnel, was ordered to conduct the earl overland and escorted him as far as the abbey of St Saviour at Redon in Brittany, 30 miles east of Vannes. The expenses of Henry's journey totalled £1,051 12s 6d *tournois*. The earls would have probably been seized if Louis had still been alive, but in the power struggle following the king's recent death, it seems that Henry and Jasper were luckily forgotten. On his return to Brittany, Henry learned of Buckingham's death, but also of the safe return to Vannes of his followers. They were now joined by a number of English nobles and gentlemen who had also fled from Richard III's revenge. Upon his return to the court at Vannes, Henry found the Marquess of Dorset, the two Courtney lords, Lord Wells, Sir John Bourchier, Sir Edward Woodville, Sir Robert Willoughby,

Sir Giles Daubeney, Sir John Cheney and his two brothers, along with several others, like Sir Richard Edgcumbe, who had fled from England. The Marquess of Dorset was Elizabeth Woodville's son by her first husband, and her three brothers, Lionel, Edward and Richard Woodville could never go back to England with Richard in power. These exiles told Henry that he must reassemble his allies and attack again, before Richard III became more firmly entrenched as king and the duke ended his hospitality.

Henry Tudor's only other main rival for the throne had been killed, as Buckingham's son and heir was just six years old. He knew that he was again in danger from Richard III, either through diplomacy or assassination. Jasper shared the danger, as he had been heavily involved in planning the multiple outbreaks across the south of England. Henry needed to enthuse his growing band of followers, and arrived at Rennes in Brittany late in 1483. He sent for his supporters from Vannes. On Christmas Day, the English exiles assembled at St Pierre Cathedral, Rennes. Henry promised to marry the Princess Elizabeth of York and unite the rival houses on becoming king. His supporters then swore homage to him as if he were already their sovereign. Present were the majority of his supporters, both Yorkist and Lancastrian, in addition to the Duchess of Brittany herself. The premier minister, Pierre Landais, was also present and through him Henry obtained Duke François' solemn promise to support and assist in the cause. Henry had entered into a pledge which he could not turn back from. If his invasion of England was successful, he would marry Elizabeth of York. It was in effect a marriage by proxy.

Henry and Jasper once again asked for aid from Brittany, promising to repay the duke's generosity when circumstances would allow. However, the 1483 uprising had been crushed, and Richard III was making friendly overtures to François. Henry's only hope probably lay with the stream of English exiles now joining him in Brittany. Further complications arose in the situation of the earls. Because of the illness of François II, Pierre Landais and his officials began running his government. Breton nobles resented Landais, and the country split into two factions. Landais saw his main hope of success in an alliance with Richard III. François' only heir was Anne of Brittany, and Edward IV had feared that if Anne married the French king, Brittany would lose its independence and France could control the Channel. Also, Louis XI had died in August 1483 and his heir Charles VIII was only thirteen. The absence of central power had fortunately allowed Jasper and Henry to pass through France after landing in Normandy.

The death of Louis was followed by an aristocratic reaction, called the 'Mad War'. The crown passed to a minor, Charles VIII, and his regency was placed in the hands of the boy's sister, Anne de Beaujeu. François II now joined in negotiations with the dukes of Orléans and Lorraine and several other feudal lords. The plan was for Louis of Orléans to marry Anne of Brittany and take over the regency of Brittany when François died. The duke was only fifty but in bad health, and would die within three years. François had already entered into an undertaking for his other daughter to marry Edward IV's heir, but the king's sudden death the previous April led to Edward V's disappearance in the Tower along with his brother. Cunningham states that Louis of Orleans 'identified Henry's position in Brittany as a source of leverage'. Thus Orléans and the rulers of France, Brittany and England all wished to use the exiles in some way to gain power and allies.

It is almost certain that the Jasper played a vital role as Richmond's closest adviser, mentor and kinsman, but the chief source of information about the exiles in Brittany, Polydore Vergil, wrote his account after Jasper's death. It obviously is centred on the qualities and history of the Henry VII, who is depicted as a good and courageous young man, while Jasper's contribution is largely ignored. However, from the rewards granted to Jasper after 1485, and the trust and authority with which he was invested – greater than that enjoyed by anyone else – we know that Henry VII understood his value.

Parliament met at Westminster on 23 January 1484, when an Act of attainder was passed against the bishops of Ely, Salisbury and Exeter, the Earl of Oxford and Jasper, Earl of Pembroke, along with other ringleaders of the late insurrection who had fled the kingdom. The attainder tells us that Buckingham had 'on the 24th September by his several writings and messages by him sent, procured and moved Henry calling himself Earl of Richmond and Jasper late Earl of Pembroke being there in Brittany, great enemies of our sovereign lord, to make a great navy and bring with them an army from Brittany'. Earls Henry and Jasper in particular were now singled out as the king's greatest enemies. Richard was empowered by the Lords and Commons to make grants of their forfeited estates. Among the persons attainted were also Henry, Earl of Richmond, and his mother, the countess dowager of Richmond. Her estate was given for life to her husband, Thomas, Lord Stanley, whom Richard had recently created Constable of England. Stanley was made responsible for keeping Margaret from all illegal correspondence for the future. Servants such as Dr Lewis Caerleon were taken away from her, some, like Caerleon, being gaoled. Richard's title to the crown was confirmed and his son Edward was declared heir apparent.

In the 1484 *Titulus Regius*, the king's deed, Richard formally declared the children of Edward IV and Elizabeth Woodville illegitimate. In it he revived the allegations of witchcraft against Queen Elizabeth Woodville, and the queen's mother Jacquetta, when he claimed that she and Elizabeth had procured Elizabeth's marriage to Edward IV through witchcraft. Richard never offered any proof to support his assertions. Along with the imprisonment and probable murder of her two sons by the king, Richard declared Woodville's marriage invalid and stripped her of her dower rights.

No longer Countess of Richmond, in consequence of the act which deprived her of title and lands, Margaret felt herself absolved from any allegiance to the king, and continued working for her son's interests. Through the services of Christopher Urswicke, her chaplain and confessor; Hugh Conway and Reginald Bray, she privately supplied her son with large sums of money, and despatched emissaries to rouse the cooperation of potential supporters. In consequence, Lord Stanley came under Richard III's suspicions. By the statement of Humphrey Brereton, his esquire, it appears that he had constant communication with Elizabeth of York about her possible marriage to Henry. Brereton was sent from London to Cheshire to communicate with Lord Stanley's sons at Lathom, and to his brother, Sir William Stanley of Holt in Denbighshire, as well as others of their connections, urging them to be prepared to support the Earl of Richmond's landing in Wales. Passing into Brittany, Brereton seems to have taken letters both from the young princess and Lord Stanley to the exiled Tudors, giving them hope again.

By 2 February 1484, Henry, Jasper, the Marquess of Dorset and Peter Courtenay, Bishop of Exeter, with other followers had returned to Vannes. Here they celebrated the Feast of the Purification of the Blessed Virgin at the cathedral, offering alms totalling £6 7s 1d *tournois*. The twenty-six-year-old Henry and the fifty-year-old Duke François had become increasingly friendly during Henry's twelve years in Breton custody. Henry needed François for security, and for any prospect of defeating Richard III. François needed Henry to become King of England in order to gain a powerful ally in his constant battles with France. However, François II had grown increasingly ill, and by 1484 his treasurer, Pierre Landais, was effectively in control of the dukedom while he recuperated.

There was a semblance of normality in Jasper's old territories. On 12 February 1484, there was a 'grant for life to the king's servant, John White the elder of the town of Tenby and his assigns of all the lands, meadows and pastures by and within the town called 'lez Demaynes', 'Fugatif Londes', 'Watellvyashyll', and 'Rigons Close', with two wind mills called 'lez Wynde Mylles', and a water mill called 'le water wynch mylle', with all appurtenances to hold to the value of £10 yearly, rendering to the king a red rose at the feast of St. Peter ad Vincula, provided that he sufficiently repair the premises'. White's father had probably helped Jasper and Henry escape from Tenby.

In March 1484, Richard attempted reconciliation with his former sister-in-law, Elizabeth Woodville. She and her five daughters were still in sanctuary in Westminster. Richard asked the Lord Mayor of London, leading peers and various aldermen to his palace. He promised that if Elizabeth and her children left sanctuary, he would protect them. They would be recognised as his kin and given a pension and dowries. Importantly, he publicly promised they would not be sent to any prisons, including the Tower of London. People at the time thought that he was planning to marry the beautiful Elizabeth of York, his niece, as his wife was in poor health.

Throughout 1484, alterations were made to the running of Jasper's former estates across Wales, with Richard Williams being particularly rewarded. Upon 11 January there was a 'grant for life to the king's servant, Richard Williams, esquire, one of the ushers of the king's chamber of the offices of constable and steward of the kings castle, town and lordship of

Pembroke with their members in South Wales, constable of the castle of
Tenby, chief forester of the forest of Coedrath, constable and steward of
the castle, town, and lordship of Cilgerran with the office of steward of the
lordship of Llanstephan and Trayne, with authority to appoint clerks of the
court and porters, with the accustomed fees from the issues of the lordship
of Pembroke executing the office of constable of the castle of Pembroke in
person'. In early 1484, Pembroke, Tenby, Cilgerran and other castles were
put in a state of readiness for invasion.

On 21 July, there was a 'warrant to the Forester of Narberth to deliver to
Richard Williams, constable of Pembroke, as much fuel and burning wood
as shall be by his direction thought necessary to be used in the said castle,
and to permit the persons assigned by him to fell and carry away the said
wood from time to time'. On 25 September, the Patent Roll recorded the
'appointment during pleasure, from Michaelmas next, of the kings servants
William Mistelbroke and Richard Lussher as auditors of all accounts of
officers and ministers of the king's castles, wardships, manors, towns,
hundreds, lands and other possessions of this principality of South Wales
in the counties of Carmarthen and Cardigan and the Castle of Pembroke'.
Richard Williams features again on 20 December in a 'grant to the king's
servant, Richard Williams and the heirs male of his body for his good
service against the rebels, of the castle, manor or lordship of Manorbier and
Penally with its members co. Pembroke of the yearly value of £100 to hold
with knights fees and all its appurtenances by knight service and a rent of
£7 10s yearly'.

Richard III had determined to teach the Bretons a lesson for accepting
rebels and not surrendering the earls, and a vigorous policy of naval warfare
was adopted. At the same time, the goods of Bretons living in London were
seized. Richard was said to be 'vexyd, wrestyd, and tormentyd in mynd
with feare almost perpetually of erle Henry and his confederates return;
wherfor he had a myserable lyfe, who to ryd himself of this inward gryefe,
determynyd fynally to pullup by the rootes all matter of fears and tumult,
and other by guyle or force to bring the same abowt'. Once more Richard
wooed Duke François of Brittany and offered, in return for a cessation of
naval warfare, the prospect of a profitable friendship, undertaking to give
the duke the revenues from lands of the English exiles in Brittany so long as
they were kept there in custody. This overture was well received by Duke
François' chancellor and chief minister, Pierre Landais, who needed allies at
this juncture to buttress his own unpopular position in Brittany. Powerful
nobles opposed Landais, and Charles VII's regency government wished to
annex Brittany to France. Landais decided that the renewal of historic ties
with England was his best hope for continuing Breton independence and
for his own preservation.

On 15 August and 8 September 1484, Henry was in Vannes with his
associates, attending Mass at the cathedral, and again making only small
offerings of alms as his finances were straitened. Richard, after attainting
the earls for treason, sent ambassadors to Brittany offering to the duke

the possessions of Richmond on condition that the earl was delivered into his hands. Landais made an agreement in mid-September with William Catesby, Richard III's principal advisor, to surrender Henry and Jasper in exchange for English protection of the Duchy of Brittany. It was Catesby who probably offered to restore the earldom of Richmond to the duke, along with other lands in Britain. We have seen earlier that one of the towers at Largoët was named La Tour du Connétable de Richemonde, Duc de Bretagne. François may have been unaware of the agreement. In 1483, Bishop Morton had escaped from Brecon Castle, where he had been in Buckingham's custody, and was now in Flanders. News of the arrangement reached Morton, who immediately despatched the priest Christopher Urswick (1448–1522) to warn Henry.

Urswick had been the chaplain to Henry's mother, Margaret Beaufort. Urswick stayed in exile with Henry and was with him at Bosworth Field, previously corresponding with Margaret Beaufort and her husband Thomas Stanley. Henry now urgently needed to escape across the border into France for asylum in the court of the new French king, Charles VIII. The utmost secrecy was required. Henry and Jasper were at Vannes, and despatched Urswick immediately to Anne of Beaujeu asking permission to enter France. Louis of Orléans was preparing an invasion backed by Brittany, Burgundy and England, and possession of the earls could be a diplomatic trump card in giving them to Richard. She gave permission and Urswick immediately headed back to Henry and Jasper. They were ready, having planned their escape in Urswick's absence but having confided only in those who would accompany them.

Jasper now led a delegation of hand-picked men, ostensibly to visit François near the French border, where he was recovering from illness. Arriving at the border, the party rode into France, heading for Anjou. Just two days later, Henry left Vannes with five followers to visit a friend in the nearby countryside. After Edward IV's death, the earls had been far freer to roam, and no suspicions were aroused, especially as over 400 of Henry's followers were still stationed within the city walls of Vannes. Five miles outside the city, having reached a forest, Henry changed into a servant's clothing and followed one of his servants, who was acting as a guide. It seems they took the horses of the other three men, who probably walked back singly to Vannes through the busy city gates without arousing any alarm. The two men rode furiously, exchanging horses as they tired: 'he travelled with such great speed, following no definite route, never stopping save to rest the horses until he had come into the territory of Anjou and rejoined his followers'. Landais, hearing of his flight, sent armed troops to head Henry off, but the Bretons arrived at the border just one hour too late. Henry's followers left behind in Vannes had no idea that he had left the duchy, such was the secrecy involved in the escape.

François was angry at Landais's secret diplomacy and treatment of the English exiles, and let them know what had happened. The disappointed duke tried to recompense by rewarding Sir Edward Woodville, Sir John

Cheyney and Edward Poynings with a gift of £100 *tournois* each, as well as £1 *tournois* for each of the 408 Englishmen still at Vannes. The duke also paid for the cost of their lodgings there, which totalled £2,500 *tournois*. He could have been richly rewarded for sending them back to England to face certain death. However, the duke had come to respect Henry and Jasper over the years. Sick as he was, he determined to undo some of Landais's damage, and allowed the rebels to join Henry in Paris. He also gave them a large gift of money, around 700 livres, to pay for their travel, in addition to their living allowance, which also paid until they entered France. Henry Tudor despatched a letter of thanks, realising that the treachery had been due to Landais, not the duke. François, having briefly recovered from his illness, was furious with Landais for losing Henry, his main bargaining device for securing English aid against France. Landais was later hanged from the walls of the Breton capital, Nantes, on 19 July 1485.

The new King of France, Charles VIII, was just thirteen, so his regents were his eldest sister Anne Beaujeu and her husband Peter II, Duke of Bourbon. In Anjou, Richmond, Pembroke and their company were well received. The royal court was at Montargis, and the governor of the Limousin was ordered by the French council to meet the English émigrés. Henry sent a messenger from Anjou to Charles VIII, then at Montargis. The king immediately sent an envoy to greet Henry and take him to Chartres. The envoy was given the generous sum of 20,000 francs for expenses on the week-long journey. Charles wanted to encourage Henry in his plan to overthrow Richard III. However, Charles may have been unnerved by the large number of Henry's English followers who needed to be housed and fed while awaiting developments. With Henry Tudor gone, Brittany had no olive branch to offer England, which weakened the Breton–English alliance. This also aided Anne of Beaujeu in her struggle against the Orléans party.

The earls were taken to the French court, where Anne de Beaujeu and her supporters welcomed them enthusiastically. Any event which would embarrass the rebels was welcome. However, there were few resources available to help Henry in his cause, as the regency council was absorbed with its own constitutional crisis. At Angers on the Loire, Henry met Jasper and was received by Charles VIII. The Tudors were useful pawns to Charles, Anne and Peter to ensure that Richard III did not interfere with French plans to annex Brittany. Only four years later, Duke François II of Brittany would die after seeing British-speaking Brittany fall to France when Charles VIII attacked and forcibly married his daughter and heir, Anne de Bretagne.

On 3 November, the French king sent out a letter to towns across France describing how Henry and Jasper had come to him 'accompanied by five or six hundred English, able to rally more as he should wish'. He said that they should give their support 'and recover the Kingdom of England from the enemies of the French crown'. Charles ordered 'great and good provision' to be made for the exiles. At Chartres, Henry was sent 2,000 francs by the king to pay his men. By 4 November Henry was in Sens, sixty miles from

Montargis, and when he finally arrived at the royal court he was 'well loved and looked after'.

On 17 November, the Royal Council authorised payment to be made to Henry of £3,000 *tournois* to help him array his men and granted him permission to assemble mercenaries for an army of invasion. According to Polydore Vergil, 'King Charles promysyd him ayd, and bad him be of good there, for he wold willingly shew his goodwill, who furthwith after departyd to Montarge (Montargis), taking Henry with him and all the trane of his nobylytie.' The earls and court had moved from Montargis to Paris by midwinter. No single faction dominated the French court during the regency, and Henry had Charles VIII 'agane to take him wholy to his tuytion, so that yf he and his confederates showld be in safetie they might all lykewyse also acknowledge the sume receavyd at his hand'.

Luckily for Henry, John de Vere, Earl of Oxford, now escaped with Viscount Beaumont from Hammes Castle near Calais, after ten years' imprisonment. Richard III had ordered Oxford's transfer to England on 28 October 1484, but before this could happen, Oxford persuaded the captain of Hammes, Sir James Blount, to leave with him and join Henry and Jasper. Blount's father, Baron Mountjoy, had been rewarded by Edward IV for services at Towton. Sir Thomas Montgomery also fled Richard's service. Henry and his supporters were in some despair after the 1483 failures, but he was said to be 'ravished with joy incredible' at Blount, Beaumont and Oxford joining his cause. Oxford immediately returned to Hammes to bring the garrison there to join Richmond. Perhaps Blount, a former retainer of William Hastings, harboured a grudge regarding the summary execution of Hastings, whose widow was one of the Neville sisters, as was Oxford's wife. Again, perhaps he, like many others, was horrified at the disappearance and probable deaths of the princes, who had been placed into Richard's care.

This was an incredible boost to Henry's bleak prospects, as Oxford was one of the greatest military men of his day. It appears that Humphrey Brereton, a retainer of Lord Thomas Stanley, Henry's father-in-law, also brought money for Henry to use in an invasion. Anne de Beaujeu, in the name of Charles VIII, now also helped to raise French troops and more money to help Henry. Richard sent out a force from Calais to regain Hammes Castle, whose garrison supported the Lancastrian cause, but Oxford and Thomas Brandon reinforced it. The whole garrison was allowed to leave on honourable terms with their arms and joined Oxford, Jasper and Henry in Paris.

Richard III was alarmed by reports from his agents about growing support for Henry, not only from former Yorkists but seemingly from the new King of France and the Duke of Brittany. Because of this, he issued a proclamation on 7 December 1484 in which he claimed that Henry's plans had been so abhorrent to Duke François that he had been forced to flee and had struck a bargain instead with Charles VIII of France. The French king would provide Henry with aid in return for a renunciation of the English claim to the French throne. A horrifying picture was painted of what Henry and his allies intended to do after their invasion: 'the moost cruell murders slaughters roberyes and disherisons that ever Were serve in any crysten Royaulme'. As a result, Richard's subjects were required 'like gode and true englisshe men to endevoir theimself at alle theire powairs for the defense of theimself … ayeinst the said malicious porposes and conspiracions'. Yorkist sympathisers today believe that the Tudors invented royal propaganda, but we can see a different picture here.

Richard was expecting an invasion, and on 8 December 1484 sent out commissions of array for his shire forces to be registered. On 18 December, Richard demanded to know how many men could be mustered on half a day's notice. Jasper Tudor, Earl of Pembroke, must have trained Henry for battle while they were in Brittany. The young man had never really experienced battle, except at Edgcote when he was not yet thirteen. Jasper, on the other hand, was an experienced soldier, having been at the first Battle of St Albans and having led the army at Mortimer's Cross.

10

The Last Successful Invasion of Britain: Bosworth Field, 1485

The war has been seen as a dispute between the richer, more populated, Yorkist South, with strong Yorkist support in London, against the Lancastrian north of England. However, the civil wars from 1455 can be seen as a series of private wars between the lords of the Welsh and Scottish Marches, with these great semi-independent barons trying to influence the kingship to their familial advantage. The Scottish Marches and the north of England had the age-old conflict of the great Percy and Neville clans, generally based in the east and west respectively. Wales and its Marches were also divided in allegiance, with a largely Yorkist east and a generally Lancastrian west. Jasper Tudor, the sole Lancastrian earl based in the west of Wales, succeeded his brother in the difficult task of securing Wales and its Marches for Henry VI. He was faced with the advances of Richard of York, followed by his son the Earl of March, later Edward IV, and the Yorkist Herberts, Vaughans, Dwnns and their retainers.

Even in exile, with nothing to offer his followers, for decades Jasper somehow kept the dying Lancastrian cause alive in Wales. He seemed to land with impunity, never being betrayed on multiple landings in what was ostensibly York-controlled territory. Jasper Tudor had been the foremost Welsh nobleman before the Yorkist William Herbert supplanted him as Earl of Pembroke. The people had seen Jasper as their saviour from the English. When Herbert was killed in 1469 at Edgcote, along with the majority of leading Welsh nobles, Jasper once again became the centre of Welsh popular support. When Richard III usurped the throne and his nephews disappeared, Henry Tudor succeeded the childless Jasper as the prophesied deliverer of Wales. We have demonstrated that Wales had never, ever really accepted English rule, from the time of its conquest in 1283. Like Jasper, Henry represented the hopes and dreams of the nation. Henry was descended from Glyndŵr's main supporters and from the royal houses of Deheubarth and Powys, as well as from French kings. Above any other factor, the support of the Welsh for a saviour of their country displaced the Plantagenets from the English Crown and ended the wars. Without the bards travelling endlessly across Wales and the Marches communicating and encouraging, the Tudor and Lancastrian hopes would have probably evaporated. Such was the importance of the bards that Henry IV banned them in 1403. Edward I had also banned them in 1283 – in tradition, he ordered their massacre.

Upon Twelfth Night 1485, Richard III received word from his agents that Henry was planning an invasion. According to the Crowland Chronicler, 'nothing could have been more pleasing to him than this news'. Now he would have the chance of extinguishing his only adult rival for the crown. All winter an invasion had been expected, and Richard had to raise levies, requisition ships, raise forced loans and impose taxes to pay for his state of readiness. Sir George Neville had one fleet patrolling the Channel and protecting Kent. Lord Lovell commanded another fleet, operating from Southampton and safeguarding the south coast. The newly ennobled Duke of Norfolk guarded the east coast. The West Country was thought safe because of the impositions after the 1483 rebellion and the loss of many gentry, some of whom were now with Henry and Jasper. Wales was thought to be safe under the control of the Herberts in the south-east, Rhys ap Thomas in the south-west and west, and the Greys and Stanleys and in the north-west and north-east respectively.

The Stanleys controlled much of North Wales, Cheshire and Lancashire. Sir William Stanley was Richard III's chief lieutenant in Anglesey, Caernarfonshire, and Merioneth, counties which made up the northern part of royal holdings in Wales. However, Henry was in touch with the Stanleys before his invasion and almost immediately upon landing in Wales. Edward IV and then Richard III had worked especially hard to gain extensive control over South Wales, knowing of Jasper's popularity. These measures would later mean that Henry did not dare march east upon landing, but was forced to march north, and away from London. Unsure of Henry's landing place, Richard travelled around the Midlands, passing through Kenilworth, Coventry and Leicester before making his base at Nottingham Castle. Here he waited in the centre of England with his court, for the news of Henry's invasion point.

Henry and Jasper had been at the king's court in Angers in the Loire Valley over the autumn and winter of 1484, and for the spring travelled 230 miles north-east with the king to Paris. Interestingly, the court at Angers was only fifty-five miles inland from the major Breton court at Nantes. On 4 February 1485, the royal party reached Paris. Jasper, Henry and Oxford must have discussed the necessity of immediate decisive action. They were in grave danger if they stayed at court, having witnessed at first hand attempts to usurp the young king. At the beginning of the reign of Charles VIII, his cousin Louis II of Orléans had tried to seize the regency, but was rejected by the States General in early 1484. In April 1484, Louis, later Louis XII, left for Brittany to join François II. He also sent a request to the pope to annul his marriage, so that he would be free to marry Anne of Brittany, François' heir. François needed security for his daughter and Brittany, and on 23 November 1484 a treaty had been made with the intention of facilitating the marriage. Returning to the royal court at Angers in November, Louis of Orléans had tried to take the young king into his custody, but his sister, the regent Anne de Beaujeu, prevented him by force. With some lords of the royal guard, she placed the Duke of Orléans under house arrest at Gien.

Having escaped from Gien on 17 January 1485, Louis led a military expedition to take Paris, but failed. He managed to escape on 3 February to Alençon, just before the king, Anne de Beaujeu and the Tudors reached Paris. Louis apologised publicly upon 12 March and he was locked up in Orléans, preventing him from returning to his allies in Brittany. Although he agreed to a truce, from August 1485 the so-called 'Mad War' occurred. The allies of François and Louis included René II, Duke of Lorraine; Alain d'Albret; Jean de Chalon, Prince of Orange; Count Charles of Angoulême; the 'Bastard of Armagnac'; and Philippe de Commines (1447–1511). Commines met Edward IV, Warwick and Henry Tudor when they were in exile, and has left an account of his meetings. Louis XII later married Anne de Bretagne, unifying France and Brittany forever.

In the spring of 1485, Henry had been in exile for almost fourteen years and the position of the French regent, Anne de Beaujeu, was far from secure. Henry's friend François of Brittany was periodically ill, with only a seven-year-old daughter to succeed him. The duke also had pressing problems with some of his nobles fighting the faction of Pierre Landais. Henry and Jasper simply could not trust Brittany to shelter them again. François, Anne of France and Louis of Orléans would each sacrifice the Tudors in return for English help in their respective crises. Henry and Jasper continuously sent urgent letters to England and Wales during the winter of 1484/85 to sound out potential allies. Their only chance of survival was a successful return to England. Richard had failed by hours to secure Henry and was waiting for his chance. He knew their situation was desperate and expected an imminent invasion, putting his coastal defences on alert, and ordering mayors and sheriffs to arrest anyone receiving or distributing Tudor messages.

On 16 March 1485, Richard's queen, Anne Neville, died aged just twenty-eight. Rumours spread across England and Europe that she was murdered in order for Richard to marry his niece, Elizabeth of York. The loss of Elizabeth's hand in marriage would hurt the alliance between Henry's Lancastrian and Yorkist supporters. Henry believed the message to be true, and desperately sent messages to the new Lord Herbert of Raglan, proposing to marry his sister Katherine. He also sent messages to the Earl of Northumberland, who had married another sister, Maud Herbert, seeking a prominent Yorkist bride. William Herbert had expected Maud to marry his ward Henry – they had grown up together – but Henry had been forced into exile. Such was the public anger and strong advice from his counsellors that Richard was forced to publicly announce that he would not marry Elizabeth. It would have been an interesting point if Richard had actually married Elizabeth as he had declared her father and brothers illegitimate and her mother an adulterer.

At this point, John Morgan of Kidwelly arrived in France to let Henry know that Sir John Savage and Rhys ap Thomas would support him, and that Reginald Bray had raised money to help pay for his troops. Without the assistance of the powerful Rhys, whose brothers and father had died in the Lancastrian cause, it would be impossible to invade through Wales. Pennant notes that Richard Kyffin, rector of Llanddwyn, was a noted Lancastrian who conspired with 'sir Rhys ap Thomas and other Welsh chieftains' to bring Henry from Brittany. Richard Kyffin was dean of Bangor from about 1480 until 1502, known as '*deon du*', the black dean, and was later rewarded by Henry for his help. It is said he used fishing boats to carry messages to South Wales and France prior to the invasion by Henry, coordinating the North Wales chiefs with Rhys in South Wales. Sir John Savage was a notable knight who fought for Edward IV at Tewkesbury, became a royal carver and Knight of the Body and was second in order of precedence when Edward was buried. He received many important grants, including that of the constableship of Hanley Castle, Worcestershire. As such close supporters of Edward IV, and associates of the Stanleys, it is unsurprising that John Savage and his father seem to have been mistrusted by Richard III. His son, Thomas Savage, may have been abroad during 1483–1485, and possibly acted as the Savage's direct contact with Henry Tudor. According to Polydore Vergil, John Savage was one of those who 'invited' Tudor to invade.

The fourteen-year-old Charles VIII and his regent Anne de Beaujeu encouraged Henry's planned invasion, but still would not commit adequate financial support. However, with the support of Philippe de Commines, an influential diplomat and agent in the French royal council, Jasper and Henry again pressed Charles to request money from the French Parliament. The king eventually did so on 4 May 1485 and returned with Jasper and Henry to Paris about a month later. Anne de Beaujeu could now commit a loan to fund this new invasion of England, and Henry and Jasper set up headquarters at Rouen to prepare an invasion fleet. The earls were provided with £40,000 *tournois* '*pour soi passaige an angleterre*'. They intensified their efforts in writing letters to nobles across England and Wales, asking for support and hoping that their messengers were not intercepted. Knowing of the disappearance of the princes, and the consequent public anger among lords and commoners, Henry now named Richard III as a tyrant and usurper. He stopped signing his documents and letters as 'Henry de Richemont', but instead with an 'H', signifying himself as the real King of England.

Despite Richard's proclamations of December 1484 and June 1485, declaring Henry and Jasper traitors and Owen Tudor and Margaret Beaufort illegitimate, Vergil tells us he relaxed many of his defensive precautions. It seems that Richard assumed through his agents that Henry would not get support from the French. He thus withdrew his naval patrols from the Channel and stood down some garrisons. Nevertheless, Vergil says, 'lest he might be found altogether unready … he commanded nobles and gentlemen dwelling about the sea coast, and chiefly the Welshmen to keep watch ... that his adversaries should not have ready recovery of the shore and come to land'. An elaborate system of beacons was placed along the south coasts of England and Wales, and possibly Milford Haven was closely watched.

Henry began gathering a force of Lancastrians, dissident Yorkists, Bretons, Scots and French mercenaries at Honfleur and Harfleur. On 23 June 1485, Richard III issued a second proclamation, similar to that of December 1484. It condemned the true king's enemies in France, summoning all loyal men to defend their country from rape and pillage. The proclamation stated that Henry's claim to the throne was now spurious for he was from illegitimate blood on both sides of his family. Henry's grandfather Owen Tudor was wrongly claimed to be a bastard. Henry's father, Edmund, the son of what today's Yorkists allege was an illegal marriage between Owen and Catherine of Valois, was not mentioned, which seems to prove conclusively that the marriage was known to be legal at that time. However, in the maternal line, Henry's mother was a descendant of John Beaufort, Earl of Somerset, the illegitimate son of John of Gaunt and Catherine Swynford. Again, this line had been legally legitimised by Parliament, but Yorkist propaganda was now calling Henry and Jasper bastards, much as Richard had called his own brothers Edward IV and Clarence bastards.

The Welsh bards were continuing to prepare the ground for the return of the Tudors. They had been valuable publicists for both the Lancastrian and Yorkist factions. The bards usually followed the allegiance of their patrons, the *uchelwyr* (high men), the landed leaders of Welsh society. However, the tradition of prophetic poetry in the fifteenth century had a strongly nationalist bias, which boosted the morale of the proscribed nation after the defeat of Glyndŵr in 1400–1420. The bards represented the conflict between York and Lancaster as one between Welsh and English leaders, and as a struggle for national liberation from English oppression. The Yorkist William Herbert had been hailed by the poet Guto'r Glyn as a potential unifier of Wales against English dominion. Edward IV himself, as a descendant through the Mortimer connection of Llywelyn the Great, had also been regarded by Guto'r Glyn and Lewis Glyn Cothi as the potential deliverer of the Welsh, and the heir to the kings of Britain. Jasper Tudor was also seen as *mab darogan*, the son of prophecy. He had been a patron of the bards since the 1450s, and was praised as a faithful supporter of Henry VI and as the man who would unite Wales under the Lancastrians.

The hour of Henry's landing drew nearer and the bards grew bolder, speaking openly and fearlessly. The fame of their vaticinations reached Richard, as in May 1485 he sent a fleet to Southampton, having heard of a prophecy that his enemy would land nearby at Milford, a small village in Hampshire. Unfortunately for him, it was Milford in Pembrokeshire that was to be Henry's landing point. The bards were confident of an immediate triumph, and in *Ceinion Llenyddiaeth Gymreig* we read,

This is the day that will save us, [the day] for the beloved Bull [Jasper] to venture forth. The Mole [Richard] will fall and a vengeance on him will go throughout the world; A Mole full of poison, a Jew of slender body ... We are waiting for him to show, when he comes, the Red Rose in high pomp. The Thames will run red with blood on that day, and then we shall be satisfied; their end will be on that day. No Saxon will go a second time to the battlefield. There is longing for Harry, there is hope for our race. His name comes down from the mountains as a two-edged sword, and his descent from high blood.

Henry Tudor had become the most credible candidate for the title of 'son of prophecy' once he became the main Lancastrian claimant to the throne. Beginning in 1483 with the usurpation of Richard III, the bards united unanimously in Henry's favour behind the Lancastrian cause. They helped condition the nation for the realisation of the prophecy. This phase in the development of vaticinatory poetry was represented by Dafydd Llwyd of Mathafarn, a well-born bard who was the most prolific advocate of Henry Tudor's cause. Contemporaneously, Dafydd denounced Richard for the murder of the Princes in the Tower: 'Shame on the hang-lipped Saracen for slaying the angels of Christ ...' Henry was depicted as a returning avenger of the princes. The current hagiographical process of cathedrals wanting Richard's bones for income-generation ignores the fact that he would never produce the princes to show they were alive, despite reports across Europe that he had killed them. Dafydd called him 'hang-lipped' as he was known at the time to have a nervous trait of chewing his lip, and he was insulted as a 'Saracen' in reference to the Islamic opponents of the Christian crusaders, a term of real contempt for a godless person. Dafydd predicted a victory for Henry as the last of the triumphant line of Brutus and Cadwaladr, kings of the Britons.

Lewis Glyn Cothi, in an ode to Jasper Tudor, told him that Wales was desperate for the return of him and his nephew. The bard asks what had become of Jasper, 'the bull of the conflict', and states that he has been expected since May 1485. The poem is dated just before Jasper's landing, in August 1485, and he pleads with Jasper to take the powerful Rhys ap Thomas, the 'Raven', into his counsels. The poet goes on to state that, by allying with the family of Rhys in the south and the gentry of North Wales, Jasper can end the claims of 'Edward's family' to the throne of England. Lewys Glyn Cothi anxiously asked when Jasper was going to land:

Jasper, what preparations do you make?
In what seas are your anchors?
When, oh Black Bull, will you turn to land?
How long shall we have to wait?

Glyn Cothi wrote several poems praising Henry, Jasper, Rhys ap Thomas and their Welsh supporters. Part of one poem addressed to Jasper just before his invasion reads:

> I [Iasbar] is beyond the sea,
> I traverses the three seas
> And nine havens dread his approach.
> I's guiding star blazes over the two glaives
> I will land,
> I will give battle,
> I will revenge his wrongs.
> After his victory
> I will offer gold
> Upon two altars to his guardian saint
> The North can understand I
> And the North men will declare for him
> There is not a Saxon from hence to Windsor
> But trembles at the thought of I across the sea ...

There is no J in the British language, so I stands for Iasbar Tudur, Jasper Tudor. Glyn Cothi is actually telling Jasper that the men of North Wales will be ready to support him.

A glaive is a pole weapon, with a single-sided blade on the end of a pole, much used in medieval warfare. The Eastern Cleddau and Western Cleddau rivers meet at 'the mouth of the two Cleddau', Aberdaugleddau, called in English Milford Haven, the great estuary. Cleddau means glaives or weapons, and the poet is actually stating that Jasper's best landing place is Milford Haven. We know that messages were being passed back and forth between the Tudors in exile and Welsh and Marcher Lords at this time. Glyn Cothi would have recited his poem at several *llysiau*, or courts. It is fascinating that, eighty years earlier, a French army in 1405 had landed in Milford Haven in support of the Glyndŵr War of Independence and invaded England through Herefordshire, stopping near Worcester, a fact seemingly airbrushed from English history. There was a stalemate between Glyndŵr's army and that of Henry IV before the Franco-Welsh force withdrew due to a of lack of supplies.

It is beyond the realm of this book to study the dozens of surviving Welsh poems from this period, which could give us a better understanding of the events leading to the march through Wales. Very many, unfortunately, have not been translated into English. Among those writing of events around the 1480s are Dafydd Llwyd of Mathafarn (*c.* 1420 – *c.* 1500), Guto'r Glyn (*c.* 1412–1493), Tudur Penllyn (*c.* 1420–1490), his son Ieaun ap Tudur Penllyn (*fl.* 1480), Lewis Glyn Cothi (*c.* 1420–1490), Ieuan Brydidd Hir (*fl.* 1450–1485), Tudur Aled (1465–1525), Huw Cae Llwyd (*fl.* 1431–1504), and his son Ieuan ap Huw Cae Llwyd (*fl.* 1475–1500). These were bards known as 'Beirdd yr Uchelwyr', Poets of the Nobility, singing the praises of their hosts and also communicating important news. Jasper will have gathered a consensus of opinion that it would be safe to land at Milford Haven in the south-west to gather a larger army, and that heading due north, then east through Grey and Stanley territories would be his best route. Thereby supporters from South Wales could march in parallel to Jasper's army to a meeting point with the men of North Wales.

At Harfleur, near the mouth of the River Seine, Henry spent about 50,000 livres to assemble around 4,000 men. Of these, around 500 were discharged soldiers from a base at Pont de l'Arche. The French soldiers were commanded by a Savoyard nobleman in French service, Philibert de Chandée, who became a good friend of Henry. De Chandée's expert soldiering during the actual battle, and the use of tactics copied from the Swiss, may have swung the Battle of Bosworth in Tudor's favour. Chandée was knighted and made the 1st Earl of Bath, being one of the very few men elevated to the peerage by Henry VII, and died after 1486 in Brittany. Perhaps 1,000 men were also apparently recruited by 'emptying all the gaols in Normandy'. There were up to 500 English and Welsh men – likely to be men-at-arms – and their households who had shared Henry's exile. Henry placed these English supporters under the command of Richard Guildford. It was later rumoured that about 1,000 Scots joined Henry's force. Whether the number is correct or not, some Scots did fight on Henry's side, including the infamous Blackadders.

On 1 August 1485, Henry and his followers left the ports of Harfleur and Honfleur near Le Havre, and sailed down the Seine into the Channel. Some sources relate that the intended landing place was at Abermaw (Barmouth) on the Mawddach Estuary in north-west Wales. Jasper had been in frequent contact with the Vaughan family of nearby Cors-y-Gedol in Dyffryn in Merioneth, who could summon the men of Ardudwy to the Lancastrian cause. Gruffydd Fychan, or Griffith Vaughan, had assisted his cousin Dafydd ap Ieuan ab Einion in the long defence of Harlech Castle from 1461 to 1468. According to W. W. E. Wynne, quoted in E. Rosalie Jones' *History of Barmouth*, he built 'Y Tŷ Gwyn in Bermo', the White House at Barmouth, in order to enable him to communicate more safely with Jasper Tudor. The story is repeated by the bard Tudur Penllyn in *Cywydd moliant Gruffydd Vychan ap Gruffydd ab Einion o Gorsygedol rhyfelwr gyda'r Brenin Henry VII*. The antiquary Robert Vaughan of Hengwrt writes that Gruffydd Vaughan was 'in great credit with Jasper Earle of Pembrok, who lay in his house at Corsygedol, when he fled to France in the tyme of Edward IV, and, as some report, Harry, the Earle of Richmond with him, who afterwards was King of England'. Griffith Vaughan's wife was Lowry, a niece of Owain Glyndŵr. Certainly the men of north-west Wales were expecting Jasper and Henry to arrive, and large numbers joined their army. Gruffydd died in 1468, as indicated earlier, and Jasper probably was with him at this time, escaping after the Battle of Twt Hill and the fall of Harlech.

The above sources indicate that storms forced the fleet into safety in the great sound of Milford Haven, instead of landing at Barmouth, but

Pembrokeshire seems to have always been the favoured destination, being in Jasper's heartland. There was obviously strong support for the Lancastrians in the area and Jasper Tudor had maintained his Welsh connections during the period of exile. Henry had been born at Pembroke Castle and was promising a great deal in return for Welsh support. At least thirty-five poets were known to be proclaiming his coming as *y mab darogan*, the man of destiny. Henry was appealing both to Welsh national consciousness and to those who hoped to gain personally.

At sunset on 7 August, Henry's fleet sailed into Milford Sound. The thirty ships were led by Guillaume de Casenove's flagship, the *Poulain de Dieppe*, into the small sandstone cover of Mill Bay, out of sight of the nearby Dale Castle. Mill Bay is the very first cove on the north side of Milford Sound. To go any further the fleet would have been seen before it disembarked. At Dale it was known, according to Vergil, that 'certain companies of his adversaries had had their station the winter by past to have kept him from landing'. Chrimes noted that Mill Bay is 'entirely invisible from Dale Point, Roads, Beach and Castle', being separated by two promontories and two much steeper coves from Dale.

Henry fell to his knees, kissed the soil and, according to *Fabyan's Chronicle*, recited all of Psalm 43, 'Judge me, Lord and fight my cause'. The force spent the night disembarking. His banners included the Cross of St George, signifying his kingship of England, and the Welsh flag of a red dragon upon a green-and-white background, the oldest national flag in the world. He knighted eight of his main followers when he landed – John Cheyney, John Lord Welles, Edward Poynings, Edward Courtenay, John Fort, the renowned James Blount, Philibert de Chandée and possibly his uncle David Owen, Owen Tudor's illegitimate son. Owen was with him, but was also said to be knighted later. These men were all chosen to be commanders in the field. Each was been issued with standards for their followers to group around and defend in fighting. A description that vividly evokes the landing is contained in a eulogy to a Carmarthenshire squire who was present, composed about a year later by Lewys Glyn Cothi:

> You conducted your king from the water, once when chieftains landed, and mustered [the cantref of] Rhos for battle. There were seen our gallant ones, and a throng like York fair, and the host of France, a large and heavy host by the sea-shore, and many a trumpet by the strand, and guns around a red banner, and mighty tracks where you passed.

There is one report that the French did not wish to land and that they had to be convinced to follow Henry. Possibly upon Jasper's advice, knowing fighting men, they were tempted on shore with fresh food and copious drink, and their spirits rose. However, the fleet's admiral, de Casenove, sailed off the following day. On 20 August, he took four Venetian galleys sailing to Flanders, an action for which Ferdinand and Isabella of Spain wrote a letter of protest. The ships contained 'a great quantity of merchandise belonging to Spanish subjects' and de Casenove had returned to England to divide up the spoils in safety after Bosworth. This was a strange invasion, and it seems that Richard underestimated the danger Henry's ragtag force posed. He seemingly believed that his loyal nobles in Wales and the Marches would easily suppress it. The series of uprisings across southern England, and Buckingham's rebellion, in 1483 had been squashed with little difficulty. There was no urgency in Richard's reaction to the invasion, as he spent his days in hunting around Nottinghamshire.

Leaving the beach, the Anglo-French-Breton-Scots-Welsh force had to carry its arms and provisions up a steep slope to Brunt Farm. It is said to be so called because Henry said 'This is brunt [hard]' about the steep quarter-mile struggle up the hill. They occupied the village of Dale and set up camp overnight on flat land near Dale Castle. The force marched quickly to Haverfordwest, the county town of Pembrokeshire, twelve miles away, crossing Radford Bridge over a branch of the Cleddau River. Haverfordwest received his force with 'the utmost goodwill of all' and the army rested a mile north of it. Neither Dale Castle, near the disembarkation point, nor Haverfordwest Castle made any known defence. Richard's main officers in South Wales, Sir William Herbert and his brother Walter, failed to move against Henry, and some of Herbert's officers, Richard Griffith and Evan Morgan, soon deserted to Henry with their men. Dennis Davies writes, in *The History of Plaskynaston* (1951), 'Henry did not receive a rapturous welcome in Wales. On 8 August 1485, at Haverfordwest, he received a crushing blow – a false report that John Savage, nephew of Henry's stepfather, and the powerful Welsh lord, Rhys ap Thomas, were not planning to support his cause.'

This may have unnerved Henry. The loyalty of Rhys, especially, was essential. Richard III had suspected both men of disloyalty. Richard has asked for Gruffydd, the son of Rhys ap Thomas, to be sent to him for security in 1484, but Rhys had replied from Carmarthen Castle that the king could be certain of his loyalty. John Savage had been attainted and arrested in Pembroke in May 1485, probably working for Jasper and Henry, and Richard had ordered Richard Williams, the steward of Pembroke, to lock him in Pembroke Castle or send him to the king. Somehow Savage was released or escaped before the invasion. John Savage (V) was the son of Sir John Savage (IV), a noble in the Stanley lordship of Cheshire, and his mother Katherine was the daughter of Lord Thomas Stanley. He had possibly been sent by the Stanleys to liaise with Henry upon his expected landing. Lord Thomas Stanley's son Lord Strange had been arrested by Richard III, and possibly had implicated Savage under questioning. Baron Stanley's sister Katherine had married John Savage (IV), so her son John Savage (V) was Lord Strange's first cousin. All of the Stanley family knew of Henry's coming.

The Crowland Chronicler tells us that Henry's route was to North Wales 'along wild and twisting tracks … where William Stanley … was in sole command'. William Stanley, the brother of Lord Thomas Stanley, had been attainted by Edward IV after the Battle of Ludlow in 1459, but managed to have this reversed. When Worcester was executed in 1470, William Stanley married his widow, Elizabeth Hopton. As the Yorkists were back in power, Stanley and his wife had joint guardianship of the estates of her son, the new Earl of Worcester. However, the boy died aged just sixteen in 1485, and the estates passed to his sisters. Suddenly, William Stanley was left with little income. Soon after this, in August, he was attainted along with his cousin John Savage. Thomas Stanley's son Lord Strange, possibly under torture, had implicated both in treason, and Richard III at Coventry announced that they were 'traitors to the king'. Richard III at Bosworth seemed to expect William Stanley's army to fight for him, which appears odd – perhaps he had promised him the reverse of his attainder. Richard also held Lord Strange to ensure that Thomas Stanley fought for him.

The misinformation about his lack of support did seemingly distract Jasper and Henry. Their fleet had left and they had little option but to progress. Both seem to have been convinced that Rhys ap Thomas would be in arms for them, because of Henry's promise of extended power across Wales. They expected him to lead an army in parallel with them, to act as a potential buffer against attacks from the east. However, there was bad news: the expected financial support from Reginald Bray, to pay the troops' wages, had not arrived as expected. Arnold Butler of Johnston, Pembroke, a relative of the powerful Butlers of Dunraven, joined at Haverfordwest, and announced that the men of Pembroke were willing to follow their lord Jasper and his nephew into battle. Vergil makes it clear that 'they were prepared to help their Earl Jasper'. After fourteen years out of power, Jasper was still seen as their traditional lord.

Butler only asked for pardon for any service given to the Yorkists, which was readily agreed. Butler had in fact accompanied Jasper and Henry on their flight to Brittany in 1471, but had soon been removed from their service, sent home by Duke François when he replaced the earls' bodyguard with Breton soldiers. It seems that he escaped punishment, as he entered the service of Rhys ap Thomas to train young gentlemen 'according to the true military discipline of those times, in which they employed much labour, accustoming them daily (as if they had been in the field) to the hardest duties of a soldier'. It may well be that Butler brought news that Rhys ap Thomas would support Henry, as promised. We must remember here that not one Welshman was attainted for his part in the Buckingham rebellion, where he led South Wales troops in 1483. South Wales was thought firmly controlled by the Herberts, Vaughans, Rhys ap Thomas, Richard Williams and James Tyrrell. Among the twenty-two Welshmen rewarded after its failure were Sir Thomas Vaughan of Tretower, whose father had been beheaded by Jasper. Jasper was thus wary of heading east across South Wales to march on London.

Jasper had suggested the landing place, believing it safe. He knew the area intimately, and now led the army north, through the counties which had accepted Yorkist rule after 1461 with reluctance. He wanted then to cross east towards the counties of Denbighshire and Cheshire, where the Stanleys were dominant. To these areas and to at least some of the Marcher lordships he sent personal letters soon after landing. They were probably written before he left France. Some letters seem to indicate that Henry was planning to head across South Wales and cross the Severn at Tewkesbury to march upon London. Perhaps these were meant to be intercepted. Richard Williams rode from Pembroke Castle to inform the king that the rebels had landed and were not as yet being opposed by the king's forces. He rode the 200 miles in just four days, fought for Richard III at Bosworth, and was attainted. Williams had tirelessly reinforced and strengthened the castles across Henry's expected route east. The march was expected in Haverfordwest, Pembroke, Tenby, Cilgerran Manorbier and right through to Goodrich in the Marches. However, Henry had marched north instead of east, resting briefly at Castell Hên-drêf, Henry's Moat, ten miles north of Haverfordwest, on 8 August before crossing the bare and exposed Preseli Hills.

Unexpectedly, en route to Cardigan, and twenty-six miles from Haverfordwest, the Lancastrian camp was swept by rumours that Rhys ap Thomas and Sir Walter Herbert were coming to attack. This may have happened because Henry's scouts spotted Rhys's army heading up the Tywi Valley, east of them. Gruffydd Rede of Carmarthen was leading men from the camp of Rhys and Walter Herbert to join Henry, which may also have sparked the panic. Henry was said to have stayed a night at Fagwr Lwyd, near Cilgwyn, Nevern. Perhaps nearby Nevern and Newport castles had to be taken, or had surrendered easily. They may have been simply bypassed, to avoid getting bogged down in sieges.

Upon 9 August, Henry and Jasper moved from Pembrokeshire into the county of Ceredigion, and were approaching its county town at Cardigan. In less than two days they had disembarked and marched forty miles from Mill Bay, bypassing any potential conflict with men based at Jasper's great castle at Pembroke. Any prolonged siege by Henry would have meant that the impetus of popular support would ebb away. It was never the intention to consolidate territory, which would have allowed Richard to gather forces and come into Wales. Jasper and Oxford knew that Henry had to quickly gather support in Wales and the counties held by his kinsmen the Stanleys, and then hopefully head to London. Messengers rode across the country rousing support, aided by the bards, urged on by Jasper, who had been exciting people for three years and proclaiming Henry as the messiah who would re-establish Welsh supremacy over the Saxons and Normans of Angle-Land. Across the wide River Teifi rose the town walls, castle towers and turrets of the port and market town of Cardigan.

Advance parties would have been sent into the town and around the local farms to arrange for animals to be brought to be slaughtered and for food and drink to be on hand for the army. Jasper and Oxford were well aware of the hostility incurred by Lancastrian armies in the past, and took care to ensure that their troops would not loot on the march. They would have to keep strict control of their foreign mercenaries and the Scots, who had no local ties. Any reports of pillage would stiffen resistance, and the earls needed the crucial target of Shrewsbury to know that they meant no harm to the townspeople or its neighbourhood. People on this route were always afraid of an oncoming army. Women and property could be harmed. Men could be conscripted. Livestock could be stolen from farms. Inns, bakeries and breweries might have to exchange their products and services for IOUs, which would be worthless if Henry was defeated. Fighting could break out in the town, fuelled by thirsty troops wanting alcohol. The earls went to great lengths to allay any such anxieties – they did not want to have to retreat through pillaged and hostile territory.

One report says that, after staying at Fagwr Llwyd, having covered thirty miles in a day over the hills, the army stayed upon a Tuesday at Cardigan. Dan Williams, in *The Story of Cardigan*, writes,

> Henry Tudor the Earl of Richmond was welcomed by Rhys ap Thomas of Carew Castle, at the head of a Welsh army devoted to his service. The combined army split to recruit on the journey northwards through Wales. Henry Tudor, with his contingent, reached Cardigan. Its royal castle had been virtually undefended since Glyndŵr's War ended seventy years before.

English kings, perpetually short of money, had more pressing priorities than spending on keeping soldiers in idleness in remote West Wales. Only during the Great Sessions was the castle properly used, otherwise there was only a janitor and prisoners. Its constable did not even live there, as the post was a reasonably paid sinecure in times of peace. His deputy was probably Thomas Bola, who had little to do but to check that the prison tower was secure. Kings fined constables heavily if prisoners escaped. The sheriff of Cardiganshire, Sir John Dwnn, did not live in the town, and for years he had been in London and elsewhere assisting Edward IV and Richard III. Incidentally, the qualities of this committed Yorkist and old enemy of Jasper were such that by 1487 he was Henry's 'trusted and well beloved counsellor'. Indeed, it says a great deal for Jasper's magnanimity that he waged no vendetta against any of his enemies when Henry came to power.

The earls were given a terrific welcome by the major families of the district. The Pryses, Lloyds, Lewes, Parrys, Colbys, Bowens and Phillips all came with their retainers to enlist in his army. It was claimed that Henry Tudor could speak Welsh as fluently as any of them as he had a Welsh nurse while at both Pembroke Castle and Raglan. Preparations had been made in Cardigan Castle to entertain the royal visitor, but, according to tradition, although lodged at the castle, he spent much of the night roistering at the Three Mariners Inn, since semi-demolished and replaced.

The army needed to buy stocks for at least another two to three days' marching to the next major town, Machynlleth. Officers of the commissariat would have gone to the port, walking down Quay Street and through New

Game, to see whether fishermen had come in from sea with a catch, or if the Teifi coracle men had landed any fine salmon, trout or sewin (sea trout), or if a ship had come in with a cargo of wine. Others would have visited the market, or gone to the inns to arrange meals. Private houses would have been enlisted to feed the men. Some would have turned to the right at the Market Cross and walked down Castle Yard, now Upper St Mary Street, passing through Wolf Gate to eat in 'the Maudlyn's hospice', where the Angel Inn now stands. There they will have seen old and infirm men being cared for by the Knights Hospitallers of St John.

Pilgrims arriving at the town to see the effigy of Mary will have been astonished to see it filled with soldiers. According to legend, a statue of Our Lady and Child was found beside the River Teifi, with a burning taper (candle) in her hand. The statue was taken to the local parish church, and moved several times before a church was specially built to house the shrine. The present St Mary's church dates back to around 1158, making the shrine more than 800 years old. Our Lady of Cardigan (Mair o Aberteifi), also known as Our Lady of the Taper, is the Catholic national shrine of Wales. The original statue is believed to have been taken to London in 1538 and destroyed along with other Marian images on the orders of Thomas Cromwell.

It is said that Sir John Savage and Richard Griffith met Henry at Cardigan. Savage would have been carrying messages from the Stanleys if this is true, because he joined with a force of men later in the march. John Morgan of Tredegar joined with followers, either between Haverfordwest and Cardigan or at Cardigan. He had been a Yorkist royal officer in Carmarthenshire and Cardigan in the 1470s. The family of Gruffudd Rede, or Richard Griffith, had estates in Staffordshire and West Wales, and he had left Walter Herbert's supposedly Yorkist force to join Henry. Once again there were rumours of Sir Walter Herbert approaching from Carmarthen with a large force, but scouts were sent out and nothing untoward was found. It appears that the approach of Griffith's or Morgan's men accidentally caused the affair. Richard Griffith and John Morgan were both friendly with Rhys ap Thomas, and probably brought news that his army was on its way to meet Henry. The march continued – led by the Welsh flag, according to Hall – to encourage support.

From Cardigan Henry wrote letters to Gilbert Talbot, the Stanley brothers and others saying that he would cross the River Severn at Shrewsbury, asking them to meet him with troops. Possibly Savage took the letters to the Stanleys. Lord Thomas Stanley controlled Cheshire and Lancashire, on the north-eastern border of Wales. His brother William possessed Shropshire, the border county south of Cheshire, and much of Denbighshire, west of Cheshire. Richard Mostyn, who had sheltered Jasper and possibly Henry, controlled much of Flint in north-east Wales. It appears that Henry knew he could get safe passage into England by passing through these lands.

One letter survives, written shortly after in Machynlleth, but the only other extant letter was written in Cardigan and demonstrates the nature of Henry's appeal for support. He states that his rightful claim to the throne was usurped by Richard. It was sent to a Welsh landowner of south Caernarfonshire, John ap Maredudd:

Right trusty and well beloved, we greet you well, and where it is so that through the help of almighty God the assistance of our loving friends and true subjects, and the great confidence that we have to the nobles and commons of this our principality of Wales, we be entered into the same, purposing by the help above rehearsed in all haste possible to descend into our realm of England not only for the adeption [*i.e.* recovery] of the crown unto us of right appertaining, but also for the oppression of that odious tyrant Richard late duke of Gloucester, usurper of our said right and moreover to reduce as well our said realm of England into his [*i.e.* its] ancient estate honour and prosperity, as this our said principality of Wales, and the people of the same to their former liberties, delivering them of such miserable servitudes as they have piteously long stood in and pray you and upon your allegiance strictly charge and command you that immediately upon the sight hereof with all such power as ye may make defensibly arrayed for the war ye address you towards us without any tarrying upon the way, unto such time as ye be with us wheresoever we shall be, to our aid for the effect above rehearsed, wherein ye shall cause us in time to come to be your singular good lord, and that ye fail not hereof as ye will avoid our grievous displeasure and answer unto at your peril.

Henry Tudor, with his reinforced army, left Cardigan and followed the coast for around eleven miles to Llwyndafydd. This is near Cwmtudu, four miles from New Quay on the Ceredigion coast. Here he was entertained by Dafydd ab Ifan (or Dafydd ab Ieuan) on 11 August. Henry was later said to have sent the Hirlas Horn, a superb drinking container, as a gesture of gratitude for the hospitality shown. The horn was supported by the greyhound of the Woodville family of Henry's queen, and the dragon of his Welsh ancestors. It was decorated with the portcullis of Henry's mother's Beaufort family and the new device of the Tudor rose.

There followed a four-mile march to the fifteenth-century Wern Newydd (Plas y Wern) at Gilfachreda near Llanarth, where the tradition is that Henry visited the home of Einion ap Dafydd Llwyd. On the left of its huge oak staircase are two large rooms, nineteen feet square, with oak-panelled walls. The dining room ceiling has heavy beams, adorned with plaster rosettes, the Tudor heraldic rose occupying a circular sunken panel in the centre. At the head of the staircase is the room in which Henry is said to have slept, only measuring fourteen by nine feet, and with one comparatively small window which cannot be entered from outside. There is a wooden plaque here, with his stay recorded in Welsh. It is thought that he would have been placed in this smaller room – both easier to guard and less likely to be suspected as his place of rest – than any of the great chambers. Also on 11 August, Henry is said to have spent the night at St Ilar's church, Llanilar, or at Llidiardau mansion, overlooking the River Ystwyth. A local tradition is that he used the mounting block at the church gate. The earls of Pembroke, Richmond and Oxford were entertained by local gentry during their progress.

The Aberystwyth Castle garrison did not immediately surrender on 12 August. Vergil noted that there had been few delays thus far, but Henry had had to overcome 'several enemy districts which had been strengthened by garrisons'. Vergil tells us that Aberystwyth belonged to Walter Devereux, Lord Ferrers, but was not strongly garrisoned and that Henry took it 'without much trouble'. Ferrers had been, with the Herberts, Jasper's main opponent in Wales for many years. From Aberystwyth Castle, Henry sent out scouts to ascertain where Rhys ap Thomas and Walter Herbert were. Richard of York was relying upon them to stop Henry entering England. Henry's most important supporter in the early stages of his invasion was Rhys ap Thomas, the most powerful lord in South Wales, although Rhys had declined to support Buckingham's revolt. When Richard III appointed officers to replace those who had joined the rebellion, he therefore made Rhys ap Thomas his principal lieutenant in South West Wales. Rhys was told to send his son Gruffydd ap Rhys to Richard III's court at Nottingham as a hostage. However, he had excused himself from doing so by claiming that nothing could bind him to his duty more strongly than his conscience.

The support of Rhys ap Thomas was crucial, and he had been in previous contact with Henry Tudor. It seems that Henry had offered him the lieutenancy of all Wales in exchange for his loyalty. Rhys had arranged beacons to be lit across his lands to summon men to his arms. From Carmarthen he travelled up the Tywi Valley past Dryslwyn Castle and Dinefwr Castle at Llandeilo to Llandovery Castle. With around 1,500 men, he headed east to Brecon Castle in the Usk Valley. At Brecon he halted, as many unsuitable men, along with women and children, had joined the march. Here he chose the 2,000 best fighting men, fully armed, on horseback. As a precaution he chose another 500 men, putting them under the command of his younger brothers David and John, and his only son, Gruffydd ap Rhys. He told them not to take to arms unless they were commanded by him, and left them to protect those who had flocked to his banner. Rhys' two older brothers and his father had already died in the Wars of the Roses and he needed to keep some reserve back in Wales in case things went wrong.

Henry had marched north at around twenty miles per day, foraging for provisions. From Aberystwyth he followed the coast to Machynlleth, arriving on 14 August, about 100 miles from his landing place. Only now did Richard seem to learn of the invasion. With hindsight, Richard should have moved immediately to force as early an engagement as possible, as Henry was daily picking up new support. From Machynlleth, Henry wrote a letter, dated 14 August, to Sir Roger Kynaston, the guardian of the Grey estates. To pass safely to Shrewsbury, Henry needed either Kynaston's support or inaction. Henry was about to head east, towards England, away from easy escape by sea, and through the large Marcher lordship of Powys, held by Lord Grey. Sir Roger Kynaston had been constable of Denbigh Castle and high sheriff of Shropshire. He was now constable of Harlech Castle, and high sheriff for life of Merionethshire. A prominent Yorkist, by personally killing James Tuchet, 5th Baron Audley, he effectively won the battle at Blore Heath in 1459. He was temporarily in charge of the estates of Edmund Grey, Lord Powys, and received the following missive from Henry:

> H By the king – Trusty and well beloved we greet you well. And forsomuch as we be credibly informed and ascertained that our trusty and well beloved cousin the lord Powys hath in time past be of that mind and disposition that at this our coming in to these parts he had fully concluded and determined to have do us service. And now we understand that he is absent and ye have the Rule of his lands and folk we will pray you and upon your allegiance strictly charge and command you that in all haste possible ye assemble his said folks and servants and with them so assembled and defensibly arrayed for the war ye come to us for our aid and assistance in this our enterprise for the Recovery of the crown of our Realm of England to us of Right appertaining. And that this be not failed as ye will that we be your good lord in time to come and avoid our gravest display sir and answer to us at your peril. Given under our signet beside our town of Machen lloyd the xiiii day of August.

While the Herberts had grown up as children with Henry and had divided loyalties, which accounted for their refusal to engage with him, Kynaston had always fought for the Yorkists, and was expected to definitely delay or even halt Henry's progress. Kynaston was defending the estates of Edmund Grey, Lord of Ruthin and 1st Earl of Kent, whose treachery had given victory to the Yorkists at Northampton. Grey raised no forces for Richard III at Bosworth, despite being JP for Merioneth and a former Lord Treasurer of England. Kent's warrior son George Grey also did not attend Richard at Bosworth, and as 2nd Earl of Kent later became one of Jasper Tudor's commanders in France and Cornwall. One must ask why so few Yorkists rallied to Richard's cause. Did they all believe that he had killed Edward V and was a usurper? Certainly, Kynaston, a man loyal to Edward IV, took men to fight for Henry against Richard.

According to Vergil, Henry sent many more messengers and letters from Machynlleth. One was to Rhys ap Thomas, assuring him of his rewards if he did not halt Henry's progress. It seems that Rhys needed an absolute guarantee of royal favour from Henry. Rhys had all to lose by supporting Henry, and needed Jasper removed from control of the region he required. Henry knew that he could obtain Crown estates from Richard's defeat with which to reward his faithful uncle, so promised what Rhys required in Wales. However, it is also doubtful if Rhys' Welsh army would have fought for an untrusted new English king against the *mab darogan*, the promised deliverer of Wales. Henry also needed the Stanley brothers to come to his cause. Thomas was his stepfather, and his brother William Stanley had been accused of treason by Richard, so Henry's hopes were high that they would honour previous agreements. Christopher Urswick, Henry's chaplain in Brittany, was despatched to his mother Margaret Beaufort and her husband Thomas Stanley at Lathom Castle, to arrange 'in what district to meet his friends'. Messages were also sent to William Stanley at Holt Castle and Lord Gilbert Talbot at Shrewsbury, among others. Henry had to pass through Grey, Stanley and Talbot estates in Merionethshire, Denbighshire, Shropshire and Cheshire en route to England.

Machynlleth was the lowest crossing point on the River Dyfi, from where the Lancastrian army quickly headed inland to rendezvous with other supporters. Four miles inland from Machynlleth, Henry met the bard Dafydd Llwyd at Mathafarn, before heading north-east to Newtown and Welshpool and then Shrewsbury. A story is told that

> the Earl is said to have lodged one night at Mathafarn, near Machynlleth, with his adherent Dafydd Llwyd. Dafydd was a bard and seer, and Henry was said to have asked what would be the issue of his enterprise. This so perplexed David that he passed a sleepless night; his wife, learning the cause, bade him good cheer, for, said she, 'Tell him the event will be both successful and glorious. If your prediction be verified you will receive honours and rewards: if it fails he will never return to reproach you.'

The army kept up its pace, hauling French artillery through the very difficult terrain of the watershed between the Dyfi and Upper Banwy valleys, resting at Mallwyd and Llangadfan. They struggled through Bwlchyfedwen Pass to Castle Caereinion, four miles west of Welshpool, where Henry is said to have stayed nearby at the now demolished Dolarddyn Hall. Simons believes that, from Llanbadarn Fawr outside Aberystwyth, the army divided into two. One force passed up the Severn Valley to Mynydd Digoll near Welshpool, while the other swung northwards via Mallwyd and Llanfyllin to reach Mynydd Digoll. The following day, Henry was joined by several forces at the agreed meeting point of Mynydd Digoll. There is an extensive plain on the summit of this mountain which would form an excellent rendezvous point, and none of the expected forces were found to be missing. This accounts for the name of the hill, 'digoll' meaning without loss.

Long Mountain, or Cefn Digoll or Mynydd Digoll, is around four miles east of Welshpool, crossing the present boundaries of England and Wales and the county boundaries of Montgomeryshire, Powys and Shropshire, rising to 408 metres at Beacon Ring, where there is a hill fort. There was a Roman road along the Long Mountain, part of a route from Wroxeter to Lavobrinta, Forden Gaer. At the southern end of the hill there are traces of Offa's Dyke, and in the eastern foothills are the remains of Caus Castle. In 630, the hill had seen the Battle of Cefn Digoll, when an alliance of the

Cadwallon of Gwynedd and Penda of Mercia defeated the invading Edwin of Northumbria.

Other forces from across north-west Wales came, bringing fatted oxen and cattle, with other stores and provisions. Henry VII had sent a letter to the Welsh gentry seeking their support before Bosworth 'to free this, our Principality of Wales of such miserable servitude as they have long piteously stood in'. It was here that substantial contingents from all parts of Wales joined him, thereby doubling the size of his army. Gwyn Alf Williams states that, in this 'highly risky venture', Henry Tudor 'depended utterly on a Welsh rally to carry him through to his supporters in England'. William Gruffudd of Cochwillian, retainer of the Stanleys and kinsman of the William Griffiths who had been imprisoned along with Lord Strange, led a force from the north-west. Many Flintshire men now joined under Richard ap Hywel of Mostyn. Richard ap Hywel led men from the north-east. The giant Rhys Fawr ap Maredudd of Golgynwal left his mansion at Foelas, outside Ysbyty Ifan, and brought the men of Hiraethog and provisions from the Conwy Valley. He was later to grasp the Welsh flag at Bosworth when its standard bearer fell.

The largest contingent was that of Rhys ap Thomas of Dinefwr from South West Wales. He had taken a more easterly route, recruiting 500 more Welshmen en route to lead about 2,000 men before uniting with Henry near Welshpool. Henry was said to have been entertained at Derwydd Mansion near Llandeilo by Rhys ap Thomas on his way to Bosworth, but it is unlikely. The connection is commemorated in a sculpture of a shield in the 'King's Room' at Derwydd. The sculpture shows a Tudor rose surrounded by Rhys' ravens in the family's coat of arms.

Rhys ap Thomas' importance was shown in the closing scenes of Shakespeare's *Richard III*, in the lines:

STANLEY: ... But tell me, where is princely Richmond now?
URSWICK: At Pembroke or at Ha'rfordwest in Wales.
STANLEY: What men of note resort to him?
URSWICK: Sir Walter Herbert, a renowned soldier,
Sir Gilbert Talbot, Sir William Stanley,
Oxford, redoubted Pembroke [Jasper], Sir James Blunt,
And Rice ap Thomas with a valiant crew;
And many other of great name and worth;
And towards London do they bend their power ...

Along the Roman road, it was only sixteen miles from Mynydd Digoll to Shrewsbury. More supporters marched to join Henry, bringing along much-needed supplies. From the south-east, Walter Herbert, a childhood friend of Henry's, joined with some forces from Gwent, despite the fact that he and his brother were prominent Yorkists and supposedly suppressing the invasion. Somewhere en route to Bosworth, Henry was joined by David Cecil, a young squire from the manor of Alltyrynys in the border lordship of

Ewyas Lacy, Herefordshire. He possibly came with Herbert's men. David, the son of David Cecil ap Philip Seisyllt, settled in England after fighting at Bosworth, becoming a yeoman of the chamber and MP for Stamford. His son Richard Cecil became a courtier and high sheriff of Northamptonshire, and his son was William Cecil, Elizabeth's Lord Burghley, the greatest of all the counsellors of the Tudors. His son Sir Robert Cecil in turn became the leading royal administrator.

William Mathew of Radyr also joined, with retainers from Llandaff, Pentyrch and Cardiff in Glamorgan. His grandfather Sir David Mathew, Dafydd ap Mathew ap Ieuan, had saved Edward IV's life at Towton in 1461. William Mathew was said to have beeen knighted at Bosworth Field, but Shaw's *Knights of England* states that this did not occur until 1513. An impressive alabaster monument in Abergavenny Priory church is that Sir Richard Herbert of Ewyas, natural son of Sir William Herbert, Earl of Pembroke. He was brought up with Henry Tudor at Raglan Castle and also joined to fight for Henry. Men had joined from every single part of Wales, and many more from the Marcher counties of Gloucester, Hereford, Worcester, Shropshire and Cheshire.

A call to arms was not always welcome, especially in winter or the harvest season. The main reason for fighting, if not bound by contract, was to keep one's home rather than being disposed by one's lord. A soldier was entitled to pay, and the medieval rate of six pence a day for an archer and one shilling a day for a mounted man who brought his horse with him was very attractive for those who could choose to fight or not. Later in the Wars of the Roses, these rates were substantially increased. Pay, perhaps as much as three months' worth, was distributed in advance at the mustering point, usually provided by the community from which the men came. The pyramidal nature of medieval society ensured that men tended to think of the king's cause as their own, and because of this hierarchy they often identified their immediate lord's dispute as the king's own. Lords in rebellion could thus sometimes raise forces without the legal compulsion of commissions of array. If one's lord thought that the wrong person was on the throne or that he was being badly advised, those who took their lead from him were usually prepared to support him. In Henry's case, the former Yorkists joining his cause in Brittany, Wales and the Marches, bringing men, believed that Richard should not be king.

Around 15 August, Henry's army crossed the border, heading for the important walled town and castle of Shrewsbury. On the march towards Shrewsbury, emissaries brought much-needed monies for the troops. The French and Scots mercenaries, in particular, would not have fought without money. They had possibly crossed the Severn on the old bridge at Buttington, hear Welshpool, but would have to cross the river again near the heavily fortified Shrewsbury. The old Montford Bridge was secured, four miles north-west of Shrewsbury, and the army encamped there, on the north side of the river at Forton Heath, with the river between them and any possible attack. Messengers were despatched to Shrewsbury to demand a peaceful entrance but the gates were shut, and the portcullis down.

Shrewsbury, in Welsh Yr Amwythig, was the possible site of Pengwern, a capital of the princes of Powys, but following Mercian expansion became an important trading town between the Welsh and the Anglo-Saxons. It may well be that the great 'Saxon hoard' recently found in Staffordshire came from the sacking of Prince Cynddylan's court there in the seventh century, as some of its gold objects are Christian in provenance. The Normans built a fort, sacked in 1069 when the town was burnt. Another Norman castle was built here in 1074, just nine miles from the present Welsh border. In 1218, the town received England's first grant of murage, a toll to build town walls. Shrewsbury fell to Welsh forces led by Llywelyn the Great in 1215 and 1234. After both attacks the defences were greatly increased. Shrewsbury also received one of the earliest grants of pavage in 1266, 'for paving the paving of the new market place' removed from the churchyard of St Alkmund and St Juliana. In 1283, Edward I held a parliament here to decide the fate of Prince Dafydd ap Gruffydd, the last free Welsh ruler of Wales. Dafydd was hanged and drawn while still alive in Edward's presence, before being quartered for the high treason of defending his country. In the late Middle Ages, Shrewsbury had national and economic significance, being a centre of the wool trade. It was an important and well-defended town.

Its western approach from Wales was defended by the Old Welsh Bridge, built around 1262 and demolished in 1795. Leland described it in 1539 thus:

> The greatest, fayrest and highest upon the streame is the Welsh Bridge having 6 great Arches of Stone, soe called because it is the Way out of the Towne into Walles. This Bridge standeth on the West Syde of the Towne, and hath at the one End of it a great Gate to enter by into the Towne, and at the other End towardes Wales a might strong Towre to prohibit Enimies to enter into the Bridge.

There was another bridge to bypass Shrewsbury, the Forton Bridge that led east to Forton outside Newport in Shropshire. Henry's men had taken this, enabling them to bypass Shrewsbury if the town did not surrender. Henry delayed his march until he held both bridges. They were not defended. Shrewsbury delayed surrendering, afraid of being sacked, but entered a day of negotiations, in which Henry's emissaries would have pointed out that their progress had been paid for as they passed through Wales.

Shrewsbury had two bailiffs, Roger Knight and Thomas Mytton, both in power for about two decades. They had prospered under Richard III, notably from the failure of Buckingham's rebellion. Mytton received Buckingham's castle there, and Shrewsbury's tax bill was significantly reduced. Blakeway's *History* relates that the senior of the magistrates was Thomas Mytton, the former sheriff of Shropshire, who had been involved in the arrest of the Duke of Buckingham. Mytton stated his loyalty to Richard, and Henry returned with his company to the house of Hugh of Forton. The next day it was arranged that Mytton's oath of loyalty to Richard would be fulfilled by Henry riding over the body of the prostrate bailiff as he entered the town. The same legend was attached to Rhys ap Thomas at Mullock Bridge near Dale. The portcullis was thus drawn up and the earls entered the town. The citizens received Henry with an 'ave chaire and God spede the wel … the streets being strowed with hearbes and flowers, and their doores adorned with greene boughs, in testimony of a true hartie reception'.

At a nearby village, Henry had composed a letter to the bailiffs promising that his men would simply march through Shrewsbury peacefully, without causing any damage or harm. He respected the oath of loyalty to Richard III and did not expect any of the townspeople to break it. The letter itself may not have altered the bailiffs' conviction, but the arrival of Rowland Warburton, a retainer of Sir William Stanley, persuaded the bailiffs to let Henry pass. *The Ballad of Lady Bessie* relates,

… then to Sir William Stanley, with 10,000 coats
In an hour's warning ready to be:
they were all as red as blood,
there their hart's head is set full high.
Sir Gilbert Talbot, 10,000 dogs
in an hours warning ready to be.
Sir John Savage, 1,500 white hoods,
for they will fight & never flee.
Sir Edward Stanley, 300 men;
there were no better in Christianity.
Rice ap Thomas, a Knight of Wales,
800 spear-men brought he.
Sir William Stanley, at the Holt [Castle] he lies,
& looked over his head so high;
'Which way standeth the wind?' he says;
'if there be any man can tell me.'
'The wind it standeth south west,'
so sad a Knight that stood him by.
'This night, yonder royal prince,
into England entereth he.'
he called that gentleman that stood him by,
his name was Rowland Warburton,
he bade him go to Shrewsbury that night,
& bade them let that prince in come.
By that Rowland came to Shrewsbury
the portcullis was letten down;
he called the Prince in full great scorn,
& said 'in England he should wear no crown.'
Rowland bethought him of a wile,

& tied the writings to a stone;
he threw the writings over the wall,
& bade the bailiffs look them upon.
Then they opened the gates wide,
& met the Prince with procession;
he would not abide in Shrewsbury that night,
for King Richard heard of his coming ...

In reality, the arrival of Rowland Warburton, sent by William Stanley to urge the opening of the city gates, was vital. The townspeople knew that the Stanleys, their local lords, were now supporting Henry. Henry promised that all acts carried out by the citizens on behalf of the Yorkists would be pardoned. Henry rode his men through the town in battle order, then rode towards Newport in Shropshire. The house in which Henry was said to have lodged in Shrewsbury, Kyle Cop, is said to be Henry Tudor House, now a restaurant and bar, with timber partitions inside dating back to the fifteenth century. At Shrewsbury, the prominent Yorkist Kynaston brought men to fight for Henry at Bosworth as did Richard Corbet.

Blakeway states,

Sir Richard Corbet of Morton Corbet, who had been a stout Lancastrian and evinced his attachment to the Earl on a former occasion by rescuing him from imminent danger at the Battle of Banbury, joined the Earl immediately on his entry into Shrewsbury. He even went the hazardous length of taking the oath of allegiance ... and collected a band of 800 gentlemen, who accompanied the Earl to the field of Redmore, or Bosworth.

Blakeway then quotes a letter from Sir Richard Corbet advancing the claims of his services after Henry had been duly invested with the regal dignity. Sir Richard's mother Elizabeth Hopton was remarried to Sir William Stanley, reinforcing Henry's Stanley support.

Written after Bosworth, 'The Petition of Sir Richard Corbet to King H. 7.' reads,

In most humble wise sheweth unto your most noble highness ... your true and faithful subject and liegeman, Ric. Corbett knight for your bodie, to consider the true faithfull service that he hath doun and hereafter entendeth for to doe to the uttermost of his power ... First. Pleaseth your Grace to call to your remembrance the first service, that after the death of the Lord Herbert after the Field of Banbury, hee was one of them that brought your grace out of danger of your enemyes, and conveyed your grace unto your towne of Hereford, and there delivered you in safety to your greate Uncle now Duke of Bedford:- and then at your comynge into England, hee was one of the first came unto your Grace at the towne of Shrewesbury, and there was sworn your liegeman, and went from thence unto the Field of Boseworth, and there jeoparded with your Grace his life, lands, and goods, and the gentlemen and others his friends that came with him in company, takinge your parte and rightwise quarrell to the number of 800 men; and at every field and jorney since hee hath byne reddy to do your Grace service to his great costs and charges, and hee, ne non of his that were with him at your first fielde, or at any other insurrections or tumolts were never noe cravers for noe rewardes nor offices as yet. The which GOD knoweth best, and your Highness.

Corbet's example was followed by Humphrey Cotes of Woodcote, who lost his life at Bosworth.

The king showed his appreciation for the services rendered him by Shrewsbury, and visited the town often. He stayed for several days in 1488, and the following year brought with him his queen and his son Prince Arthur, and kept the Feast of St George, on 23 April, in the church of St Chad. Some citizens of Shrewsbury also joined Henry, and the army camped for one night near Newport, Shropshire, on 16 August, where Sir Gilbert Talbot joined. Talbot was the uncle and guardian of the young Earl of Shrewsbury, and was said to have brought 500 retainers, or alternately 'two thousand tall men', vassals or dependants of the Earl of Shrewsbury. Others came with Roger Acton. Thomas Croft of Herefordshire, who had been brought up with Edward IV, brought a contingent of followers. He was one Yorkist among many who believed that Edward V had been murdered by Richard III. John Hanley of Worcestershire, who had probably served Clarence, arrived with troops, as did Robert Pointz of Gloucestershire.

Companies came from the executed Buckingham's Marcher lordships, having been based around Caus and Talgarth castles. Of the ninety-seven men attainted for the Buckingham revolt in South Wales, not one was Welsh, which shows how the nation was transformed from apathy to rebellion with a Welsh rather than English leader. More deserters from Richard's forces joined. Although accounts of numbers joining were exaggerated, the army had grown substantially since the landing. However, Henry's army was not yet large enough to fight, and Jasper Tudor slowed down the pace of the army through Staffordshire, trying to gather more recruits.

Richard had known of Henry's impending invasion since 22 June, and had ordered his lords to maintain a high level of readiness. News of Henry's landing had reached Richard on 11 August, but it took three or four days for his messengers to notify his lords of their king's mobilisation. Only on 16 August did the Yorkist army begin to gather, eight days after Henry had begun his march across Wales. The Duke of Norfolk headed for Leicester, the Yorkist assembly point. Simultaneously, Northumberland was gathering men and heading south.

After the fall of Shrewsbury, Henry's forces were attended from a distance by Richard's 'scurriers', mounted scouts, while Jasper and Oxford were using the same means to study Richard's movements. There is a legend that Henry's soldiers began to adopt the leek at this time. When parties of troops met, with loyalties unsure and no distinct uniforms, Henry's men were said to display a leek, or in its absence a daffodil, hyacinth or onion, the white root being recognised.

Henry's strategy of landing in Wales and heading east into central England had depended on the reactions of his kinsmen Sir William Stanley, chamberlain of Chester and North Wales, and Lord Thomas Stanley, who owned much of Cheshire and Lancashire. Learning of the invasion, Richard III had ordered the Stanleys to raise the men of their region to fight Henry. Henry had been communicating on friendly terms with the Stanleys for months, and the Stanleys had actually mobilised their forces upon hearing of Henry's landing, days before the message from Richard. The Stanley armies now ranged themselves ahead of Henry's march through the English countryside, meeting twice in secret with Henry as he slowed his progress through Staffordshire. Henry's force was following Watling Street from Shrewsbury to London.

Richard's seemingly dilatory response seems to have occurred because he thought that Henry's little army would be overcome in Wales, mainly because of his trust in William Herbert, who was inactive. Herbert's father, a great warrior known as 'Black William', had been executed by Warwick after Edgcote Moor, so it was expected that his son William would have strongly supported the Yorkist cause. However, in 1467, William Herbert had married Elizabeth Woodville's sister Mary Woodville (*c.* 1456–1481). The bride was about ten or eleven years old, and William Herbert was fifteen. This link between Herbert and the Woodvilles may well have affected his decision not to attack Henry on his invasion. Herbert was governing South Wales for York, but he had been forced by Edward IV to give up the second earldom of Pembroke in 1479 in exchange for that of Huntingdon, and a less valuable endowment in Somerset and Dorset. In 1484, Herbert took as his second wife Katherine Plantagenet, the illegitimate daughter of Richard III. Whether this was a forced marriage is unknown, and there were no children. Thus not only did William Herbert have links with the Woodvilles, his incomes and estates had in fact been slashed by the Yorkist king he faithfully served. He had also grown up with Henry Tudor, so his loyalties would have been mixed at best.

Henry's wardship in the Herbert household seems to have played a massive role in his path to the kingdom. Indeed, upon acquiring the throne, Henry remained on extremely friendly terms with Anne Devereux, the widow of 'Black William'. She had been as a mother during Henry's years at the great Raglan Castle, when Henry was aged between four and twelve. Pembroke's daughter Maud Herbert, whom Pembroke had wished to marry Henry, had married the Earl of Northumberland at some time between 1473 and 1476. Northumberland did not engage his reserve army at Bosworth, possibly because of the influence of Maud Herbert and his receipt of letters from Henry in exile in France.

In Henry's eight years in custody at Raglan until 1469, he aged from four to twelve, while Maud went from thirteen to twenty-one, the eldest son and heir William from ten to eighteen and the second-eldest son Walter from nine to seventeen. In effect, Henry Tudor grew up with Herbert's children, learning martial arts and courtly behaviour along with them. When William succeeded his father in 1469, he had been growing up with Henry for almost a decade. William Herbert was ordered to intercept Henry's invasion army in Wales, but did not move, and his younger brother Walter Herbert actually took a force of men from Gwent to join Henry's invading force. The Herberts were Yorkists but felt no loyalty to Richard III, especially as he had not returned the earldom of Pembroke to them, taken by Edward IV. It is recorded that Richard was thrown into 'a fierce rage' when he found that Henry had 'traversed Wales unopposed'. He had expected loyalty from the Herberts, Rhys ap Thomas, Kynaston, Grey and the Stanleys.

On 15 August, Lord Thomas Stanley had left Lathom with his army, making for Newcastle-under-Lyme. On 17 August, Lord Thomas Stanley entered the cathedral city of Lichfield with an army estimated at 5,000 men, but left the next day. Henry's army switched its route south-east on 18 August, and Richard feared it was heading to London. Henry passed through Rugeley and camped outside the town walls of Lichfield, not wishing to alienate its citizens. It appears that Thomas Stanley had smoothed the way for him. On 20 August, Henry was welcomed into the city. He then marched to Tamworth and the castle surrendered, with Henry probably taking its cannon. Not until this day did Richard begin moving from Nottingham. Unfortunately for him, only twenty-eight peers, fewer than half of those available, had answered his call to arms and possibly only six actually took part.

Thomas Stanley's men marched quickly to Atherstone along Watling Street, leaving Henry's men a clear path in front of them. Stanley could always say to Richard's scouts that he was rushing to join the king's forces. William Stanley's force reached Lichfield early upon 20 August, and actually met up with some of Henry's rearguard. *The Ballad of Bosworth Field* tells us that Henry and William now met and celebrated, but a message arrived from Thomas Stanley informing them that Richard's army was near, and fighting was expected in the next three hours.

On the evening of 20 August, Sir Thomas Bourchier joined Henry, as did Sir Walter Hungerford, who had possibly deserted from Robert Brackenbury's Yorkist force as it made its way from London to Nottingham. Bourchier was the nephew of Cardinal Thomas Bourchier, Archbishop of Canterbury and former Lord Chancellor of England. The archbishop had been asked by Richard III to procure Richard of Cornwall from sanctuary with his mother, to join his brother Edward V in the Tower, whence they vanished. It is likely that the nephew had the archbishop's blessing to fight against the usurper Richard. Walter Hungerford of Farleigh was the youngest son of the 3rd Baron Hungerford, the Lancastrian who had been captured and executed after Hexham in 1464. Walter Hungerford was MP for Wiltshire in 1477, and, as a Lancastrian partisan in earlier days, obtained a general pardon from Richard III on his accession in 1483. He had been, nevertheless, arrested by Richard on the landing of the Henry Tudor in 1485, but escaped from custody, and joined Richmond's army. At the forthcoming battle he slew, in hand-to-hand combat, Sir Robert Brackenbury, lieutenant of the Tower of London, under whose command he had previously served. Brackenbury, a close associate of Richard III, had joint command of the vanguard. Again, perhaps Hungerford knew of the princes' fate in the Tower and had singled out their captor.

Also on the evening of 20 August, Henry disappeared with a few companions while his army camped outside Tamworth Castle. He had probably just been lost, but he told his army that he had received good news from secret friends. On the morning of 21 August, Richard's scouts returned, informing the king that Henry Tudor's position was near Atherstone. As Richard prepared to lead out his force for its final journey towards Atherstone, he knew that there was still one baron missing. In spite of his promise to be with the king, Thomas Stanley had failed to join his army. Richard had ridden out of Leicester with the crown upon his head, flanked by the Earls of Norfolk and Northumberland. At some time on 21 August, at the second Stanley–Tudor meeting, they conferred 'in what sort to arraign battle with King Richard, whom they heard to be not far off'. According to tradition, Henry met with the Stanleys at the Three Tuns pub in Atherstone, where he is also supposed to have lodged.

However, it seems more likely that he stayed at Merevale abbey and also conferred with his stepfather and uncle there. According to Polydore Vergil's report, 'Henry and Stanley took each other by the hand and yielding mutual salutation, both were moved to great joy and after which they entered in counsil in what sort to arraigne battle with King Richard'. *The Ballad of Bosworth Field* tells us that the Stanley armies were to amalgamate, with Lord Thomas Stanley commanding the vanguard, Sir William Stanley the rearguard and their brother Edward Stanley the wing. Prior to the Battle of Bosworth, the Stanleys were camped near each other at Atherstone, while Henry Tudor's army camped on the lands of the nearby Cistercian Merevale Abbey. By Bosworth, Henry had survived three shipwrecks. He attributed his good luck to the intervention of the Breton Saint Armel, whom this author has associated with the legendary Arthur. Henry later commissioned a stained-glass window for Armel at Merevale Abbey.

Henry's army was around three miles from Richard's chosen position at dawn on 22 August. Henry did not seem to get an agreement for the Stanley armies to link up with his, as the Stanleys wanted to keep control of their own troops, but Lord Thomas ordered four of his best knights and their retainers to reinforce Henry's vanguard. Thus Sir John Savage (V) of Cheshire, Sir Robert Tunstall of Lancashire, Sir Hugh Persall of Horseley and Sir Humphrey Stanley of Clifton and Pipe in Staffordshire rode into Henry's camp. All were knighted by Henry. Persall (or Peshall or Peshale) was knighted on the field of battle and appointed sheriff of Staffordshire. He was married to the daughter of Henry's supporter Richard Corbet of Moreton Corbet. Humphrey Stanley was the son of Sir John, a Knight of the Garter, and is buried in Westminster Cathedral. He shared a grandfather, another Sir John Stanley, with William and Thomas Stanley. Like Persall, he was appointed sheriff of Staffordshire. His brass plate shows him in plate armour but helmetless.

John Savage (III) had served as deputy to Sir Thomas Stanley, afterwards Baron Stanley, as steward of the duchy lordship of Halton, Cheshire. His son John Savage (IV) was knighted at Elizabeth Woodville's coronation in May 1465, and he probably became a Knight of the Body to Edward IV, and a banneret after the Scottish campaign of 1482. He was very prominent in affairs in Cheshire and the north Midlands. In 1484, as mayor of Chester, he presided when his sons were made freemen of the city. John Savage (IV) married Stanley's daughter Katherine. Their children included the heir John Savage (V), and Thomas Savage (d. 1507), who rose to be Bishop of Rochester in 1492, of London in 1497, and Archbishop of York in 1501. John Savage (V) certainly played an important role at Bosworth, where he commanded the left wing. The author of *Bosworth Field* described him and his men, clad in their distinctive white livery and hoods at Bosworth:

Sir John Savage, that hardy Knight,
deathes dentes he delt that day
with many a white hood in fight,
that sad men were at assay.

Sir John Savage led the force that seized Humphrey Stafford from sanctuary at Culham in 1486, and was killed at the siege of Boulogne in 1492.

Bosworth was a poorly recorded battle, and its site has just been rediscovered away from its traditional location. We know that it was over quickly, in about two hours, but the actual sizes of the five small armies involved are difficult to estimate. Descendants of Henry's followers exaggerated their accounts of the numbers who supported the Tudor army. Both sides had artillery, Henry's being laboriously transported from his ships across Wales. While we think of the heavily armoured knights of the time as being on horseback, they normally dismounted to fight. This was because of the target that a man on horseback presented to missiles, especially special armour-piercing arrows. A good archer could despatch around twelve arrows a minute, and would specifically aim at horses, as a thrown man in armour was almost helpless. Shafts fitted with broad hunting heads ripped through flesh, and horses became unmanageable, even when not mortally wounded. Thus, although a knight or man-at-arms had been trained to fight with a lance when mounted, it was often more effective to have most dismount and to keep only a small mounted reserve. Mounted men were very useful in a rout, for they could catch a fleeing enemy and cut him down with minimum risk to themselves, especially if he was lightly armoured.

Archers usually sought protection beyond stakes, hedges or ditches, making a charge potentially lethal for cavalry, as the French had discovered at Agincourt, Crecy and Poitiers. When armies clashed, the danger of the archery fusillade was minimised as they would not risk firing at their own men. For the combatants, plate armour had replaced chain, and a shield was no longer needed. The men-at-arms no longer needed to hold a rein or a shield, and the weapon of choice in hand-to-hand fighting was some type of long, two-handed polearm. They still carried a sword at their side for use in closer fighting. One of the most popular polearms was the pollaxe or poleaxe, designed to dent or crush the plates of armour, either to wound or knock down the wearer or so damage the plates that they ceased to function properly.

Armies tended to be organised into three divisions or 'battles': the vanguard or 'van', the main battle and the rearguard. Each division included soldiers of all types who served their various lords or the king directly. The king and his lords were recognised by their banners, a large, rectangular or square flag bearing their coat of arms. Knights generally served lords in turn, and were divided into knights banneret and knights bachelor. A knight banneret carried a banner, generally possessed more fiefs than a knight bachelor, and was obliged to serve in war with a greater number of attendants. The dignity of knight banneret was sometimes conferred by the king in person on the field of battle. Lords and knights might also wear a surcoat bearing their arms, at this time generally a loose tabard with loose elbow-length sleeves. However, surcoats were being used less and less and, with a lack of shields, it was essential that the banner bearer remained close to his master. The rallying flag was the standard, a long flag ending in a point or swallowtail. It was usually divided horizontally into the two principal colours from the lord's coat of arms, which also formed the livery colours worn on the jackets of his retainers. A lord might give the order not to move more than ten feet from the standards, as Oxford did at Bosworth. If the line slightly shifted, it would not be too difficult to strike out accidentally at an ally in the confusion of battle. At times, the lack of uniforms made fighting confusing. While helmet visors helped defensively, they also made vision difficult, and Norfolk died at Bosworth because his visor, or faceguard, had been broken off while fighting Oxford.

Soldiers were paid wages, but their 'profit' came from plunder, usually obtained while fighting overseas, such as in the Hundred Years' War. With an internal war, like the Wars of the Roses, it was difficult to acquire such profits, and men were more reluctant to fight unless under such duty. Thus battles now involved a few great magnates raising relatively small forces. As the war progressed, more fighting men died or declined to fight, and wages had to rise. The remaining lords had seen their families decimated and had less income because of the effects of war, and armies declined in size. Even Richard III's personal army at Bosworth was small, because of the financial difficulties resulting from trying to defend his coastlines against a potential invasion. His 1484 parliament granted him less money than he needed, and he had to borrow from Yorkist lords.

While Henry Tudor may have gained an army of over 5,000 men marching through Wales, Richard may himself have had no more than 9,000 men, with the Duke of Norfolk in command of his vanguard. The size of Henry's army is difficult to assess. Some reports say he left France with 5,000 men, and others that he landed at Mill Bay with 2,000. Around 3,000 men would have joined him on his march through Wales and England. After repeated calls to array, the Earl of Northumberland had belatedly arrived with perhaps 4,000 men to act as Richard's rearguard, but very few, if any, had arrived from York with Northumberland. Northumberland had been approached by Jasper or Henry by letter, and he was married to Maud, who had grown up with Henry and had been meant to marry him.

The Stanley brothers each had armies of over 3,000 men, supposedly to fight for Richard. Thus Richard potentially had four armies consisting of 20,000 men: his personal force of 3,000 troops; Norfolk with the main battle of 6,000; Northumberland with 4,000 soldiers; and 7,000 men in two Stanley forces, against Henry's single army of around 5,000 troops.

Thomas Stanley had turned down Henry's request to join his army, and 'answered that the earl should set his own forces in order while he would come with his (own) army well appointed'. Despite this setback, Jasper and Oxford mustered their troops into marching order and headed to Atherstone. They would have brought their French guns but not their baggage train, which they could easily retrieve if they won and would not need if they lost. They probably arrived on the battlefield at about 8.00 a.m. Tudor is said to have used local guides on this journey. William Burton, a local man writing in the seventeenth century, said that his ancestor John de Hardwick, lord of the nearby manor of Lindley and a commissioner of array for Leicestershire, joined Tudor on the day before the battle with men and horses, and served as a guide on the morning of the battle.

Two other men in Henry's army, Sir Robert Harcourt and Sir John Cheyne, were also local and may have helped to guide Tudor's army. With Henry were also most of the prominent gentry and clergy who had fled to him in 1483. They included John, Lord Welles; Edward Woodville, the queen's brother; John Cheyne; Piers Courtenay, Bishop of Exeter; and Robert Morton, who had been Master of the Rolls until 1483, when he joined the Buckingham rebellion. He was the nephew of John Morton, Bishop of Ely, who had played an active part in planning the invasion. Also present were Christopher Urswick and Richard Fox, who were to be prominent in the new Tudor administration.

The route Henry took to the battlefield may be traced by the payments he subsequently made to a number of villages because they sustained losses of corn and grains 'by us and our company at our lat victorious field', just as he also recompensed Atherstone and the Abbot of Merevale for damage. Most of the compensation was given to the village of Witherley, which was perhaps in the direct route of the army, but Fenny Drayton received a good sum, with Mancetter and Atterton receiving less. Some of the damage may have been caused by troops foraging before the battle, or perhaps some troops quartered in these villages. At Witherley, Tudor knighted more of his followers. These included William Brandon, who would not long enjoy his new status since he was shortly to die on the battlefield. By the time Henry reached the battlefield, Richard must have been waiting for an hour. Once on the battlefield, Tudor 'made a slender vanward for the small number of his people; before the same he placed archers of whom he made captain John Earl of Oxford, in the right wing of the vanward he placed Gilbert Talbot to defend the same, in the left verily he set John Savage and himself, trusting to the aid of Thomas Stanley, with one troop of horsemen and a few footmen did follow'. The position described, with Talbot on the right of the vanward and Savage on the left, might indicate that the rebel army was arranged in the normal way with three battles, but there may have been only one 'slender' battle, with Oxford in overall command. However, in Beaumont's poem on Bosworth, he says that both wings came to join with Oxford in a crucial point in the battle when he deployed a wedge formation.

A fascinating but little-known fact about the ensuing battle is that William Gardyner, one of Rhys ap Thomas' Lancastrian force, is thought by some to have been the mercenary and 'Welsh halberdier' who killed Richard III. An acquaintance of Gardyner's for many years was fellow mercenary Roland Warburton. Warburton's arrival, as a known retainer of William Stanley, was vital in Shrewsbury opening its gates to Henry Tudor. Warburton was next noted for his arrival at Bosworth Field on 21 August, 1485, the eve of the battle, with money to pay the 3,000 men under William Stanley's command. His arrival did much to lift the morale of the troops, making them more eager for action. Was this money sent by Margaret Beaufort?

Jasper remained close to his nephew. Colin Richmond has estimated that only six peers turned out for Richard at Bosworth, several for Henry, and around forty did not bring men. Many of Richard's Northerners may have been in Northumberland's inactive ranks. They had supported his brother Edward, but, with the mysterious disappearance of Edward V and his brother Richard of Cornwall, may have been unenthusiastic about battle. Kendall believes that Northumberland's inertia was due to dislike for Richard, and perhaps also there had been a tacit agreement with Henry before the battle. Ross observes that the two had had been arguing from the early 1470s. He also notes that the Percys were among the oldest of the noble families, and that Richard was more closely linked with their rival Nevilles.

It may be that Richard chose his position because the Stanleys were already stationed on the slopes of Crown Hill when the royal army reached the battlefield, and he was trying to find a position for his army that could counter any hostile movement from the Stanleys while still keeping the Lancastrians in sight. Vergil describes the battle preliminaries with both armies lined up opposite one another, and a 'marsh between both hosts, which Henry of purpose left on the right hand that it might serve his men instead of a fortress, by the doing thereof he left the sun on his back'. If Henry's army reached the battlefield by 8.00 a.m., the sun would probably have been at their back by the time they lined up on the field, and there was certainly a marsh between the two hosts, although only on one flank. According to Molinet, the armies were about a quarter of a league apart. If this was a French league, this would put the two sides about 800 yards apart, beyond bow shot of about 250 to 300 yards, the normal distance apart for opposing armies. With Richard on a hill, his artillery would have a major advantage.

We are unsure of the placement of the two Stanley armies. Some believe that they were stationed alongside one another, but William had been declared a traitor and Thomas had a history of hedging his bets in battle and not committing to either side. Thomas Stanley had so far been reluctant to openly ally himself with Henry. It seems he placed himself south of the main action, on Northumberland's flank, perhaps on a slope from which he could watch the fighting develop. There was no action here, with the Crowland Chronicler recording that 'where the Earl of Northumberland stood, however, with a fairly large and well equipped force, there was no contest against the enemy and no blows given or received in battle'. Sir William Stanley may have been lower down on the slope of the hill, to the west of his brother and nearer Henry's forces. Just before the fighting started, Richard became suspicious of the Stanleys and ordered the execution of Lord Stanley's eldest son, Lord Strange:

> However, those to whom the task was given, seeing that the matter in hand was at a very critical stage and that it was more important than the elimination of one man, failed to carry out that king's cruel command and on their own judgement let the man go and returned to the heart of the battle.

A little-known fact is that another of Edward IV's Yorkist followers, the Welsh lord William Griffith of Penrhyn Castle, was held with Lord Strange. William Griffith had married Joan Troutbeck, whose mother was Margaret, the sister of Thomas and William Stanley. He was thus a nephew by marriage to the Stanleys. In 1476 he is described as 'king's servant' and 'marshall of the King's Hall' (an office earlier held by his father) in a grant to him by Edward IV of an annuity of £18 5s. At Michaelmas 1483, he was appointed chamberlain of North Wales by Richard III, and his annuity was renewed by Richard III in March 1484. His record suggests that he followed very closely the lead of his kinsman Thomas Stanley, and poems by Lewis Môn and Tudur Aled prove that, immediately before Bosworth, he shared with Lord Strange imprisonment at Nottingham as hostage for the Stanleys' uncertain loyalty. Griffiths must have shared the same narrow escape from death, for within a month of Bosworth his appointment as chamberlain was confirmed by Henry VII. The Stanleys, Griffiths and Tudors had been strongly interlinked for decades.

Both the contemporary *The Ballad of Lady Bessie* and *The Ballad of Bosworth Field* say that Richard could see Lord Stanley's banner, which he could have interpreted as Stanley taking up arms against his sovereign. This is perhaps the implication of the words, in the *Ballad of Bosworth Field*, 'I see the banner of Lord Stanley he said, Fetch hither the Lord Strange to me, for doubtless he shall die this day.' Vergil says that, as soon as the king saw the enemy forces pass the marsh, he ordered his men to begin battle, which they did, with 'great shouts'. Molinet states that the royal army fired on the Tudor troops as soon as they came within range. The Tudor army would have replied with arrows when in range, and recent evidence of the pattern of cannonballs being found shows that Henry's army also had some artillery. Molinet tells us that 'the French, knowing by the king's shot, the lie of the land and the order of his battle, resolved in order to avoid the fire, to mass their troops against the flank rather than the front of the king's battle'.

Jasper, Oxford and the French and Scottish commanders would have seen that the royal army was larger than their own. They seemingly could not rely on a Stanley intervention, so, from what Molinet says, it appears that the invading army was forced to launch a flank attack. However, archaeological evidence in the form of shot found on the royal position suggests that at least part of the Tudor army was ranged in front of the royal army. A flank advance and attack would have had the element of surprise and would have been a difficult tactic to counter. It would also lessen Richard's numerical superiority in artillery and men, since he could not bring his whole force to bear against the enemy. Richard's men advanced downhill, but would have been cut in numbers by Henry's archers, commanded by Oxford, who also led Henry's vanguard. Richard's archers would have been moved out of the way to allow Richard's troops to advance, whereas the Lancastrian archers would have been deployed in front of Henry's men, firing up to twelve arrows a minute, until the last seconds of the troops clashing. If Henry had, say, 500 longbowmen, and it took the armoured Yorkists seventy seconds to cover the 300 yards of bowshot range, the longbowmen could have poured 7,000 deadly arrows into Richard's army. By the time they had engaged in hand-to-hand combat, they were probably in disarray and lacking leadership in their ranks, whereas Oxford's men were in good order.

Shortly after the battle began, there seemed to be an impasse. It was thought that the Yorkist army lacked morale – Richard was never a popular king. On the other hand, Henry's mixed army knew that defeat would mean probable death, and may have fought harder. As both lines were fighting, Oxford ordered 'in every rank that no soldier should go above ten feet from the standards; which charge being known, when all men had thronged together and stayed awhile from fighting the adversaries were therewith afraid supposing some fraud and so they all forebore the fight a certain space'. Henry's troops were thus ordered to go into close order, and while they did this the fighting slackened off. It seems that this confused the royal troops, who were wary of some subterfuge, perhaps another flank attack or a cavalry charge. Beaumont believes that at this stage the wings of Talbot and Savage joined to make a larger mass and break through Norfolk's line. In his *Poly-Olbion: Song the Twenty-Second*, Michael Drayton noted Jasper at Bosworth:

> The middle battle, he [Henry] in his fair person graced; With him the
>   noble earl of Pembroke,
> Their countrymen the Welsh, (of whom it mainly stands
> For their great numbers found to be of greatest force),
> Which but his guard of gleaves [glaives], consisted all of horse ...

Rhys ap Thomas' troops were said to all be mounted and probably formed up around Henry, behind Oxford and between the wings of Talbot and Savage. There was also a bodyguard of men bearing polearms, with a blade eighteen inches long on top of a six- or seven-foot-long pole.

Oxford now ordered his men into 'array triangle', a wedge formation popular on the Continent, where the flanks of the wedge were protected by pikemen. It is believed that many of the French and Scottish mercenaries in the rebel army were pikemen. The earl now ordered an advance. Neither troops using long pikes, pikemen, nor wedge formations were familiar to English soldiers. This was not like the earlier schiltrons, which were defensive 'shield-wall' formations, often with pikemen, but a terrifying offensive manoeuvre, as if a vast hedgehog was approaching with jabbing long pikes. It may well be that Richard's archers and artillery could not fire through his men at Oxford's array triangle, while Henry's bowmen and cannon were still placed to fire into the Yorkists at this point. Beaumont describes this occurring, and says that the experienced Norfolk made his line more 'slender' to help minimise the heavy casualties before what he calls Oxford's 'trigon', or wedge, advanced. Oxford's attack was a success, according to Vergil, and Richard could see his demoralised forces being pushed back. It seems than some of his men began to desert, seeing that Northumberland's army remained impassive, and the two Stanley forces were not joining the battle. Henry Percy, Earl of Northumberland, had spent some time with Henry Tudor as a boy in Raglan Castle, after his father, the Lancastrian third earl, had been killed at Towton in 1461. Percy not only knew Henry Tudor, but had shared a similar childhood. He had also married Maud Herbert, Henry's intended wife.

Henry Tudor's men may have fought better, as on their long march to Bosworth the different groups of soldiers had time to bond with one another and their commanders. Quite possibly, most of the troops in the rebel army were professional French and Scottish soldiers, whereas Richard's troops had been hastily recruited and were probably less experienced and less well equipped. At some point in the fighting, the Duke of Norfolk was killed – by Sir John Savage, according to the *Ballad of Lady Bessie* – perhaps while trying to rally his men. After this, the royal army's vanguard started to collapse. According to the *Ballad of Lady Bessie*, Norfolk was killed near a windmill while fleeing with his troops. The Dadlington windmill was well over 1,000 yards from the main action, so if Norfolk was killed there it must certainly have been during a rout, but it seems probable that Norfolk was killed in the battle. Richard knew that his main commander's death would cause a collapse of morale, and seemed to sense that men were leaving the field. He possibly had no option but to try and end the battle very quickly, before a rout ensued. As Vergil states, 'King Richard understood, first by espialls [observation] where Earl Henry was far off with a small force of soldiers about him, then after drawing nearer he knew it perfectly by evident signs and tokens that it was Henry, wherefore all inflamed with ire he struck his horse with spurs and runneth out of the one side without the vanwards against him.' He may have charged around Northumberland's right wing, avoiding the great marsh that protected Henry's men from a direct cavalry charge. Richard possibly hoped that Northumberland would follow him.

It seems that Henry, probably with Jasper in attendance, was riding towards the Stanley armies, asking for help to end the battle. Richard had with him probably several hundred elite mounted knights and soldiers, formed from the royal household and bodyguard. Vergil says that Henry saw Richard coming at him, and fought the king with great determination. Richard killed Sir William Brandon, the standard bearer. Rhys Fawr ap Maredudd, Rhys the Mighty, immediately picked up Henry's red dragon banner. Richard also knocked to the ground Sir John Cheyne. Henry refused to give up his position, and his Welsh bodyguard fought ferociously, bringing Richard's onslaught to a near standstill. Richard's own standard bearer, Sir Percival Thirlwall, was unhorsed and had both legs hewn off. Seeing Richard and his detachment separated from his army, Sir William Stanley and his red-coated men swept into the melee to surround the king. Richard began crying 'Treason! Treason! Treason!' according to John Rous of Warwick.

Molinet says that a Welsh halberdier then slew the unhorsed Richard. Sir William Stanley's infantry was composed mainly of Welshmen. A Welsh tradition credits Rhys ap Thomas with killing the king, and Rhys Fawr ap Maredudd also claimed that he killed Richard. The family of Ralph Rudyard, from Rudyard near Leek in Staffordshire, also claimed afterwards that he had killed Richard. Richard's army saw his standard fall and began to flee. Northumberland left the field without striking a blow. Both Northumberland and Thomas Stanley may have stayed out of the battle because the marsh was blocking their path. Equally, if either moved position, they could have been subjected to a flanking attack by the other.

It seems likely that, along with Henry's Welsh bodyguard, the French troops of Philibert du Chandée played a major part in blunting Richard's desperate cavalry charge. Henry's personal footmen may well have been some of the French pikemen fighting in the Continental style. Information on the part played by these mercenaries comes from a letter written by one of them on the day after the battle. Only a small part of this letter is known, and in it Richard is quoted as saying, 'These French traitors are today the cause of our realm's ruin.' The letter also says that Tudor was protected on foot in the middle of the mercenaries, presumably within the partial pike square. There were probably not enough pikemen to make a full defensive square.

Sir William Stanley's late intervention quickly swung the battle in Henry's favour, although the outcome may well have been a Lancastrian victory anyway. He was not well rewarded by Henry. Bacon wrote that although Stanley arrived in time to save his life in the battle, Henry must have been aware that he had stayed his hand quite long enough to endanger it. Vergil reported that Richard 'could have saved himself by flight'. Diego de Valera repeats this, saying that Juan de Salazar, who was present at Richard's side during the battle, saw the treason being committed and urged the king to flee in order to fight again another day. De Valera goes on to say that at this point Richard put his royal crown over his helmet, donned his surcoat with the royal coat of arms and fought valiantly for a long time, heartening those who remained loyal. The ballads repeat the story, stating that an unnamed knight told Richard that his horse was at hand and he could with honour retreat and fight again another day. All sources except Molinet have Richard 'fighting manfully in the thickest press of his enemies'. Molinet, however, claims that Richard tried to flee and was killed when his horse became stuck in the marsh.

The recent discovery of Richard III's bones was described by this author in *Richard III: The King in the Car Park*. His death almost certainly came from a halberd 'shaving' the skull. The blow, if it did not kill him, would have been sufficient to knock him down, when he would have suffered other wounds to kill him. A poem of Guto'r Glyn, *In praise of Sir Rhys ap Tomas of Abermarlais*, describes Richard's death by 'chopping' his head:

… I love the dubbed knight of Carmarthen,
the hawk of the fortress of gold and wine is loved by all.
I have loved Sir Rhys – and why would I not love him?
… Now a young man has come to protect us from violence,
a lord from York to the river Tawe.
The saint is a roofbeam over the three counties,
over lands, of Elidir's lineage.
All his factions are flowers for us,
and Sir Rhys himself is a rose.
A host is inadequate to maintain a court
compared to one who could feed a whole island.
One hundred men together would not give
as much as he has given this long while.
He is a man too in war,
greater than a duke wherever he comes.
The mighty one knows well how to scatter an army,
dagger of battle, he was a fearless young man.
There was a battle, like that of Peredur,
the ravens of Urien prepared it.

King Henry won the day
through the strength of our master:
he killed Englishmen, capable hand,
he killed the boar, he chopped off his head,
and Sir Rhys like the stars of a shield
with the spear in their midst on a great steed ...

For some reason, the last successful invasion of England is thought by the vast majority of its population, and many historians, to have been in 1066. However, a small army of French, Breton and Scottish troops, assisted by a few hundred English and Welsh exiles, was almost doubled in size by Welsh forces in 1485. The vast majority of Henry's army was not English, and the vital defection during the Battle of Bosworth was made by Stanley's Welshmen of Denbighshire.

According to the proclamation issued by Henry afterwards, Richard died at 'Sandeford'. The fighting was then over in a matter of minutes as the royal army broke ranks and fled. As described, Oxford was already getting the better of the van after much hard fighting. The death of Norfolk would further have disheartened the royal troops, and great numbers of them are said to have thrown away their weapons with relief and submitted themselves to Henry, the new king. Most of the sources say that many of the royal troops were there reluctantly and were pleased to stop fighting. Some members of Richard's army did not apparently want to fight for him, as shown by the petition of Roger Wake of Blisworth, Catesby's brother-in-law, against his attainder on the grounds that it was against his 'will and mind' to fight for Richard. Another appeal against attainder was that of Geoffrey St German, who died the day after Bosworth, probably of wounds. His daughter and heiress said that he was only with the royal army because he was 'so threatened by the same late duke's [*i.e.* Richard III's] letters that unless he came to the same field he should lose his life, lands and goods, that for dread of the same he was most unwillingly at the same field'.

As the royal army fled, Northumberland and his troops were probably still standing in their position on the left wing of the royal army. Molinet says Northumberland should have charged the French (as he describes Henry's army) but did nothing, because he had an understanding with the Tudors. Northumberland was arrested after the battle but released by early December and never prosecuted or fined. As well as Norfolk, the other Yorkists killed included Walter Devereux, Lord Ferrers, whose sister had cared for Henry. Sir Richard Ratcliffe, Sir Robert Percy (Controller of the Royal Household), Sir Robert Brackenbury (Constable of the Tower), and Richard's secretary John Kendall also died. Lord Lovell fled east, because he is next heard of in sanctuary at Colchester, together with Humphrey and Thomas Stafford. The Earl of Surrey, son of the Duke of Norfolk, was arrested and attainted, but was released in 1489 and restored to his earldom. Vergil says 1,000 of the king's troops died and only about 100 of Henry's men, but we have no real idea of casualties.

Rhys ap Thomas' troops found Richard's crown in the hands of William Gardyner and brought it to Henry. Henry knighted William Gardyner, Gilbert Talbot, Humphrey Stanley and Rhys ap Thomas on the battlefield as well as a number of his captains. It is to be noted that neither Thomas nor William Stanley were honoured. All present cried 'God save King Henry'. He was then crowned with Richard's crown – that is, the coronet from Richard's helmet – by Thomas Stanley. Traditionally, he is said to have been crowned on the hill now known as Crown Hill, on the slopes of which the Stanleys were probably stationed. The crown is traditionally said to have been found in a hawthorn bush, where it had rolled when Richard was finally struck down. The hawthorn was to feature in heraldry for Henry Tudor from the beginnings of his reign.

William Stanley was given the spoils carried by Richard – tapestries from his royal tent and the like. A flag fragment recently auctioned in Derby had been one of three decaying parts originally hung above the tomb of Sir Robert Harcourt, who was standard bearer to Henry during the battle. Sir Robert, a Knight of the Bath, was buried in St Michael's church in Stanton Harcourt, Oxfordshire, after he died in 1490. The remnant was then passed to a local family who passed it down through generations before deciding to sell it. The new king ordered the battlefield cleared and set off in the evening for Leicester, which he entered wearing his new crown. Henry was anxious to reach London with his troops. He left the cleaning-up operations to the Stanley brothers, who had not given him the support they had promised. He was to take no revenge on Thomas for his mother's sake.

It may be that Thomas Stanley had an ulterior motive for wanting Henry to be defeated. He only entered the battle when it was finished to chase fleeing troops. Henry's mother, Margaret Beaufort, had been attainted by Richard, who gave all of her considerable wealth to Thomas Stanley. With Henry dead, he would have continued to own these lucrative assets. Stanley had been Margaret Beaufort's fourth husband after John de la Pole, Edmund Tudor and Sir Henry Stafford. Tellingly, in her will, she specified that she be buried alongside Edmund when she died just two months after Henry VII, in 1509. (Despite this, she is buried in the Henry VII Lady Chapel at Westminster Abbey.) However, there may well have been a covering march mounted by Lord Stanley, and it is possible that he may have dispersed and defeated royal levies in Leicestershire and Warwickshire two days before the battle. The facts are to be uncovered. It may also be that, as mentioned above, he was placed in an awkward position, not being able to join battle without being overcome by Northumberland. Another intriguing point is that a note was placed upon Norfolk's tent overnight, warning him that there would be treachery in Richard's camp. Hall recorded that Norfolk was warned 'to refrain from the field, insomuch that the night before he should set forward toward the king, one wrote on his gate: "Jack of Norfolk be not too bold / For Dickon thy master is bought and sold."' The actions and motivations of the Stanley brothers and Northumberland, and the extent of their agreements with Henry before the battle, may never be known.

None of the great Northern magnates – Northumberland, Westmorland, lords Scrope, Greystoke, Fitzhugh, Dacre or Lumley – were attainted for their possible presence fighting for Richard. Either they did not attend the battle, or they stood still in his rearguard, refusing to fight. Several chronicles relate that many of Richard's army watched the fighting, with others deserting before and during the battle. According to Skidmore,

> Four-fifths of the nobility, twenty-eight men, decided it best to remove themselves from the conflict altogether. Of those who chose to fight, two abstained from joining the fray, and only two attainted earls, Oxford and his uncle Jasper, fought for Henry. Only six can be proved to have joined Richard and fought for his cause. Norfolk and Lord Ferrers gave their lives during the battle, yet both were elderly men. Norfolk's son and heir, Thomas Howard, Earl of Surrey, Francis, Viscount Lovell, Lord Scrope of Bolton and John, Lord Zouche, also fought, yet most, it seems, did so because they owed their livelihoods to the king. Francis Lovell, for instance, the king's closest friend, had been rewarded with grants of land estimated at £400. Lord Scrope of Bolton had been given lands in Devon and Cornwall worth over £200 annually, and had been given an annuity of £156 as well as a salary as the king's councillor.

Also, Norfolk and Surrey had recently been given a dukedom and earldom respectively by Richard. Not one soldier from his supposedly faithful city of York is known to have come to battle, and the only peers who actually fought were the very few that he had rewarded with honours. The vast majority of peers and nobles wanted little to do with the usurper king, but had strongly supported his brother Edward IV in all his years of battle. The present groundswell of public opinion in favour of Richard as a good and heroic king ignores the feelings of the time. Neither lords nor commoners trusted the usurper, and all the nation's lords except Lord Lovell quickly came to an accommodation with the new dynasty.

11

Jasper and the Last Battles of the Wars of the Roses, 1485–1487

There was little or no retaliation by Henry after Bosworth. His benevolent response astonished European diplomats and commentators. Henry concentrated on mending bridges with Yorkists, giving many of them offices of state. Jasper knew that Edward IV had attempted to make his government more effective, so many of his civil servants were useful men in any efficient transition to a new administration. The Lancastrians who had been attainted were given back their lands. Henry and his uncle had never known peace, and they seemed to sense that the ending of these decades of internecine wars, in reality beginning with Henry IV's usurpation in 1399, gave the nation the opportunity for a real change. France was effectively lost, there were no real rivals for the crown, and the great noble families were exhausted. There was the prospect of peace after over a century of strife.

Lewys Glyn Cothi celebrated that 'the cold boar to the grave has gone', and Dafydd Llwyd exulted that the bards were much happier, as 'the world is all the better for the killing of little Richard'. Bernard André, the French poet and friar, noted Henry's descent from the British King Cadwaladr and wrote of Henry's duty to 'tame the ferocity of the English'. The Italian poets Giovanni dei Gigli (1434–1498) and Pietro Carmeliano (1451–1528), along with the Scot Walter Ogilvie (1460 – c. 1508), extolled Henry as Cadwaladr's heir. In 1486, the citizens' pageant in Worcester to welcome Henry extolled,

Cadwaladr's blood lineally descending,
Long hath been told of such a prince coming,
Wherefore friends, if that I shall not lie,
The same is the Fulfiller of the Prophecy.

The Venetian ambassador wrote to the Council of Ten that 'the Welsh may now be said to have recovered their former independence for the most wise and fortunate Henry VII is a Welshman'.

Henry's quarter-Welsh ancestry had been of critical importance in easing his path to the throne, for his only possible route to battle was through

Wales, picking up followers. Henry recognised the Welsh role in his success. He issued his first proclamation as king three days after Bosworth, on 25 August, and the opening words were 'Henry, by the grace of God, King of England and of France, Prince of Wales and Lord of Ireland'. This was the very first time that any king who had not himself been invested as Prince of Wales, as heir apparent, had appropriated the title. Henry could now begin to heal the millennium-old racial tension between the British/Welsh and the Saxon/Norman/Scandinavian English, and he developed deliberate policies to this effect. Henry VII showed some favour to Wales, and his granddaughter Elizabeth I had a strong Welsh presence at court. The new dynasty of the House of Tudor ruled England, Wales and Ireland from 1485 to 1603.

On 3 September at St Paul's Cathedral, Henry offered to God the three main banners his forces had carried in battle – the arms of St George (symbolising his right to the crown by virtue of victory in battle), the Tarteron and Duncow (representing the houses of Lancaster and Beaufort) and the red dragon of Cadwaladr (proclaiming his British ancestry). According to Hall, this was 'a red firye dragon beaten vpon white and grene sarcenet' – the Welsh national flag, the oldest national flag in the world. Henry's most immediate problem was in the North, as war was being threatened from Scotland. He had no desire to alienate any former Yorkists who might wish to join the Scots. On 25 September, the sheriffs and gentlemen of the Northern counties were ordered to hold themselves in readiness to repel an anticipated Scottish invasion. In York, his proclamation of 8 October pardoned all the men of the North for their treason against Henry VI. It asked men to defend the land against the Scots, and forgave them 'all manner of riots, murders, treasons, felonies, insurrections, conspiracies against their allegiances done and committed' before 22 September.

Henry had also commissioned men in the south and east of England to be prepared for an invasion, but by 20 October the Scottish danger was over. James IV saw, by the new king's rapid response, that any element of surprise was lost and there was little chance of pardoned men flocking to his banner. Feeling more secure, Henry decided to be crowned before Parliament met, but the 'sweating sickness', previously unknown, appeared in London. This extremely contagious plague or fever had broken out between Henry's landing on 7 August and Bosworth on 22 August. Shortly after the arrival of Henry, Jasper and Oxford in London on 28 August, it broke out in the capital and was blamed upon Henry's French troops. The new king almost immediately paid off and sent home his French and Scottish mercenaries, feeling confident in his Anglo-Welsh support and not wishing to alienate the citizens of London and elsewhere.

However, the French were not to blame – it had not affected Henry's army in the three to five weeks of mustering, sailing and marching to Bosworth. Indeed, Thomas Stanley had excused himself from Richard III's court before Bosworth on account of the 'sweating sickness', and he had not then come into contact with Henry's forces. Several thousand people died, and, strangely, the upper classes seemed to suffer more, as it killed two lord mayors, three sheriffs and six aldermen of London. It did not attack small children. Symptoms of sweating sickness included 'a sense of apprehension', shivers, dizziness, headaches, pain in the arms, legs, shoulders and neck, and fatigue or exhaustion. The illness had a cold, shivery stage followed by a hot, sweating stage and could kill in hours. It was distinct from other epidemics in its rapidity, lasting twenty-four hours; if a person survived a day, they usually recovered. The illness then spread into Europe, where it was known as the 'English Sweate', with a series of epidemics between 1485 and 1551. Its cause is unknown and it disappeared entirely after 1578.

Henry had withdrawn to a king's manor at Guildford to be beyond danger of contagion, but before the end of October the sickness swiftly disappeared. The plague was regarded as portending 'a stern rule and a troubled reign', and was considered an inauspicious beginning to the new dynasty. Preparations for the coronation began again, with Henry wanting to make it spectacular to cement his destiny as the founder of a new dynasty. On 19 October, the office of Lord High Steward of England was given to the Earl of Oxford. Preparations for the coronation were made under the direction of Oxford as Lord Chamberlain, Lord Stanley as Lord High Constable, and the Earl of Nottingham as Earl Marshal of England. There were unusually and significantly very few honours granted to celebrate the coronation. Henry did not want to create any powerful lords, but on 28 October Jasper, Earl of Pembroke, was created Duke of Bedford, Lord Thomas Stanley was made Earl of Derby, and Sir Edward Courtenay was created Earl of Devon. The only other dukedoms to be granted by Henry VII were those of York, Cornwall and Somerset to his own sons Henry, Arthur and Edmund, as the ducal title was still almost exclusively reserved for the king's close kinsmen.

Jasper was dressed in the 'habit of estate of a duke' on 28 October when he was presented before the king, who was sitting beneath the cloth of estate in his presence chamber. The new duke was led in by the Duke of Suffolk and the Earl of Lincoln, signifying that Henry wanted members of the Yorkist royal household to serve the new regime. Viscount Berkeley bore Jasper's cap of estate, and the Earl of Shrewsbury carried his sword, pommel facing upwards. We read that 'in the entering of the chamber door he did his first obeisance, and in the midst of the chamber the second, and in the king's presence the third'. John Writhe, as Garter King of Arms, handed the letters patent to Oxford, who, as Great Chamberlain, delivered them to Henry. Henry passed the letters to his secretary, commanding that they be read out to all in the chamber. As they were read out, Henry placed a girdle around Jasper's neck, and his cap upon his head.

Henry was not the first to reward individual Welshmen, but this was on a greater scale, not only in terms of those in the upper ranks who were rewarded, but also in the number of lesser men appointed as sheriffs, bailiffs, etc. Jasper was also made Justice of South Wales, while Rhys ap

Thomas was knighted, and he and William Gruffydd (Griffith) of Penrhyn were appointed chamberlains of South and North Wales respectively. William ap Gruffydd of Cochwillan and Huw Lewys of Prysaeddfed had each brought contingents to Bosworth and became sheriffs of Caernarfon and Anglesey. After almost a century, Welsh bishops were appointed: John Morgan and Edward Vaughan at St David's and Dafydd ab Ieuan and Dafydd ab Owain at St Asaph. Sir Mathew Cradock of Swansea now virtually ruled Glamorgan and Gower as Somerset's deputy. Henry rewarded John Puleston of Hafod-y-Wern, who fought at Bosworth, an annuity of 20 marks for life, and made him a gentleman usher of the king's chamber. Lewis of Caerleon, noticeable in the service of Margaret Beaufort and in carrying messages, was made Henry's doctor, and Sir David Owen his carver. Piers Lloyd, one of his yeomen at Bosworth, became customer of Calais, and Edward ap Rhys was given a beerhouse in Fleet Street, which he named 'The Welshman'. David Seisyllt of Alltyrynys, noted as having 'fled out of England with Henry of Richmond' became sergeant of the guard, a landowner in Northampton and the father of the remarkable Cecil family, which effectively ruled Elizabethan England. Richard ap Hywel of Mostyn's decision to stay in Wales and 'dwell among my own people' was 'a rare exception' to those Welsh supporters offered places at court.

There was also a transformation in the ownership of Wales and its Marches. In 1461, the counties of Anglesey, Caernarfon, Merioneth, Flint, Cardigan and Carmarthen were outside the Principality of Wales. As such, few lordships in these counties were held directly by the Crown. In his capacity as Duke of Lancaster, Henry held some small areas in South Wales, but the bulk of Marcher territory was still ruled by independent lords. The Marcher lordship of Pembroke now reverted via Jasper Tudor to the new royal family. Warwick had held the vast lordship of Glamorgan and the smaller one of Elfael in Mid Wales, and his death meant that the Crown had assumed them. The House of York held the lordship of Denbigh and the earldom of March, critically situated on the border and incorporating much of present-day Shropshire, including Ludlow. After Bosworth, all these huge Marcher estates reverted to the Crown, preventing powerful lords from creating disturbances again and threatening the Crown. Henry wanted peace, and with over-powerful great magnates, as Warwick had been, there would always be a threat to his rule.

The northern Marcher lordships of Westmorland and Northumberland had always seen disputes between the Nevilles and the Percys. John Neville, Earl of Westmorland, had died fighting for Henry VI at Towton in 1461, and his family had been eclipsed by the Yorkist Percys. However, the Earl of Northumberland was in comfortable lodgings in the Tower of London until Henry accepted his loyalty and sent him back to control the eastern border against the Scots. The Earl of Westmorland, whose father had been killed at Towton, entered into bonds to Henry of £400 and 400 marks, and on 5 December 1485 gave the king the custody and marriage of his eldest son and heir, Ralph Neville. Westmorland held a command in the royal army sent into Scotland in 1497. Under Henry, both these lordships remained loyal.

Almost as soon as Henry arrived in London, he took firm control of Crown affairs in order to make things financially viable. 'Land was leased out at improved rents, and overseers of works and reparations were appointed in many royal castles and lordships. He ensured that the royal castles were granted into the hands of faithful servants, appointed keepers of parks and forests, bailiffs of royal towns, and so on. Henry rewarded the men who had been with him in exile, and who supported him at Bosworth. Nearly all of his grants of estates or office contained a clause stating that the gift was made "in consideration of his services against the king's rivalling enemy and adversary, Richard, late Duke of Gloucester, the usurper of the king's right and crown aforesaid".' In later legal documents, the shorter form 'King in deed but not in right' was used in any reference to Richard III's name.

The Bishop of Exeter became Keeper of the Privy Seal, and Thomas Lovell Chancellor of the Exchequer. New judges and law officers were appointed, with John de Vere, Earl of Oxford, becoming Constable of the Tower of London for life. Sir William Berkeley became 'master and operator of the king's monies and keeper of the king's exchange', while Sir Richard Guildford became Master of the Ordnance and Keeper of the Armoury in the Tower of London. These were immediate acts of sovereignty, with which Henry asserted that his kingship was totally independent of Parliamentary sanction.

Henry IV had usurped the throne from Richard II, Edward IV from Henry VI, and Richard III from Edward V, but all had waited for a Parliamentary Act of Settlement to agree their claims to the throne by inheritance. However, Parliament now agreed to Henry's right to the Crown, by him being king de facto, before it had even met. Although Henry declaimed to the Speaker of the House of Commons that his right was by both conquest and descent, these are not mentioned in the Act that grounded his right to the crown. Henry had even transferred the estates of some dead or escaped Yorkists before they were legally forfeited by Parliamentary Act. He also arranged for the collection of the customs before Parliament had granted them to him. Henry decided from the start that he would not be at the mercy of the lords in Parliament, and Parliament acquiesced, agreeing after the event to his actions. It appears that Henry was guided in his actions by Jasper, who had witnessed the problems of both Henry VI and Edward IV. Henry and Jasper had also learned from the French kings and Breton dukes, who ran their domains far more despotically than did the English kings.

There is evidence in Henry's ordinances that both he and his council feared treachery, so by the day of his coronation on 30 October 1485 he had formed his 'Body Guard of the Yeomen of the Guard', which made its first appearance at the coronation. Hall writes,

Wherefore for the safeguard and preservation of his own body he constituted and ordained a certain number, as well of good archers as of divers other persons, being hardy strong, and of agility, to give daily attendance on his person whom he named Yeomen of his Garde, which precedent men thought that he learned of the French King when he was in France, for men remember not any King of England before that time which used such a furniture of daily soldiers.

Bacon related that the king, for the security of his person, instituted a permanent band of fifty archers to attend him under a captain, naming them the Yeomen of the Guard. It is thought that Henry followed the precedent of Louis XI, King of France, who, ten years previously, had established for himself a 'Grand Guard' of 100 knights and 200 attendants, the latter being armed as archers when in the battlefield but carrying a halberd of a peculiar shape at state ceremonies, the hook at the back resembling the beak of a crow.

It may be, however, that Henry formed this bodyguard, composed mainly of Welshmen, for the Battle of Bosworth. By surrounding his person with guards, copying the King of France, Henry emphasised his special royal dignity. The bodyguard was increased by Henry and maintained until his death, and became a permanent perquisite of the king or queen. It was also the original nucleus of an English standing army. Under Henry VII they fought at Stoke Field in 1487, Boulogne in 1492 and Blackheath in 1497. The Yeomen of the Guard were chosen men, often given posts of responsibility, being keepers of royal castles, surveyors of ports, and so on. Their wages were fixed at sixpence a day. Now called the Queen's Body Guard of the Yeomen of the Guard, it still acts as the monarch's bodyguard and is the oldest British military corps in existence. The present sixty yeomen still wear red-and-gold uniforms of Tudor style. One of the symbols on their uniform is a crowned hawthorn bush and the letters 'HR', the letters representing Henry Rex and the bush referencing the story that Richard's crown was discovered in a hawthorn bush after Bosworth by one of the bodyguard supplied by Rhys ap Thomas.

The 'Yeomen Warders' are often incorrectly referred to as Yeomen of the Guard, which is the distinct corps of royal bodyguards formed by Henry Tudor. In fact, with their full title of the 'Yeomen Warders of Her Majesty's Royal Palace and Fortress the Tower of London, and Members of the Sovereign's Body Guard of the Yeoman Guard Extraordinary', popularly known as the Beefeaters, they are ceremonial guardians of the Tower of London. In principle they are responsible for looking after any prisoners in the Tower and safeguarding the Crown Jewels, but in practice the thirty-eight Yeomen Warders act as tour guides.

On the eve of the coronation the king held a Chapter of the Bath, where he created twelve new knights. Two cartloads of clothing and hangings were brought from Richard III's royal castle at Nottingham. Twenty-one tailors and fourteen skinners were employed to create new robes for Henry and his leading nobles. For instance, Oxford's robe was cut from forty-one yards of crimson velvet costing an amazing £61 10s. In total, £1,506 18s 10d was spent on the ceremony – Henry wanted to impress upon Londoners and the nation that his was to be a dynasty of some splendour. Another estimate of the cost of the coronation to the Treasury is £1,556 18s 10d and three farthings. This latter estimate would today be worth almost £9 million in estimated labour value, and its economic status value is calculated at around £33.5 million.

On 30 October, Henry left the Tower in procession to Westminster to be crowned

over a doublet of cloth of gold and satin in the Tudor colours of white and green the king wore a 'long gowne of purpure velvet, furred with ermyns poudred, open at the side and purfiled with ermyns, laced with gold and with taselles of Venys gold, with a riche sarpe and garter'. He rode a charger with trappings of cloth of gold, and a golden canopy was held above him, 'riding opyn-heded', by four noble knights. Seven horsemen, in crimson and gold, riding bareheaded and leading a spare charger, followed the king. His henchmen and footmen wore liveries of white and green, and there was a long line of heralds and trumpeters in their gorgeous clothing.

The red rose of Lancaster and the crowned portcullis of the House of Tudor appeared everywhere. The scene in the Abbey was full of colour and splendour. The most important posts at the ceremony were filled by Henry's personal friends. The new king's crown was held by Jasper, Duke of Bedford; his sword was borne by the Earl Stanley of Derby, and his spurs by the Earl of Essex. He was supported on his right and left hand by the faithful Bishops Fox of Exeter and Morton of Ely.

Henry's mother, Margaret Beaufort, was seen to burst into floods of tears at her son's coronation. After the crowning, en route to the Tower for a great banquet, the new king was shown to the cheering crowds. Jasper, as steward, rode up and down before the king. Sir Robert Dymoke, the king's champion, rode decked with the red dragon of Cadwaladr, challenging all comers, as he had for Richard III and would do for Henry VIII.

Between his coronation and the opening of Parliament, Henry probably formed his council. Henry and Jasper did not bring an exiled governmental machine with them, nor was there such an organisation settled in England. Henry thus had to rely heavily on former servants and ministers of the Yorkist kings. Henry invited to his council competent men of the middle class, upon whose gratitude and obedience he could rely, instead of the great nobles with their traditions of aristocratic defiance, who assumed it their natural right to counsel the king. The peers summoned to the council were earls like Jasper, Oxford, Stanley and Devon and lords Willoughby de Broke, Daubeney, Dynham and Strange, all bound to the king by ties of blood or known loyalty. Prominent were also two great churchmen: John Morton, Bishop of Ely, who became Archbishop of Canterbury, and Bishop

Richard Fox of Exeter, who had been with Henry in Paris and became Lord Privy Seal.

Henry VII came to hold the rights and lands of many noble titles, which came to the Crown through royal and personal inheritance, escheats and attainder. Unlike earlier kings, he generally avoided granting these titles to favoured subjects he thought worthy of ennoblement. This helped to avoid any jealousy of court favourites. Also, by retaining control of the territories himself, he solidified his control on the kingdom, avoiding the prospect of overmighty subjects and rebellion. Just some of the Crown lands he held included the Principality of Wales, the duchies of Cornwall, Lancaster and York and the earldoms of Chester, March, Pembroke, Richmond, Salisbury, Suffolk and Warwick. Each former incumbent had been a great noble, but Henry accrued their lands and power for his heirs. The Marcher lordship of Glamorgan was given to Jasper Tudor.

At last Jasper, again Earl of Pembroke and also Duke of Bedford, was in a position to marry. It has been said that he had always been in love with his brother's widow, Margaret Beaufort, which accounted for his not marrying, but there was a forbidden degree of consanguinity between them. In the Church's eyes, her marriage to Edmund made Jasper and Margaret officially brother and sister. More likely, he had no real opportunity. Aged around fifty-four, Jasper wed Katherine Woodville on 7 November 1485. She was Buckingham's widow, an aunt of Henry VII's queen, and the queen dowager Elizabeth's youngest sister. Katherine (1458–1509) was aged around twenty-seven and already had four children, who became the Duke of Buckingham, Earl of Wiltshire, Countess of Sussex and Countess of Huntingdon respectively. Not long after his ennoblement in 1453, Jasper's brother Edmund had been provided with a wife by Henry VI in the person of Margaret Beaufort, but his tumultuous life led to Jasper being still unmarried in 1485. The importance of good marriages in fifteenth-century society was considerable. The social connections and landed wealth of both spouses were scrupulously examined before a match was arranged. Age, looks and disposition were generally of secondary importance, which is why Edward IV's supporters were shocked when he married the 'commoner' Elizabeth Woodville for love instead of a French princess. Thus, in January 1465, Sir John Woodville had married Catherine Neville, senior of the two dowager duchesses of Norfolk, a wealthy old lady in her mid-sixties, Sir John being only twenty years old. Interestingly, Earl William Herbert of Huntingdon, the son of William Herbert, Earl of Pembroke, married Katherine Woodville's sister Mary, linking the Herbert and Tudor families.

Like the king's own forthcoming marriage with Katherine Woodville's niece Elizabeth of York, Jasper's was a union between the rival houses of York and Lancaster. From Henry VII's marriage, said Hall, it was hoped that 'pesce was thought to discende oute of heaven into England, consideryng that the lynes of Lancaster and Yorke, being both noble families equivalent in ryches, fame and honour, were now brought into one knot and connexed together'. Related marriage alliances, like that between Duke Jasper and

Katherine Woodville, would support the Tudor policy of uniting former enemies. After her husband's execution in 1483, Duchess Katherine had not been awarded her dowry by Richard III, who had kept the forfeited Stafford estates in his own hands. These estates were very considerable as the Stafford family was one of the richest in the land. Marriage to Katherine Woodville was therefore extremely valuable, as she had been granted her rightful dowry by Henry VII.

Jasper had benefited greatly as the guardian of Lady Margaret Beaufort in the years between the death of Edmund Tudor in 1456 and the dowager countess's remarriage around 1459. His own marriage to Katherine Woodville was to give him more wealth. In the parliament that opened on 7 November 1485, the duchess was granted both the jointure of 1,000 marks per annum bequeathed to her in her husband's will and extensive dower lands in England and Wales, consisting of six major groups of property concentrated in the Home Counties and South East England. These consisted of the lordship, castle and borough of Tunbridge and the manors of Hadlow, Brasted, Yalding, Edenbridge, Penshurst and Bayhall (Kent), with the office of bailiff of the liberty of the Honour of Gloucester in Kent and Surrey. The second and neighbouring group included the manorial borough and lordship of Bletchingley, and the manors of Titsey and Oxted in Surrey, with a tenement in Thames Street, London. East of London were the dowager duchess's third group of estates, the Essex manors of Writtle, Boyton, Hatfield Broad Oak, Broomshawbury, Fobbing, Heydon, Ongar and Harlow, with a marsh called Palmers Things and the hundreds of Ongar and Harlow.

The fourth group of lands lay in Norfolk and was made up of the manors of Wells, Warham, Wiverton Sherringham, Stafford and Berningham. The fifth group acquired by Duchess Katherine included the castle, manor, soke and lordship of Kimbolton, and the manors of Tilbroke, Swineshead and Hardwick in Huntingdonshire and Bedfordshire, as well as the office of feodary of the Honour of Gloucester in those counties. The sixth block of property assigned to the duchess lay farther to the west in Gloucestershire, and consisted of the manors of Thornbury, Harefield, Eastington, Alkerton and Rendcombe, and the office of bailiff of the liberty of the Honour of Gloucester in the same county. This impressive last was completed by the addition of the lordship of Callilond in Cornwall, the castle, manor and lordship of Newport in the Marches of Wales, and the office of bailiff of the Honour of Hereford.

Jasper's marriage thus brought him an additional thirty-five lordships and manors, so that his estates extended from Milford Haven in the west to the North Sea in the east. Within a year of the Battle of Bosworth, Jasper had become the pre-eminent figure in the English magnate class. There is an intriguing indenture that shows how Jasper was now enjoying the trappings of wealth. Upon 21 December 1487, Jasper and Katherine concluded an indenture with Robert Litton, Under Treasurer of England, and John Beverley, citizen and skinner of London, who were thereby granted a £20 annuity, as well as the lease of a Stafford manor in Essex, until a debt of £230 was paid, which the duke and duchess owed John Beverley for furs.

Although his new duchess was young enough to have children, there is no record of any children for Jasper and Katherine. This was either fortunate or deliberate, as it ensured that there were no other Tudor claimants to the new dynasty. There may have been a stillborn son around 1490, however. Jasper possibly had illegitimate daughters, one proposed being Helen Tudor, born in Wales around 1459 to a woman named Myfanwy. The other was Joan Tudor, born around 1479, who married William ap Yevan Williams. Their son Morgan ap William, born in Llanishen, Cardiff, married Catherine Cromwell in 1499, an older sister of Thomas Cromwell, Earl of Essex. Their direct descendant was Oliver Cromwell, also known as Oliver Williams.

Henry's first parliament reinstated his mother, Margaret Beaufort, Countess of Richmond and Derby, with the lands and grants taken from her by Richard III. She was also given the rights and privileges of a 'sole person, not wife nor covert of any husband', allowing her personal control over her extensive properties. This was very unusual for the time. Beaufort was just thirteen years older than her son, and would become probably his closest counsellor. Immediately after Bosworth, Henry spent two weeks in close consultations with his mother, learning about the ways of government, the powers at court and the like. Called at court 'my Lady the King's mother', she now signed herself 'Margaret R' and became extremely influential at court. Some recent sources state that there was thus friction between Henry's Lancastrian mother and his Yorkist wife, but it is difficult to find any real evidence.

Favours extended by Henry to his mother's husband, Thomas Stanley, such as making him the Earl of Derby, seemed perhaps only to enhance her status. When Henry reversed the attainder of his mother and curtailed the marital power of Stanley over her estates, he enabled his mother to run her own financial affairs. This could be seen as the equivalent of a virtual divorce. Henry's mother took a vow of chastity, further isolating Stanley. The measures taken against Stanley had the effect of not allowing him to remarry. Neither mother nor son ever quite forgave Stanley for his lack of support at Bosworth, and Margaret Beaufort made a will asking to be buried alongside Edmund Tudor, not Stanley. Henry may have been minded at one time to attaint Stanley, but that would have meant that his beloved mother was married to a traitor.

Henry annulled many of Edward I's and Henry IV's penal laws upon Welshmen, to the annoyance of English burgesses in Wales. In the early sixteenth century, letters of denizenship began conferring English status upon Welshmen, charters of privileges were granted and various civic disabilities imposed by the penal laws of both Henry IV and Henry V were removed. Welshmen were now allowed to settle in the bastides, or walled plantation boroughs.

An Act was passed in this first parliament specifically in favour of Jasper, whereby all letters patent granted to him by Henry VI were to be 'of as good strength, force and effect, and to the same Duke as available, as they should or might have been, if no Act of Resumption, nor other Act of Parlement, had been made to the hurt our adnullation of the same Lettres patents'. Theoretically, therefore, these Acts enabled Duke Jasper to recover all the estates he had held in the period 1453–1461 either in fee tail, fee male or in survivorship with his elder brother Edmund. In practice, however, it was impossible for him to be restored to all his own lands because of the way in which they had been granted away in the preceding quarter-century.

Fortunately, the honourial lands of the earldom of Pembroke were recoverable. Granted to William, Lord Herbert, in 1462, they were inherited in 1469 by his son, who had been forced to exchange them, and the title of Earl of Pembroke, with the Prince of Wales in 1479 in exchange for the title of Earl of Huntingdon, with estates in the west of England. Thus the lordships of Pembroke, Cilgerran, Llanstephan, Ystlwyf, Trane Clinton and St Clears were still in royal hands in 1485, and there was no problem about their restoration to Jasper. Jasper seemed to spend some time back in Pembroke Castle, overseeing much renovation, and adding a fine oriel window to the private chamber or solar. Its ruined Perpendicular Gothic window can be seen, but its mullions have collapsed. Chimneys were added everywhere as Jasper tried to restore the castle to its former splendour. A broad flight of processional steps were added against the redundant great tower. A detached, private 'mansion house' that formerly stood in the outer ward was also thought to have been his work. The mansion was demolished during the English Civil War, sometime between 1642 and 1649. At some point in Jasper's tenure, the Great Gatehouse was converted to hold out against the rest of the castle, in case the garrison could not be trusted.

Jasper stayed very close to Henry in his first few years of kingship, becoming a Privy Councillor. He was also made Lieutenant of Calais for a time, and had many grants from the king. From 1485 to 1493 Jasper was High Steward of Oxford University, and from 1486 to 1494 he was Lord Deputy of Ireland. In the Easter term of 1486, Duke Jasper's patent of creation was enrolled on the Exchequer. He was granted the style and dignity of Duke of Bedford in tail male, but since there were no estates attached to the title he was given a £40 annuity instead from the issues of the counties of Bedford and Buckingham. A similar process had occurred when he had been granted a £20 annuity in 1452 after he was granted the title, but not the estates, of the earldom of Pembroke. From now on, when the heralds cried Jasper's title, or in the opening sentence of his own letters patent and on the legends of his seals, the fifty-five-year-old Duke Jasper was styled 'the high and mighty prince, Jasper, brother and uncle of kings, Duke of Bedford and Earl of Pembroke'.

There had been no real reprisals. Estates were not randomly confiscated by the Crown. Possibly the most pragmatic of English kings, Henry rewarded his own supporters only in the short term. As he came to understand his kingdom and the power factions, he began to appoint and promote the brightest and best and those who best served his interests. Yorkists could see that Henry was never vindictive and was attempting to heal the nation. The great Northern Yorkist nobles were left virtually untouched as Henry tried to reconcile the competing parties. Northumberland, Westmorland, Scrope of Castle Bolton, Scrope of Masham, Dacre, Fitzhugh and Lumley all kept their lands and honours. Henry needed the North to be kept secure against the Scots. It is notable that Richard Charlton of Edmonton, who died at Bosworth, was the only Southerner to be attainted, in his very limited Act of attainder.

The House of York had its greatest support in the South, but the South had rebelled against Richard almost immediately upon his usurpation. Richard's closest advisors were attainted, but Kendal, Brackenbury, Catesby and Ratcliffe were not part of the great families of England, and their punishment would not cause any harmful resentment. Eight of the mere twenty-eight men attainted were dead, and another two, Lovell and Zouche, had escaped from the battle. Nearly all were later pardoned and their estates returned. Of the thirty-eight great peers in Richard's 1484 parliament, only five were attainted. These men were the dead Norfolk and Ferrers, the imprisoned Surrey, Lord Lovell, who escaped to sanctuary, and Zouche, who was captured after the battle. Zouche slowly regained his lands and titles by 1495, and died in 1526. More than anything, the Act shows how limited Richard's support was at Bosworth among the noble houses of England, and how generous Henry was to the Yorkists. Lord Lovell was to cause the first major difficulty in Henry's reign.

However, another Lovell, Sir Thomas, was the fifth son of a Lancastrian Norfolk family, and had been attainted in Richard III's first parliament. He had returned to England with Henry, fought at Bosworth and had his attainder reversed. In 1485, he was appointed Chancellor of the Exchequer for life. Thomas Lovell represented Northampton in Parliament, became Speaker of the House of Commons, Secretary of the Treasury and treasurer of the king's and queen's chambers. He was made a Knight of the Body. Thomas Lovell headed the Commons on 10 December 1485, when it requested the king to marry Elizabeth of York.

The agreed wedding to Elizabeth of York had been delayed until after Henry's coronation on 30 October 1485. He wished to established himself firmly enough in his own right as king, to halt any further attempts on the kingship from Elizabeth's relations. Perhaps a majority of people still saw Elizabeth, the daughter of Edward IV, as having the stronger claim to the crown. Henry and Elizabeth married on 18 January 1486. The story of the ubiquitous Tudor rose, symbolising the union of Elizabeth and Henry, is an interesting one. When the deposed Henry VI was again briefly king in 1470, the Grocer's Company in London wisely pulled up the white roses they had planted for Edward IV, and replaced them with red ones as a mark of their loyalty to Henry VI. Henry VI's half-nephew, Henry Tudor, was then in London and possibly knew of the event. He left within days and only returned in 1485, after having defeated Richard III at Bosworth.

It was only after Bosworth that Henry Tudor chose the red rose as his favoured badge. The religious symbolism was important as Henry regarded the Virgin Mary as his special protector. The red rose also represented Christ's Passion – the five petals of the heraldic rose corresponding to the 'five wounds' on Christ's crucified body. This also had a special meaning for Henry. Years later, when the dying king ordered thousands of masses to be said for his soul, he asked for a quarter of them to be dedicated to the five wounds. Henry could have chosen other religious symbols for his badge, but seems to have chosen the red rose in the knowledge that he was to marry Elizabeth of York, the heir of the white rose dynasty. Within weeks of this marriage, the Royal Mint had issued a coin featuring the double union rose, commonly known as the 'Tudor rose', in which the red petals of the Lancastrian rose surround the white petals of the House of York. It became immensely popular with artists and poets, symbolising as it did the healing of the nation after the civil wars.

In 1486 and 1487 came what is known as the Stafford and Lovell rebellion. Francis, Lord Lovell, had replaced the executed Hastings as Lord Chamberlain in 1483, and along with Catesby and Ratcliffe had been the closest friend of Richard III. Lovell, together with the Stafford brothers Humphrey and Thomas, had escaped from Bosworth, finding sanctuary at Colchester Abbey in Essex. In April 1486, the king left London to tour the north of England, and Lovell and the Staffords escaped sanctuary to seek support to overthrow Henry in favour of Clarence's son the Earl of Warwick, who was in comfortable quarters in the Tower. They were followed by Henry's agents. In March 1486, Henry left London without his queen on a progress through the eastern counties to York, where he was received with great cheering. Henry heard of the rebellion while in Lincoln, and moved to suppress it. Lord Lovell headed to Yorkshire and Middleham Castle, where a few Yorkist retainers came out to support him. With a small force, Jasper was now sent ahead of Henry's main army into Yorkshire, promising to pardon everyone except Lovell. He quickly scraped together around 3,000 men from the king's own following and from local tenants and yeomen. Jasper was also armed with a papal bull dated 27 March, which threatened excommunication of all who rebelled against the king. The rebels quickly disbanded and accepted Jasper's terms. In previous times a lord might have wished to make examples of rebels, seeking battle and executing leaders, but Jasper, like the new king, did not share the bloodlust of their predecessors. They were sick of war, hiding, fear and death, especially Jasper, who was now around fifty-five. He seems to have exerted a temperate influence on his nephew when he assumed the crown. Jasper had seen the alternative to peace. Henry now sent Sir Richard Edgecumbe and Sir William Tyler to seek and arrest Lovell. Lovell rode west to Furness Fells in Cumberland and passed some time in hiding with Sir Thomas Broughton. Broughton and Sir John Huddleston had briefly kept Yorkist resistance going in the north-west of England.

There was then a rebellion by the Vaughan family at Brecon in April 1486, when Sir Thomas Vaughan and disaffected Yorkists attacked Brecon, Hay and even Tretower Castle, their former property, burning deeds and documents. It was possibly timed to coincide with the Lovell rising. Jasper raced to his lordship, and with Sir Rhys ap Thomas, who brought 500 men, was instrumental in swiftly suppressing the rising. Thomas Vaughan was the son of Sir Roger Vaughan, beheaded by Jasper in 1471, but he was allowed to return to court in 1487, showing that Jasper was not vindictive toward the son of the man had tried to kill him and who had killed his father, Owen.

Lovell managed to flee to Richard III's sister, Margaret of York and Burgundy, in Flanders. The Stafford brothers had escaped from sanctuary in Colchester at the same time as Lovell, and rode to Worcestershire. Here they tried to stir up a rising, but few people joined them. Hearing that Lovell had fled and that Henry's army was moving west towards them, the Staffords were followed by Henry's scouts to Culham Abbey, where they again claimed sanctuary. They were forcibly removed from the abbey on the night of 13 May 1486 by Sir John Savage.

Bacon's account of Henry's initial dismissal of the rebellion, and of Jasper's actions are thus:

> For he was no sooner come to Lincoln, where he kept his Easter, but he received news, that the lord Lovel, Humphrey Stafford, and Thomas Stafford, who had formerly taken sanctuary at Colchester, were departed out of sanctuary, but to what place no man could tell: which advertisement the King despised, and continued his journey to York. At York there came fresh and more certain advertisement, that the lord Lovel was at hand with a great power of men, and that the Staffords were in arms in Worcestershire, and had made their approaches to the city of Worcester, to assail it. The King, as a prince of great and profound judgment, was not much moved with it; for that he thought it was but a rag or remnant of Bosworth-field, and had nothing in it of the main party of the house of York. But he was more doubtful of the raising of forces to resist the rebels, than of the resistance itself; for that he was in a core of people, whose affections he suspected.
>
> But the action enduring no delay, he did speedily levy and send against the lord Lovel, to the number of three thousand men, ill armed, but well assured, being taken some few out of his own train, and the rest out of the tenants and followers of such as were safe to be trusted, under the conduct of Jasper the duke of Bedford. And as his manner was to send his pardons rather before the sword than after, he gave commission to the duke to proclaim pardon to all that would come in: which the duke, upon his approach to the lord Lovel's camp, did perform. And it fell out as the King expected; the heralds were the great ordnance. For the lord Lovel, upon proclamation of pardon, mistrusting his men, fled into Lancashire, and lurking for a time with Sir Thomas Broughton, after sailed over into

Flanders to the lady Margaret. And his men, forsaken of their captain, did presently submit themselves to the duke. The Staffords likewise, and their forces, hearing what had happened to the lord Lovel, in whose success their chief trust was, despaired and dispersed. The two brothers taking sanctuary at Colnham, a village near Abingdon; which place, upon view of their privilege in the king's bench, being judged no sufficient sanctuary for traitors, Humphrey was executed at Tyburn; and Thomas, as being led by his elder brother, was pardoned. So this rebellion proved but a blast, and the King having by this journey purged a little the dregs and leaven of the northern people, that were before in no good affection towards him, returned to London.

Rather than being summarily executed, as would have occurred under Plantagenet rulers, the Stafford brothers were put on trial. They were found guilty of treason, with the judges declaring that the rules of sanctuary did not apply in such cases. Pope Innocent VIII supported Henry VII and declared that sanctuary could not be claimed by rebels against the king. The judges also stated that it was unreasonable for attainted traitors to be allowed sanctuary a second time. The Staffords were sent to the Tower, with the elder brother, Humphrey, being beheaded at Tyburn in July 1486. Humphrey was not hanged, drawn and quartered, the normal penalty for treason. The younger brother, Thomas, pledged allegiance, was pardoned and remained loyal to Henry. Other rebels were also treated with leniency. Sir John Conyers, who was suspected of being involved in the Lovell revolt and was a major office holder in Yorkshire, lost his stewardship of Middleham and had a £2,000 bond imposed. The Abbot of Abingdon, who had secured sanctuary for the Stafford brothers, was given a 3,000-mark allegiance bond.

Henry had advanced on Worcester, making the Staffords take flight, and at its Cathedral Bishop Alcock preached before him on Whitsunday. After the sermon, Alcock declared that certain bulls received from Rome confirmed the king's title and his marriage. The king then visited Bristol before returning to his palace at Sheen in London in June. Henry then took Queen Elizabeth to Winchester, where on 20 September 1486 she gave birth to Prince Arthur. The new prince was titled in Welsh the same as Llywelyn the Great: 'Tywysog Cymru ac Arglwydd Eryri' (Prince of Wales and Lord of Snowdonia). Arthur was probably conceived before the couple wed, and recent Ricardian novelists are attributing this to a 'forcible rape' by the king, without any shred of evidence. Bacon wrote,

In September following, the Queen was delivered of her first son, whom the King, in honour of the British race, of which himself was, named Arthur, according to the name of that ancient worthy King of the Britains, in whose acts there is truth enough to make him famous, besides that which is fabulous. The child was strong and able, though he was born in the eighth month, which the physicians do prejudge.

There was one major noble who had escaped at Bosworth: John de la Pole, Earl of Lincoln. Henry did not wish to alienate Lincoln's powerful family, and Lincoln had taken an oath with others in 1485 not to maintain felons. On 5 July 1486, he had been appointed a justice of oyer and terminer. However, he suddenly left England in the early part of 1487 to sail to Brabant. Here he was joined by Lord Lovell at Margaret of Burgundy's court at Mechelen (Malines) in Flanders, and came to threaten Henry's reign. Margaret of Burgundy was Richard III's sister, also known as Margaret of York. The rebels had a priest instruct Lambert Simnel, a ten-year-old boy, to impersonate Edward Plantagenet, Earl of Warwick. The young Warwick had been imprisoned in Sheriff Hutton as a potential rival to the crown by Richard III, and Henry had taken him to royal apartments in the Tower.

The twenty-three-year-old Earl of Lincoln also had a claim to the throne, seemingly having being named by Richard III as his heir in 1485, although there was no public proclamation. Lincoln's mother was Richard's sister Elizabeth. Under *Titulus Regius*, Clarence's son Warwick, who had a superior claim, had been attainted so could not succeed. Lincoln had travelled across France and Ireland looking for support for a Yorkist rebellion in the name of Edward, Earl of Warwick. Lincoln's followers started a rumour that Warwick had escaped from the Tower. Lincoln probably wanted to use the Warwick impersonator Simnel as 'the true heir' to gain support, and then could have reverted to reusing the *Titulus Regius* to proclaim himself the true king.

With an army paid for by Lincoln's aunt Margaret, and led by Martin Schwarz, Lincoln and Lovell followed the pretender Lambert Simnel to Ireland. Schwarz was a German mercenary who had commanded Swiss and other troops for Charles the Bold and Maximilian. Some English refugees from Margaret's court joined them. Here they were supported by Gerald FitzGerald, Earl of Kildare, who wished to see a return of Yorkist rule in England. The army rapidly increased in size, gaining Irish recruits led by FitzGerald's brother Thomas. The Yorkist kings had allowed Irish self-government, with FitzGerald as almost the 'uncrowned king of Ireland'. On 24 May 1487, Lincoln, Lovell, Margaret and others installed Simnel as Edward VI in a ceremony in Dublin. Their army then landed at Piel Island in north Lancashire on 4 June 1487, and were joined by a number of the local gentry. These were led by Sir Thomas Broughton and included Sir Thomas Pilkington, James Harrington and Robert Hilton. The first three had all been pardoned after Bosworth. Henry promptly had Edward of Warwick taken from the Tower and displayed in public at St Paul's Cathedral, in response to the presentation of Lambert Simnel as the 'Earl of Warwick' in Ireland. This is exactly what Richard III could have done if he had not killed the Princes in the Tower, Edward V and Prince Richard.

Lincoln's Yorkist army of 8,000 included around 2,000 well-trained German, Swiss and French mercenaries and 4,500 Irishmen. The army moved to York, which refused to surrender. It had marched over 110 miles across the north of England in just five days to Bramham Moor, near Tadcaster in Yorkshire, an incredible speed across the unforgiving Lake District and Yorkshire Moors on poor roads. On 10 June, Lovell led 2,000 men on a night attack against a force of 400 Lancastrians led by Lord Clifford, routing it. The Earl of Northumberland, having been restored to his estates after a few weeks in the Tower after Bosworth, now employed delaying tactics for the Lancastrians, refusing to give battle.

Jasper Tudor, as Earl Marshal, gathered the king's army. Thomas Stanley's son Lord Strange and the Earl of Shrewsbury arrived with seventy knights and about 6,000 troops, while Devon and Sir Rhys ap Thomas also brought men. Sir Edward Woodville, Lord Scales, led cavalry attacks to constantly harass the Yorkist rebels in their movements, and then led his men to rendezvous with Henry's army, now up to 12,000 strong, at Nottingham on 14 June. On 16 June 1487, Henry's vanguard, commanded by the experienced Oxford, found the Yorkist army. It had moved south, crossed the River Trent and set up camp on a hilltop near East Stoke. Schwarz probably commanded the rebels, as Lincoln, Lovell and Fitzgerald had no real experience of leadership in battle. The battle was bitterly contested for over three hours, but the lack of body armour on the Irish troops meant that they were cut down in increasing numbers, being especially vulnerable to the king's archers. Jasper commanded the centre and Henry the rearguard. Rhys ap Thomas, with Oxford, was in the thick of the action. Henry and Jasper did not commit the other two battles, leaving Oxford's vanguard to win by attrition, with his men being repeatedly reinforced as Lancastrian contingents came up from the centre, directed by Jasper.

Unable to retreat, the mercenaries fought to the last. Lincoln, Schwarz, Fitzgerald and Broughton were killed at the Battle of Stoke Field, and Simnel was captured. He was pardoned by Henry in a gesture of clemency, as Henry realised that Simnel was merely a puppet for the leading Yorkists. It is notable how little support the English nobility gave to the Yorkists at this last battle of the Wars of the Roses. Duke Jasper had been involved in the first battle, at St Albans in 1455, and at the last in 1487.

Bacon recounts Jasper's role in the rising:

And first he [Henry] did conceive, before he understood of the earl of Lincoln's sailing into Ireland out of Flanders, that he should be assailed both upon the east parts of the kingdom of England, by some impression from Flanders, and upon the north-west out of Ireland. And therefore having ordered musters to be made in both parts, and having provisionally designed two generals, Jasper earl of Bedford, and John earl of Oxford, meaning himself also to go in person where the affairs should most require it, and nevertheless not expecting any actual invasion at that time, the winter being far on, he took his journey himself towards Suffolk and Norfolk, for the confirming of those parts ...

From St Edmond's-Bury he went to Norwich, where he kept his

Christmas. And from thence he went, in a manner of pilgrimage, to Walsingham, where he visited our lady's church, famous for miracles, and made his prayers and vows for help and deliverance. And from thence he returned by Cambridge to London. Not long after the rebels, with their king, under the leading of the earl of Lincoln, the earl of Kildare, the lord Lovel, and colonel Swart, landed at Fouldrey in Lancashire; whither there repaired to them Sir Thomas Broughton, with some small company of English. The king by that time, knowing now the storm would not divide, but fall in one place, had levied forces in good number; and in person, taking with him his two designed generals, Jasper duke of Bedford, and the earl of Oxford, was come on his way towards them as far as Coventry, whence he sent forth a troop of light horsemen for discovery, and to intercept some stragglers of the enemies, by whom he might the better understand the particulars of their progress and purposes, which was accordingly done; though the king otherwise was not without intelligence from espials in the camp.

Henry gave Simnel a job as a turnspit in the royal kitchens, and he later became a falconer, dying a free man in his fifties. The Irish nobles who had supported Simnel were also pardoned, as Henry needed their support to govern Ireland effectively. Unusually, no one seems to have been executed after the battle, and Henry's clemency to Simnel was remarked upon across Europe. Here was a new type of monarch who did not believe in precedent, and preferred accommodation to revenge. Lovell was reported to have been killed at Stoke, but was seen trying to swim the Trent on horseback, and may have escaped to his house at Minster Lovell, Oxfordshire. Again, perhaps Lovell escaped to Scotland or returned to Burgundy. On 4 November 1488, James IV of Scotland issued safe conducts to forty-two exiled Yorkists, including Lovell, but it is unknown if he ever collected it. Lovell had been attainted after Bosworth, but not until after the Battle of Stoke Field were his lands confiscated, being later granted to Sir William Stanley. The mansion of Minster Lovell was given to Lord Strange, the heir of Thomas Stanley. Most of Lovell's Northamptonshire estates were given to Henry's mother, the Countess of Richmond.

In the autumn, Henry was at Leicester when he received an embassy from Charles VIII, sent to explain the reasons for the French attack on Brittany and the siege of its duke in Nantes. Henry arrived in London on 3 November 1487, and Parliament met on 9 November. It voted for a subsidy, in case Henry wished to aid Brittany. Henry did not have Elizabeth of York, now aged twenty-one, crowned as his queen consort until 25 November 1487, over two years after Bosworth Field, ensuring that he was seen as the true king and not merely as king consort. They had been married on 18 January 1486. Jasper was made high steward for her splendid coronation, and bore her crown at the ceremony. The queen was borne from Greenwich upon a great decorated barge, which breathed fire over the surface of the Thames from the mouth of a large Welsh dragon.

Elizabeth was then carried in a litter with a canopy of cloth of gold to Westminster, wearing a dress of white and gold, and the ceremony was followed by a great banquet in Westminster Hall. Her ladies-in-waiting sat at her feet, and Jasper was in the leading place at the banqueting table among all the great peers. Henry and his mother watched the proceedings from a platform especially erected outside a window. It was common practice for those not entitled to be present to watch proceedings unseen from above. Two days of feasting and celebrations followed. After Elizabeth's coronation, she gave birth to six more children: Margaret became Queen of Scots; Henry succeeded his father as Henry VIII; Elizabeth Tudor died in infancy; Mary became Queen of France; Edmund, Duke of Somerset, died in infancy; and Katherine died as a baby, shortly followed by her mother in 1503 after a post-partum infection. Henry VII was utterly devastated by her death, and courtiers were worried about his health.

By his marriage, Jasper had acquired a large share of the Stafford estates, including the lordship of Newport in Monmouthshire. Royal grants gave him Glamorgan and Morgannwg, with the lordships of Abergavenny, Builth, Caldicot, Cilgerran, Haverfordwest, Llanstephan and Magor. Glamorgan and Abergavenny had formerly been part of the great Beauchamp inheritance which Anne Beauchamp had brought to her husband Richard Neville, Earl of Warwick. Jasper was hardly in Wales, but had developed a team of loyal men to look after his new estates. His professional council was headed by his chamberlain, Sir Edmund Montfort (or Mountford), along with two lawyers, John Morgan of Kidwelly and William Fisher. (Another Morgan Kidwelly, a Westcountryman, had been Richard III's attorney general when he was Duke of Gloucester and king, but had lost the position in 1485.) Kidwelly also served Henry VII as a royal councillor and became Jasper's chancellor of Glamorgan. Montfort had been steward of the household of the executed Duke of Buckingham, and Fisher had been Buckingham's receiver general.

Before his attainder in 1461, Jasper had held several estates formerly shared with his elder brother. The most valuable and extensive of these were in Nottinghamshire and Derbyshire: the manors of Mansfield and Linby and the lordship, castle and town of Clipstone, all in the Sherwood area of Nottinghamshire, and the castle and lordship of Horston, the manor of Bolsover and the office of bailiff of the wapentakes of Morleston and Litchurch, all in Derbyshire. The Tudor earls had also been granted jointly the Warwickshire manors of Solihull and Sheldon. As well as the restoration of most of his estates, the new Duke of Bedford was able to recover the two fee farms of London and Hereford, which Henry VI had granted him, worth respectively £20 and £42 per annum. Jasper also acquired very extensive and valuable new lands, partly by royal grant, and partly by marriage. In Wales, Jasper was also able to recover the lordship of Caldicot, which had been granted in tail to Lord Herbert in 1465.

Similarly, he recovered possession of the 'manor' of Magor in modern Monmouthshire, which had been jointly granted to him and his brother in 1453. The duke seems to have been less successful with the 'manors' of Cloigyn and Pibwr in Carmarthenshire, and with the lordship of Aber in Caernarfonshire. The former was granted to 'John Don' (John Dwnn) in tail male on 9 November 1467 and safeguarded to him in the Acts of resumption of 1468 and 1473. Although a loyal Yorkist until 1485, Dwnn quickly embraced Henry VII's cause and soon became a trusted servant of the new government. The services of such a man were essential to the Tudor cause, which could not afford to alienate those knights, gentlemen and esquires upon whom later medieval government relied. Noticeably, Jasper had named Dwnn among those Welshmen who cost him the Battle of Mortimer's Cross, but again he seems not to have wished to pursue any vendetta.

On 2 March 1486, the king rewarded Jasper with the lordship of Sudeley in Gloucestershire and scattered properties which had formerly belonged to Francis, Viscount Lovell, and Sir William Berkeley, both attainted supporters of Richard. On 21 March 1488, the grant of these properties to Jasper was reconfirmed and augmented by the addition of the castle, town and lordship of Haverfordwest. Jasper thereby became the undisputed master of South Wales, while the lordship of Sudeley gave him a foothold in the Severn Valley. In addition to Sudeley, the Lovell and Berkeley estates gave Jasper considerable territorial power along the Welsh border, in the Severn Valley and across the Cotswolds. The Lovell lands consisted of the manors of Minster Lovell, Brize Norton, Cogges, Hardwick, Rotherfield Greys, Somerton, Banbury and Widford in Oxfordshire; Acton Burnell, Holdgate, Longden, Woolstaston, Smethcott, Abdon, Millichope and Uppington in Shropshire); and the manor of Little Rissington in Gloucestershire and some pasture land at Wanborough in Wiltshire. Several of Sir William Berkeley's properties similarly fell to Jasper: Stoke, Kingsweston, Aylburton, Rockhampton, Sheperdine, Uley and Bradley in Gloucestershire, and the manors of Brigmerston in Wiltshire and Kingsmoor in Somerset. His great estates were concentrated in a triangle of land with its apex in Derbyshire, and its corners at Milford Haven in the west and the Thames estuary in the east. The strategic centre of this widespread domain was the Severn Valley, where the duke now spent much of his time.

12

The Honoured Elder Statesman, 1488–1495

By the time of Bosworth, Jasper Tudor had been a political refugee for almost a quarter of a century. Although he had made brief visits to England, Scotland, Ireland, France, Brittany, Flanders, Burgundy and Wales in Edward IV's two reigns of 1460–1470 and 1471–1483, his longest period in England was probably for a few months during Henry VI's readeption from 30 October 1470 to 11 April 1471. After being a political prisoner in exile, Duke Jasper now held a pre-eminent position in England and, along with Henry's mother, was probably Henry VII's closest and most trusted adviser. He had saved the new king by taking him to Brittany and France, and Henry had known him all his life. Now aged around fifty-eight, and with the crown seemingly secure, Jasper could rest at ease. He was probably the richest peer in the kingdom. On 14 July 1488, Jasper was named as one of the conservators of the truce with France, and was spoken of as Lieutenant of Calais 'for the time being'. His grateful nephew had not only restored his old title and lands, but had also granted Jasper massive new estates as well as the title of Duke of Bedford. From 11 March 1485 to 1 November 1494 he was Lord Lieutenant of Ireland, but it does not appear that he ever went there. He was reported to be High Steward of Oxford University from 1485 to 1492, before Reginald Bray, and Earl Marshal of England from 1492 to 1494.

Under Henry VI, as Earl of Pembroke, Jasper had needed a household and council to administer his affairs and disparate landholdings. After he became Duke of Bedford, Jasper generally relied upon former servants of Buckingham, his wife's late husband. These men had experience of handling Buckingham's great estates, many of which had passed to Jasper through marriage. Edmund Montfort of Coleshill, in Warwickshire, had begun his career around 1444 in the household of Henry VI, and was a loyal servant of the houses of Lancaster and Tudor. In 1461, Montfort had fought for Queen Margaret at the Battle of Towton and shared her exile in Scotland and France for the next decade. At this time, he would have often come into contact with Jasper. Montfort must have made his peace with Edward IV after the restoration of 1471, for he had become steward of the household of Henry Stafford, Duke of Buckingham by 1475. In the following year he was acting as an itinerant justice in the Stafford lordship of Newport.

Montfort was granted a pardon by Richard III on 8 November 1484, so had probably been involved in Buckingham's 1483 rebellion. Sir Edmund was associated with Jasper on various commissions concerned with the administration of the Welsh Marches and the border shires, and by 1491–1492 was being described as one of his councillors. As well as being Jasper's chamberlain, Montfort was also steward of the Stafford (Buckingham) lordship of Thornbury in Gloucestershire from 1485 until 1494, one of Jasper's favourite homes. He was also MP for Gloucestershire in 1491–1492, as well as a Gloucestershire JP from November 1490 until his death in 1494, only a year before that of his master. Jasper and his wife held extensive estates in Gloucestershire, and it is probable that Montfort's prominent position there was the result of their local influence.

While all seemed relatively settled domestically, Jasper's nephew became faced with foreign policy issues. Although the Lancastrians had not pursued the kingship of France as much as the Yorkists, Henry and Jasper knew intimately the rulers of the warring France and Brittany. Henry was in no position to adopt any major aggressive foreign strategies. The civil wars had diminished manpower and finances, and with an inclination to prudence, diplomacy and security brought on by his upbringing Henry was more inclined to peace than war. However, there had been clashes with France since 1066, with English holdings of lands in France leading to the Hundred Years' War of 1337–1453. By 1485, the French monarch had virtually brought all the separate duchies and feudal territories into a single cohesive state, with around three times the resources of England in terms of manpower and revenue. France had always been a repository of those gathered to oppose the English throne, as Henry knew full well, so one of his first acts as king was to sign a year's truce with France, soon extended to 1489. Henry also wished for good relations with James III of Scotland, and James' willingness to accommodate Henry led to a rebellion of the Scottish border nobles. James III died fighting them at Sauchieburn in June 1488. Henry now agreed truces with the Scots in 1488, 1491, and 1492, while supporting opposition to the new regency. The reason for this was that the regency of the young James IV began supporting Yorkist plots.

Brittany had been Henry's primary place of exile, while France helped to finance his successful invasion. Brittany, governed by the ageing Duke François, was the last independent territory that France needed to implement plans for a unified nation. Anne of Beaujeu, as Regent of France, decided to marry her eight-year-old brother, Charles VIII, to Anne of Brittany, the twelve-year-old only daughter of François. At the same time, the recently widowed King of the Romans, Maximilian, stated his intention of marrying Anne of Brittany. Henry did not wish to be involved, but in the spring of 1488 Lord Scales, Sir Edward Woodville, the queen's uncle, went over without authorisation with a band of volunteers in aid of the duke. Henry endeavoured to pursue a peaceful course, and repudiated Lord Woodville's act, prolonging for one year the truce with France, which would have expired in January 1489. Henry sought to act as mediator, but had hardly signed the renewal of the truce when Brittany was completely defeated at the Battle of St Aubin on 28 July 1488. Lord Woodville was slain with nearly all his men, mainly archers. Brittany made peace with France, being compelled to become a vassal state, and François died soon after.

It was in England's interests to preserve the independence of the duchy, which now passed to Anne, a girl of twelve. Various marriage projects were formed for her by her guardian, Marshal de Rieux, with a view to an alliance against France. Henry sent men in aid of the duchy, purely for defensive purposes so long as his truce lasted but prepared, by alliances with other powers, to make war on France if necessary as soon as the truce expired. Parliament met in January 1489 and voted an unprecedented subsidy. It was assessed on wealth and incomes, and was to continue in succeeding years without further consultation, should the war continue. It was to be collected in addition to the more traditional fifteenth and tenth tax also levied in that year. On 14 February 1489, the Treaty of Redon promised 6,000 English troops to defend Brittany at the duchess's expense, but also provided for Breton assistance should Henry wish to reassert English rights in France.

For Maximilian, this treaty brought English military assistance under Giles, Lord Daubeney, against the rebel Flemish cities. Daubeney had been with Henry's invasion army, having escaped to Brittany in 1483. In 1486, Daubeney had negotiated at Calais with the ambassadors of Maximilian, and in 1489 led an expedition of 1,800 English troops to assist Maximilian against the Flemings and their French allies. On 13 June Daubeney attacked the Flemish siege lines outside Dixmude, wading through ditches in water up to his armpits to defeat the besiegers and capture many of their guns. The *Chronicle of Calais* records that 'the battayle of Dickysmewe [Dixmude or Dixmew in Flanders] was on the xiij. day of June, that day beyng satterday, and the 4. yere of Henry the Seventh, anno 1489, where the Ynglishe men had great vyctorye, for there was taken and slayne a greate nombar, and there was slayne the lorde Morley an Englishe man'.

In March and April 1489, Henry's troops, some 7,400 strong under Robert, Lord Willoughby de Broke, crossed to Brittany. Most had returned by Christmas 1489, but in July Willoughby led a second expedition, fewer in men but stronger in ships. That year and the next brought English raids on the French coast and French attacks on Dorset. The war was complicated by Breton civil strife, in which Henry tended to support his old host Jean de Rieux. Henry's alliance with Maximilian was broken when the latter settled with the French at Frankfurt in July 1489, but was renewed at Woking in September 1490, a reconciliation marked by Maximilian's acceptance of investiture with the Order of the Garter in December. The final crisis of Breton independence came in 1491, as the French captured Nantes in March. Henry called a great council and levied a benevolence in July, funding a third, smaller expedition.

The Breton army was led by Jean de Rieux, friend of Henry and tutor of Duchess Anne. Facing heavy odds, the Bretons withdrew to Rennes. The dukedom was rent by internal arguments, and the duchess was obliged to rely largely on mercenary troops. After besieging Rennes for several months, Charles bribed the garrison to surrender. He entered the town and, after long and strenuous negotiation, persuaded Anne to marry him. Breton independence was at an end. Anne married Charles VIII on 6 December 1491, with the marriage ending Brittany's thousand-year independence. Henry had spent some £124,000 for nothing.

On the domestic front, in January 1489 a new parliament had met, and granted Henry another subsidy for a force of 10,000 archers for defence of the kingdom. When the commissioners began to levy it in Yorkshire they were openly resisted, and the Earl of Northumberland, who came to support their authority, was slain on 28 April.

In response, Henry marched north from Hertford through Leicester and Nottingham, gathering an impressive army before entering York on 23 May. The rebels had already dispersed, but trials and executions followed. When Henry returned south in June, he compensated for Northumberland's loss by leaving Thomas Howard, Earl of Surrey, as his lieutenant in the North, a role he performed with distinction, for example in his rapid suppression of another tax revolt in 1492. After being released from the Tower, where he had been imprisoned after Bosworth, Surrey served Henry faithfully and regained all his titles and estates. The insurrection was prolonged for a while under Sir John Egremont and John à Chamber, but Egremont soon fled to Flanders and Chamber fell into Surrey's hands. The king accordingly returned southwards and established a council for the government of the North under Surrey.

Princess Margaret was born on 29 November 1489. The three-year-old Arthur was ceremoniously created Prince of Wales on the following day, and a second prince, the future Henry VIII, was born on 28 June 1491. Jasper was to act as Prince Arthur's deputy in Wales and the Marches. Jasper's last acquisition of land was on 15 May 1491, when Henry enfeoffed his uncle with the castle and lordship of Builth in the Marches of Wales, which was part of the earldom of March. It had been incorporated in the royal demesne by Edward IV and remained in the Crown's hands and was thus available to Henry VII to give to his uncle as a final reward. Apart from visiting Wales to restore order in the Vaughan revolt of 1486, Jasper appears to have spent the rest of his life on his English estates. The strategic centre of his widespread estate was the Severn Valley, so Jasper spent much of his time here. The favoured home of the new Duke and Duchess of Bedford was Sudeley Castle. Sudeley became the property of the Crown when Edward IV granted the estate to his brother Richard, Duke of Gloucester, who held the estate until 1478. When he acceded to the throne, Richard III took ownership of Sudeley for a second time. It was during this period that the magnificent banqueting hall and the now ruined state rooms were built. When Jasper died in 1495, the property reverted back to the Crown. During the Tudor period, Sudeley was to become closely associated with the intrigues surrounding the Tudor court.

The couple also spent time at Thornbury Castle. Its best-known ghost is said to be that of Jasper Tudor. In Jasper's day, the area on the first floor of the castle now occupied by offices was said to be reserved for gentlemen only. The castle is now a hotel and restaurant and its website tells us the following:

> It seems Jasper is unhappy that today's office ladies have invaded his space, and makes his presence felt. He turns on the photocopier and pushes objects off shelves – once he dropped a first aid box from the top shelf right in front of Julie, former PA to the Baron of Portlethen. A clairvoyant who visited the offices claimed she could see Jasper Tudor, dressed in a long dark coat and a pointed hat, indicating to her to keep her distance. Interestingly, a quieter time was enjoyed by all when there was a man working in the office. Jasper may also operate in the Library, where books have been known to jump out of bookcases. Now and again, guests report noticing people in their rooms in the middle of the night. A little girl who stayed in the Mary Tudor room drew a picture of a man she said had visited her in the night, and the picture bore a remarkable resemblance to Jasper Tudor.

Rudder's *History of Gloucestershire* notes that adjoining the gallery leading to Thornbury church was originally a suite of rooms called 'the Earl of Bedford's lodgings'. *The History of Thornbury Castle* tells us that 'the Earl of Bedford's lodgings' contained 'thirteen rooms, whereof six are below, three of them having chimneys in them; and seven above, whereof four have chimneys likewise. All of which houses, buildings and rooms aforementioned are for the most part built in freestone, and covered with slate or tile.'

Jasper also appears to have spent money restoring churches. He assumed the lordship of Cardiff after the accession to the throne of Henry VII. At Llandaff Cathedral in Cardiff, the north-west tower was added by him between 1485 and 1490 and is now named after him. Llandaff, along with Bangor, St David's and St Asaph, is one of the four oldest cathedrals in Britain. This notable 'Jasper Tower' replaced a detached bell tower. The bell tower had been built 200 years earlier at the top of a small hill which in pre-Norman times had provided the original church, based on St Teilo's holy well. Until the time of Henry VIII, pilgrims thronged to the shrine of St Teilo, whose tomb and reputed skull fragment are still in the sanctuary, and their gifts supported the church. It appears Jasper may have contributed towards St Mary's in central Cardiff, and to some rebuilding of the west wing of apartments at Cardiff Castle.

He may also have paid for the completion of the tower at St Gwynlliw's Cathedral, Newport, now called St Woolos' Cathedral. St Woolos' is a large, multi-period church with a twelfth-century nave and late fifteenth-century tower and aisles. The church was probably badly damaged during Owain Glyndŵr's revolt, which laid waste the lordship of Newport in 1402–1403. The nave and aisles have a complete set of late medieval wagon roofs, and the building of the tower is attributed to Jasper Tudor, Lord of Newport.

In 1491, Jasper was in London for the birth of the future Henry VIII. Here he will have met the new prince's governess, Jane ap Hywel. Jane had been in Jasper's household in Pembroke when Margaret Beaufort arrived, heavily pregnant and awaiting the birth of her child. Jane may have even helped in Margaret's birthing chamber, and then took care of the infant Henry Tudor, being appointed as his governess. Jasper had been forced to flee to Scotland from Pembroke when his nephew Henry of Richmond was only four years old, and it is extremely likely that Jane stayed with her charge. It seems that she moved with him when Henry was taken into the wardship of William Herbert.

Jane became friendly with Anne Devereux, the wife of Herbert, who cared for Henry as if he was one of her own sons. As king, Henry VII thanked Anne Devereux for her hospitality. Around 1470, when Jasper had retaken Pembroke and Herbert had been killed, Jane rejoined his household with Henry, and was now married to another servant, Philip ap Hywel. She may have been with Henry when he visited Henry VI during the brief readeption of 1470–1471. It is not known whether Jane was with Henry and Jasper when they fled to Brittany, but after Bosworth Jane and Philip were granted rewards by the new king and invited to court. We do not know for how long she was governess to Henry, Duke of York. It may be that Jasper had recommended her for the position of caring for Henry VII's second son. Margaret Beaufort, the new king's mother, was a strong presence at court, and will have known Jane ap Hywel's capabilities in bringing up her beloved Henry.

There were still Yorkist conspiracies, often fuelled by French patronage. Sir Robert Chamberlain of Kingston near Cambridge was caught at Hartlepool in January 1491 while attempting to leave for France. He was attainted and beheaded at the Tower on 3 March for plotting against the king, but his son inherited his estates. Most threatening was the conspiracy gathering in Ireland around a new pretender, Perkin Warbeck. He was alleged to be Richard of Shrewsbury, the younger of Edward IV's sons, supposedly having escaped from the Tower. He was at Charles VIII's court by March 1492, which led Henry to prepare for war. In June 1492, Daubeney and Bishop Fox led negotiations with the French. Henry had adopted a more aggressive foreign policy, knowing that France was more interested in expanding its power in northern Italy. He announced his intention to assert his claim to the French throne. An attempt to liberate Brittany faltered, and Henry's fleet was at length repulsed from Normandy after raids in June and July. He sent troops under Sir Edward Poynings to assist Maximilian's siege of the rebel stronghold of Sluys, but, despite what seem to have been good intentions on Maximilian's part, received no immediate help in return. Yet he continued to gather an army of 15,000 men, with which he crossed to Calais in October, rejecting the advice of his councillors to again postpone the campaign.

Mortimer recounted that Jasper, Duke of Bedford, was one of Henry's two main commanders:

By this treaty the town of Berwick, with its territory, was to be declared a neutral town; and the lordship of Lorn, in Scotland, and the little island of Lundy belonging to England, were excepted out of the truce. Henry ratified the treaty on the ninth of January, 1492, but the king of Scotland, whether bribed by France, or from some other motive, refused to confirm it; he agreed, however, to a much shorter truce, on the twentieth of February following, which was to last only eleven months. His next step was to send ambassadors to summon Maximilian and Ferdinand of Spain to assist him in invading France, according to treaty; but, notwithstanding the high and lofty strain in which Henry affected to talk to his parliament, it is pretty evident he had no intention to push the war with vigour; for, at the very time we are now speaking of, viz. the months of February and March, when the flame of his resentment seemed to blaze highest, we find him opening a negotiation with two agents from his cousin of France.

On the third of May, however, the staff-officers and purveyors of the army were appointed; sir Reginald Bray, knight of the Garter, being made pay-master of the troops. On the ninth of the same month, Henry entered into an indenture with his principal officers for their quotas of men, which were to serve in the ensuing campaign, at the rate of eighteen pence for every man at arms, with a servant and page; and sixpence for every archer on foot or horseback. As we have but imperfect accounts of the art of war in those days, it is not easy to say in what manner these troops were formed and disciplined; it is not unlikely that every contractor acted as colonel of the men whom he had indentured to raise; and that the whole, being divided into vanguard, centre, and rearward, flanked by the horse in two bodies, as wings, were commanded by the general officers, who, upon this occasion, were the king himself, the duke of Bedford, and the earl of Oxford. Mention is also made of the Marquess of Dorset, the earls of Kent, Devonshire, Devonshire, Surry, Arundel, Derby, Shrewsbury, Suffolk, Essex, and Ormond; the lords Latimer, Powis, Barnes, Grey, Scroope of Bolton, Scroope of Upsal, Audley, and Strange; the viscount Wells; sir Reginald Bray, sir Charles Somerset, sir Roger Cotton, sir Richard Hole, sir William Courtney, sir Richard Corbet, sir William Stanley, sir John St. John, sir Walter Hungerford, with several other gentlemen, all of them contractors for furnishing men and arms, and also a brave body of Welsh troops under the command of Richard Thomas.

The rendezvous of the whole army was appointed to be held near London, and upon a review it appeared to amount to the number of twenty-five thousand foot and sixteen hundred horse, or men at arms, which, allowing two servants to each man at arms, make in the whole an army of about twenty-nine thousand eight hundred fighting men. But before this army could be got together, and through Henry's affected delays, the season for fighting was over. It was the twentieth of September before Henry got to Canterbury, where he made sir Robert Nanfan judge-advocate of the navy, with a power of punishing capitally all offences committed in the same; and sir Robert Willoughby de Brooke (as he is called in his commission) marshal of the army, with the like powers. On the second of October, Henry, being ready to embark at Dover, appointed his son Arthur, prince of Wales, guardian of the realm. On the sixth of the same month he embarked with his army, and next day landed at Calais. Henry had scarcely landed on the continent when the ambassadors he had sent to the king of the Romans arrived, and told him that Maximilian was wholly unprepared to enter France, as he had promised; this news was immediately made known to the whole army. Some days after, he received from his ambassadors in Spain, letters, which were likewise made public, importing that Ferdinand had concluded a peace with the king of France, upon that monarch's promising to restore to the crown of Castile the province of Roussillon, without receiving the three hundred thousand crowns, which Lewis XI had lent upon that county.

Jasper was thus one of the commanders of the army that invaded France in 1492. Bacon recorded that

by this time was drawn together a great and puissant army into the city of London; in which were Thomas marquis Dorset, Thomas earl of Arundel, Thomas earl of Derby, George earl of Shrewsbury, Edmond earl of Suffolk, Edward earl of Devonshire, George earl of Kent, the earl of Essex, Thomas earl of Ormond, with a great number of barons, knights, and principal gentlemen; and amongst them Richard [Rhys ap] Thomas, much noted for the brave troops he brought out of Wales. The army rising in the whole to the number of five and twenty thousand foot, and sixteen hundred horse; over which the King, constant in his accustomed trust and employment, made Jasper duke of Bedford and John earl of Oxford generals under his own person. The ninth of September, in the eighth year of his reign, he departed from Greenwich towards the sea; all men wondering that he took that season, being so near winter, to begin the war; and some thereupon gathering, it was a sign that the war would not be long. Nevertheless the King gave out the contrary, thus: 'That he intending not to make a summer business of it, but a resolute war, without term prefixed, until he had recovered France; it skilled not much when he began it, especially having Calais at his back, where he might winter, if the season of the war so required.' The sixth of October he embarked at Sandwich; and the same day took land at Calais, which was the rendezvous, where all his forces were assigned to meet.

The army crossed the Channel and, on 18 October 1492, besieged Boulogne. The earldom of Boulogne had been the property of Burgundy and it was not until 1478 that Louis XI had finally united it with the French crown. On the northern extreme of the French kingdom, Boulogne and its surrounds formed a salient, with its base on the River Somme, stretching along the north-west coast towards Calais and as far east as Thèrouanne. Defended by the great castle of Montreuil, it sat on the eastern flank of the Spanish invasion route from the Habsburg Netherlands, just twenty miles south of the English possession of Calais and within sight of the Kent coast. It was strategically important and the English coveted and besieged it twice. The first siege of 1492 took the lightly defended lower town.

The advisors of Charles VIII wanted to get rid of Henry to leave them free to concentrate all resources in northern Italy. The result was the Treaty of Étaples on 3 November 1492. Henry received a promise from Charles that he would no longer give any assistance to any pretenders to the English throne. Henry also received a total of 745,000 crowns, the cost of the venture, to be paid at 50,000 crowns a year. There was a generous annual payment in compensation for English expenses in the Breton war, and a French promise to expel Warbeck and his supporters. As his father had done when making the similar Treaty of Picquigny with Edward IV in 1475, Charles VIII also granted pensions to eight of Henry's councillors, an additional incentive to England staying pacific while he pursued his Italian expansion plans.

Unfortunately for Henry, Warbeck moved from France to the Burgundian court of Margaret of York, the sister of Edward IV, Richard III and Clarence, who welcomed him as her 'nephew' and gave fresh impetus to his followers. Henry knew that Ireland would be his recruiting ground, and, from 1491, English troops were sent there on several occasions. Henry further increased the influence of the Butlers to countervail that of the Fitzgeralds, who had done little to stop Warbeck and had supported Simnel. From early 1493, senior figures at the English court such as John Radcliffe, Lord Fitzwalter and even Sir William Stanley were apparently drawn into plots in favour of Warbeck. Henry's agents must have suspected something, as he spent the summer of 1493 in central England at Warwick, Kenilworth and Northampton, poised to meet an invasion. His trusted lords were instructed to have troops ready to march at one day's notice. He also increased his personal security by creating a privy chamber, staffed by servants of humble origin, into which he could withdraw from the pressures of the court. In May, commissioners were appointed to investigate suspected treason across fifteen counties. Some plotters were arrested, but in June Sir Robert Clifford and others slipped away to Margaret's court.

In July, Sir Edward Poynings and Dr William Warham were sent to Burgundy, in what is now the Netherlands, to denounce Warbeck's imposture. However, they could not persuade the councillors of the young

Philip the Fair of Burgundy, recently emerged from the regency of his father Maximilian, to restrain the support for the pretender. Henry mixed persuasion with coercion, suspending all direct trade to the Netherlands, the staple market for English cloth exports, in September 1493.

In Wales, an administrative machinery for order and justice was required. Prince Arthur's council, based at Ludlow Castle, was specifically required to superintend to this. In its absence, Jasper Tudor filled the role. A wide-ranging commission on Edward IV's Yorkist model was issued to Arthur and Jasper on 20 March 1493 to superintend the execution of justice throughout Wales and the shires of Shropshire, Worcester, Hereford and Gloucester. At the same time Arthur received military powers to facilitate law enforcement, and he was authorised to replace unsatisfactory officials. Jasper and his counsellors effectively ran this as Arthur was six years old.

In mid-November 1494, a series of arrests began that brought in the leading suspects accused by Sir Robert Clifford. Clifford was almost definitely the king's agent, having been sent to Margaret's court as a Warbeck supporter but having returned to provide evidence. Sir William Stanley was tried on 6–7 February 1494 and executed. Lord Fitzwalter was convicted on 23 February but imprisoned at Guisnes outside Calais, only to be executed in 1496 after trying to escape. With fighting in Dublin, Henry dismissed the Earl of Kildare, who had fought for Edward IV. Kildare had effectively ruled Ireland as Jasper's deputy Lord Lieutenant. A force of 1,000 men was raised to subdue Ireland, but Jasper was too ill to lead it. Henry instead sent Sir Edward Poynings and made his four-year-old son Prince Henry Lord Lieutenant.

Men lived to an average age of about fifty at this time, and only about one-fifth lived into their sixties. Infant mortality was extremely high, it is possible that up to half of all children did not live to be twenty. Jasper was now around sixty-five and seemed to know he was dying, writing a will a few days before his death. It is dated 15 December 1495, written at his manor of Thornbury, and bequeaths his 'soul to almighty God to our blessed lady his mother the Virgin Mary and to all saints'. Most of the rest is concerned with monetary bequests to religious houses and provisions for the welfare of his own soul, those of his parents and that of his brother Edmund. Jasper asked that land be amortised 'for the finding of four priests to sing perpetually'. They were to sing masses for his soul, and for those of his father and mother. Jasper Tudor, Earl of Pembroke and Duke of Bedford, died at Thornbury on 21 (or possibly 26) December 1495. Margaret Beaufort, Henry VII, Katherine Wydeville and possibly Elizabeth of York were present at the great man's passing.

Jasper left most of his possessions to his nephew, King Henry. A number of religious houses received rich garments. Keynsham Abbey received his best gown of cloth of gold, which was to be made into vestments 'to the honour of God and his blessed mother'. The monastery of St Kenelme in Winchcombe received a gown of crimson velvet for a cope. The church at

Thornbury had a black velvet gown for the same purpose. A second gown of cloth of gold was given to the Grey Friars of Haverford, as Hereford was then called, where Owen Tudor was buried, for a cope or vestments. Another black velvet gown went to the church of Pembroke for a cope. Jasper left the Blessed Trinity of Crichurch (the Priory of Holy Trinity in London) a jacket of cloth of gold, which was to be used to make two jackets. He left £4 to two orders of friars at Cardiff and a pound to the Austin friars at Newport.

Jasper gave all his household servants a year's wages and asked that his household be kept from the day of his death until the following Easter. The land that Jasper held in fee simple was to be retained for twenty years for the payment of his debts and the satisfaction of his will, after which it was to go to Jasper's nephew, King Henry VII, 'and to his heirs kings of England forever'. Jasper also asked that Henry see the will executed 'for my old since devotion to his Grace'. Jasper placed the residue of his goods in the hands of his executors and asked that 'my Lady my wife and all other persons have such dues as shall be thought to them appertaining by right law and conscience'. He appointed the Archbishop of Canterbury, the Bishop of London, Lord Daubeny and Lady Agnes Cheyne, the incumbent of Chenies Manor House, as his executors. When the will was probated on 2 July 1496, Daubeney and Kidwelly were appointed the executors.

Lady Agnes Cheyne had bequeathed Keynsham Abbey in Somerset to Jasper in 1494. Here Henry VII and his queen attended the duke's funeral, held before the end of the year. In the Dissolution of the Monasteries, Henry VIII did not spare Jasper's effigy or the abbey, which was destroyed, although his grandmother Margaret Beaufort's chapel at Holywell in Flintshire was spared. Just two months after Jasper's death, Jasper's wife Katherine married, without royal licence, Richard Wingfield, a young man probably around twelve years her junior. Just before Jasper's death, Parliament passed an Act that strengthened Katherine's hold on her jointure, which suggests that Jasper either did not think that she was going to remarry, or perhaps did not mind if she did. He was well into his fifties when he had married her as his only wife.

Just before or after Jasper's death, on 23 December 1497, Sheen Palace, the chief residence of Henry VII and located about nine miles south-west of Westminster, was destroyed. It burned down during the night, with the destruction of not only large parts of the palace, but vast amounts of expensive furniture and tapestries. An alarm was raised in time for the royal couple and their children to escape to safety, along with the remainder of the court. The destruction of Sheen gave Henry VII the opportunity to construct a magnificent new palace on the same site, which he named Richmond after his hereditary earldom. Henry died there in 1509, and the royal palace was demolished after the execution of Charles I in 1649. Only the wardrobe, trumpeters' house and gatehouse remain, all Grade I listed.

Jasper was the last Earl of Pembroke in the old manner. In 1536, the earldom of Pembroke was abolished with all the other Marcher lordships in the Act of Union between England and Wales. Jasper's earldom instead became the basis of a new government shire under government control.

Postscript

In 1915, Howell Evans wrote of Jasper,

None showed more unselfish loyalty to the cause of the Crown, or greater resource in defending it. Sleepless in his devotion to his party for nearly thirty years, he laboured more assiduously than any other to shape its destiny. His achievements in the open field were negligible; the only victory in which he could claim a share was the final triumph of his cause at Bosworth. But, from his entry into political life he displayed extraordinary skill and tenacity in reorganizing his forces after defeat, as well as a keen zest for the shifts of statecraft. His strategy was that of timely retreat when victory had eluded his grasp. He alone of the leaders on either side lived through the struggle and witnessed its close. Sometimes lurking in caverns and woods, sometimes traversing lonely mountain paths, sometimes stranded on a deserted shore, he continued to hold in his hands the thread of Lancastrian hopes. Shrewd, adroit, and persevering, he was undaunted by the caprice of fortune, and successfully braved the perilous vicissitudes incident to his arduous undertaking. And in an age of brutal passion he emerged with his fame untarnished by any deed of cruelty or wrong; while the affectionate care he bestowed upon his fatherless nephew, Henry Tudor, throws into relief the hideous ferocity that surrounded him.

'There is a sayle-yeard fulle good and sure,
To the shyp a grete tresour,
For alle stormes it wolle endure,
It is trusty atte need.
Now the sayle-yeard I will reherse,
The Erle of Pembroke, curtsy and fierce,
Across the mast he hycthe travers,
The good ship for to lede.'

Following his almost secret birth around 1431, from the first battle of the Wars of the Roses in 1455 until the last in 1497, Jasper Tudor lived in dangerous times. His incredible feats of survival in losing campaigns, interspersed with being chased into exile and returning into peril, led to him being the single thread holding the Lancastrian party together. His tenacious support of Henry VI, his wife Margaret of Anjou and their heir Edward of Westminster segued into protecting and mentoring his nephew Henry as the sole remaining adult Lancastrian claimant to the crown. We must remember that from 1461 until Henry VII's coronation after Bosworth twenty-five years later, there had been six different kingships with four kings, three of whom died by violence. Even the fourth, Edward IV, may have been poisoned. More than anyone else, Jasper, travelling tirelessly across Britain and Europe, held out hope for Lancastrian resistance in the 1470s and early 1480s after the death of Henry VI and his son. His loyalty and determination never once faltered, even with the deaths of his only brother Edmund and father Owen, and several promises of pardon. Without Jasper Tudor there would have been no Tudor dynasty.

And we must remember that this dynasty gave us the beginning of the British Empire, the concomitant international sea power and the flowering of the finest period of English culture – the English Renaissance. Henry left behind him a stable country and a full Treasury. Simons well describes the terrible state of the little nation of 3 million souls that Henry took over:

> The crown was no longer a symbol of unity and nationhood. So many invaders had landed in England determined to win her that from one day to the next the common folk hardly knew whether King Log or King Stork was their master. The nobles had shown themselves not chivalrous, disinterested lovers of their native land but greedy tyrants, bursting with envy, hatred and ambition. The feudal customs had exposed themselves as merely convenient arrangements whereby the lords could call upon their servants and retainers at will for their own private wars. They were as likely to find themselves fighting men from the next county as the foreigner.
>
> The towns were choked with the helpless, hopeless residues of the armies – the blind, the lame, the disabled, the sick, the diseased and the mendicants. Lepers were not uncommon. There was little or no money with which to repair damage or maintain collectively-owned edifices such as market halls. Pirates roamed the Channel and raided the southern ports. The Treasury was almost empty, and even the crown jewels had been pledged to pay for guns and munitions. Exports and imports had declined from the swelling torrents of Edward IV's latter days to thin trickles. The island was regarded in Europe as the home of warring barbarians, even its lords being often unable to read and write. As an ally she was considered negligible by all but a few minor princes in desperate straits, such as the Duke of Brittany.

Against this background, we can see one man who stands out as never changing sides, standing loyal throughout the wars where the Plantagenets virtually wiped each other out. Half-British and half-French, Jasper constantly faced terrible odds but never gave up or betrayed anyone. His sole act of vengeance was against the man who was sent to kill him and who ensured that his father was beheaded. His alternative at the time was to set him free, as Jasper was escaping to exile, trying to save his nephew. He could neither imprison Roger Vaughan, nor take him with him. When he returned to power briefly in 1470, he did not retaliate against the Yorkists who had killed his brother Edmund. When he came to power in 1485, still there was no thirst for revenge. He mentored his nephew in exile to become Britain's greatest king, in this author's perspective, a king whose achievements were not built upon the heroism of war and bloodshed, but upon peace, accommodation and prosperity.

Tudor writers gloried in their new monarchs, leaving little space for Jasper. In his *Mémoires* about Henry VII, de Commines wrote, 'The English, who were powerful and rich, and governed by a wise, graceful, and valiant Prince, Henry, who had several sage and brave men under him, and very good commanders, as the Earl of Salisbury, Talbot, and others I pass by, etc.' By the 'Earl of Salisbury', Commines meant Jasper Tudor. There was some confusion around the title of Earl of Salisbury, as Henry attainted the earl in 1485 after Bosworth and intended to confer his title and lands on Jasper. Henry eventually executed the holder of the title in 1499. Jasper was made Duke of Bedford instead.

While in exile in France and Brittany, Jasper and Henry learned diplomacy and a different method of running a nation. They both knew that, for a new dynasty to succeed, they had to curb the independence of the great nobles, especially those in the Marches of Wales. In retrospect, the years of restricted freedom in exile might have come to be considered time well spent by Jasper and Henry. The Breton and French courts were political hotbeds where, without direct personal involvement, both men had been able to observe and learn how modern, centralised kingdoms could be fashioned out of feudal conglomerates. Francis Bacon, in his *History of the Reign of King Henry VII*, bracketed Henry with Louis XI and Ferdinand of Spain as the 'three wise men' of the age, and historians still debate the extent to which Henry VII emulated the political strategies of his powerful contemporaries.

Polydore Vergil related that Henry 'was moderate, honest, frugal, affable, and kindly. He hated pride and arrogance so much that he was rough and harsh towards men marked by those vices. No man enjoyed such sway with him that he dared to act as he please … he said this was his practice, so that he would be called a king who chose to rule rather than be ruled.' Henry thus began to reduce the power of great nobles in their feudal localities. Jasper, Oxford, Morton and Fox were experienced and loyal advisors. Henry appointed to important local offices lesser lords who were more dependent on royal favour. He made no distinction between Yorkists and Lancastrians – loyalty and ability were the major qualities required. Unlike earlier kings, the Tudors did not choose their chief secular advisors from the higher ranks of the nobility. That would cause more problems from the great magnates. Instead, advisors were promoted on the basis of merit.

To some extent, Henry was successful because the great houses had been weakened by decades of war. There were fifty-five great nobles at Henry's accession. However, when added to natural wastage as families died out without heirs, there were only forty-two nobles by Henry's death. Henry was reluctant to hand out titles, making those servants he wanted to reward Knights of the Garter rather than hereditary noblemen. The great estates of the houses of York and Lancaster, and of Warwick the Kingmaker, all fell to the new king.

The Yeomen of the Guard became the first permanent royal guard, but Henry relied on the system of levying militias from the shires when military force was needed. Henry VII recognised the weakness of England relative to France and Spain, so he allied with Spain and avoided aggressive adventures in France. There was little support within the political nation for a rebellion against Henry. During the Wars of the Roses there had been a declining interest from the nobility and leading gentry in engaging in factional conflict and struggles for the crown: the risk of backing the wrong side meant that there was too much to lose. From the high point of 1459–1461, when some fifty-five noble families had been engaged in the Wars of the Roses, eighteen fought in 1471 and only twelve turned up at Bosworth in 1485.

As David Starkey notes in his recent biography of the young Henry VIII, 'The story of how Henry Tudor survived against the odds, and won his throne and bride against even greater odds, is one of the world's great adventures.' The importance of Jasper's tutelage of his nephew has only recently been fully appreciated by historians. While Henry's mother, Margaret Beaufort, was an indispensable agent of his interests in England, Jasper was his political mentor in the years spent in exile. Between them, Margaret and Jasper nurtured Henry's rights, first, to be restored to his lands and title, and, after the death of Henry VI and Edward of Westminster, as Lancastrian claimant to the crown. Complex and skilful diplomacy, attention to financial detail and the vital support of men like Jasper Tudor all played their part. Henry's kingship was assisted by skilful visual and verbal image making, and the arts of prophecy and propaganda – Henry and Jasper both believed Henry was the chosen one, destined for glory. Henry was possibly the first king to leave a full Treasury, and his three surviving children were linked to the other royal dynasties of Europe.

Both Jasper's support in Wales and the bards' songs were vital in Henry's success. Emyr Wyn Jones asked why Dale was chosen as the landing point for the Tudor invasion fleet:

Hazardous undertakings involving such high stakes are not embarked upon without much careful preparatory work. Wales was emotionally prepared for Henry's arrival on its shores; the long years of encouraging prognostication by the bards had not been in vain. The long period of skilled and indefatigable political scheming, mainly in Wales, by Jasper

Tudor, Henry's uncle, was about to bear fruit. It is no exaggeration to assert that Henry's arrival was an event of 'messianic' significance where Wales was concerned. It was an event that culminated in the enthusiasm and prowess of the powerful army of Welshmen who accompanied 'a descendant of their ancient British princes' from Dale to Bosworth, or joined him along the march.

The Welsh gentry had known Jasper to be operating in and around Wales for three decades, and many were related to him. They knew he was an honourable man, battle hardened and also fortunate, perhaps destined, to stay alive in these years. Across the whole of Yorkist-dominated Wales, men flocked to join his young nephew's banner. Jasper's role in educating Henry in diplomacy and warfare in the years of exile, and his importance in taking Wales for the future king has always been underplayed. Henry's biographers and later writers have always focussed upon the king, bypassing the role of Jasper.

Jasper was not only a great influence on the young Henry but he also saw the potential of the north-west and south-west of Wales as strategic bases and centres of support. He had great influence in South Wales and was a great patron of the bards, including Lewys Glyn Cothi and Dafydd Llwyd. The *canu darogan*, songs of prophecy, were a peculiarly Welsh phenomenon which reflected a national struggle for British independence, the desire to regain sovereignty over lands conquered by the pagan English invaders. Its roots go back at least to Nennius' *Historia Brittonum* of around 800, and the encounter at Vortigern's court between the red dragon of the British and the white dragon of the Anglo-Saxons. In this tale the red dragon was defeated but regained superiority, and the similar expectation was that, following defeat, the English and then the French-Normans would be expelled back overseas.

The *Armes Prydain*, 'Prophecy of Britain', of around 930 wanted the Welsh, Bretons, Cornish and Strathclyde British, all speaking the same language of P-Celtic (today's Welsh), to join with Scotland, Scots from Ireland and Norsemen to fight the West Saxons under two sons of prophecy, Cynan and Cadwaladr. The belief even survived the final conquest of the remaining Britons of Wales in 1282–1283, propelling the Glyndŵr Rising between 1400 and 1415. The persistence of hope for a British king once more, after a millennium of fighting, was crucial for the change of regime. A note of some interest is that many vaticinatory poems prophesy a rescuer named Owain. The name associated with Owen of Manaw, Owen ab Edwin, Owen Lawgoch, Owen Glyndwr and Owen Tudor passed, like Cadwaladr, into a figurative designation for the long-expected leader. Even in the Wars of the Roses, Owain was still mentioned. In his history, Ellis Griffith relates that Henry Tudor was first named Owen, and, although the name was changed by the command of Margaret Beaufort, the Welsh continued to call him Owen rather than Henry.

Emyr Wyn Jones added, 'By the fifteenth century, national sentiment in Wales had taken deep root, finding expression in the literature and especially the prophetic literature of the period. These prophecies, cast in the cywydd metre of the period and often in allegorical form, took on a more purposeful character, and towards the end of the Wars of the Roses this literature tended to rally round Henry Tudor, who could appeal to his countrymen, both Yorkists and Lancastrians, in a truly national cause. It was this great wave of national sentiment in Wales which was to carry Henry to victory at Bosworth.' As W. Watkin Davies wrote in *Wales* in 1924, 'It was as much a Welsh conquest of England as the expedition of 1066 was a Norman conquest of England.' It was more than this. It was a British conquest, and the first British royal dynasty – and without Jasper Tudor it could never have happened.

Notes

Limitations of space preclude an in-depth analysis of Welsh writings in this period, which are essential to an understanding of how the Tudors came to power. It is also impossible to describe in depth Jasper Tudor's time in several countries. Equally, to reference each fact would require a book several times as large as this volume. It is hoped that the following brief notes are of some interest to the reader.

The Original Tudor Church

The church at Penmynydd, Anglesey, where Gronw (Goronwy) Fychan ap Tudur Hen ap Gronw is buried, is dedicated to St Gredifael, who founded a Celtic church here in the sixth century. A stone church was first built here in the twelfth century. It is now gone, although some of its stones, with chevron markings, are thought to have been reused in the current building. The present church dates from the fourteenth century, with restorations taking place in 1848 and 1969. The Tudor tomb is in a separate chapel, which also contains a stained-glass window with the symbols of the Tudor family. The motto reads '*UNDEB FEL RHOSYN YW AR LAN AFONYDD AC FEL TŶ DUR AR BEN Y MYNYDD*', which translates as 'Unity is like a rose on a river bank, and like a House of Steel on the top of a mountain'. The phrase 'Tŷ Dur' (House of Steel) refers to the name Tudur, and 'Ben y Mynydd' (mountain top) is a mutation of Penmynydd. In 2007, Vandals broke into St Gredifael church and destroyed the Tudor stained-glass window, as well as three other windows with original glass dating to the Elizabethan period.

Geography of Yorkist and Lancastrian Support

Winston's doctoral thesis explains that there was no easy delineation of power or sides as there was in, say, in the American Civil War. No geographical line can be drawn separating the towns faithful to York from those that favoured Lancaster. Winston tried to contrast the distribution of the great lords who supported the rival factions with the location of certain towns:

> It has come to be almost a commonplace of historians to refer to the struggle between Lancaster and York as one between the more backward north and west and the more highly developed south and east. Only in a rough sense is this an accurate representation of the division of parties; for while it is true that the strength of the Lancastrians lay in the extreme north and west, and York drew its partisans largely from the south-eastern counties and the Marches, yet the facts do not warrant the division of the realm in so precise a fashion between the adherents of the two rival factions.
>
> ... For instance, the Yorkists were strong in the north, nor were there wanting adherents of the White Rose faction among the magnates of the southwest. On the other hand, Margaret drew supporters from counties in which a majority of the lords were Yorkist in sympathies. The very fact that the estates of the great lords were not compact, but were scattered in different counties confuses the conflict and renders difficult an alignment of parties corresponding to precise geographical units. No section of England presents a uniform political complexion in the struggle between Lancaster and York. To some writers the struggle was a war of the more populous and more advanced south against the more baronial and wilder north; others represent the conflict as one between the democratic element of the south and the aristocratic north. If the facts do not warrant the drawing of a hard and fast line between those portions of the realm which sided with Lancaster, and those which favoured York, still more is this true in the case of the boroughs.
>
> The statement which has been repeated by different writers that the great towns of the south were steady for the house of York is only partially true. For as has been shown, the party of the Red Rose found warm partisans among the burghers of some of the southern cities. At the same time it is undoubtedly true that a majority of the townsmen south of the Trent espoused the cause of the White Rose. Perhaps the safest general statement which can be made – and it is a commonplace one – is that the towns of the realm as a whole were divided in their allegiance, the attitude of any particular town being determined by a variety of considerations.

Lewys Glyn Cothi, *c.* 1420–1490

The *gogynfeirdd*, bards of the princely courts, practised a highly complicated verse form, which was gradually replaced during the fourteenth century by a more flexible type of poetry based on the cywydd, the rhyming couplet. Their practitioners, the *cywyddwyr*, still used the strict patterns of alliteration and internal rhyme known as *cynghanedd*, which poets like Gerard Manley Hopkins would later try to emulate in English. The great houses in Wales generally retained their own bards. In the fifteenth century there evolved two other classes of poet. The 'gentlemen bards' were literary-minded gentry who practised the art for entertainment, not needing to earn a living from it. There were also itinerant bards, professional *cywyddwyr* who travelled between the homes of the gentry, earning their livelihood by their reputation.

Also known as Llywelyn y Glyn, Lewys Glyn Cothi was one of the most important representatives of the *Beirdd yr Uchelwyr* (Poets of the Nobility) or *cywyddwyr*, the itinerant professional poets of the period between the 1284 Statute of Rhuddlan and around 1600. He was possibly born at Pwllcynbyd farm, near the remote hamlet of Rhydycymerau, a few miles from Llanybydder in Carmarthenshire, now a forest of massive wind-power generators. He may have been educated at Carmarthen Priory, and compiled the internationally important *White Book of Hergest*, kept at Hergest Court by his patrons, the Vaughans.

Glyn Cothi was a Lancastrian, although he also composed poetry proclaiming the Herberts and Vaughans. After Mortimer's Cross, when he was probably in the company of Owain ap Gruffudd ap Nicolas, he was forced into outlawry with Owain in Snowdonia. He may have accompanied Jasper Tudor from the battlefield, and was a strong supporter of Jasper Tudor and his nephew Henry. There is a story, originating in a note on a manuscript copy of his poetry, that Lewys settled at Chester and was later ejected from the city by its burgesses for marrying a widow without their consent. Other stories attached to different manuscripts state that he was driven out of the staunchly Yorkist city for making a verse prophecy that Henry Tudor would become king. Although unconfirmed, it seems certain that something occurred for him to satirise Chester's citizens mercilessly in an *awdl*, describing them as the offspring of 'eight kinds of intercourse in the bushes' and calling the vengeance of a pro-Lancastrian Welsh noble, Rheinallt ap Gruffydd ap Bleddyn of Mold, on their heads. His works have not been translated.

Section of a Contemporary Dafydd Nanmor Poem Addressed to Jasper and Edmund

Y ddeuwr arglwyddïaidd	The two lords
O Droya a Groeg, da yw'r gwraidd,	From Troy and Greece, the ancestry is good,
O dalaith, hyd i delon,	From crown to talon,
Rhodri Mawr, ymerodyr Môn;	Rhodri Mawr, emperor of Anglesey;
Iarll Rismwnd, Edmwnd, iaith	Earl of Richmond, Edmund, of the language of
Gydwalader, ag o'i dalaith.	Cadwaladr and from his crown lands.

Penvro yw, penav o'r iaith.	Pembroke is the most skilful champion of the language.
Imp îr o frenin Paris	A healthy graft descended from the King of Paris
A dail our a fflowrdilys.	With golden leaves and fleur-de lis.
Siasbar yw darpar y dawns,	Jasper is prepared for the dance,
Nai Siarlys o ddinas Orliawns.	Charles' nephew from the city of Orléans.
Iarll hydyr, o hil Llur Llediaith,	The brave earl of the lineage of Llyr Llediaeth,
Penvro yw, penav o'r iaith.	Pembroke, the greatest of the nation.

The Scots at Bosworth

There is very little information on the Scots at Bosworth Field. Bernard Stewart or Stuart, Alexander Bruce, John de Haddington and Henderson of Haddington are said to have led Scottish mercenaries from France to fight for Henry. The latter was said to be captain of the Scots Foot. Sir Alexander Bruce of Earlshall, said to be captain of the Scots Horse, led a contingent of Scots from France and was given an annuity of £20 after Bosworth by Henry VII, 'in gracious remuneration of his good, faithful and approved services and his great labours in various ways heretofore'. He was also made *familiari armiger* to James III of Scotland, who also rewarded him for supporting Henry's invasion. James gave Bruce some of the Duke of Albany's confiscated Berwickshire estates. John Major's *A History of Greater Britain*, written before 1521, tells us that the King of France supplied Henry Tudor with 5,000 men, including 1,000 Scots, for the invasion of England, and that 'John son of Robert Haddington was chief and leader of the Scots'.

Robert Lindsay of Pittscottie's *Chronicles* of the 1570s, drawing on oral tradition, states that

Henry Tudor arrives in England with 10,000 men, including 3,000 Englishmen, 6,000 Frenchmen and 1,000 Scots, namely the Scots company under Sir Alexander Bruce of Earlshall. Richard raises a vast army to resist him, numbering 100,000. Henry secretly tries to win over key nobles, most especially Lord Stanley, who was 'captain of 1,000 bows of ordinance which was a great part of King Richard's vanguard', promising to make him the greatest lord in the land, and Sir Edward Brackenbury, lieutenant of the Tower of London, captain of the ordnance in the royal vanguard. The two lords first demand of King Richard that he restore the lands of certain friends, formerly in the service of Edward IV. When he refuses, telling them to ask for rewards when they have performed service, they offer their support to Henry Tudor and promise to 'set the crown upon his head'. Henry is pleased and arrays his men, now 30,000 strong, with the vanguard of 10,000 men under the command of Alexander Bruce. Richard has to give battle, and determines to wear his crown. While in a tent, it is stolen for a short while by a Highlander called MacGregor.

The next day the two armies meet. Richard positions his vanguard with his great artillery. Henry marches forward first, but the royal vanguard 'that should have opposed them gave them place and let them go by, themselves turned around and faced King Richard as if they had been his enemies'. The two battle lines fight stoutly for a long while with uncertain victory, but at last many of King Richard's battle fled from him and passed to Prince Henry dreading that victory should fall to him at length. Some others of King Richard's army stood and looked on while they saw who had the victory. But this King Richard fought so cruelly that he was slain, for he would not be taken, and there was slain on his party with him the duke of Norfolk with many other lords and gentlemen and in like manner was taken alive his son the earl of Surrey and had to the Tower of London and put in prison where he remained a long time ever he was relieved. By this King Henry passed over this battle and won the victory thereof, and that by the Scots' and Frenchmen's support.

Bernard Stewart, 3rd Lord of Aubigny (*c.* 1452–1508), is the most intriguing character. He was a Franco-Scot, commander of the *Garde Écossaise*, and belonged to the Scottish family of Stewart of Darnley, which produced the English Stuart monarchs. Because of his family background and high favour with the French king, he was chosen as the envoy to James III of Scotland to announce the accession of Charles VIII of France. He was also given the task of signing a treaty with the Scots that renewed the Auld Alliance on 22 March 1483. The Lord of Aubigny was also the medium of communication for the section of Scottish lords who favoured Henry Tudor. Henry needed King Charles to finance the army and to be able to provide foot soldiers capable of fighting. In 1485, Bernard Stewart was said to be chosen to command the French troops that accompanied the invasion. A poem by John Beaumont describes his participation at Bosworth.

Blackadder at Bosworth

The pilot episode that began the TV comedy series *Blackadder* (1983–1989) begins with an alternative aftermath to Bosworth. According to Rowan Atkinson, the choice of the name *Blackadder* was fairly random – he needed a name that sounded devious. With truth being stranger than fiction, the 'Black Band of the Blackadders' figure in the Scottish Border feuds with the English. Cuthbert Blackadder and his seven sons were styled thus from their dark complexion, and took part in the Wars of the Roses, falling at Bosworth while fighting for the Lancastrians. The crest of the Blackadders includes three Tudor roses because of support given to Henry at Bosworth.

In a violent manner this family,

with the view of acquiring the lands of [Blackadder], having, by rapacity and fraud, appropriated to themselves, in course of time, the greater part of Berwickshire. The person on whom James the Second conferred the lands, and who from them took the surname of Blackadder, as a reward for military services, was named Cuthbert, styled the 'Chieftain of the South.' The royal grant is dated in 1452. On his expeditions against the English who crossed the borders for plunder he was accompanied by his seven sons who, from the darkness of their complexion, were called the 'Black band of the Blackadders' (*Writs of the Family*, quoted in Crichton's *Life of the Rev. John Blackadder*). When the country required to be put in a posture of defence against the preparations of Edward the Fourth, the Blackadders raised a body from among their kindred and retainers, the Elliots, Armstrongs, Johnstons, and other hardy and warlike borderers to the number of two hundred and seventeen men, all accounted with jack and spear.

Their castle, a fortress of some strength, was planted with artillery, and furnished with a garrison of twenty soldiers (*Ibid*. Redpath's *Border History*). Cuthbert and his sons joined the train of adventurers from Scotland, who had embarked in the wars of York and Lancaster, marshalling themselves under the banner of the Red Rose, and fighting for the earl of Richmond, afterwards Henry the Seventh, at Bosworth, where the father and three of his sons were left dead on the field. Andrew, the eldest of the surviving brothers, succeeded to the barony of Blackadder. Robert and Patrick entered into holy orders. The former became prior of Coldingham, the latter was made dean of Dunblane. The fourth brother, William, remained in England, where he obtained a title and opulent possessions (*Writs of the Family of Blackadder*). In memorial of their services at Bosworth, King James granted the family permission to carry on their shield the roses of York and Lancaster. It was afterwards quartered with the house of Edmonstone; field, azure; cheveron, argent; upper left hand, gules; crest, a dexter hand holding a broadsword; motto, 'Courage helps fortune.'

The Discovery of the Location of Bosworth

Until fieldwork in 2009, the battle's exact location was unknown, but the discovery of a small lead ball led to the finding of other small cannon projectiles from the battle. The pattern of distribution of the three dozen lead projectiles unearthed suggests an exchange of artillery fire by both sides. This probably influenced the way the battle was fought, encouraging the Lancastrian army to make a flank attack on Richard rather than face a frontal approach under heavy fire. Jean Molinet in 1490 wrote, 'The king had the artillery of his army fire on the earl of Richmond, and so the French, knowing by the king's shot the lie of the land and the order of his battle, resolved, in order to avoid the fire, to mass their troops against the flank rather than the front of the king's battle.' However, these weapons were not yet a battle-winning force, as the main action would have consisted of archery and then hand-to-hand fighting. Not until the Battle of Pinkie Cleugh in 1547 would an English army win a decisive victory in a major battle chiefly through the use of firepower. Most of the lead round shot discovered at Bosworth ranges in diameter from less than 30 mm up to 94 mm. Thus the train of artillery at Bosworth already contained some guns as large as a saker, the largest mobile field piece normally deployed on battlefields in succeeding centuries.

In contrast, only two or possibly three lead bullets – likely to have been fired by 'hand cannons', an early type of handgun with a large bore – have so far been recovered from the site. With one or two notable exceptions – such as at St Albans in 1461, when a company of foreign 'handgunners' were deployed – handheld firearms seem rarely employed by English armies until the mid-sixteenth century. The effectiveness of the English longbow meant that the introduction of the early handgun was not a priority here compared to other parts of Europe. There are so many different diameters of round shot at the site that there must have been at least ten pieces of artillery and perhaps two hand cannons present.

The finds show us that the battle was fought not far from Stoke Golding, two miles or so south-west of Ambion Hill, the traditional location of the action. In addition to locating the battlefield, the archaeological survey has unearthed the largest group of cannonballs and lead shot ever found on any medieval battlefield across Europe, ranging from bullets fired from handguns to round shot from substantial artillery pieces. In fact, the site features more lead round shot than on all the other battlefields of the fifteenth and sixteenth centuries in Europe put together. The scatter of round shot from artillery and bullets from handguns extends over a distance of more than a kilometre. The combined evidence proves that the battle was fought in the area between the villages of Dadlington, Shenton, Upton and Stoke Golding. Bosworth was not fought on the heights of Ambion Hill but two miles away in low-lying ground close to a Roman Road and beside a marsh known later as Fen Hole. Richard might have chosen this terrain because he was an artillery enthusiast and on this flat ground it could be used to best effect. But Henry's troops simply manoeuvred behind the protection of the marsh to attack the flank of Richard's army and so avoid the heavy artillery fire. Other finds from the new battle site include the evidence of a silver gilt badge in the shape of a boar, the emblem of the doomed king. It would almost certainly have been worn by one of the knights who rode with Richard to his death on his cavalry attack.

Dafydd ap Owen, Henry's Uncle, *c.* 1459–1535

Dafydd (or David or Davy) Owen was born at Pembroke, the illegitimate son of the widowed Owen Tudor. He seems to have originally been called

Dafydd Tudor. David Owen was with Henry when he landed in Wales, and fought with his half-brother Jasper and Henry at Bosworth. He seems to have married three times, firstly to Anne, daughter and heir of William Blount. She was co-heiress to Baron Mountjoy. Secondly he married Mary, daughter and co-heir of John de Bohun, of Midhurst, by whom he had three sons and a daughter. It is thought that Henry arranged this prosperous marriage for him. His sons were named Henry, Jasper and Roger. His daughter Anne married Sir Arthur Hopton.

David's third wife was Anne, sister to Walter Devereux, Lord Ferrers, of Chartley. It appears that he had two sons, Henry and John, esquire, and one daughter, Elizabeth, by this wife. Elizabeth married Sir Thomas Burgh. However, the *Book of Baglan* records that 'the wife of Sir David ap Owene, the 3 son to Owen Tudyr, was Joyes, the daughter of Sir Edward Crofte'. This appears to be wrong, for his son by Mary de Bohun, Sir Harry (or Henry) Owen, married Joyce Croft of Croft Castle. By an unknown mistress (or mistresses), David Owen also had one illegitimate son, William, and one illegitimate daughter, Barbara.

Henry granted his uncle Sir David Owen the manor of Oxhill, Warwickshire, following the forfeiture of John Catesby of Lapworth in 1485. David Owen was one of the twelve knight bachelors who held the canopy at the coronation of Queen Elizabeth of York in 1487. In 1489, he was granted the manors of Little Creaton and Old, Northamptonshire, forfeited by William Catesby. He was probably made a knight banneret in 1493. In 1526, he was among those who escorted the king to Petworth. He became the king's carver, and Knight of the Body to Henry VIII. Sir David was a knight of Westminster, Middlesex; Old, Northamptonshire; Lagham (in Godstone) and Wotton, Surrey; Oxhill, Warwickshire; Southwick (in North Bradley), Wiltshire; and, in right of his first wife, of Cowdray (in Midhurst), Clemping, Easebourne, Ford, and Newtimber, Sussex. His effigy is in Easeborne church, near Midhurst, Sussex.

The Lost Tudor Plays

On 8 November 1599, the Admiral's Men at the Rose Theatre had paid £8 for a play by Robert Wilson called *Henry Richmond, Part 2* about Owen Tudor's grandson. The Admiral's Men bought this play while they were still performing at the Rose, before moving to the Fortune in the fall of 1600. Across Maid Lane, they could see the newly built Globe in operation, where a likely offering was (or had recently been) Shakespeare's *Henry V*. They bought *Owen Tudor*, a play related in historical and genealogical subject matter, the following January. This is shown in *Henslowe's Diary*, where we read of payments to playwrights: 'Lent vnto mihell drayton antony monday mr hathwaye & mr willsone at the apoyntment of Thomas downton in earneste of a playe Boocke called owen teder the some of ... iiijli.' From the same source, we read, 'Ye 10 of Jenewary 1599 – Receyved in pt of payment & in er[e]nest of a playe called Owen Tweder the somme of foure poundes wittnes or hands ... iiijli Ri: Hathwaye R Wilson. An: Mundy – witnes Robt Shaa.'

Englishmen took little interest in the Welsh connection of their rulers. *Owen Tudor* was commissioned by the London impresario Philip Henslowe, who paid an advance of £4 to the playwright Anthony Munday and three collaborators. It must have been a poor investment, for there is no trace of any performance. Owen Tudor was ignored by Shakespeare in his histories: perhaps he judged it too indiscreet to dwell on the circumstances of the mésalliance. However, in 1603 the Welsh writer Hugh Holland published the first (and only) book of his *Pancharis*, which related the love between Owen Tudor and Katherine of Valois.

In 1751, a novel entitled *The Life and Amours of Owen Tideric, Prince of Wales Otherwise Owen Tudor* was published. Its unnamed author claimed that the novel was based on history and its story widely current in France. The narrative is that Owen Tudor was sent to the court of France as a representative of Wales. He and Katherine fell in love before Henry V invaded France and defeated the French forces, but, believing himself unworthy, Owen went away, leaving Katherine at the disposal of her father, at which point Henry claims her as a war prize. The novel has enough conventions of the romance – a relatively lowborn but morally superior foreigner falls in love with an unattainable beauty and chooses exile over rejection – to remove any doubt that the story is not historical, but if its elements were also known in England as early as 1599, it could nonetheless have provided the Admiral's Men with a counter-narrative to that in the Globe play by Shakespeare, *Henry V*.

Pancharis

Hugh Holland (1571–1633), son of the Welsh poet Robert Holland, was a contemporary of Ben Jonson who travelled on the Continent and in the Middle East. After his conversion to Catholicism, he was imprisoned in Constantinople for abusing Queen Elizabeth. Holland was patronised by Buckingham and contributed a sonnet to the Shakespeare's First Folio. Much of his 1603 work *Pancharis: The Love Between Owen Tudyr and the Queen* features Jasper Tudor speaking about the circumstances of his father's romance, for instance:

> JASPER: They all together in the wardrobe met,
> And them among (though far above them all)
> The gentle Owen was: a man well set;
> Broad were his shoulders, though his waist but small;
> Straight was his back, and even was his breast,
> Which no less seemly made him show then tall.
> Such as Achilles seemed among the rest

Of all his army clad in mighty brass:
Among them such (though all they of the best)
The man of Mone [Anglesey], magnifique Owen, was.
He seemed another oak among the briars;
And as in stature, so did he surpass
In wit, and active feats, his other peers.
He nimbly could discourse, and nimbly dance,
And aged he was about some thirty years:
But armed had ye seen him go to France,
Ye would have said, that few on foot or horse
Could have so tossed a pike, or couched a lance,
Wherewith to ground he brought full many a corpse;
That oft alone when I recount the fame,
My tender heart cannot but have remorse:
To write it then, alas! I were too blame.

The Ghost of Jasper

This is an intriguing entry in Bacon, as Jasper had died in December 1495, which nevertheless shows Jasper's extended deathly service to the king. It refers to the Cornish rebels at Blackheath in June 1497:

REBELS AT BLACKHEATH

Nevertheless both Tate the lord mayor, and Shaw and Haddon the sheriffs, did their parts stoutly and well, in arming and ordering the people. And the King likewise did adjoin some captains of experience in the wars, to advise and assist the citizens. But soon after, when they understood that the King had so ordered the matter, that the rebels must win three battles, before they could approach the city, and that he had put his own person between the rebels and them, and that the great care was, rather how to impound the rebels that none of them might escape, than that any doubt was made to vanquish them: they grew to be quiet and out of fear; the rather, for the confidence they reposed, which was not small, in the three leaders, Oxford, Essex, and Daubeney; all men well famed and loved to amongst the people. *As for Jasper duke of Bedford, whom the king used to employ with the first in his wars, he was then sick, and died soon after.* It was the two and twentieth of June, and a Saturday, which was the day of the week the King fancied, when the battle was fought; though the King had, by all the art he could devise, given out a false day, as if he prepared to give the rebels battle on the Monday following, the better to find them unprovided, and in disarray...

Henry's Illegitimate Son? Sir Roland de Velville (1471?–1535)

An extract from an elegy to Sir Roland de Velville by Daffyd Alaw in 1535 describes him as 'gwr o lin brenhinoedd / ag o waed ieirll i gyd oedd' (a man of kingly line / and of earl's blood). As this was broadcast in the reign of Henry VIII, just twenty-six years after Henry VII's death, we must give the claim some consideration. Roland de Velville (also spelt Vielleville, Veleville or more correctly, Vieilleville) was constable of Beaumaris Castle from 1509 to 1535. He was reputed to have been a natural son of Henry VII, born to a Breton lady while Henry was in exile in Brittany. He definitely accompanied Henry from France on his invasion, being aged possibly between eleven and fourteen. It is possible that Henry Tudor had actually been married to de Velville's mother, who may have died shortly after the marriage or in childbirth. Prior to 1483, Henry had virtually no prospect of succeeding to the throne of England as there were several legitimate heirs living at that time. He even had very little prospect of ever returning to England without being imprisoned or killed. He therefore had little incentive to remain unmarried.

However, Roland Velville figures insignificantly in the records of the reign of Henry VII, whose servant he was. He was given 'by way of reward' ten marks in 1488, and figures among the esquires who took part in the tournaments held at the creation of Prince Henry as Duke of York in 1494. De Velville was given, as 'king's servant', a grant for life of an annuity of 40 marks out of the issues of the county of Wiltshire. After the Battle of Blackheath, he was knighted on 17 June 1497, and as Sir Roland he was summoned to attend upon the king during the prolonged reception of the Archduke Philip in 1500. After Blackheath, de Velville married Agnes Griffith, a distant cousin of the king, a daughter of the most powerful family in North Wales at the time, the Griffiths of Penrhyn. The Tudor patrimony at Penmynydd in Anglesey was granted away, partly to the abbey of Conway and partly to de Velville.

Under Henry VIII he was appointed to be constable of Beaumaris Castle in 1509, making him one of the richest men in North Wales, and was given during pleasure an annuity of twenty pounds. In 1512, as 'a native of Brittany', de Velville was granted letters of denization for himself and the heir of his body, probably to assist him in acquiring new estates. He was summoned to attend Henry VIII during his meeting with Charles V at Gravelines in 1520. Even after his allowance of nearly £300 a year for soldiers' wages at Beaumaris was discontinued in 1516, his income from his annuities and constable's fee was over £240 a year. Altogether, during Henry VIII's reign de Velville received £6,176 13s 4d from the chamberlain of North Wales and a further £1,236 13s 4d from Exchequer revenues. In his will, de Velville directed that he should be buried in the monastery of the Friars Minor of Llanfaes, the burial place of Goronwy ap Tudor (d. 1382).

For twenty-five or more years he lived at court, clearly a favourite of the king, participating in numerous jousts and accompanying the king out hunting. He was a courtier, not a 'servant', and mixed on equal terms with the highest members of the aristocracy, including the Duke of Buckingham. Rumours concerning his royal parentage were certainly current in North Wales during his own lifetime and it appears that he was believed to be Henry VII's son by his family and immediate circle, as well as by his notable descendants, such as Katherine of Berain, the 'Mother of Wales'.

Jasper's Widow

Katherine Woodville passed away on 18 May 1497, aged around forty. She had been the wife of the executed Henry Stafford, Duke of Buckingham, then Jasper Tudor, Duke of Bedford and Earl of Pembroke, and finally Sir Richard Wingfield. She was a sister to Queen Elizabeth Woodville and, out of around thirteen children, she was probably the youngest daughter of Jacquetta of Luxembourg and Richard Woodville, 1st Earl Rivers. She first married when still a child, sometime in 1465, to Henry Stafford, Duke of Buckingham, with whom she had four children. The oldest, Edward, was born in 1478, and succeeded his father as Duke of Buckingham, followed by Elizabeth, Henry, Humphrey (who died young) and Anne. The marriage was, according to Dominic Mancini, said to be unhappy. Mancini declared that Henry Stafford 'had his own reasons for detesting the queen's kin; for, when he was younger, he had been forced to wed the queen's sister, whom he scorned to wed on account of her humble origin'.

Katherine's life changed drastically in 1483. Buckingham, along with Richard, Duke of Gloucester, was responsible for the illegal capture and execution of Katherine's brother and nephew Anthony Woodville (Earl Rivers) and Richard Grey. Gloucester then seized the crown as Richard III, whereupon Buckingham rebelled against the monarch he had given all of his support. He was executed on 2 November 1483. The newly widowed Katherine found herself in a difficult situation, with four very young children.

Just two years later, on 7 November 1485, Katherine married Jasper Tudor. Jasper and Katherine's marriage was a one of strategic benefits and whether they were happy together is unknown. Jasper's will left her little, and Katherine, now in her late 30s, very hastily married Richard Wingfield, twelve years her junior, without a royal licence. Perhaps she had an affair with Wingfield before Jasper's death and Jasper knew about it. Henry VII fined the couple £2,000 for marrying without his consent. Katherine had probably known Wingfield for some time. Wingfield's mother was connected to Anthony Woodville's second wife, Mary, and two of his brothers – and perhaps Richard himself – had served in Katherine's household. She died of unknown causes barely one year after remarrying, and her burial place is unknown. Wingfield remarried and had many children with his second wife, Bridget Wiltshire. In his will of 1525, Wingfield requested masses to be said for Katherine's soul.

Select Bibliography

Abbott, Jacob, *Margaret of Anjou, Queen, consort of Henry VI, King of England 1430–1482* (Harper, 1871).

Alexander, Michael Van Cleave, *The First of the Tudors: a study of Henry VII and his reign* (Rowman & Littlefield, 1980).

Allanic, J., *Le prisonnier de la tour d'Elven ou la jeunesse du Roy Henri VII* (Vannes, 1909).

Arthurson, Ian, 'Espionage and Intelligence from the Wars of the Roses to the Reformation', *Nottingham Medieval Studies*, XXXV (1991).

Ayton, Andrew, 'Arms, Armour, and Horses' in Maurice Keen (ed.), *Medieval Warfare* (Oxford University Press, 1999).

Baird, Ian Forbes, *Poems concerning the Stanley Family (Earls of Derby) 1485–1520* (unpublished PhD thesis: Birmingham University, 1989).

Blakman, John, *Henry VI, King of England 1421–1471*, ed. M. R. James (Cambridge University Press, 1919).

Boardman, Andrew W., *The Medieval Soldier in the Wars of the Roses* (Stroud, 1998).

Breverton, Terry, *Owain Glyndŵr: The Last Prince of Wales* (Amberley, 2013).

Breverton, Terry, *Richard III: The King in the Car Park* (Amberley, 2013).

Carr, A. D., 'Gwilym ap Gruffydd and the rise of the Penrhyn estate', *Welsh History Review*, 15 (1990–91).

Chrimes, S. B., *Henry VII* (Eyre Methuen, 1972).

Christie, Mabel E., *Henry VI* (Houghton Mifflin, 1922).

Cunningham, Sean, *Henry VII* (Routledge, 2007).

Cymmrodorion, Honourable Society of, *The Poetical Works of Lewis Glyn Cothi: A Celebrated Bard* (Oxford, 1837).

Davies, J. S. (ed.), *An English Chronicle of the Reigns of Richard II, Henry IV, Henry V and Henry VI 1377–1461* (Camden Society, 1856).

DeVries, Kelly, *Medieval Military Technology* (Broadview Press, 1992).

Dockray, Keith, *Henry VI, Margaret of Anjou and the Wars of the Roses: A Source Book* (Sutton, 2000).

Domville, Lady Margaret, *The King's Mother: Memoir of Margaret Beaufort, Countess of Richmond and Derby* (London, 1899).

Drayton, Michael, *Englands Heroicall Epistles* (1597) in J. W. Hebel (ed.), *The Works of Michael Drayton* (Oxford, 1961).

Duncumb, John, *Collections towards the History and Antiquities of the County of Hereford* (Hereford, 1804).

Ellis, Henry (ed.), *Polydore Vergil's English History [1525], Comprising the Reigns of Henry VI, Edward IV and Richard III* (Camden Society, 1844).

Ellis, Richard, *The History of Thornbury Castle* (John Wright, 1839).

Evans, H. T., *Wales and the Wars of the Roses* (Alan Sutton, 1995).

Fabyan, Robert, *The Chronicles of England and France*, ed. Henry Ellis (London, 1811).

Foarde, Glenne & Anne Curry, *Bosworth 1485: A Battlefield Rediscovered* (Oxbow, 2013).

Gairdner, James (ed.), *A Short English Chronicle in Three Fifteenth Century Chronicles* (Camden Society, 1809).

Gairdner, James (ed.), *The historical collections of a citizen of London in the fifteenth century (Gregory's Chronicle)* (Camden Society, 1876).

Gairdner, James (ed.), *The Paston Letters 1422–1509* (London, 1900).

Gairdner, James, *Henry the Seventh* (1889).

Gasquet, Cardinal Francis, *The Religious Life of King Henry VI* (London, 1923).

Goodman, Anthony, *The Wars of the Roses: Military Activity and English Society, 1452–97* (Dorset Press, 1981).

Griffith, Ralph A. & Roger Thomas, *The Making of the Tudor Dynasty* (St Martin's Press, 1985).

Griffiths, Ann, *Rhai agweddau at y syniad o genedl yng nghyfnod y cywydwyr 1320–1603* (unpublished PhD thesis: Aberystwyth, 1988).

Griffiths, Ralph A. & James Sherborwe, (eds), *Kings and Nobles in the Later Middle Ages* (St Martin's Press, 1986).

Griffiths, Ralph A., 'Wales and the Marches' in S. B. Chrimes, C. D. Ross & Ralph A. Griffiths (eds), *Fifteenth-Century England, 1399–1509* (Alan Sutton, 1995).

Griffiths, Ralph A., *King and Country: England and Wales in the Fifteenth Century* (Hambledon Press, 1991).

Griffiths, Ralph A., *The Principality of Wales in the Later Middle Ages* (Cardiff, 1972).

Griffiths, Ralph A., *The Reign of King Henry VI: The Exercise of Royal Authority 1422–1461* (University of California Press, 1981).

Gruffudd, Elis, *Cronicl o Wech Oesoedd* (Chronicle of the Six Ages of the World) (*c.* 1545).

Haigh, Philip A., *The Military Campaigns of the Wars of the Roses* (Sutton Publishing, 1995).

Hall, Edward, *Chronicle containing the History of England from Henry VI to Henry VIII*, ed. Henry Ellis (London, 1809).

Halliwell-Phillipps, James Orchard (ed.), *Warkworth's Chronicle of the first thirteen years of the reign of King Edward IV* (London, 1839).

Halsted, Caroline, *Life of Margaret Beaufort, Countess of Richmond and Derby* (London, 1839).

Harrison, Wilfred, *Some Aspects of Tenby's History* (Tenby Museum, 1985).

Harriss, G. L. & M. A. (eds), 'John Benet's Chronicle for the years 1400 to 1462', *Camden Miscellany*, 24 (Camden Society, 1972).

Heywood, Thomas, *Song of Lady Bessy, the eldest daughter of King Edward IV; and how she married King Henry the Seventh of the House of Lancaster* (London, 1829).

Hodges, Geoffrey, *Ludford Bridge and Mortimer's Cross the Wars of the Roses in Herefordshire and the Welsh Marches* (Logaston Press, 2001).

Holland, Hugh, *Pancharis: The Love Between Owen Tudyr and the Queen* (1603).

Humphreys, Emyr, *The Taliesin Tradition* (Seren, 2000).

Jones, Emyr Wyn, 'Bosworth Field: A Selective Historiography', *National Library of Wales Journal* (Summer 1979).

Jones, Michael K., 'Sir William Stanley of Holt: Politics and Family Allegiance in the Late Fifteenth Century', *Welsh History Review*, 14(1–4) (1988–1989).

Jones, Michael K., *The King's Mother: Lady Margaret Beaufort, Countess of Richmond and Derby* (Cambridge University Press, 1992).

Jones, W. Garmon, 'Welsh Nationalism and Henry Tudor', *Transactions of the Honourable Society of Cymmrodorion* (1917–1918).

Kingsford, C. L., *Chronicles of London* (Oxford, 1905).

Lindsay, Robert of Pittscottie, *The Historie of Scotland from the Slauchter of King James the First to the Ane Thousande Fyve Hundreith Thrie Scoir Fyftein Yeir*, ed. A. J. G. Makay (Scottish Text Society, 1899–1911).

Lloyd, Jacob Youde William, *History of the Princes, the Lords Marcher and the Ancient Nobility of Powys Fadog* (T. Richards, 1882).

Owen H. & J. B. Blakeway, *A History of Shrewsbury* (1825).

Major, John, *A History of Greater Britain*, in A. Constable (ed.) (Scottish Historical Society, 1892).

Mirehouse, Mary Beatrice, *South Pembrokeshire: Some of its History and Records* (David Nutt, 1910).

Nicholas, Thomas, *Annals and Antiquities of the Counties and County Families of Wales* (Longmans, 1872).

Prestwich, Michael, *Armies and Warfare in the Middle Ages: The English Experience* (Yale University Press, 1996).

Rees, David, 'Sir Rhys ap Thomas', *The Journal of Pembrokeshire Historical Society*, 2 (1986–1987).

Rees, David, *The Son of Prophecy: Henry Tudor's Road to Bosworth* (Black Raven Press, 1985).

Richards, W. Leslie, *Gwaith Dafydd Llwyd of Fathafarn* (Gwasg Prifysgol Cymru, 1964).

Roberts, Peter, 'The Welshness of the Tudors, *History Today*, 36(1) (1986).

Roberts, G., 'Wyrion Eden: the Anglesey descendants of Ednyfed Fychan in the fourteenth century', *Transactions of the Anglesey Antiquarian Society and Field Club* (1951).

Roberts, G., 'Teulu Penmynydd', *Transactions of the Honourable Society of Cymmrodorion* (1959).

Roberts, Thomas & Ifor Williams, *The Poetical Works of Dafydd Nanmor* (Cardiff, 1923).

Simons, Eric N., *Henry VII, the First Tudor King* (1968).

Skidmore, Chris, *Bosworth: The Birth of the Tudors* (Weidenfield & Nicholson, 2013).

Starkey, David, *Henry, Virtuous Prince* (Harper Press, 2008).

Temperley, Gladys, *Henry VII* (London, 1917).

Thomas, Lawrence Beckley, *The Thomas book, giving the genealogies of Sir Rhys ap Thomas, K. G., the Thomas family descended from him, and of some allied families* (New York, 1896).

Thomas, Roger Stuart, *The Political Career, Estates and 'Connection' of Jasper Tudor, Earl of Pembroke and Duke of Bedford* (unpublished PhD thesis: Swansea, 1971).

Tout, Thomas Frederick, *The Collected Papers of Thomas Frederick Tout with a Memoir and Bibliography* (Manchester University Press, 1934).

Vergil, Polydore, *English History* (Camden Society, 1844).

Warkworth, J., *A Chronicle of the First Thirteen Years of the Reign of King Edward the Fourth 1461–1474*, in J. O. Halliwell (ed.) (Camden Society, 1839).

Watts, John, *Henry VI and the Politics of Kingship* (Cambridge University Press, 1999).

Waurin, Jehan de, *Recueil des Chroniques, etc., Vol. V.*, in William Hardy (ed.) (Rolls Series, 1864–91).

Weir, Alison, *Lancaster and York: The War of the Roses* (London, 1995).

William of Worcester, *Annales Rerum Anglicarum*, in Joseph Stevenson (ed.) (Rolls Series, 1864).

Williams, Gruffydd Aled, 'The Bardic Road to Bosworth: A Welsh View of Henry Tudor', *Transactions of the Honourable Society of Cymmrodorion* (1986).

Williams, John, *Ancient & Modern Denbigh: A Descriptive History of the Castle, Borough & Liberties* (Williams, 1836).

Williams, A. H., *The Early History of Denbighshire* (1950).

Williams, Glanmor, *Harri Tudur a Chymru (Henry Tudor and Wales)* (Gwasg Prifysgol Cymru, 1985).

Williams, Glanmor, *Renewal and Reformation: Wales, c. 1415–1642* (Oxford University Press, 1993).

Williams, Neville, *The Life and Times of Henry VI* (Weidenfield & Nicolson, 1973).

Winston, J. E., *English Towns in the Wars of the Roses* (unpublished PhD thesis: Princeton and Oxford, 1921).

Wolffe, Bertram, *Henry VI* (Methuen, 1983).

Wright, Thomas (ed.), *Political Songs and Poems Relating to English History*, Vols I and II (Rolls Series, 1859–1861).

List of Illustrations

Genealogical Tables

The royal descent from Edward I. (Author's collection)
The Lancastrian line of descent from Edward III. (Courtesy of Amy Licence)
The origins of the Tudors. (Author's collection)

1. Jasper Tudor and his wife from stained-glass windows in Cardiff Castle. (Author's collection)
2, 3 & 4. The coats of arms of Owen Tudor, Edmund Tudor and Jasper Tudor respectively. Jasper and Edmund were given the arms of England, quartered lions and lilies, by Henry VI with the augmentation of a border. Though very similar, on closer viewing the coats of arms of Jasper and Edmund are different – to distinguish the brothers, while Jasper's arms had the addition of *abordure azure with martlets or* (a blue border featuring golden martlets), for Edmund the martlets were alternated with the lilies of France in honour of the firstborn of Catherine of Valois. The martlets were a device used by their father, Owen Tudor. (Courtesy of Sodacan under Creative Commons 3.0)
5. Jasper Tudor's mother, Catherine of Valois (1401–1437), the daughter of Charles VI of France. Here she is marrying her first husband, Henry V (1386–1422), on 2 June 1420. He died young, never seeing his infant son, Henry VI. Catherine later married Jasper's father, Owen Tudor. (© Jonathan Reeve JR1729b90fp85 14001500)
6. Pembroke town walls and castle were repaired by Jasper Tudor. The walls run almost two miles around a narrow peninsula in which the town lies, with the castle at its tip. Remains include four of the six flanking towers and one of the three gatehouses. Barnard's Tower is the most complete survivor, overlooking the great mill pond. (Author's collection)
7. Pembroke Castle from the air. The double-towered Great Gatehouse is on the left, with the Henry VII Tower the first guard tower on the left of it. The domed, circular Great Keep is seventy-five feet high, with walls twenty feet thick at its base. The castle and its earldom were granted to Jasper Tudor in 1452. (Author's collection)

18. View in the morning mist from Wigmore Castle, the great stronghold of the Mortimers in the Marches, where Edward IV stayed before the Battle of Mortimer's Cross in 1461. (Author's collection)

19. Battlefield site at Mortimer's Cross, taken from the bridge over the Lugg. The Lancastrians did not wish to fight but were forced to as they wished to cross the river and join Margaret's northern army. Some 4,000 out of 9,000 men who fought are said to have died. (Author's collection)

20. Memorial monument at Mortimer's Cross, near the battlefield, erected in 1799. The battle was fought in the River Lugg's water meadows between here and Kingsland. (Author's collection)

21. Harlech Castle, one of Edward I's 'Iron Ring of Castles'. The World Heritage Site, which was then lapped by the sea, held out for seven years against various sieges and attacks from 1461 to 1468. (Author's collection)

22. Twt Hill in 1461 was the scene of the defeat of Jasper in 1468. It is a small hill, the site of a previous battle outside the walls of Caernarfon Castle, where Glyndŵr unfurled his golden lion flag for the first time in 1401. (Courtesy of Paul Remfrey)

23. Chepstow Castle, showing the lower bailey from Marten's Tower. After hearing of the defeat at Tewkesbury in 1471, Jasper returned here. In the lower bailey he may have beheaded Sir Roger Vaughan, who had been sent to kill him. (Author's collection)

24. Tretower Court Main Hall – this fortified manor house alongside Tretower Castle was renovated and extended by Sir Roger Vaughan, when granted to him by William Herbert. (Author's collection)

25. Tomb of Thomas and John White. In St Mary's Church, Tenby, lie the effigies of father and son Thomas and John White, both merchant and mayor. Thomas was mayor in 1471 and is said to have hidden Henry and Jasper in his house in that year. Each man lies with a peacock at his head and a hart at his feet. Their wives and children are depicted on the sides of the alabaster tombs, coffins denoting those that died in infancy. (Author's collection)

26. Underground medieval passage from the demolished White's House, next to the church of St Mary's in Tenby, leading under Upper Frog Street to Jasperley House, now Boots the Chemist. (Author's collection)

27. Engraving by Charles Norris in 1812 of the ruins of White's House next to the medieval church of St Mary in the walled town of Tenby. (Author's collection)

28. Cellar under Mayor White's House, Tenby, where Jasper and Henry hid for three days while waiting for a boat and favourable winds and tide to take them to France. (Author's collection)

29. Tenby Harbour – a tunnel led from Jasperley House to the harbour to allow the easy escape of Henry and Jasper. Tenby was an important

More Kings and Queens of England from Amberley Publishing

THE TUDORS
Richard Rex

'The best introduction to England's most important dynasty'
DAVID STARKEY

£9.99   978-1-4456-0700-9   272 pages PB 143 illus, 66 col

RICHARD III
David Baldwin

'A believably complex Richard, neither wholly villain nor hero'
PHILIPPA GREGORY

£9.99   978-1-4456-1591-2   296 pages PB 80 illus, 60 col

KATHARINE OF ARAGON
Patrick Williams

'Williams has the courage to march in where most biographers have feared to tread'
BBC HISTORY MAGAZINE

£25.00   978-1-84868-325-9   512 pages HB   70 col illus

WILLIAM THE CONQUEROR
Peter Rex

'Rex has a real ability to communicate difficult issues to a wide audience'
BBC HISTORY MAGAZINE

£12.99   978-1-4456-0698-9   304 pages PB 43 illus, 30 col

ENGLAND'S QUEENS: THE BIOGRAPHY
Elizabeth Norton

'A truly enlightening read' **THEANNEBOLEYNFILES.COM**

£16.99   978-1-4456-0904-1   432 pages PB 241 illus, 184 col

HENRY VIII
David Loades

'David Loades Tudor biographies are both highly enjoyable and instructive, the perfect combination' **ANTONIA FRASER**

£12.99   978-1-4456-0704-7   512 pages PB 113 illus, 49 col

CATHERINE PARR
Elizabeth Norton

'Norton cuts an admirably clear path through tangled Tudor intrigues'
JENNY UGLOW

£9.99   978-1-4456-0383-4   304 pages PB 49 illus, 39 col

ANNE BOLEYN
Lacey Baldwin Smith

'The perfect introduction'
SUZANNAH LIPSCOMB, BBC HISTORY MAGAZINE

£20.00   978-1-4456-1023-8   240 pages HB 60 illus, 40 col

THE KINGS AND QUEENS OF ENGLAND
David Loades

£25.00   978-1-4456-0582-1
512 pages HB   200 illus, 150 col

ELFRIDA
Elizabeth Norton

£20.00   978-1-4456-1486-1
224 pages HB   40 illus

ELIZABETH OF YORK
Amy Licence

£20.00   978-1-4456-0961-4
272 pages HB   40 illus, 10 col

EDWARD THE CONFESSOR
Peter Rex

£12.99   978-1-4456-0476-3
256 pages PB   30 col illus

More Kings & Queens of England from Amberley Publishing

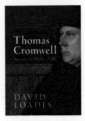  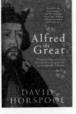 

THOMAS CROMWELL
David Loades

'Fresh, fair, lucid and a pleasure to read'
HILARY MANTEL

£25.99   978-1-4456-1538-7   352 pages HB 27 illus, 20 col

INSIDE THE TUDOR COURT
Lauren Mackay

'A superb, sound, engagingly written & much needed study...
highly recommended'
ALISON WEIR

£20.00   978-1-4456-0957-7   288 pages HB

ALFRED THE GREAT
David Horspool

'If you have time to read just one book about the great man, you
should make it this one'
THE DAILY TELEGRAPH

£9.99   978-1-4456-3936-9   272 pages PB 40 illus, 30 col

THE PRINCES IN THE TOWER
Josephine Wilkinson

'Wilkinson investigates the prime suspects, asks wether they might have
survived and presents her own theory about what really happened to them'
ALL ABOUT HISTORY

£18.99   978-1-4456-1974-3   192 pages HB

 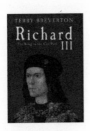  

QUEEN VICTORIA & THE STALKER
Jan Bondeson

'The amazing story of the first celebrity stalker' **THE SUN**

£12.99   978-1-4456-0697-2   224 pages PB 47 illus

RICHARD III
Terry Breverton

£16.99   978-1-4456-2105-0   200 pages HB 20 col illus

CATHERINE HOWARD
Lacey Baldwin Smith

'Beautifully written'
SUZANNAH LIPSCOMB, BBC HISTORY MAGAZINE

£9.99   978-1-84868-521-5   288 pages PB 25 col illus

JANE SEYMOUR
David Loades

£20.00   978-1-4456-1157-0   192 pages HB 40 illus, 20 col

RICHARD III	THE KINGS AND QUEENS OF ENGLAND	ANNE OF CLEVES	RICHARD III
Amy Licence	Robert J. Parker	Elizabeth Norton	Peter Rex
£9.99 978-1-4456-2175-3	£9.99 978-1-4456-1497-7	£9.99 978-1-4456-0183-0	£12.99 978-1-4456-0476-3
96 pages PB 75 col illus	128 pages PB 80 illus	224 pages PB 57 illus, 27 col	256 pages PB 30 col illus

Also available as ebooks
Available from all good bookshops or to order direct
Please call **01453-847-800 www.amberleybooks.com**

Tudor History from Amberley Publishing

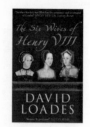

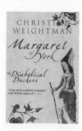

THE TUDORS
Richard Rex

'The best introduction to England's most important dynasty'
DAVID STARKEY
'Gripping and told with enviable narrative skill... a delight'
THES
'Vivid, entertaining and carrying its learning lightly'
EAMON DUFFY
'A lively overview' *THE GUARDIAN*

£9.99   978-1-4456-0700-9   256 pages PB 143 illus., 66 col

CATHERINE HOWARD
Lacey Baldwin Smith

'A brilliant, compelling account' *ALISON WEIR*
'A faultless book' *THE SPECTATOR*
'Lacey Baldwin Smith has so excellently caught the
atmosphere of the Tudor age' *THE OBSERVER*

£9.99   978-1-84868-521-5   256 pages PB 25 col illus

MARGARET OF YORK
Christine Weightman

'A pioneering biography of the Tudor dynasty's most
dangerous enemy'
PROFESSOR MICHAEL HICKS
'Christine Weightman brings Margaret alive once more'
THE YORKSHIRE POST
'A fascinating account of a remarkable woman'
THE BIRMINGHAM POST

£10.99   978-1-4456-0819-8   256 pages PB 51 illus

THE SIX WIVES OF HENRY VIII
David Loades

'Neither Starkey nor Weir has the assurance and command
of Loades' *SIMON HEFFER, LITERARY REVIEW*
'Incisive and profound. I warmly recommend this book'
ALISON WEIR

£9.99   978-1-4456-0049-9   256 pages PB 55 illus, 31 col

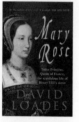

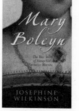

MARY ROSE
David Loades

£20.00 978-1-4456-0622-4
272 pages HB 17 col illus

MARY BOLEYN
Josephine Wilkinson

£9.99 978-1-84868-525-3
208 pages PB 22 illus, 10 col

JANE SEYMOUR
Elizabeth Norton

£9.99 978-1-84868-527-7
224 pages PB 53 illus, 26 col

HENRY VIII
Richard Rex

£9.99 978-1-84868-098-2
192 pages PB 81 illus, 48 col

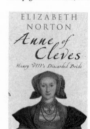

THOMAS CROMWELL
Patrick Coby

£20.00 978-1-4456-0775-7
272 pages HB 30 illus (20 col)

ANNE BOLEYN THE
YOUNG QUEEN TO BE
Josephine Wilkinson
£9.99 978-1-4456-0395-7
208 pages PB 34 illus (19 col)

ELIZABETH I
Richard Rex

£9.99 978-1-84868-423-2
192 pages PB 75 illus

ANNE OF CLEVES
Elizabeth Norton

£9.99 978-1-4456-0183-0
224 pages HB 54 illus, 27 col

Available from all good bookshops or to order direct
Please call **01453-847-800** www.amberleybooks.com

More Tudor History from Amberley Publishing

HENRY VIII
David Loades

'David Loades Tudor biographies are both highly enjoyable and instructive, the perfect combination' *ANTONIA FRASER*

£12.99   978-1-4456-0704-7   512 pages HB 113 illus, 49 col

ANNE BOLEYN
Elizabeth Norton

'Meticulously researched and a great read'
THEANNEBOLEYNFILES.COM

£9.99   978-1-84868-514-7   264 pages PB 47 illus, 26 col

THE TUDORS VOL 1
G. J. Meyer

'His style is crisp and popular'
PROFESSOR DAVID LOADES

£12.99   978-1-4456-0143-4   384 pages PB 72 illus, 54 col

THE TUDORS VOL 2
G. J. Meyer

'A sweeping history of the gloriously infamous Tudor era'
KIRKUS REVIEW

£12.99   978-1-4456-0144-1   352 pages PB 53 illus, 15 col

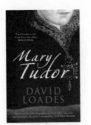

ANNE BOLEYN
P. Friedmann

'A compelling and lively biography... meticulously researched and supremely readable classic of Tudor biography' *DR RICHARD REX*
'The first scholarly biography' *THE FINANCIAL TIMES*

£20.00   978-1-84868-827-8   352 pages HB 47 illus, 20 col

MARY TUDOR
David Loades

£12.99   978-1-4456-0818-1   328 pages HB 59 illus, 10 col

CATHERINE PARR
Elizabeth Norton

'Norton cuts an admirably clear path through tangled Tudor intrigues'
JENNY UGLOW
'Wonderful... a joy to read'
HERSTORIA

£9.99   978-1-4456-0383-4   312 pages HB 49 illus, 30 col

MARGARET BEAUFORT
Elizabeth Norton

£9.99   978-1-4456-0578-4   256 pages HB 70 illus, 40 col

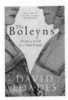

IN BED WITH THE TUDORS
Amy Licence

£20.00   978-1-4456-0693-4
272 pages HB   30 illus, 20 col

THE BOLEYNS
David Loades

£10.99   978-1-4456-0958-4
312 pages HB   34 illus, 33 col

BESSIE BLOUNT
Elizabeth Norton

£25.00   978-1-84868-870-4
384 pages HB   77 illus, 75 col

ANNE BOLEYN
Norah Lofts

£18.99   978-1-4456-0619-4
208 pages HB   75 illus, 46 col

Available from all good bookshops or to order direct
Please call **01453-847-800 www.amberleybooks.com**

More Tudor History from Amberley Publishing

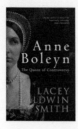

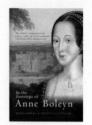

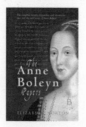

ANNE BOLEYN
Lacey Baldwin Smith

'The perfect introduction'
SUZANNAH LIPSCOMBE

£20.00   978-1-4456-1023-8   240 pages HB 60 illus, 40 col

INSIDE THE TUDOR COURT
Lauren MacKay

'Superb... highly recommended'
ALISON WEIR

Feb 2014 £20.00   978-1-4456-0957-7   240 pages HB

THE ANNE BOLEYN PAPERS
Elizabeth Norton

'A very useful compilation of source material on Anne'
ALISON WEIR

£12.99   978-1-4456-1288-1   384 pages PB

IN THE FOOTSTEPS OF ANNE BOLEYN
Sarah Morris & Natalie Grueninger

£20.00   978-1-4456-0782-5   288 pages HB 100 illus, 70 col

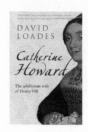

KATHARINE OF ARAGON
Patrick Williams

£25.00   978-1-84868-325-9   512 pages HB 70 col illus

THOMAS CROMWELL
J. Patrick Coby

£20.00   978-1-4456-0775-7   292 pages HB 30 illus, 10 col

ELIZABETH OF YORK
Amy Licence

£20.00   978-1-4456-0961-4   272 pages HB 40 illus, 10 col

CATHERINE HOWARD
David Loades

£20.00   978-1-4456-0768-9   240 pages HB 27 illus, 19 col

JANE SEYMOUR
David Loades

£20.00   978-1-4456-1157-0
192 pages HB   40 illus, 20 col

THE BOLEYN WOMEN
Elizabeth Norton

£20.00   978-1-84868-988-6
304 pages HB   40 illus, 20 col

Available from all good bookshops or to order direct
Please call **01453-847-800** **www.amberleybooks.com**

Coming soon from Amberley Publishing

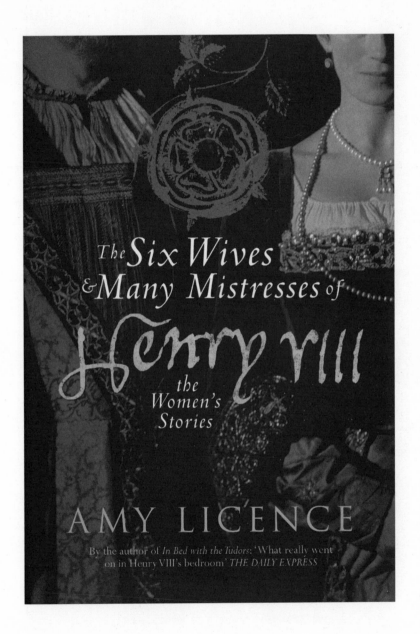

The *Six Wives*
&*Many Mistresses* of

Henry VIII

the
Women's
Stories

AMY LICENCE

By the author of *In Bed with the Tudors*: 'What really went
on in Henry VIII's bedroom' *THE DAILY EXPRESS*

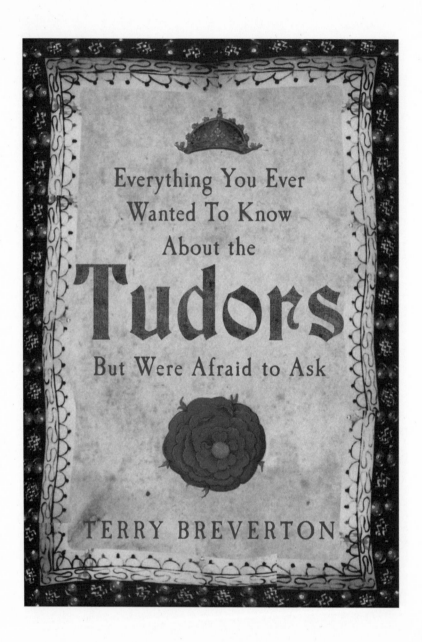